Understanding Whole Language

with Diane Stephens and Janet Vance

University of Illinois   Spring Independent School District

Spring, Texas

Understanding Whole Language

From Principles to Practice

Constance Weaver
Western Michigan University

Heinemann
Portsmouth, NH

Irwin Publishing
Toronto, Canada

HEINEMANN EDUCATIONAL BOOKS, INC.
361 Hanover Street   Portsmouth, NH   03801-3959

Published simultaneously in Canada by
IRWIN PUBLISHING
1800 Steeles Avenue West
Concord, Ontario L4K 2P3
Canada

Acknowledgments begin on page xvii.
Every effort has been made to contact the copyright holders for permission to reprint borrowed material. We regret any oversights that may have occurred and would be happy to rectify them in future printings of this work.

Library of Congress Cataloging-in-Publication Data
Weaver, Constance.
    Understanding whole language : from principles to practice /
Constance Weaver.
        p.   cm.
    Includes bibliographical references and index.
    ISBN 0-435-08535-2
    1. Language experience approach in education—United States.
I. Title.
LB1576.W34   1990
428'.007'073—dc20   90-37835
                                                                         CIP

Canadian Cataloguing in Publication Data
Weaver, Constance.
    Understanding whole language

Includes bibliographical references.
ISBN 0-7725-1815-7

1. Language arts (Elementary).   2. Language
experience approach in education.   3. English
language—Study and teaching (Elementary).
I. Stephens, Diane.   II. Vance, Janet.   III. Title.
LB1576.W43 1990   372.6'044   C90-095057-9

Cover design by Jenny Greenleaf
Front-cover photo by J.D. Willison
Printed in the United States of America
90 91 92 93 94   9 8 7 6 5 4 3 2 1

Contents

List of Figures

In Appreciation

I can do no more than begin to thank the many individuals who have contributed to and supported the writing of this book: my family and friends; students and colleagues; the many educators across the United States and Canada with whom I have worked and talked; and, of course, the wonderful people at Heinemann. Nevertheless, certain individuals deserve more than generic recognition and thanks.

Among my students, I particularly thank Debbie Benefiel, Jackie Bienas, Anne Michelle Dailey, and Amy Schroeder; they have made specific and significant contributions to the book. Colleagues at Western Michigan University who have shared materials and/or read parts of the manuscript are Ellen Brinkley, Ruth Heinig, and Jeanne Jacobson; their assistance has been most helpful. I also appreciate all those teachers and researchers throughout the United States and Canada who contributed ideas and materials. In having such generous students and colleagues, here and elsewhere, I am indeed fortunate.

I am especially grateful to Diane Stephens for co-authoring with me the chapter on whole-to-part research, which draws significantly on her report and book on whole language research. Diane also critiqued two of the other chapters, providing valuable insights. I am also indebted to Jannie Vance for researching and writing Chapter 8 on developing comprehension and thinking in whole language classrooms. The book is richer for this contribution, which aids particularly in conveying the flavor of whole language learning and teaching. In addition to being outstanding scholars, teachers, and writers, both Diane and Jannie are wonderful people with whom to work. I am privileged indeed.

I am deeply indebted also to the wonderful individuals who contributed their "voices of experience" to Chapter 11 on implementing a whole language philosophy: Jane Bartow, Linda Cameron, Lee Dobson, Yvonne Freeman, Yetta Goodman, Linda Henke, Kitty Kaczmarek, Julie Kniskern, Peter Krause, Sharon Otto, Lynn Rhodes and Nancy Shanklin, Mary Snow, and Ardis Tucker. From differing vantage points, their individual voices have nevertheless combined to present a unified concept of what does and does not work well in attempting to implement a whole language philosophy in the schools. These individuals' willingness to share their stories has contributed immeasurably to the chapter and the book. I am grateful.

The criticisms and suggestions of Michael Ginsberg were a tremendous help. Michael demonstrated an unerring instinct for locating weak spots in the manuscript. Surely it goes without saying, however, that the remaining flaws and lapses in conceptualization are my own.

Working with Philippa Stratton, Editor-in-Chief of Heinemann, has again been a delight. She immediately recognized the need for such a book and patiently supported me throughout the writing and production of it, even providing a ''writer's conference'' when I needed it. Others at Heinemann have been unfailingly helpful as well: Nancy Sheridan, who managed the production of the book, and Kathy Traynor, who helped prepare the Acknowledgments. Thanks, too, to Fran Bartlett of G & H Soho for her thorough and conscientious editing. I am appreciative and thankful.

Most important has been the patience, love, and support of Rolland, who has persistently encouraged my work on this book. I am blessed indeed, and my life has been greatly enriched.

Connie Weaver
May 1990
Western Michigan University

Acknowledgments

We are grateful to the publishers and individuals below for granting permission to reprint material from previously published works.

Chapter 1

Page 8: From ''A Research Base for Whole Language.'' Authors: Rhodes, Lynn K., and Nancy L. Shanklin; Coordinators/Consultants, Applying Whole Language, Denver; Studies and Research Committee, Colorado Council of the International Reading Association. Denver, CO: LINK, 1989.

Figure 1.3: Reproduced with permission from Lucy McCormick Calkins: *The Art of Teaching Writing* (Heinemann Educational Books, Inc., Portsmouth, NH, 1986).

Pages 20–21: From ''When Children Want to Punctuate: Basic Skills Belong in Context'' by Lucy McCormick Calkins. In *Language Arts* 57 (May 1980): pp. 567–73.

Chapter 2

Pages 43–44: Watson, Dorothy, and Paul Crowley, ''Determining Lesson'' in *Reading Process and Practice*, edited by Constance Weaver. Portsmouth, NH: Heinemann Educational Books, Inc., 1988, pp. 232–279. Reprinted by permission of the authors.

Pages 44–45: Edelsky, Carole, Draper, Kelly, and Smith, Karen. ''Hookin' 'Em In at the Start of School in a 'Whole Language' Classroom.'' Reproduced by permission of the American Anthropological Association from *Anthropology & Education Quarterly* 14:4, 1983. Not for further reproduction.

Chapter 3

Figure 3.3 and Appendix 3.1: From ''Basal Readers and the State of American Reading Insturction: A Call for Action.'' Position Statement, Commission on Reading, National Council of Teachers of English, 1988. Reprinted by permission.

Appendix 3.2: From *Developmentally Appropriate Practices in Early Childhood Programs Serving Children from Birth Through Age 8*, edited by S. Bredekamp. Reprinted by permission of NAEYC: Washington, DC, 1987.

Chapter 4

Figures 4.2 and 4.3: Reproduced with permission from Denny Taylor and Catherine Dorsey-Gaines: *Growing up Literate: Learning from Inner-City Families* (Heinemann Educational Books, Inc., Portsmouth, NH, 1988).

Figure 4.4: Reproduced with permission from Mary W. Hill: *Home: Where Reading and Writing Begin.* (Heinemann Educational Books, Inc., Portsmouth, NH, 1989).

Figures 4.5 and 4.8: Newman, Judith. *The Craft of Children's Writing.* Reprinted by permission of Scholastic-TAB Publications Ltd: Richmond Hill, ONT, 1984.

Figure 4.6: From Temple, Charles, N.; Nathan, Ruth; Burris, Nancy; and Francis Temple. *The Beginnings of Writing*, 2d ed. Boston: Allyn and Bacon, 1988. Reproduced by permission.

Figure 4.7: Reprinted by permission of the publisher from *Children's Drawing* by Jacqueline Goodnow. Cambridge, MA: Harvard University Press, Copyright © 1977 by Jacqueline Goodnow.

Figure 4.10: Chomsky, Carol. "Approaches to Reading Through Invented Spelling." In *Theory & Practice of Early Reading*, by Resnick, Vol. 2. Reprinted by permission of the publisher, Lawrence Erlbaum Associates, Inc., Publishers.

Pages 99–101, 102: Doake, David. *Reading Begins at Home.* Reprinted by permission of Scholastic-TAB Publications Ltd: Richmond Hill, ONT, 1988.

Pages 99–100: From pages 7–14 of *Prince Bertram the Bad* by Arnold Lobel. Copyright © 1963 by Arnold Lobel. Reprinted by permission of Harper & Row, Publishers, Inc.

Page 101: From *Where the Wild Things Are.* Copyright © 1963 by Maurice Sendak. All selections reprinted by permission of Harper & Row Publishers, Inc.

Figure 4.14: "Greedy Cat" from Joy Cowley's *Greedy Cat*, illustrated by Robyn Belton. Department of Education, Wellington, NZ, 1988. Distributed in the United States by Richard C. Owen Publishers, Inc., Katonah, NY. "In a Dark Dark Wood," adapted by June Melser and Joy Cowley. From THE STORY BOX®, published in the U.S.A. by The Wright Group, 10949 Technology Place, San Diego, CA 92127.

Chapter 6

Pages 130–32: From Lee Gunderson and Jon Shapiro, "Some Findings on Whole Language Instruction." *Reading-Canada-Lecture* 5, i:22–26. Reprinted by permission of the publisher.

Page 139: Stice, C. F., and N. P. Bertrand (1988, December). *The Texts and Textures of Literacy Learning in Whole Language versus Traditional/Skills Classrooms*. Paper presented at the meeting of the National Reading Conference, Tucson, AZ.

Chapter 7

Page 157: "Alphabet Stew" by Jack Prelutsky. From *The Random House Book of Poetry for Children*, selected and introduced by Jack Prelutsky. Copyright © 1983 by Random House, Inc. Reprinted by permission of the publisher.

Page 158: "Mist" by Sarah Kelly. Reprinted with permission from *Big Dipper Rides Again*, June Epstein, June Factor, Gwendda McKay, and Dorothy Richards, eds. Published by Oxford University Press, Australia, 1982. "The Pines" by Margaret Mahy from *The First Margaret Mahy Story Book*. Published and reprinted by permission of J. M. Dent & Sons Ltd, Publishers, London.

Chapter 9

Figure 9.3: Adapted from Sheila Valencia and David P. Pearson, "Reading Assessment: Time for a Change," *The Reading Teacher*, April 1987, pp. 726–32.

Figure 9.4: From Charles W. Peters and Karen K. Wixson, "Smart New Reading Tests Are Coming." *Learning 89* 17: pp. 43–44, 53. Published by Springhouse Corporation: Bethlehem, PA. Reprinted with permission.

Chapter 10

Figure 10.3: Figure 1 from "Assessment of Young Children's Reading: Documentation as an Alternative to Testing," Edward Chittenden and Rosalea Courtney, from *Emerging Literacy: Young Children Learn to Read and Write*, Dorothy Strickland and Lesley Mandel Morrow, eds., 1989. Reprinted with permission of Edward Chittenden and the International Reading Association.

Figure 10.4: From *Journeys into Literacy* by Moira McKenzie. Reprinted by permission of the publisher, Schofield & Sims Ltd, Publishers, London, 1986.

Figures 10.5 and 10.14: Reprinted from the *Primary Language Record Book* by kind permission of the Centre for Language in Primary Education, Webber Row, London, SE1 8QW.

Figure 10.6: From *A Camel in the Sea* by Lee Garrett Goetz. Published by McGraw-Hill Publishing Company, New York. Copyright © 1986. Reprinted with permission.

Figure 10.7: Appendix C in Yetta M. Goodman, Dorothy J. Watson, and Carolyn L. Burke, *Reading Miscue Inventory: Alternative Procedures*. Katonah, NY: Richard C. Owen, 1987.

Figure 10.10: From Orin Cochrane, Donna Cochrane, Sharen Scalena, and Ethel Buchanan, 1984. *Reading, Writing and Caring*. Winnipeg: Whole Language Consultants, p. 108. Reprinted with permission.

Figure 10.11: From Jane Baskwill and Paulette Whitman, *Evaluation: Whole Language, Whole Child*. Copyright © 1988 by Jane Baskwill and Paulette Whitman. Reprinted by permission of Scholastic-TAB Publications Ltd.

Figure 10.12 and page 238: Reproduced with permission from Lucy Calkins: *The Art of Teaching Writing*. (Heinemann Educational Books, Inc., Portsmouth, NH, 1986).

Pages 240–41: Reproduced with permission from Lucy Calkins: *Lessons from a Child* (Heinemann Educational Books, Inc., Portsmouth, NH, 1983).

Figure 10.15: Reproduced with permission from Karen Sabers Dalrymple, " 'Well, What About His Skills?': Evaluation of Whole Language in the Middle School." In *The Whole Language Evaluation Book*, Kenneth Goodman, Yetta Goodman, and Wendy Hood, eds. (Heinemann Educational Books, Inc., Portsmouth, NH, 1989, pp. 111–131).

Figure 10.18: Reprinted with permission from Rene Galindo " 'Asi No Se Pone Si': That's Not How You Write 'Si'." In *The Whole Language Evaluation Book*, Kenneth Goodman, Yetta Goodman, and Wendy Hood, eds. (Heinemann Educational Books, Inc., Portsmouth, NH, 1989, pp. 55–67).

Figure 10.19: Reprinted from Mary Ellen Giacobbe, "Helping Children Become More Responsible for Their Own Writing." *LiveWire* 1, i (August 1984): pp. 7–9. Copyright © by the National Council of Teachers of English. Reprinted with permission.

Figure 10.22: Reprinted by permission of Charles Scribner's Sons, an imprint of Macmillan Publishing Company from the illustration by Jackie Aher in The Young Learner's Handbook by Stephen Tchudi. Copyright © 1987 by Stephen Tchudi.

Understanding Whole Language

INTRODUCTION

Philosophy as a Basis for Reform

As the 1980s faded into the 1990s, there was a new excitement among educators about whole language learning and teaching. We heard that in whole language classrooms, children actually *want* to read and write; that teachers close to burnout have embraced the challenges of teaching with new enthusiasm; and that entire schools and school systems, states, and provinces have turned to this kind of teaching, which has been hailed as holding great promise for developing literate citizens and lifelong learners.

But what *is* "whole language"? As the term becomes more widely used, it seems to become less clearly understood. Thus, among whole language educators, there is growing concern that a whole language philosophy is in danger of being increasingly misunderstood, misapplied, and therefore unjustly maligned. There is concern that this reform movement will be curtailed because practices that are totally contrary to a whole language philosophy are being given that label, and instructional materials that are likewise contrary to the philosophy are being promoted in the name of whole language.

To prevent whole language education from being locked out of the schools through misunderstanding is, then, one aim of this book. But the major aim, of course, is positive: to demonstrate that whole language is indeed good education. More specifically, the aim is to provide people wanting to know more about whole language education with a reasonably succinct introduction to what a whole language philosophy is, what kinds of research support whole language education, how a whole language philosophy may be carried out in practice, and how to go about implementing a whole language philosophy in a school or school system.

Most of the professional literature on this topic is directed toward teachers. This book, however, is designed for a broader audience of not only teachers and teacher educators but curriculum supervisors and specialists, principals and superintendents, parents and members of school boards. Note, however, that the book does not offer any "quick fix'' for the country's educational ills. Though individual teachers may institute, almost overnight, changes that produce significant growth in literacy and learning among their students, even individual teachers usually make such changes slowly, as they develop increased understanding of the need for change. Significant educational reform on a large scale requires a substantial amount of time and concentrated effort—typically at least five to ten years at the school or school system level. What I hope to demonstrate in this book is that whole language education is well worth the sustained effort that large-scale reform inevitably requires.

The order of the chapters reflects my original intent to write a book especially for administrators. Thus, the chapters progress, logically enough, from defining whole language to fostering the development of whole language teachers and creating whole language classrooms and schools—that is, from principles to practice. Throughout the book, however, several themes recur: that the most meaningful and thus the most effective and enduring learning is that in which learners are actively engaged; that therefore, skills are best developed through engagement in authentic acts of reading and writing; that research and assessment need to reflect a broader concept of literacy than that measured by standardized tests; and that our educational means need to be congruent with our long-term goals of developing literate and lifelong learners, in order to promote rather than subvert those goals. Another major theme, more implicit than explicit until the last chapter, is that significant change can be facilitated but not forced.

Attempting to exemplify my own philosophy of change, then, I invite you to share what I currently understand about whole language, and why I believe it is crucial to transform our schools into places where whole language, literacy, learning, and life are valued and actively promoted.

CHAPTER 1

What Whole Language Is, and Why Whole Language

This chapter addresses the question of *what whole language is*, partly by discussing it within the context of broader, contrasting philosophies of teaching and learning and then by providing examples of how these philosophies are manifested in practice. The kinds of research supporting whole language education are discussed more fully in later chapters: Chapter 4 on developing language and literacy, and Chapters 5 and 6, which compare the effectiveness of contrasting approaches. As a prelude to that discussion, however, the present chapter touches briefly on research demonstrating that skills are learned better in a functional context. This is part, but only a small part, of whole language educators' response to the question "*Why whole language?*" Much more broadly, whole language is simply good education.

WHAT WHOLE LANGUAGE IS

First, it is important to emphasize that whole language is a *philosophy*, a belief system about the nature of learning and how it can be fostered in classrooms and schools. It is not an approach per se, though of course some kinds of activities can reasonably be characterized as whole language because they are consonant with this philosophy, while others are logically rejected by the philosophy. When, occasionally, I use the phrase "whole language approach," what I am referring to is a teaching/learning environment in which the activities reflect, predominantly, a whole language philosophy. But there is no single set of activities, much less a prepackaged program, that could be said to define whole language.

> **ff** First, it is important to emphasize that whole language is a *philosophy*, a belief system about the nature of learning and how it can be fostered in classrooms and schools. It is not an approach per se, . . . **jj**

Unity and Diversity within an Evolving Philosophy

Whole language is not a static entity but an evolving philosophy, sensitive to new knowledge and insights. It is based upon research from

3

a variety of perspectives and disciplines—among them language acquisition and emergent literacy, psycholinguistics and sociolinguistics, cognitive and developmental psychology, anthropology, and education. It is also based upon the successful practices of teachers who have implemented in their classrooms some of the insights from these disciplines—or who are "natural" whole language teachers, based upon their own insights and observations of how children learn.

Because of the common research base, whole language educators hold many key beliefs in common. On the other hand, each practitioner has developed his or her own perspective on what whole language is and means. How, then, do we characterize both the unity and the diversity—or rather, the unity *within* the diversity?

The best approach may be to listen to the "voices" of whole language educators, as reflected in the starter bibliography in Figure 1.1. Each of these writers emphasizes one or more aspects of what whole language is—and isn't—all about.

Articles

Altwerger, Bess, Carole Edelsky, and Barbara M. Flores. November 1987. Whole language: What's New? *The Reading Teacher* 41:144–54.

Fields, Marjorie V. May 1988. Talking and writing: Explaining the whole language approach to parents. *The Reading Teacher* 41:898–903.

Kline, Lloyd W. June 1988. Reading: Whole language development, renewed focus on literature spur change. Association for Supervision and Curriculum Development newsletter, *Curriculum Update* pp. 1–4, 9–12.

O'Neil, John. January 1989. "Whole language": New view of literacy gains influence. Association for Supervision and Curriculum Development newsletter, *Update* 31,i:3, 6–7.

Articles on various aspects of whole language were published in a variety of educational journals during the late 1980s or are being planned for the early 1990s, including not only specialized journals like *Language Arts* and *The Reading Teacher* but teacher magazines such as *Learning* and *The Instructor* and educational journals such as *Educational Leadership* and *Phi Delta Kappan*.

Books

Goodman, Kenneth. 1986. *What's Whole in Whole Language?* Portsmouth, N.H.: Heinemann.

For numerous additional books, see starter bibliographies in Chapters 2, 4, and 10.

Figure 1.1 **Starter bibliography on understanding whole language**

Learning and Learners

Kenneth Goodman is one of the leading advocates, worldwide, of a whole language philosophy of learning and literacy. As he notes in *What's Whole in Whole Language?* (1986), this educational philosophy is based upon research from converging disciplines that together provide a strong theory of learning and of language, a view of teaching and the role of teachers in fostering learning, and a language- and learner-centered view of the curriculum. The following is an abbreviation of the points Goodman outlines and then discusses under the heading "Learning Theory" (1986, p. 26):

1. Language learning is easy when it's whole, real, and relevant; when it makes sense and is functional; when it's encountered in the context of its use; when the learner chooses to use it. . . .
2. Language is both personal and social. It's driven from inside by the need to communicate and shaped from the outside toward the norms of the society. . . .
3. Language is learned as pupils learn through language and about language, all simultaneously in the context of authentic speech and literacy events. . . .
4. Language development is empowering: the learner "owns" the process, makes the decisions about when to use it, what for and with what results. Literacy is empowering too, if the learner is in control with what's done with it.
5. Language learning is learning how to mean: how to make sense of the world in the context of how our parents, families, and cultures make sense of it. . . .
6. In a word, language development is a holistic personal–social achievement.

K Goodman

Goodman contrasts the practical consequences of a whole language theory with those of a more traditional approach to instruction. Language and literacy develop easily, he argues, when the principles just listed are understood and respected; language is hard to learn, and literacy difficult to develop, under contrasting conditions—which unfortunately are more typical of our schools (K. Goodman 1986, p. 8).

A Philosophy and "Approach" That Facilitates Whole Learning

Elsewhere I have described what seem to me some of the key features of a whole language philosophy and some of the ways it is actualized in whole language classrooms (adapted from Weaver 1988, pp. 44–45):

1. Children are expected to learn to read and write as they learned to talk—that is, gradually, naturally, without a great deal of direct instruction, and with encouragement rather than the discouragement of constant correction.
2. Learning is emphasized more than teaching: the teacher makes detailed observations of the children's needs, then assists their development accordingly. It is assumed that the children *will* learn to read and write, and the teacher facilitates that growth.
3. Children read and write every day—and they are not asked to read artificially simplified or contrived language, or to write something that does not have a ''real'' purpose and a receptive audience.
4. Reading, writing, and oral language are not considered separate components of the curriculum or merely ends in themselves; rather, they permeate everything the children are doing in science and social studies, and they are integrated with the so-called creative arts.
5. There is no division between first ''learning to read'' and later ''reading to learn.'' From the very beginning, children are presented with predictable and repetitive *whole* texts and are encouraged to compose *whole* texts of their own, however brief—real language written for real purposes and a real audience.

Thus, my own answer to *''What is whole language?''* would include a characterization of what is ''whole'' in whole language: *language* is kept whole, not fragmented into ''skills''; *literacy* skills and strategies are developed in the context of whole, authentic literacy events, while reading and writing experiences permeate the whole curriculum; and *learning* within the classroom is integrated with the whole *life* of the child. Thus a whole language philosophy may also be referred to as a *whole or authentic literacy* philosophy, which promotes whole learning throughout students' whole lives.

Teachers Defining and Redefining Whole Language

All of this sounds idealistic—and it is. But it is also intensely practical, as demonstrated by the hundreds and thousands of teachers who have joined whole language support groups and organizations. For example, the April issue of *Learning 89* included an article by Wendy Hood describing the rise of such groups, beginning with the first TAWL group (Teachers Applying Whole Language) in 1978. She gives the addresses of the eleven largest TAWL groups in North America and those of five whole language newsletters. An international Whole Language Umbrella has recently been formed as a confederation of whole language support groups.[1] There is a Whole Language Special Interest Group within the International Reading Association and a Whole Language Assembly within the National Council of Teachers of English. The Canadian Council of Teachers of English has adopted a policy statement on language development and early literacy that reflects a whole language philosophy.

The fact that whole language is a philosophy whose time has come is well demonstrated by teacher after teacher in such publications as *Breaking Ground* (Hansen, Newkirk, and Graves 1985), *Whole Language: Theory in Use* (Newman 1985), *The Art of Teaching Writing* (Calkins 1986), *When Writers Read* (Hansen 1987), *Stories to Grow On: Demonstrations of Language Learning in K–8 Classrooms* (Jensen 1988), *Risk Makers, Risk Takers, Risk Breakers* (Allen and Mason 1989), *The Whole Language Evaluation Book* (Goodman, Goodman, and Hood 1989), and numerous others. See, for example, the starter bibliography on reading, writing, and literacy in the classroom (Figure 10.13, p. 240).

As Jerome Harste has put it (1989), whole language is ''practical theory''; it has evolved from the successful practices of teachers who began implementing what they were learning about how children learn, how they learn language, and how they develop literacy in settings outside of school. Research and theory have stimulated practice, which in turn refined theory.

Because implementation of the philosophy depends upon the teacher's understanding of it, as well as upon his or her ability and

1. The Whole Language Umbrella can be reached through any of its officers. The addresses of the current (1990–91) president, immediate past president, and membership chairs are as follows:

Orin Cochrane, President	Dorothy Watson, Past President
Whole Language Umbrella	Whole Language Umbrella
14 Regula Place	University of Missouri—Columbia
Winnipeg, Manitoba R2G 3C1	212 Townsend Hall
	Columbia, Missouri 65211
Debbie Manning, Membership	Lorraine Krause, Membership
Whole Language Umbrella	Whole Language Umbrella
4848 N. Fruit	961 Fairview Road
Fresno, California 93705	Huntington, Quebec J0S 1H0

One of the major whole language newsletters is issued by a commercial publisher of whole language materials:

Teachers Networking
Richard C. Owen, Publishers
135 Katonah Avenue
Katonah, New York 10536
$15/year, 4 issues
$18 in U.S. funds for
Canadian residents

willingness to depart from traditional methods, in one sense there are as many definitions of whole language as there are whole language practitioners. Classroom teachers themselves define and redefine whole language as they increasingly manifest their philosophy in their teaching:

> Though there are some instructional techniques that may be commonly found in whole language classrooms, no one technique or set of techniques makes up something called a "whole language" method. Instead, teachers make decisions about what reading and writing techniques to use based on their ideas of establishing a literate environment, research-based theories about the nature of reading and writing, and the observations they make about students' learning. What whole language teachers have in common is a theoretical underpinning about literacy learning and instruction and a commitment to a continued exploration of theory and practice. The classroom implementation of whole language philosophy may be very different from teacher to teacher and evolves as teachers continually reflect on their evolving philosophies of learning and teaching. (Rhodes and Shanklin 1989)

This partly explains, then, the diversity that exists within the unity. Indeed, one key tenet of the unity among whole language educators is that diversity is both inevitable and desirable.

WHOLE LANGUAGE WITHIN A BROADER PERSPECTIVE

❝ . . . from one perspective, a whole language philosophy is in effect a particular manifestation of a much broader conception of learning.❞

As the preceding discussion suggests, a whole language, whole literacy perspective is broadly concerned with whole learning and the whole lives of children and teachers. It should not be surprising, then, that from one perspective, a whole language philosophy is in effect a particular manifestation of a much broader conception of learning. This broader educational philosophy stems from the recognition that meaningful and enduring learning occurs most readily as the result of an active process of meaning-making, rather than a passive process of filling in blanks or repeating or recopying information presented by the teacher or the text.

Transactional Rather Than Transmission Model

Research from a wide variety of disciplines now supports this active concept of learning, which is sometimes called a *transactional* model, reflecting the fact that the learner actively engages with—or transacts with—the external environment, including people and books, in order to learn (see Holdaway 1979, Hall 1987, Cambourne 1988, Smith 1988b and earlier books). Figure 1.2 contrasts the transactional and transmission models of teaching. (For discussions of contrasting models, see Clark 1988 and Weaver 1988 and 1985; for discussion of the model underlying basals, see K. Goodman et al. 1988 and Shannon 1989.)

Though we rarely stop to consider the educational philosophy implicit in materials for instruction and assessment, reflective examination of such materials suggests that many traditional materials and associ-

Transmission Model	Transactional Model
Emphasis is on direct teaching, which is controlled first by the program and second by the teacher.	Emphasis is on learning, which is facilitated but not directly controlled by the teacher.
Basis is the behaviorist model of learning (for example, Skinner).	Basis is the cognitive/social model of learning (for example, Vygotsky, Halliday).
Learning is viewed as a matter of building from simple to complex, from smaller to larger skills.	Smaller "parts" of a task are seen as more readily learned within the context of a meaningful whole.
Learning is viewed as habit formation; thus verbalizing/writing correct responses and avoiding incorrect responses are seen as crucial.	Learning is seen as the result of complex cognitive processes that can be facilitated by teachers and enhanced by peer interaction.
Since correctness is valued, risk-taking is discouraged and/or penalized.	Risk-taking, and hence "errors," are seen as absolutely essential for learning.
All learners are expected to master what is taught when it is taught; thus, most children experience varying degrees of failure.	Learners are expected to be at different stages and to develop at their own pace and in their own ways; thus, there is no concept of "failure."
Ability to reproduce or verbalize a predetermined correct response is taken as evidence of learning.	Ability to apply knowledge and to think in novel ways is considered evidence of learning, as is the ability to use general strategies across a wide range of tasks and contexts.

Figure 1.2 Contrasting models of education: transmission versus transactional

ated practices reflect a passive and even failure-oriented transmission model of education rather than an active, success-oriented transactional model. With the traditional basal reading series particularly, teachers have been told what to say and what responses to expect of students. For their part, students have been assigned the task of completing workbooks—page after page, workbook after workbook—and/or required to write answers to questions accompanying story after story (see K. Goodman et al. 1988). And the usual standardized tests that report scores as "grade-level" norms consign literally half the children, by definition, to being "below grade level"—to being considered inadequate to greater or lesser degree, if not downright failures (see Chapter 9 of this book).

Some of the implications of the contrasting transactional model of education that whole language teachers try to implement are as follows:

1. That although certain developmental patterns and trends are common among children, each child develops idiosyncratically, with his or her own particular configuration of intellectual strengths, learning styles, and strategies. Thus, it is unrealistic and child-defeating to expect children to develop in prespecified ways, much less at predetermined rates. The teacher needs the knowledge and the flexibility to facilitate individual growth.

2. Genuine (enduring) learning, as opposed to what we often take as evidence of learning (for example, test scores), can be facilitated but not forced. Students must be immersed in a situation that encourages them to engage themselves emotionally in the learning task, not merely to go through the paces of completing assignments. Thus, the teacher can best facilitate learning by providing learning opportunities in which children choose to engage and invest themselves.

3. People rarely engage or invest themselves in learning tasks they consider boring or irrelevant to themselves personally. (They may *do* such tasks, but they don't engage themselves in the doing.) Thus, teachers need to offer children many opportunities to choose activities that interest and challenge them, as well as to recognize that skills will most readily be learned as children understand the need for them, and then are given appropriate assistance.

4. People do not engage or invest themselves in learning tasks that they perceive as threatening to their self-esteem. Thus, teachers need to create learning climates in which students can take risks without fear of "failure." Among other things, this means that criterion- and norm-referenced tests must be minimized in favor

of systematic observation and documentation of children's progress and needs, which will provide teachers with information needed to facilitate continued growth.

What is true for children as learners is equally true for teachers and administrators, of course. They too progress at their own rate and in their own way, in coming to understand how to foster learning. Their learning can also be facilitated, but not forced; and in order to engage themselves in a learning task, they must perceive it as personally worthwhile and not threatening to their self-esteem or to their job. Obviously the *they* is *we*: all of us.

Contrasting Models of Education

Of course, in actual practice, most teachers and classrooms fall somewhere between the extremes of the transmission and transactional models. Though many if not most of our instructional materials implicitly reflect a passive transmission concept of learning and teaching, in practice most teachers provide some classroom experiences that actively engage children in learning. In fact, many teachers who generally are quite "traditional" do a superb job of developing exciting projects that engage students. Conversely, though whole language teachers typically strive to implement a transactional model of education, in practice most whole language teachers also assign students some tasks that do not reflect that philosophy.

As a matter of definition, though, what I have chosen to call traditional classrooms and teachers are those that reflect a transmission model more than a transactional model, while whole language classrooms and teachers are those that reflect more the transactional model. Nevertheless, these categories only partially characterize the possible relationships between teachers teaching and students learning.

In *The Art of Teaching Writing* (1986), Lucy Calkins offers a grid that helps clarify how a transactional model of education, and whole language teaching, differ from other explicit and implicit models (see Figure 1.3). Quadrant 1, low teacher and low student input, represents a transmission model of education. At its extreme, this model is exemplified by much of what is advocated under the name of *direct teaching*. Neither the teacher nor the students are much involved—the teacher follows a script, and the students repeat or respond minimally; later, the students demonstrate "mastery" on tests that require equally little thought or learning. Though not nearly so extreme, the teaching and learning encouraged by many of our instructional materials and programs require little more of either the teacher or the students.

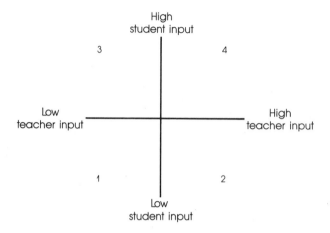

Figure 1.3   Contrasting models of education: student/teacher input (Calkins 1986, p. 164)

Quadrant 2, high teacher input with low student input, may characterize the kind of teaching that many of us have engaged in, as relatively traditional teachers. We have prepared interesting lessons and activities—or so we have thought; we have carefully defined what students are to do and guided them step-by-step in doing it; in short, we have offered fail-safe recipes for success. *We* have worked hard, and the students have fared well, but we have left little to the initiative or ingenuity of the learners. Our students have been challenged only minimally. Thus, our teaching has reflected a transmission model more than we ever might have thought.

Quadrant 3, low teacher input but high student input, seems to have characterized the early "process writing" classrooms in which students wrote one personal narrative after another, often with multiple drafts, but received from their teachers little stimulus to enlarge their repertoire of writing strategies or to broaden their command of genres. The students maintained ownership of the learning process, but learned less than they could have with greater teacher assistance and direction. Because the teacher was so little involved, this early process teaching reflected a transactional model at less than its full potential.

Quadrant 4 represents whole language classrooms, with high teacher input as well as high student input. Whole language teachers have high expectations for students and facilitate their taking significant responsibility for their own learning. At the same time, they provide students with strong support: See, for example, the classroom described in Chapter 8. Such teaching reflects a transactional model at its best.

DIRECT TEACHING WITHIN THE TRANSMISSION AND TRANSACTIONAL MODELS

Within whole language classrooms, much of the learning is only indirectly stimulated and facilitated by the teacher. The teacher creates a learning environment in which students learn to read and write largely by reading and writing; in which students learn from their peers as much as from the teacher; and in which students are allowed and encouraged to take significant responsibility for their own learning.

Not surprisingly, then, the direct teaching that occurs in whole language classrooms is significantly different from direct teaching in more traditional classrooms, because of the differences in the underlying educational models. Thus, the following sections will contrast direct teaching reflecting a transactional model and direct teaching reflecting a transmission model in order to clarify the differences between the underlying principles as well as to characterize some of the direct teaching that occurs in whole language classrooms.

Direct Teaching in a Transactional Model

Some of the direct teaching within a whole language, transactional classroom consists of demonstrations in which the teacher is personally involved and in which the students are invited to engage. Other direct teaching occurs in response to students' demonstrated needs—a matter of seizing the "teachable moment." A third kind of direct teaching occurs more or less incidentally within the context of authentic literacy events in which students are engaged. Still another common kind of direct teaching takes the form of "mini-lessons" on topics that at least some members of the class seem ready to take advantage of. These lessons are presented briefly and succinctly, on the assumption that such information will be added to the "class pot" of ideas, strategies, and skills, to be drawn upon as needed. Of course, these examples do not exhaust the kinds of direct teaching found in whole language classrooms; they are merely representative.

The first two kinds of direct teaching are illustrated here, while the second two kinds are illustrated in Chapter 7, "Developing Phonics Knowledge in Whole Language Classrooms," and Chapter 8, "Developing Comprehension and Thinking in Whole Language Classrooms."

Like many colleagues in the public schools, I am attempting to implement a whole language philosophy in my classes; therefore, examples of the first two kinds of direct teaching in whole language education are drawn from my own classes for preservice elementary teachers.

Scene 1: The Demonstration. I walk into class and almost immediately start a discussion about difficult words we encounter in texts.

"Look at this interesting word I ran into yesterday." I write it on the board: *fissiparous*. "Anybody know what it means?" Nobody does. "Anybody know how it's pronounced?" They make guesses: "fissy-parous," "fis-sip-arous."

"Would knowing how it's pronounced tell you what it means?" I ask. No, of course not. What, then, can we do?

My students wisely ask how it was used in context. Good for them! I write on the chalkboard what appears to be a minimal context:

> the seamless robe of "high education" was divided even further into narrower and increasingly insular departments and disciplines. This *fissiparous* tendency can be linked, perhaps, to the reductionism inherent in "science."

Well, they reason, it looks as if the word has something to do with dividing and narrowing. Fair enough.

"Are there any other clues?" I ask. We look at word parts: *fissi-* reminds me, if not them, of the words *fissure* and *fission*, as in nuclear fission. I get a mental image of a crack, a division. It fits.

So they/I/we determined the meaning of the word from context, supported by the apparent meaning of a part of the word. I confessed that, curious as to the word's derivation, I had ultimately used a dictionary. Sure enough *fissiparous* is related to *fissure* and *fission*.

This demonstration, in which I attempted to engage the students, led on subsequent days to further discussion of what we as mature readers do when we meet problem words, and of what recognition of our own preferred strategies ought to tell us about helping children develop productive word-handling strategies. We tried to generalize from our own experience, see how research confirmed our experience, and draw conclusions about how to help children develop similar strategies.

Exploring our own resources and strategies for dealing with problems in "real" situations was the foundation for learning, yet I directed that learning in key ways: by sharing a problem I had actually encountered and demonstrating how I had gone about solving it; by asking critical questions and engineering certain learning experiences; by contributing my understanding and experience to the exploration of ideas; and ultimately by developing a handout with a more coherent version of what I thought we had concluded from discussion (see Figure 1.4). However, the students were also actively involved in reasoning, reflecting, making hypotheses, and drawing tentative conclusions. The teaching/learning situation involved a transaction between and among teacher and students.

WHAT GOOD READERS DO MORE OR LESS AUTOMATICALLY BUT OTHER READERS MAY NEED HELP IN LEARNING TO DO

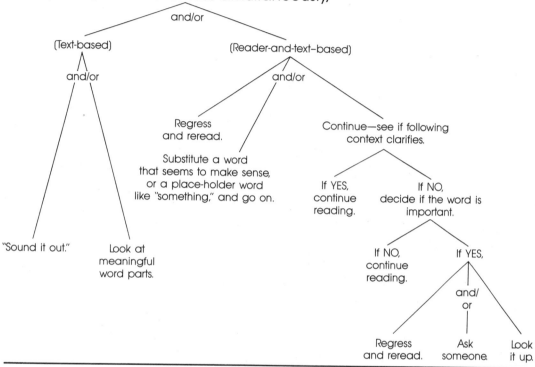

Figure 1.4 **Strategies for dealing with problem words, as discussed among classes of preservice teachers**

Scene 2: Seizing the Teachable Moment. On other occasions, we had impromptu vocabulary lessons: Once again, I was attempting to model not only how my students could solve problems as readers but how they could help their own students do so.

One recent example of seizing the teachable moment occurred when a group of my preservice teachers, struggling to make sense of a difficult article on dyslexia, admitted that they did not know what the author meant when she mentioned grouping children into *heterogenous* groups. Perhaps context would have clarified the word, but I decided this time to focus on meaningful word parts.

''Does the author contrast *heterogenous* grouping with any other kind of grouping?'' I inquired. Of course: *homogenous* grouping. So, we brainstormed for words containing *hetero-* and *homo-*. The class came up with more words than I can remember, but the major keys to meaning were the words *homosexual* and *heterosexual*, which naturally led students to the conclusion that *homo-* means ''the same'' and, therefore, *hetero-* must mean ''different.''

''Okay, so what are *heterogenous* groups and what are *homogenous* groups?'' I queried. No problem: This time, the students could explain it. I also used the occasion to explain why the milk we buy is called *homogenized* milk; the students understood that the first part of the word means ''the same,'' but their prior knowledge was not adequate for them to understand in what respect milk might be ''the same.''

Again, the discussion reflected a transaction among teacher and students, not the teacher lecturing, much less orchestrating students in passive repetition or recall.

Commentary. In both lessons, I directly modeled certain kinds of inquiry behaviors that I wanted my students to develop in themselves and in the children they will teach. The level of engagement was relatively high, in comparison with what one ordinarily observes in a typical lesson based on a transmission model of education.

Direct Teaching in a Transmission Model

❝The following example is admittedly not typical of the transmission model as it operates in most traditional classrooms. Rather, it is an example designed to characterize the transmission model at its extreme . . . ❞

The following example is admittedly not typical of the transmission model as it operates in most traditional classrooms. Rather, it is an example designed to characterize the transmission model at its extreme—what I would consider its worst. Examples of whole language teachers cited in Chapters 2 and 8 characterize a transactional model at its extreme best. Thus, the contrasting examples clarify the parameters within which most teachers and teaching fall.

I have chosen to illustrate the extreme of the transmission model by using lesson formats designed for third-graders in a program written by personnel from a local school system. The two lessons focus on vocabulary: one on inferring vocabulary meaning from context, the other on expanding vocabulary meaning through other means. I cannot resist teaching ''my'' words *fissiparous* and *heterogenous* within the lesson formats and frames, though, of course, much simpler words would actually be used with third-graders. I have shortened the lessons and altered the formats somewhat, but only slightly: by focusing on a single word rather than a set of words and occasionally by adding clarifying comments in brackets. Lesson 1 teaches the use of context to determine the meaning of words:

Lesson 1: Vocabulary Meaning
  Format: Vocabulary Meaning
  Signal: Hand-drop

1. Hold your hand as if stopping traffic.
2. Ask a question.
3. Pause.
4. Pull your hand up slightly and drop it quickly [students are to respond in unison as the teacher's hand falls].

[*Directions to the teacher*] Next to the words listed for vocabulary discrimination, write the sentence from the story in which the word appears.

Teacher	Students
1. Today we are going to use the context to figure out the meaning of words. (Explain what "using the context" means, if necessary.)	
2. "Let's talk about what this word means."	
3. "This word is *fissiparous*."	
4. "I'll read this sentence. You are to listen as I read it." Read the sentence in which the word appears. [Next to the word in isolation, I would have written the sentence in which it occurred.]	
5. "Now read this sentence with me."	Students read the sentence in unison.
6. "Look at the words in the sentence around the un-	

Teacher	Students
known word."	
"I'll name some of the words in the sentence that help determine the meaning of the word. [The words *divided* and *narrower* look like the best clues.] Underline each word in the sentence as you say it."	
"Say each word with me."	Students repeat the words underlined.

The lesson continues through three more steps, followed by a "corrective procedure."

Lesson 2: Vocabulary Expansion

Format: Vocabulary Expansion	
Signal: Point-touch	1. Point to the word on the board.
	2. Say, "What word?"
	3. Pause (one second).
	4. Touch the word.

Use the same words presented in vocabulary meaning.
[Assume, then, that *heterogenous* was also taught using the above format.]

Teacher	Students
1. "Today we are going to work on increasing our vocabulary."	
2. "This word is *heterogenous*."	
"What word?" (Point-touch signal.)	Students say word.
3. "This word is an adjective."	Students repeat part of speech.
4. Use any of the following statements that describes the form of expansion appropriate for the word.	

Teacher	*Students*

NOTE: Explain/define each
   form of expansion
   being taught.

5. ''An antonym for this   Students repeat the antonym.
   word is *homogenous.''*

[I have eliminated the other options, which seem less useful with this word.]

Commentary. Of course, I have distorted these lessons somewhat by using ''adult'' words with lesson formats intended for third-graders. But the lessons would be just as insulting and inappropriate, I contend, if words more appropriate for third-graders were used. Ironically, this particular program was developed in order to teach children *active* reading strategies, such as predicting, using context to determine meaning, monitoring comprehension, and so forth.

While such lessons reflect a transmission model at its passive extreme, this example is not, unfortunately, an isolated one. In fact, the procedures are modeled after *A Direct Instruction Series: Reading Mastery* (Engelmann and Hanner 1982). In this well-known program, children are treated as if they were no more than robots, and the ability to repeat-after-me is taken as evidence of learning.

Fortunately, most instructional materials are not nearly so extreme, yet the lessons in commonly used materials, such as virtually all of our traditional basal reading series, resemble these examples in significant respects. They typically tell teachers exactly what to do and say, as well as what to expect students to do and say; and they reward the repetition or copying of ''correct'' answers more than critical or divergent thinking. While this problem may be lessening somewhat as criticisms of basal programs become more widespread, traditionally such programs have done little to encourage either students or teachers to actively engage in learning.

It is significant that a transmission model of education can be readily if not best illustrated with examples of instructional materials, whereas a transactional model is best illustrated by examples from actual classroom exchanges among teachers and students.

TRANSMISSION VERSUS TRANSACTIONAL MODEL: THE LEARNING OF SKILLS

It seems evident that students will become more active and more engaged in their own learning when the learning environment reflects a transactional model. Some of the many benefits of a whole language, transactional model are clarified in Chapter 6, which deals with research from a whole-to-part perspective. That chapter, however, focuses on the development of reading specifically rather than on the development of both reading and writing. Here, then, by way of illustration and balance, is an example comparing the effectiveness of a transmission versus a transactional model in the teaching of writing and writing "skills."

In a significant article, "When Children Want to Punctuate: Basic Skills Belong in Context," researcher Lucy Calkins (1980) compared the approaches to learning punctuation that were adopted in two third-grade classrooms, one clearly reflecting a transmission model and the other a transactional model.

In the first classroom, Ms. West teaches language mechanics through daily drills and workbook exercises:

> "I start at the very beginning, teaching them simple sentences, periods, capitals," she [Ms. West] explains. "Everything that is in the book, I do a whole lesson on it." Ms. West writes sentences on the chalkboard and asks her children to insert missing punctuation. She makes dittos on question marks and gives pre-tests and post-tests on periods. Her children rarely write. (p. 569)

Ms. West's class reflects a transmission model, in which teachers often teach isolated skills, students practice them, and then are tested for mastery of the skills. It is simply assumed—but rarely proved—that skills so learned will later be put to effective use. Furthermore, the extensive teaching/practicing/testing of skills often leaves little time for students to engage in the behaviors wherein they are expected to apply those skills: in this case, writing. This was the situation in Ms. West's class.

In the second classroom, Ms. Hoban, another third-grade teacher in the same school, did not have the children study punctuation from workbooks and dittos or do exercises on the chalkboard. Instead, they wrote for an hour a day, three days a week. Ms. Hoban taught individual children and groups of children punctuation skills directly, but only as they needed various kinds of punctuation to clarify their writing. The children also learned punctuation from each other and from books and other printed materials in the classroom. The classroom environment was transactional in several ways: the teacher facilitated learning and even taught punctuation directly, but not in a teach/practice/test format; learning was in many respects social, both stimulated and effected by peers; skills were learned not in isolation, but within the context of a meaningful whole; learners were expected to be at different stages of writing development and to have different needs; risk-taking was encouraged, and the concept of "error" was discarded as inimical to learning.

The result? At the end of the year, Calkins interviewed all the children in each class to determine what they knew about punctuation. The children who studied punctuation day after day could explain, on the average, only 3.85 punctuation marks. Most could explain the period and the question mark, and half explained the exclamation mark, typically by reciting the rules they'd learned. In contrast, the writing-only group explained, on the average, 8.66 punctuation marks. More than half explained the period, question mark, exclamation mark, apostrophe, paragraph sign, caret sign used in editing, dash, quotation marks, and comma; nearly half could explain the colon, parentheses, and asterisk. These chidren tended to explain punctuation marks not by reciting memorized rules but by explaining or demonstrating how they used the marks in their own writing.

For example: third-grader Alan says, " 'If you want your story to make sense, you can't write without punctuation. . . . Punctuation tells people things—like if the sentence is asking, or if someone is talking, or if you should yell it out.' " According to Chip, another third-grader, punctuation " 'lets you know where the sentence is heading, so otherwise one minute you'd be sledding down the hill and the next minute you're inside the house, without even stopping' " (Calkins 1980, p. 569). The children use punctuation for special effects, as well as for clarity. " 'I keep putting in new kinds of punctuation,' " confides 8-year-old Andrea, " 'because I need them. Like sound effects—it takes weird punctuation to put *thud-thud* or *splat!* onto my paper' " (Calkins 1980, p. 571). Calkins summarizes: "When children need punctuation in order to be seen and heard, they become vacuum cleaners, sucking up odd bits from books, their classmates' papers, billboards, and magazines. They find punctuation everywhere, and make it their own" (1980, pp. 572–73).

In the transmission classroom, the children learned to parrot back the definitions they had learned for three to four punctuation marks. In the transactional classroom, children learned to *write*—and in the process, they learned to use and explain an average of eight to nine punctuation marks.

A TRANSACTIONAL MODEL
IN METAPHORICAL PERSPECTIVE

A metaphor might help to clarify what a transactional model is and is not. Let us liken children to flowers. Those who adhere to a *transmission* model of gardening would assume that every flower must grow in the same way and at the same time. Though such gardeners might have planted several varieties of flowers with differing needs, growing styles, and life cycles, each flower would be accorded the same amount of sunlight and water, the same amount and kind of fertilizer, the same insect sprays, and the same artificial aids such as stakes or trellises.

At the opposite extreme would be gardeners adhering to what might be called a naturalistic or *autogenous* concept of gardening, according to which each flower would be left to grow naturally; the gardener would in effect be only a bystander, watching the flowers grow or wither, flourish or die.

Those adhering to a *transactional* model of gardening would reflect a middle philosophy, recognizing that each flower is unique and must be expected to grow accordingly, but also believing that flowers must be nurtured in ways appropriate to their own nature and in ways that maximize their growth, rather than merely be left to grow wild.

WHAT WHOLE LANGUAGE IS: COMMON PRINCIPLES AND PRACTICES

The following discussion of whole language both summarizes some important observations made previously and looks ahead to topics addressed in subsequent chapters. This section will be followed by a contrasting section intended to clarify further what whole language is, by considering what it is not.

1. *Whole language is a philosophy rather than an approach*. This philosophy stems from research converging from various disciplines, including cognitive psychology and learning theory, psycholinguistics and sociolinguistics, anthropology and philosophy, and, of course, education. Whole language is a way of thinking about children and their learning, a set of beliefs that increasingly guides instructional decision-making for those committed to this educational philosophy. Thus, if we talk about a whole language approach, we mean instructional practices that stem from this philosophy, not a system that can be embodied in sets of prepackaged materials.

2. *A whole language philosophy is based upon the observation that children grow and learn most readily when they actively pursue their own learning*. Many children can memorize factual information and learn to respond correctly to worksheets and tests that assess ''mastery'' of relatively minute and isolated skllls. Their learning of concepts and strategies and their mastery of complex processes like reading and writing, however, is best facilitated by active involvement: in the case of literacy development, by actually reading and writing authentic texts that have meaning for

the children. They need to be psychologically *engaged* in what they are doing.

3. *To foster emergent reading and writing in particular, whole language teachers attempt to replicate the strategies parents use successfully to stimulate the acquisition of language and the ''natural'' acquisition of literacy.* Parents and whole language teachers recognize that it takes years for children's oral language to become like that of adults in their language community, and they accord emergent readers and writers the same gift of time. They do not expect ''correct'' word identification in reading or ''correct'' spelling in writing from the very outset; instead, they reward children's successive approximations toward adult norms—just as parents do in encouraging their children to speak.

4. *Whole language teaching is based upon the observation that much of what children learn—such as functional command of the structure of their native language—is learned with little, if any, direct instruction.* Thus, whole language teachers give students the opportunity to engage in the processes of reading and writing, even when their ''reading'' as yet involves only reconstructing a story from text and pictures, or their ''writing'' consists only of putting letterlike marks on paper to express their thoughts. Just as children developed functional command of spoken language by listening to others model adult speech and by speaking and receiving feedback mainly on the truth of their utterances rather than on the form, so they gradually progress toward adult norms in reading and writing.

5. *Recognizing students' incredible ability to learn complex processes by engaging in those processes, whole language teachers conceptualize direct teaching much differently than traditional teachers.* Direct teaching frequently occurs in response to students' demonstrated readiness and need: for example, when a writer is using dialogue and finds that readers cannot tell who said what, the writer is typically ready to learn the function and use of quotation marks. Other direct teaching may occur incidentally (whether preplanned or not), in the context of an authentic literacy event in which an entire group or the class is engaged. These and other kinds of direct teaching are important in whole language classrooms, but the majority of students' time is spent in reading, writing, discussing, and otherwise exploring concepts and ideas.

6. *Whole language learning—and the teaching that stimulates it—proceeds more from whole-to-part than from part-to-whole.* With the guidance of their teacher and the accompaniment of their peers,

❝Parents and whole language teachers recognize that it takes years for children's oral language to become like that of adults in their language community, and they accord emergent readers and writers the same gift of time. They do not expect "correct" word identification in reading or "correct" spelling in writing from the very outset . . .❞

as needed, emergent readers read and reread favorite texts: familiar songs, rhymes, or repetitive stories that contain few new words from stanza to stanza or episode to episode. Gradually, with appropriate instructional help and with concomitant writing experience, they learn to distinguish more and more words—that is, they develop a growing repertoire of sight words—and they learn basic letter/sound relationships and patterns. Thus, whole language learning and teaching proceeds from wholes toward parts, in sharp contrast to both a phonics approach and a sight word or "look-say" approach. As in other areas of learning, children develop literacy by beginning with function and gradually developing control over form, by starting with gross features and gradually learning finer distinctions, by more and more closely approximating the complex behavior of adults rather than trying to master that behavior skill by isolated skill.

7. *Knowing that language and literacy are best developed through functional use, whole language teachers thus engage students in reading and writing, speaking and listening, for a variety of authentic purposes.* In primary classrooms, children may use writing to "sign in" at the beginning of the day, to label things in the classroom, to take telephone "messages" and write grocery lists and menus at a home center, and so forth; they read what they and others in the classroom have written, as well as familiar environmental print (for example, labels on cans and packages), familiar songs and rhymes, and stories with repetition that makes them easy to read. Gradually they come to use a variety of written materials— textbooks and popular books, biographies, articles, newspapers—to gather information and to explore ideas across all aspects of the curriculum. *In whole language classrooms that are "littered with literacy" and in which children daily engage in the complex processes of reading, writing, discussing, and of course thinking, children simultaneously develop language and literacy, and learn about and through these processes.*

8. *A whole language philosophy asserts that in order to grow and learn, teachers and children must all be learners, risk-takers, and decision-makers, taking significant responsibility for learning within the classroom.* No prepackaged program can become the curriculum. Teachers must be sufficiently informed to select and develop teaching materials and practices that stem from the whole language philosophy, and they must have sufficient autonomy to reject materials and practices that conflict with that philosophy.

To a significant extent, the curriculum is "negotiated" with children: that is, it evolves as teachers and children together explore topics and themes, generating new interests and goals. Whole language teachers ensure that children develop needed skills and cover mandated areas of the curriculum, but these objectives are realized by integrating language and literacy with other aspects of learning.

9. *In whole language classrooms, learning is often fostered through social interaction.* Whole language teachers recognize that social interaction among students—discussing, sharing ideas, working together to solve problems and undertake projects—enhances learning. Therefore, whole language teachers facilitate productive interaction among children. Whole language teachers know that emphasizing cooperation rather than competition helps each child develop his or her potential.

10. *In whole language classrooms, children are treated as capable and developing, not as incapable and deficient.* Whole language teachers do not give students batteries of tests in order to determine in what isolated skills they might be deficient, nor do they constantly try to ferret out and criticize children's weaknesses. Rather, they notice and praise children's strengths and their developing competence as learners and literate individuals. Building upon the children's strengths, whole language teachers create a climate in which children are eager to take risks and grow, rather than afraid to respond for fear of making "errors" and revealing weaknesses that will subject them to remediation. Not surprisingly, then, the students who seem to exhibit the greatest growth in whole language classrooms are the ones traditionally considered deficient.

11. *In whole language classrooms, typically there are few behavior problems, not only because students are more actively involved in learning but because students are given the opportunity to develop self-control rather than merely submit to teacher control.* Instead of controlling children by their demands, whole language teachers develop learning communities characterized by mutual respect and trust—communities in which many decisions are made cooperatively, and students have numerous opportunities to make individual choices and take responsibility for their own learning. In such environments, learning flourishes and behavior problems subside.

12. *In whole language classrooms, assessment is intertwined with learning and teaching; though periodic assessment may be preplanned and struc-*

tured, daily learning experiences also provide opportunities for assessment—which in turn leads to the modification of teaching, as necessary. Knowing that standardized, state-mandated, and basal reading tests are inadequate, inappropriate, and even invalid measures for making educational decisions, whole language teachers develop a variety of means for assessing and evaluating students' progress, as well as their own teaching. Such measures include not only periodic performance samples of reading and writing, but think-aloud protocols, recorded observations, conferences and interviews, inventories and questionnaires, dialogue journals and learning logs, and student-kept records. Taken together, several such means are far more valid indicators of student progress than prepackaged tests.

13. *A whole language philosophy reflects and encourages a far different concept of literacy than that reflected in traditional classrooms.* In traditional classrooms, becoming literate is operationally defined as practicing reading and writing skills that are all too often divorced from the context of their use. And literacy is implicitly— if unintentionally—defined as high scores on tests of reading and writing skills; certainly, beyond the classroom, these scores tend to be equated with the development of literacy. Though students in whole language classrooms frequently score as well or better on such tests, raising test scores is not the primary aim of whole language teachers, nor are high test scores their definition of literacy. In whole language classrooms, the daily learning experiences as well as the assessment measures define literacy much differently. Students do not "practice" skills in order to become literate; rather, they use such skills and strategies daily in reading and writing a variety of materials for various purposes—in thinking and discussing and creating. In short, they daily engage in the kinds of behaviors that characterize the literate adult.

14. *Whole language classrooms foster the kinds of attitudes and behaviors needed in a technologically advanced, democratic society.* From the outset of their schooling, children in whole language classrooms learn to think of themselves as competent, as readers and writers rather than as mere children who have yet to master the skills of reading and writing. This mind-set has a powerful effect upon their self-concept, motivating them to engage actively in learning and encouraging the fulfillment of that prophecy—as they learn to think of themselves as readers and writers, they become effective readers and writers. Furthermore, students in whole

language classrooms are thinkers and doers, not merely passive recipients of information. They learn to think critically and creatively and to process and evaluate information and ideas rather than merely to accept them. Thus, whole language classrooms prepare students to participate actively in a democracy, rather than to submit passively to authority.

WHAT WHOLE LANGUAGE IS NOT: COMMON MYTHS AND MISUNDERSTANDINGS

In attempting to clarify what whole language *is*, it may help to discuss what whole language is not. Clearly, some of the following characterizations of what whole language is *not* derive logically from the preceding statements about what whole language *is*. However, the concepts bear repeating from the opposite perspective because of current confusions about whole language. Thus, the following comments are couched in terms of common myths and misunderstandings regarding whole language education. Most of these issues are considered more fully in subsequent chapters.

1. *Whole language is just another name for the whole word, or ''look-say,'' approach*. Not true. First, whole language is a philosophy, not an approach. In a whole word approach, teachers emphasize learning basic sight words before reading meaningful text. In whole language classrooms, on the other hand, teachers assist children in reading predictable and meaningful text, from which they develop a repertoire of interesting as well as basic words they can recognize. What whole language teachers *don't* do, however, is emphasize the identification of words at the expense of constructing meaning.

2. *Whole language is the same as language experience*. Not true. Whole language is not the same as language experience, nor is it similar enough to be lumped together with whole language, as if the two were essentially the same. Language experience involves taking children's dictation. Usually, a class or group engages in a shared learning experience (for example, science experiment, field trip, cooking activity) and then dictates what the teacher will write about that experience, sentence by sentence. Sometimes an individual child will dictate what someone else will write: a caption or sentence describing a picture the child has drawn, for example. Although language experience may indeed

be one activity within a whole language classroom, it is only that: one of many varied kinds of literacy activities in which children are engaged. At most, language experience is only a very small part of whole language.

3. *Whole language education is just another name for the ''open education'' of the 1960s.* Not true. Though there are philosophical similarities, there are also significant differences. One important difference is that whole language educators emphasize learning as a social phenomenon rather than an activity pursued by the individual in isolation. Another is that whole language teachers play more active roles in facilitating learning. What whole language teachers *don't* do is simply wait for learning to happen.

4. *Whole language teachers don't teach skills, such as phonics.* Not true. They teach *needed* skills and strategies, *if or as necessary*, within the context of reading a variety of genres and writing for a variety of purposes and audiences. What whole language teachers *don't* teach is skills isolated from their use or artificially contrived skills lessons.

5. *Whole language teachers don't do any direct teaching.* Not true. They teach directly, but often within the context of reading and writing and exploring concepts across the curriculum, rather than in isolated lessons. What whole language teachers *don't* do is teach bits and pieces of language in a teach/practice/test format or teach lessons unrelated to students' demonstrated needs.

6. *Whole language education is just a matter of teaching skills in context, rather than in isolation.* Not true. A whole language philosophy derives in part from evidence that, with opportunity and appropriate assistance, students readily *learn* needed skills and strategies while engaging in authentic acts of reading and writing. Artificially contrived lessons for teaching skills in context are therefore rarely needed. Furthermore, whole language is much more than teaching, or learning, skills in context.

7. *Whole language teachers don't assess or evaluate students.* Not true. They do evaluate, and they base their evaluations on a much broader range of assessment measures than do most traditional teachers. Evaluation is, in fact, an integral part of whole language learning and teaching. What whole language teachers *don't* do is test students on isolated and irrelevant skills.

8. *There is no structure in whole language classrooms.* Not true. In fact, whole language teachers provide substantial and consistent structure in order to enable their students to take increased

responsibility for their own learning. What whole language teachers *don't* do is adopt a structure imposed by a prepackaged curriculum.

9. *There are no specified expectations for students in a whole language classroom.* Not true. Whole language teachers expect children to grow in their competence as readers and writers and thinkers, in their use of oral language, and in understanding and control of their world. Whole language teachers have sufficient understanding of literacy development to facilitate, recognize, and document growth. What whole language teachers *don't* do is expect each child to learn the same things, at the same time, according to a predetermined scope and sequence chart or curriculum guide.

10. *There is no research supporting whole language education.* Not true. There is a solid foundation of research stemming from cognitive psychology and learning theory, psycholinguistics and sociolinguistics, and language acquisition and emergent literacy, as well as from education. There is also a growing body of comparative research suggesting that whole language learning/teaching fosters a much richer range of literacy attitudes, abilities, and behaviors than more traditional approaches.

11. *Anything anybody chooses to call "whole language" is whole language.* Not true. Despite the diversity among whole language practitioners, there is a common core of beliefs that characterizes a whole language philosophy. This core of beliefs provides a benchmark against which to assess the practices of educators who claim to be implementing a whole language philosophy, or the materials touted as "whole language" by publishers.

12. *You can buy whole language in a package.* Not true. Whole language is a philosophy, and unless teachers have internalized that philosophy of learning/teaching, they may not use even the most holistic of materials appropriately. Holistic materials and activities do not by themselves constitute a whole language program or guarantee holistic teaching.

13. *Only the best teachers can "do" whole language.* This statement comes closer to being true than the preceding ones, but the implicit assumption—that teachers cannot *become* more effective—is emphatically rejected by whole language educators. Whole language educators believe in each individual's ability to grow and become, and this includes teachers and administrators, as well as students.

> **"**There is also a growing body of comparative research suggesting that whole language learning/ teaching fosters a much richer range of literacy attitudes, abilities, and behaviors than more traditional approaches.**"**

14. *All you have to do to implement whole language is mandate it.* Nothing could be much further from the truth. Becoming a whole language teacher requires developing a whole language philosophy, which often requires rejecting a *transmission* concept of learning in favor of a *transactional* one. This process typically takes time and requires substantial encouragement and support.

SUMMARIZING AND LOOKING AHEAD

This chapter has characterized whole language as a dynamic, evolving philosophy of learning and teaching. While whole language teachers share a common core of beliefs, they are continually refining and re-defining the theory through classroom practice and research. The core of beliefs derives from the understanding that language and literacy are best developed when language (oral or written) is not fragmented, but kept whole; when listening and speaking and reading and writing are not isolated for study, but permeate the whole curriculum; when students are encouraged and allowed to develop language and literacy as they engage in authentic language/literacy events; and when the whole curriculum, instead of being isolated from the perceived needs, thoughts, and feelings of students, is integrated with their whole lives.

A whole language philosophy is from one perspective a particular manifestation of a broader, transactional model of education. In sharp contrast to the transmission model that underlies much of what occurs in our classrooms, the transactional model reflects a recognition that the most meaningful and enduring learning takes place when learners are actively involved and engaged in that learning. And as reflected in Calkins' punctuation study comparing Ms. Hoban's transactional approach to developing writing and writing skills with Ms. West's transmission approach to teaching merely punctuation, there is growing evidence that a whole language, transactional model of education is far more effective in developing literacy and learning than a transmission model.

Chapter 2 will continue the comparison by suggesting how the transmission and transactional models lead to vastly different conceptions of literacy and literacy development, as these are defined by the day-to-day activities in which students are—and are not—engaged. Chapter 3 builds upon the first two chapters by demonstrating the widespread impetus for educational reform in general, and for a transactional concept of education in particular. Subsequent chapters further clarify what whole language is and is not, as well as why whole language may be viewed simply as good education.

CHAPTER 2
Defining and Redefining Literacy

Most educators have very similar long-range goals regarding students' development of literacy. They want students to become able to read and write various kinds of texts, for various purposes, so that as adults they will be able to participate fully in the economic, political, social, and cultural life of their communities and nation. They want students to learn to read and write not only critically and creatively, but with pleasure and for personal satisfaction. Most of all, perhaps, they want literacy to become an integral part of their students' lives as adults.

There is a vast difference, however, between how literacy is taught in traditional classrooms reflecting a transmission model of education, on the one hand, and how it is developed in whole language classrooms reflecting a transactional model. Despite the similarity in educators' long-range goals and verbalized definitions of literacy, there is considerable difference in how literacy is defined through day-to-day activities in the contrasting classrooms. And it is this *operational* definition of literacy that many children seem to internalize. This internalized definition affects not only how students perceive reading and writing and how they perceive themselves as readers and writers, but also how, and how well, they develop as readers and writers.

LITERACY AS OPERATIONALLY DEFINED IN TRANSMISSION, "SKILLS" CLASSROOMS

In traditional classrooms strongly reflecting a transmission, "skills" concept of education, children may too often develop a limited understanding of what reading and writing are, which in turn may inhibit their actual development of literacy. This is particularly true in classrooms where the teaching is tightly controlled by rigid and detailed curriculum guides and objectives and/or by the demand that the traditional basal reader program be used in lock-step fashion, with no room for teacher decision-making as to what materials should be used, when, and with whom.

Students' Concepts of Reading and Writing

When an outstanding second-grade teacher from a school with a tightly controlled "skills" curriculum interviewed one of her students regarding his concepts about reading, for instance, here was the result:

TEACHER: What is reading?

STUDENT: It's like when you, when the teacher ask you questions and you have to answer them back and when you have to read sometimes, read directions and stuff, and sometimes it be like a group and they read and stuff, and like that.

TEACHER: Okay. What do people do when they read?

STUDENT: They read the story and sometime it be questions they have to answer.

TEACHER: Okay. Why do we read?

STUDENT: Why do we read?

TEACHER: Um-hmm.

STUDENT: It's part of a minimal skill so we can get to third grade.

TEACHER: Any other reasons?

STUDENT: Not that I know of.

TEACHER: When you're at home, you told me [before] that when you're at home you like to read. You're not reading for minimal skills at home.

STUDENT: I read to get to third grade and stuff.

Further prodding did reveal that sometimes the student would read a story book at home "to see if it's any fun or interesting or something." However, his overriding concept of literacy, the definition he inferred from what occurred in the classroom, was that reading meant answering questions and mastering minimal skills.

Unfortunately, such concepts are all too readily developed by children who daily complete skills work rather than in reading materials for their own enjoyment or to obtain information relating to their own purposes and interests. For example, Harste's research suggests that in response to the question "What is reading?" many children give definitions such as these (Harste 1978, p. 92; see also Burke 1980):

"It's filling out workbooks."

"Pronouncing the letters."

''It's when you put sounds together.''

''Reading is learning hard words.''

In an article reviewing thirty years of inquiry into students' perceptions of reading, Johns (1986) mentions, among others, a study of 1,655 students from grades 1 to 8. The results must be interpreted with caution, Johns points out, because students often know more than they reveal in brief interviews. Even so, the results of this study are disconcerting. In responding to the question ''What is reading?'' fewer than 20 percent of the students made any reference to getting meaning (the percentage was higher with the older students and lower with the younger ones). Most described reading as decoding (for example, sounding words out) or as an activity involving a textbook and occurring in a classroom or school environment (Johns and Ellis 1976, as reported in Johns 1986, p. 36). But the students interviewed did not typically define reading as a meaningful activity or one in which they voluntarily engaged.

Evidence also suggests that just as many students conceptualize reading as getting the words or saying the words with as few errors as possible, so they also conceptualize writing as the avoidance of errors when putting words on paper. For example, *un*skilled writers—even at the college level—typically are preoccupied with technical matters of spelling and punctuation, see revision mainly as ''error hunting,'' stop revising when they think they haven't violated any rules, and/or tend to conceptualize revising merely as ''making neat copy in ink'' (see Glatthorn 1981, p. 40, where he has summarized a significant body of research). Such writers do not conceptualize writing as coming to understand, express, or communicate ideas and feelings through the written word.

Of course, educators have not usually intended for students to develop such limited and detrimental concepts of literacy. Rather, these concepts or definitions result from what students do—and don't do—day after day in the classroom.

> **Of course, educators have not usually intended for students to develop such limited and detrimental concepts of literacy. Rather, these concepts or definitions result from what students do—and don't do—day after day in the classroom.**

Concept of Literacy in Transmission Classrooms

If, then, we were to characterize the implicit concept of literacy *operationally* defined by the materials and practices in the more traditional, skills-oriented, transmission classrooms, such an extended definition might look something like this:

1. Literacy is circling correct answers on worksheets.
2. Literacy is filling in blanks.

3.   Literacy is writing out answers to questions at the end of the story.
4.   Literacy is identifying words.
5.   Literacy is reading aloud, word perfectly.
6.   Literacy is spelling words correctly.
7.   Literacy is doing exercises on mechanics and grammar.
8.   Literacy is practicing ''skills.''
9.   Literacy is giving the correct answers on tests.
10.   Literacy is learning not to think.

Of course, students themselves might never *consciously* define literacy in quite this way, but this is the sort of implicit definition promoted by many instructional materials and practices. Reading and writing are too often taught as a matter of mastering discrete, isolated skills rather than as the ability to construct meaning from language (reading) and through language (writing). Surely it is no wonder, then, that many students believe literacy has little to do with real life, or that many students fail to become the avid readers and prolific writers that we hoped they would.

Reading Taught as Worksheets and Skills: The Evidence

The widely cited *Becoming a Nation of Readers* addresses many of these concerns, pointing out that even for beginners ''reading should not be thought of as a 'skill subject''' (Anderson et al. 1985, p. 61). The problem, of course, is that reading—and writing—will likely be thought of that way by the children, if it is taught that way.

The report *Becoming a Nation of Readers* is worth reading and rereading for the advice the authors give against teaching literacy from what I have called a transmission model, emphasizing skills rather than thoughtful, joyful engagement with the text. Drawing upon research to support their points, they discuss the inappropriateness and ineffectiveness of such practices as round-robin reading, asking numerous literal recall questions focused on details, and completing workbooks and skills sheets.

Because the authors of *Becoming a Nation of Readers* have done such an excellent job of discussing the problem of ''skilling and drilling'' our nation's children, I will quote extensively from their work (Anderson et al. 1985, pp. 74–76), leaving it to the interested reader to check the research they cite. The authors begin their discussion as follows:

> Students spend up to 70% of the time allocated for reading instruc-
> tion in independent practice, or ''seatwork.'' This is an hour per day in

the average classroom. Most of this time is spent on workbooks and skill sheets. . . . In the course of a school year, it would not be uncommon for a child in the elementary grades to bring home 1,000 workbook pages and skill sheets completed during reading period. . . .

Analyses of workbook activities reveal that many require only a perfunctory level of reading. Children rarely need to draw conclusions or reason on a high level. Few activities foster fluency, or constructive and strategic reading. Almost none require any extended writing. Instead, responses usually involve filling a word in a blank, circling or underlining an item, or selecting one of several choices. Many workbook exercises drill students on skills that have little value in learning to read. . . .

As an example of a useless activity, the authors cite the following exercise from a second-grade workbook:

Read each sentence. Decide which consonant letter is used the most. Underline it each time.

1. My most important toy is a toy train.
2. Nancy, who lives in the next house, has nine cats.
3. Will you bring your box of marbles to the party?

Commenting on this activity, the authors of *Becoming a Nation of Readers* note:

It is peculiar to suppose that, if children can already read the sentences, their reading ability will be improved by asking them to underline consonants. Furthermore, though the children are directed to "read each sentence," they don't need to read anything but the directions to do the task. *The one certain conclusion is that the exercise is time-consuming and extremely tedious.* (emphasis mine)

If such useless activities were the exception rather than the rule, educators would have little reason for concern. But unfortunately, workbooks abound with such "skills" activities that not only do not promote literacy but that in fact keep valuable time from being spent on the actual reading and writing that does promote literacy.

The authors of *Becoming a Nation of Readers* continue:

Even young children often see the futility of doing workbook page after workbook page. One researcher asked children what they were doing when they were occupied with workbooks. Most saw the pages as something to do to get finished. As one boy, age 6, said, "There! I didn't understand that, but I got it done." Students frequently don't read all the material in worksheets. Instead, they attempt to use shortcuts that allow them to answer in a mechanical fashion. If options *a* and *c* have been used to answer two of three questions, for example, some children will write down *b* for the third question without reading it.

Similarly, children often don't read the story that accompanies the so-called comprehension questions. They read the questions, look for the answers within the text, and copy down what appears to be correct. They—often the most "successful" students—take standardized tests in similar fashion: read the question and possible answers, then look for the "right" answer within the passage.

When students spend a significant portion of their day completing such tasks, is it any wonder that they become confused about what literacy is? Or that they fail to become emotionally and intellectually engaged in the activities the schools operationally define as literacy? Is it any wonder that they consider literacy education irrelevant to their lives? Or, since other subjects are frequently taught in a similar manner, is it really surprising that a sizable percentage of students drop out of school?

What Has Happened to Real Reading and Writing?

The authors of the *Report Card on Basal Readers* reinforce the observation that in the basal reading programs that have traditionally dominated reading instruction, reading is indeed taught as skills, as completing worksheets that have little if any bearing upon reading itself (K. Goodman et al. 1988). The authors' careful examination of the most widely used basal reading series in the mid-1980s confirms many of the points made here, including the point that reading is taught and tested as if it were a matter of identifying words, especially in the primary grades; that comprehension is taught and tested as a limited "skill" rather than as a cognitive process; and that reading instruction in American basal readers clearly reflects what I have called a *transmission* model of education based upon precepts from the behavioral psychology of the 1920s.

What happens to *real* reading and writing when such a model underlies instruction and implicitly and operationally defines literacy?

After examining the components of and activities within the leading basal reading programs, the authors of the *Report Card* concluded that "In the programs we studied, it is likely that only 10 to 15 percent of the instructional time will actually be spent in silent reading of cohesive texts" (K. Goodman et al. 1988, p. 73). How much time does this actually amount to? The authors of *Becoming a Nation of Readers* note that "An estimate of silent reading time in the typical primary school class is 7 or 8 minutes per day, or less than 10% of the total time devoted to reading. By the middle grades, silent reading time may average 15 minutes per school day" (p. 76).

The situation is similar, or perhaps worse, with respect to writing. Even in secondary schools, writing has typically consisted more of filling in blanks than of composing connected text (Applebee 1981).

In short, real reading and writing have virtually been crowded out of the curriculum, mainly by the voluminous amount of skills work that children are assigned.

WHAT BEST PROMOTES READING, WRITING, AND LITERACY?

If there were evidence that these nonreading behaviors actually promote reading and writing more than engaging in the processes themselves, we might grudgingly tolerate them. The evidence demonstrates quite the contrary, however: even when literacy is measured narrowly as scores on standardized tests.

With reading, for example, "Classroom research suggests that the amount of time devoted to worksheets is unrelated to year-to-year gains in reading proficiency," while, on the other hand, "research suggests that the amount of independent, silent reading children do in school is significantly related to gains in reading achievement" (Anderson et al. 1985, p. 76).

"Research also shows that the amount of reading students do out of school is consistently related to gains in reading achievement" (Anderson et al. 1985, p. 77). In fact, research suggests that independent reading is the major contributor to reading comprehension vocabulary growth, as well as to gains on tests of "reading achievement" (ibid.). Unfortunately, most children rarely read. They read very little in school, and outside school they read—books, anyhow—only a few minutes a day, if at all. In fact, one study of the after-school reading of fifth-graders noted that "50% of the children read books for an average of four minutes per day or less, 30% read two minutes per day or less, and fully 10% never reported reading any book on any day. For the majority of the children, reading from books occupied 1% of their free time, or less" (Fielding et al. 1986, as cited in Anderson et al. 1985, p. 77).

Not surprisingly, "Research suggests that the frequency with which students read in and out of school depends upon the priority classroom teachers give to independent reading" (Anderson et al. 1985, p. 79). But the basal *programs* have traditionally given priority to workbooks and skills sheets, not to independent reading. And, if anything, some teachers may give even more priority to the worksheets—at least, publishers claim that the demand for seatwork activities is "insatiable." Classroom observers have noted that many teachers use the exercises of several publishers, as well as ones they have prepared themselves (Anderson et al. 1985, p. 74).

To estimate the cost of seatwork, Jachym et al. (1989) asked principals in five schools to complete a questionnaire designed to uncover the costs, overt and hidden, of purchasing and preparing seatwork for the second-graders in their schools. Costs varied widely—and, of course, the study was limited to just one grade level in only five schools. But at least for these schools, Jachym et al. estimated that if the total seatwork costs were cut in half and the remaining money used for paperback books, the schools would be able to purchase between eight and thirty paperbacks books per child each year. Thus, the authors suggest that schools reduce the cost of materials that have *not* been reliably demonstrated to enhance reading acquisition in favor of independent reading materials that *have*. The authors conclude:

> If we value the reading of books, we will incorporate books into our reading program. We have been told too often it is an issue of inadequate funds and inadequate time for books. It is neither. Rather, it is an issue of what we value. If we have no funds, nor time for books in school, why should we expect children to value reading or books, in school or out? (Jachym et al. 1989, p. 34)

Research suggests that seatwork materials must give way to books and other authentic reading materials if the majority of children are to develop either the desire to read or the ability to read more than minimally.

What of writing? Just as independent reading fosters reading ability, so actual writing for real purposes and audiences fosters writing ability—and reading ability as well. Again, even considering only very limited measures of literacy, "Opportunities to write have been found to contribute to knowledge of how written and oral language are related, and to growth in phonics, spelling, vocabulary development, and reading comprehension" (Anderson et al. 1985, p. 79). The authors of *Becoming a Nation of Readers* further note, however, that

> Unfortunately, every recent analysis of writing instruction in American classrooms has reached the same conclusion: Children don't get many opportunities to write. In one recent study in grades one, three and five, only 15% of the school day was spent in any kind of writing activity. Two-thirds of the writing that did occur was word for word copying in workbooks. Compositions of a paragraph or more in length are infrequent even at the high school level. (Anderson et al. 1985, p. 80; they cite Bridge and Hiebert 1985 and Applebee's 1981 landmark study.)

The "recent" research cited is, of course, no longer quite so current, and the growing popularity of the writing process approach, fostered in part by the National Writing Project centers as well as by educators like Donald Graves and Lucy Calkins, has surely modified the situation in some classrooms and schools.

In general, however, the traditional transmission concept of education has resulted in extensive and relatively ineffective skills instruction in reading and writing, at the expense of the real reading and writing that fosters literacy development.

Whole language classrooms offer a sharp contrast to those that teach reading and writing as the mastery of isolated skills.

LITERACY AS OPERATIONALLY DEFINED IN TRANSACTIONAL, WHOLE LANGUAGE CLASSROOMS

In whole language classrooms, students daily engage in real reading and writing, with skills learned and taught in the context of these authentic literacy events. They typically read and write a far greater variety of genres and forms than the students in skills classrooms: everything from labels, lists, letters, and memos to personal narratives and poetry; from various kinds of fiction to an even wider array of nonfiction, including both informative and persuasive writing—all at even the earliest grades. Figure 2.1 lists many kinds of reading and writing that may engage students in whole language classrooms, whether elementary or secondary. The atmosphere too is vastly different in whole language classrooms. Students are actively engaged in learning and in taking responsibility for their own learning. They work cooperatively with peers, often learning as much or more from them than from the direct instruction or intervention of the teacher. The classroom climate reflects mutual respect and trust, with each individual valued as both learner *and* teacher. Students are treated as competent rather than as deficient, as readers and writers rather than as children who have not yet learned prerequisite skills. In such a climate, students freely take the risks necessary to learn and develop.

Concept of Literacy in Transactional Classrooms

Thus, literacy operationally defined in whole language classrooms might be characterized something like this:

1. Literacy is seeing yourself as a reader and writer.
2. Literacy is enjoying reading and writing: through independent reading and writing, and through working and sharing with others.
3. Literacy is gaining insight into yourself and others through books.

❝In general, however, the traditional transmission concept of education has resulted in extensive and relatively ineffective skills instruction in reading and writing, at the expense of the real reading and writing that fosters literacy development.**❞**

adaptations, adventure stories, advertisements, allegories, alphabet books, anecdotes, applications, arguments, articles, autobiographies

ballads, biographies, books

caricatures, cards, cartoons, case studies, catalogues, chants, children's books, comedies, commercials, complaints, commentaries, critiques

descriptions, dialogues, dialogue journals, diaries, descriptions, dictionaries, directions, directories, drama

editorials, elegies, epigraphs, epistles, epitaphs, essays, eulogies

fables, fact books, fairy tales, fantasies, feature articles, folktales, futuristic tales

giftbooks

haiku, hero tales, histories, how-to books, horror stories, hymns

informational books, interior monologues, interviews, invitations

jingles, jokes, journals, jump-rope rhymes

kennings, knock-knock jokes

lab reports, labels, letters (real and imaginary), lists

magazines, memos, menus, monographs, monologues, mysteries, myths

narratives, newspapers, news reports, notes, notices, novellas, novels

observations, odes

parables, parodies, plays, proposals, proverbs, poems, pourquoi tales

quatrains, quotable quotes, quips

raps, recipes, reports, résumés, reviews, rhymes, romances

satires, scripts, soliloquies, songs, stories, summaries, synopses

tall tales, technical reports, thumbnail sketches

utopian proposals

video scripts, vignettes

written conversations and debates

x-rays (penetrating verbal descriptions)

yarns

zanies, zoophabets (alphabet books of zoo animals)

Figure 2.1 **Forms for writing and reading: from A to Z. Note that in addition to some atypical coinages, there is considerable overlap among the forms, resulting from the attempt to give examples for each letter of the alphabet.**

4. Literacy is gaining information from various kinds of environmental print (signs, labels, menus, maps) as well as from books, magazines, and newspapers.

5. Literacy is taking responsibility and risks—for example, ''having

a go'' at reading a book, even though you don't know all the words, and attempting to convey your thoughts, feelings, and experiences through writing, even though you haven't mastered all the conventions of the language.

6. Literacy is developing a flexible repertoire of strategies for constructing meaning, monitoring your own comprehension, and solving problems encountered in trying to construct meaning.

7. Literacy is writing for various purposes and audiences.

8. Literacy is developing a repertoire of increasingly sophisticated and flexible strategies for generating ideas, drafting, revising, editing, and ''publishing'' what you write.

9. Literacy is developing an appreciation for different kinds of literature, as well as using the conventions of various literacy genres in your writing.

10. Literacy is learning strategies for reading and accepted conventions for writing in the context of authentic literary events: because you have an immediate need for the strategies and skills.

11. Literacy is using written language to think and to create.

In whole language classrooms, students often find that literacy engages their whole being.

The concept of literacy operationally defined in whole language classrooms can be inferred from reading about those classrooms, from anecdotal glimpses into how teachers ''teach'' and how and what the students learn. Figure 2.2 presents a starter bibliography of books that include descriptions of whole language classrooms and/or classroom activities. The list includes books on both reading and writing—mostly together rather than separately; on whole language across ages and grades, from primary school to secondary school; and on whole language as implemented in a variety of classrooms, including classes with ESL (English as a second language) students and students termed ''learning disabled'' or ''remedial.'' And these do not begin to exhaust the list of books, much less articles, that demonstrate how a whole language concept of literacy is operationalized, day to day, in a rapidly increasing number of classrooms.

We shall see in Chapter 6 that an emerging body of research is beginning to document, in a different way, the fact that students in whole language classrooms *are* internalizing various aspects of this transactional, whole language concept of literacy and learning. Here, I will briefly share two anecdotal descriptions of whole language teachers and their students. Chapter 8 presents a more detailed description of whole language teaching and learning, focusing more on the teacher and students in one classroom.

The following list is chronologically ordered in order to give some idea of how whole language has increasingly spread in the past decade. To save space, the publisher is listed only for those books that are *not* published by Heinemann Educational Books, Portsmouth, New Hampshire.

Graves, Donald. 1983. *Writing: Teachers and Children at Work.*

Calkins, Lucy McCormick. 1983. *Lessons from a Child.*

Hansen, Jane, Thomas Newkirk, and Donald Graves, eds. 1985. *Breaking Ground: Teachers Relate Reading and Writing in the Elementary School.*

Calkins, Lucy McCormick. 1986. *The Art of Teaching Writing.*

Newkirk, Thomas, and Nancie Atwell, eds. 1986. *Understanding Writing: Ways of Observing, Learning, & Teaching.* Second edition 1988.

Atwell, Nancie. 1987. *In the Middle: Writing, Reading, and Learning with Adolescents.*

Routman, Regie. 1988. *Transitions: From Literature to Literacy.*

Cambourne, Brian. 1988. *The Whole Story: Natural Learning and the Acquisition of Literacy in the Classroom.* Richmond Hill, Ontario: Scholastic.

Harste, Jerome, Kathy Short, and Carolyn Burke. 1988. *Creating Classrooms for Authors: The Reading–Writing Connection.*

Gilles, Carol, et al. 1988. *Whole Language Strategies for Secondary Students.* Katonah, N.Y.: Richard C. Owen.

Rhodes, Lynn, and Curt Dudley Marling. 1988. *Readers and Writers with a Difference: A Holistic Approach to Teaching Learning Disabled and Remedial Students.*

Enright, D. S., and M. L. McCloskey. 1988. *Integrating English: Developing English Language and Literacy in the Multilingual Classroom.* Reading, Mass.: Addison-Wesley.

Johnson, D., and D. Roen, eds. 1989. *Richness in Writing: Empowering ESL Students.* New York: Longman.

Newkirk, Thomas. 1989. *More Than Stories: The Range of Children's Writing.*

Allen, JoBeth, and Jana Mason, eds. 1989. *Risk Makers, Risk Takers, Risk Breakers: Reducing the Risks for Young Literacy Learners.*

Watson, Dorothy, Carolyn Burke, and Jerome Harste. 1989. *Whole Language: Inquiring Voices.* Richmond Hill, Ontario: Scholastic.

Jensen, Julie M., ed. 1989. *Stories to Grow On: Demonstrations of Language Learning in K–8 Classrooms.*

Rigg, Pat, and Virginia G. Allen. 1989. *When They Don't All Speak English: Integrating the ESL Student into the Regular Classroom.* Urbana, Ill.: National Council of Teachers of English.

Figure 2.2 Starter bibliography of books on whole language classrooms and activities

OPERATIONALIZING A TRANSACTIONAL DEFINITION OF LITERACY: TWO BEGINNINGS

The best way to convey a sense of whole language classrooms is to show them in action, through teachers and children. Here, I have chosen to present sketches of how two teachers, a first-grade teacher and a sixth-grade teacher, began creating a different atmosphere for literacy development and learning the very first day of school. As their activities and the children's are described, one senses that already on that first day, children had begun conceptualizing literacy and learning as holistic and personally rewarding.

Kittye Copeland: First-Grade Teacher

Three years ago at a conference in Toronto when I first met Kittye Copeland, I exclaimed, "Oh, so *you're* Chapter 12." Kittye looked at me blankly. She didn't know that Dorothy Watson had described her transformation from traditional to whole language teacher in Chapter 12 of my (our) *Reading Process and Practice* (Weaver 1988). What I want to share first, then, is Watson's description of why and how Kittye began implementing a whole language philosophy (Watson 1988):

> The teacher we want to describe is Kittye Copeland, who for ten years on the first day of school passed out worksheets, workbooks, basals, and other texts, and then spent the year trying to get her students to master all the first-grade information. Kittye loved teaching, but what she had done for ten years could only be described as routine; she was nearing burnout. This dedicated teacher decided to try once again; she spent the summer studying socio-psycholinguistic research and theory, including miscue analysis, and she began to develop a whole-language alternative to her traditional reading program.
>
> Kittye's eleventh year of teaching started as no other year had. The first major difference was attitudinal; Kittye focused on what her students did *right* rather than what they did *wrong*; she truly respected their efforts. This enlightened observer of children developed literacy across the curriculum based on the strengths of her students. She valued the individual and the group, and she promoted both.
>
> On the first day of school, the children were surrounded with meaningful print. They chose their nametag off the bulletin board and helped other children who had trouble reading their own name. There were letters from Kittye in their class mailbox, and on that first day they wrote back to their teacher. The children were constantly encouraged to take linguistic risks (with reading, "Put in something that makes sense"; with writing, "What would you like to tell us through writing?"; with spelling, "Spell it the best you can—think how it looks, sounds, feels in your mouth").

On the first day of school, the children listened to stories, read by themselves and with partners, wrote letters, and dictated a finger play ("Eensey Weensy Spider") to their teacher. On their own initiative they acted out "Eensey Weensy Spider"—learning concepts such as *water spout/faucet*. Interest in spiders led to some research in the science corner reference books. "Eensey Weensy Spider" became a chant that all the children could easily read as a group and individually.

As the children moved from a large-group sharing of the highly predictable book, *The Bus Ride*, to reading the book with their partner, the rhythm of the class began to emerge—even on that first day. The children knew that they could consult with other students; they knew that if they needed to try out an idea, or get help and encouragement from others, it was permissible to do so.

The classroom and materials were arranged for the students. There were large and small group work areas as well as spots where children could find a quiet place if one were needed. Unexpected events, such as a note from the cafeteria manager, were turned into literacy events in which the children shared in both receiving a message and replying to it.

At the end of the day, 26 first graders left their classroom eager and happy—not one tear, not one squabble, not one deflated and defeated learner. These children did not take home a handful of worksheets and memories of a disappointing school day. Rather, they proudly presented their parents with a copy of their finger play, a real book, a letter from their teacher, and the unshaken notion that they happily were readers and writers.

Karen Smith: Sixth-Grade Teacher

Another teacher I have come to know and admire is Karen Smith, whose methods of creating a whole language environment are described in "Hookin' 'Em in at the Start of School in a 'Whole Language' Classroom" (Edelsky, Draper, and Smith 1983):

August 30, the afternoon of the first day of school for sixth graders at Laurel School. Twenty-five children, many of whom have failed two different grades somewhere between kindergarten and today, several of whom have reputations as "bad kids" in this inner city school, have an assignment. They are to take potting soil and plant a bean in each of two milk carton containers. They will use their plants to begin the first of many experiments. The teacher tells everyone where to find the soil, seeds, and scissors. Children are to pace themselves for coming to the sink for soil and planting: "If there are five people at the sink already, use your own judgment about what else to work on. Work in your journals or decorate your folders."

Forty-five minutes from the presentation of the assignment, with no reprimanding, no step-by-step directions, no close teacher monitoring of the clean up, the children have filled 50 milk cartons with soil and seed, put them on trays near the window, cleaned the sink area, and put finished journal entries on the teacher's desk. By the end of the first school day, these children look like self-directed, conscientious "good kids," able to perform an intricate, efficient dance choreographed, but seemingly not directed, by the teacher. (pp. 257–58)

Though it may seem strange to describe a science activity as exemplifying a whole language philosophy, in whole language classrooms that philosophy pervades the entire curriculum. Karen Smith's assumptions—and hence the expectations she communicated to the students—reflected a whole language, transactional concept of how people learn best. Among the goals that she began to achieve this first day were these (pp. 263–64):

1. To get students to think and take pleasure in using their intellects.
2. To help students learn to get along with and appreciate others.
3. To manage the day-to-day environment smoothly so other goals could be accomplished.
4. To get students to be self-reliant and sure of themselves.

In such classrooms, children are likely to develop concepts of literacy and learning as involving risks and responsibility, and to think of themselves as competent readers, writers, thinkers, and learners. Such concepts promote the development of literacy and the desire to be lifelong learners.

In Karen Smith's classroom, both literacy and the students flourished. For example:

Despite these students' prior histories, KS and the students succeeded together. Absentee rates were low; in some months there were no absences. Visitors frequently commented that students were almost always engaged in appropriate tasks. Parents reported a sudden and dramatic turn to book reading and story writing as at-home activities. Students whose September journals had entries such as "I don't got nuthin to write" were writing full pages by October. Previous "nonreaders" read award-winning children's literature and revised and edited multiple drafts of long, involved stories. By spring, children spontaneously discussed the literary merits of their own writing and of books they read, commenting on style, point of view, plot structure, and other literary elements. (p. 260)

Clearly, the students had come to enjoy reading and writing and to perceive themselves as capable readers and writers—many, perhaps, for the first time. They had developed a sophisticated understanding of literature by engaging in authentic literacy events rather than in worksheet activities. They had, in short, become engaged learners, taking significant responsibility for their own learning.

ALIGNING OUR METHODS WITH OUR GOALS

❝Children develop positive attitudes toward learning when they are encouraged to view themselves as competent and responsible.❞

These two descriptions of learning and teaching in whole language classrooms should begin to suggest the value of a whole language concept of literacy and literacy learning, of a whole language, transactional philosophy as it is operationalized in a growing number of classrooms and schools. Children develop positive attitudes toward learning when they are encouraged to view themselves as competent and responsible. And in an atmosphere where they engage in actual reading and writing for a multiplicity of purposes, they become not only competent readers and writers but avid and prolific readers and writers, both inside and outside of school. In fact, competence is a by-product of engagement, rather than a prerequisite.

The traditional transmission-oriented skills model of teaching and learning that underlies much of what passes for education promotes a limited and limiting concept of literacy. In such classrooms and schools, learners are likely to conclude that reading and writing consist mainly of completing worksheets and taking tests, and that success in reading and writing is achieved mainly by avoiding or minimizing errors. There is little time in these classrooms to engage in reading and writing that demonstrably promote a broader, more functional, or more humanistic concept of literacy. Nor are learners treated in ways that encourage engagement in learning, or that promote responsibility, group cooperation, and self-determination—all characteristics our society needs.

As Chapter 3 shows more fully, the traditional, transmission concept of education is not succeeding well in developing students and adults who are literate in the sense of being able to read, write, and think critically—much less in developing citizens who through literacy can participate fully in the economic, political, social, and cultural worlds available to the literate. Not only the assessment data from the 17-year-olds who have remained in school but the statistics on the rate at which students have dropped out, many before their seventeenth year, bear witness to the inadequacy of our traditional model of education. In the inner city, the drop-out rate is often around 40 percent.

While whole language is no magic cure for our educational ills, it seems likely that more of our youth will engage themselves in the learning enterprise, as Kittye's and Karen's students have, when they participate in activities that they themselves value, when they are respected and given the opportunity to take risks and responsibility as learners, and when their strengths are emphasized instead of their weaknesses being constantly pointed out, criticized, and "remediated."

As Chapter 3, "Impetus for Revision and Reform," further suggests, we as educators must align our instruction with our goals. We are not succeeding in developing adults who reflect a transactional concept of literacy by adopting a transmission model of education in our schools. The whole language, transactional model is significantly more promising as a means of making literacy an integral part of *students'* everyday lives, and thereby of promoting the kind of literacy that will enable them as adults to participate fully in the economic, political, social, and cultural life of their world.

CHAPTER 3

Impetus for Revision and Reform

Further evidence of the inadequacy of the typical transmission model of education is presented at the outset of this chapter. First, the model is viewed from the perspective of numerical data from the National Assessment of Educational Progress and then from the perspective of the individual student. All too often a student is not merely shortchanged by the transmission approach but considered a failure by the system—when we might better consider the system itself a failure and the model upon which it rests as inappropriate for effective education.

More specifically, the chapter considers why the transmission model is an inaccurate, inappropriate basis for education and how it breeds failure. The chapter then discusses briefly the impetus and a blueprint for reform in Canada, specifically in British Columbia, before emphasizing the widespread recognition of the need for a transactional model of education in the United States. This recognition, in turn, gives impetus to a whole language philosophy and its implementation within our schools. The final section touches briefly upon how this impetus for revision and reform might be affected by the drive to create national goals and standards in education.

FAILURE OF THE TRANSMISSION MODEL: FURTHER EVIDENCE

Chapter 2 noted that the transmission model of education encourages publishers to produce workbooks and worksheets for teaching reading as the mastery of skills and similarly encourages teachers to assign an incredible number of such worksheets to children—particularly in the primary grades. We have seen also that research does not support the use of such materials; that is, there is no evidence that they are effective in promoting the development of reading. On the contrary, such seatwork preempts valuable time that might better be spent actually reading and writing.

Data from the National Assessment of Educational Progress and case studies of individual children further clarify the inadequacy of this model. While failing to develop the kind of literacy that our society requires, our schools are simultaneously misteaching and mislabeling our youth. By expecting students to fit into a single, predetermined mold and model of education that is not well supported by either research or experience, we find ourselves labeling some children as learning disabled or even as failures. Yet it is our concept of education—particularly our concept of reading and literacy development—that should be viewed as faulty (see Smith 1989).

National Assessment of Educational Progress Reports

For some time now, the business community and government officials, as well as educators, have been aware of the findings from the National Assessment of Educational Progress (NAEP). Data from five reading assessments over nearly two decades are presented and discussed in *The Reading Report Card, 1971–88* (Mullis and Jenkins 1990). These data show that though the reading proficiency of 9- and 13-year-olds improved somewhat through the 1970s and that of 17-year-olds improved during the 1980s, nevertheless, few of our youth are able to perform reading or writing tasks that go beyond the relatively simple and simplistic.

Figure 3.1 shows the percentage of students at or above certain identified proficiency levels on the NAEP scales. These statistics suggest what everyday observation confirms: that few of our students are able to draw more than the simplest of inferences from what they read—at least, when they have inadequate background knowledge, or inadequate motivation, or perhaps stress that mitigates against successful performance (see Gentile and McMillan 1987). Nor do many students seem able to analyze, evaluate, or extend their reading into other contexts.

Of course, part of the problem may be the artificiality of the tests and testing situations, or the heightened fear of failure, as compared with tasks required in everyday life outside of school. Another possibility is that questions requiring more sophisticated reading and thinking normally generate a wider range of well-reasoned responses, only one of which is considered right on such tests. Ironically, the more demanding the test, the greater the probability that the best thinkers will give "wrong" answers. Thus, we must be cautious about drawing scores from even—or perhaps especially—the best of multiple choice tests. Even so, however, everyday observation suggests that there is consider-

	Reading Skills and Strategies	Age	1971	1975	1980	1984	1988
Can carry out simple, discrete reading tasks.	Rudimentary (Level 150)	9	90.5*	93.2	94.6	92.5	93.0
		13	99.8	99.7	99.9	99.8	99.8
		17	99.6	99.7	99.8	100.0	100.0
Can comprehend specific or sequentially related information.	Basic (Level 200)	9	58.2*	62.2	67.6*	61.9	62.5
		13	92.8*	93.3*	94.9	94.1	95.1
		17	95.9	96.4	97.2	98.3	98.9
Can search for specific information, interrelate ideas, and make generalizations.	Intermediate (Level 250)	9	15.3	14.6	17.2	17.0	17.0
		13	57.9	58.6	60.9	59.1	58.0
		17	78.5*	80.4*	81.0*	83.1*	86.2
Can find, understand, summarize, and explain relatively complicated information.	Adept (Level 300)	9	1.0	0.5	0.6	1.0	1.2
		13	9.8	10.3	11.3	10.9	10.6
		17	39.2	39.1	38.5	40.0	41.8
Can synthesize and learn from specialized reading materials.	Advanced (Level 350)	9	0.0	0.0	0.0	0.0	0.0
		13	0.1	0.2	0.2	0.2	0.2
		17	6.6*	6.1*	5.3	5.5	4.8

Figure 3.1 **Percentage of students at or above the five levels of reading proficiency, 1971–1988 (* = statistically significant difference from 1988). Data from NAEP assessments of reading (Mullis and Jenkins 1990, p. 24)**

able cause for concern about our students' ability to read and reason critically and creatively.

The situation with respect to writing is no more encouraging. The authors of *Crossroads in American Education* generalize that although the writing achievement of 13- and 17-year-olds climbed between 1979 and 1984 after declining between 1974 and 1979, "writing proficiency across the ages generally appeared to be no better in 1984 than it was 10 years earlier" (Applebee et al. 1989, p. 10). Figure 3.2 presents the highest percentage of students performing at or above the minimal and adequate levels on various types of writing tasks in the 1988 and 1984 assessments.

At grade 4, most children wrote at or above a minimal level on imaginative tasks and in reporting information, but few were able to write even minimal pieces in response to the other tasks. Few eighth-

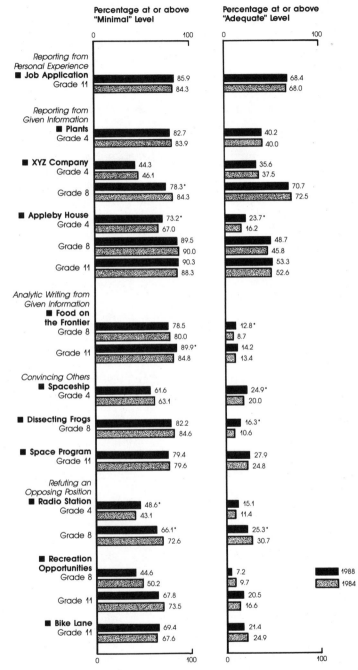

Figure 3.2 **Trends in informative and persuasive writing on selected NAEP tasks (* = statistically significant difference between years at the .05 level) (Applebee et al. 1990, pp. 12 and 27)**

grade students were able to write adequate pieces in response to most of the tasks, and less than a third of the eleventh-grade students were able to write adequate pieces in response to the analytic or persuasive tasks. Thus, "The results suggest that a vast number of students nearing high-school graduation do not have a sufficient command of written language to move beyond straightforward explication and communicate a reasoned point of view" (Applebee et al. 1989, p. 25). The results for the 1988 assessment of writing are somewhat better for the younger students, but even less impressive for the eleventh-grade students, overall.

At the "adequate" level, the data from *Crossroads in American Education* suggest that the situation is similar in the disciplines of literature, history, mathematics, and science. Thus, not only in literacy education but in the content areas, the transmission model of education that dominates our classrooms is simply not fostering the sophisticated kinds of reasoning that our society has come to demand.

Students Who Don't Fit the Transmission Model or Mold

Typically, then, the transmission model shortchanges students, not only encouraging a limited concept of literacy and learning, but actively promoting it. Students are rewarded more for "correct" answers than for critical and creative thinking, as so many of us who have taught honors freshmen in college can attest: All too often these bright students have applied their intelligence merely to the task of playing the academic game. They are appalled and afraid of "failure" when we insist that they reason for themselves.

Other students, however, either will not or cannot play the traditional academic game, so they actually come to be labeled failures in a system dominated by a transmission model. All students in such classrooms implicitly are expected to learn the same things at the same time, in the same way—and complex processes like reading and writing are taught as if they first involved the mastery of discrete skills.

Often, a kindergartener well on the way to becoming a reader and writer finds his or her progress thwarted by a *skills* approach to literacy in the first grade. Here is part of one teacher/parent's report of her son's transition from a "very eager, caring, sensitive" child in a whole language kindergarten to a "very negative, frustrated, defiant" child in a skills-oriented first grade. The change apparently resulted from the difference in instructional philosophies and methods:

> In the whole language kindergarten, Eric considered himself a reader. He was able to successfully use functional productive reading skills and strategies to read stories both at home and at school. He was

genuinely excited about story themes and authors, and frequently shared his enthusiasm with friends and family.

In a phonics approach to reading in first grade, he came home one day to express his concern that they "didn't have time to read a story today," though they did "do lots of work." His functional reading strategies began to recede with phonics, because reading was episodic or truncated. He was required to complete so many worksheets on beginning, ending, and short vowel sounds before a book or story was introduced that attention to meaning was lost. His oral reading became segmented and halting because he was concerned about sounding everything out. He was given word-list worksheets—sight words which he was required to memorize in isolation. He was also given worksheets with 25–30 words which he was required to pronounce, distinguishing between the short and long vowel sounds. Each week, the teacher sent home for practice child-made tachistoscopes using rhyming words dictated by the teacher. Reading in class was not meaning-centered, but was used to apply phonics skills previously practiced. Stories were almost meaningless, but reflected a large number of the phonics skills to be practiced.

In writing, the differences between the two classes were much the same. In kindergarten, Eric wrote daily in his journal at home and in school. In first grade, the only writing done on a regular basis was fill-in-the-blank comprehension questions, copying weekly spelling words three times each, or copying a class language experience activity from the board. The children were never encouraged to write independently. (M. Graves 1990)

Thus, Eric's transition from eager to frustrated learner should not be surprising. And given Eric's personality change from kindergarten to first grade and his new reluctance to engage in reading and especially writing, his mother understandably fears that Eric might soon be labeled as deficient in reading and writing skills.

As another example, take the case of Tom, reported in Carbo's "Deprogramming Reading Failure: Giving Unequal Learners an Equal Chance" (November 1987):

At the age of 7, Tom was wrongfully branded as "learning disabled" and "severely emotionally disturbed" and shipped off to a school for the handicapped. At the end of third grade, after four years of intensive phonics instruction, Tom could read only a few words. He was convinced that he was "stupid" and "bad," and he began to have recurrent stomach pains.

The destruction of Tom's natural desire and ability to learn to read had begun in kindergarten and had continued throughout the intervening years. He had been inappropriately taught, embarrassed by his poor performance, and teased and taunted by his schoolmates. Tom's steady academic decline was temporarily halted in fourth grade, when his teacher's approach to teaching matched his reading style. That year, Tom encountered for the first time holistic reading methods, tactile/kinesthetic materials, and no phonics. Within eight months, he was reading on a second-grade level, and his stomach pains were a thing of the past.

Unfortunately, that breakthrough was not enough to save Tom. His family relocated, and he had to attend a different school. The reading program in his self-contained fifth-grade classroom for the hand-icapped consisted of worksheets and more phonics. Since Tom could not learn through these approaches, he never advanced beyond a second-grade reading level. Eventually he dropped out of school to join the swelling ranks of adult illiterates. (pp. 197–98)

This, as Carbo says, should have never happened: Tom had a normal IQ and attended a "good" suburban school. "Like millions of other students, however, Tom was a victim of an unspoken presumption in our schools: that there is one right way to teach children to read—and that there is something inherently wrong with any student who cannot learn to read by that method" (Carbo November 1987, p. 198).

One need not subscribe to the concept of *reading styles* to realize that something was indeed wrong with the position that if Tom could not learn phonics as taught using worksheets, he could not learn to read by any other means. In the case of both Eric and Tom, it is the skills model of education that is the problem, not the children.

WHY THE TRANSMISSION MODEL IS AT FAULT

The transmission model is at fault simply because it does not re-flect how children actually learn complex processes. Despite what is "taught" and what may appear to be learned, children's actual cogni-tive processing proceeds in idiosyncratic and uncontrollable ways, not typically one skill at a time. Janet Emig has summarized this relationship between teaching and learning: "That teachers teach and children learn no one will deny. But to believe that children learn *because* teachers teach and only what teachers explicitly teach is to engage in magical thinking" (Emig 1983, p. 135). In effect, then, even students who seem to succeed with a transmission approach may be learning in far different ways than they appear to be, and may be learning very different lessons than those the schools are trying to teach.

In a significant article, "Toward a Unified Theory of Literacy Learn-ing and Instructional Practices," ethnographer Denny Taylor (1989) discusses insights gained from the literacy profiles or "biographies" developed from anecdotal and other records on the daily activities and progress of individual children. Drawing upon such detailed records of children's literacy development in what are essentially whole language classrooms, Taylor concludes that both the stage theory of development and a related linear, hierarchical approach to developing literacy severely distort the learning process. While evidence for the idiosyncratic nature of children's literacy development doesn't mean there are no trends in how children develop literacy, it does mean that stage theory is far too tidy a concept to account for the messy reality encountered when we observe and document the learning of individual children.

Without explicitly mentioning a transmission model of education, Taylor is in effect condemning that model in her discussion of the necessity for giving up simplistic notions about complex behaviors:

> The methods of instruction that are now dominant dictate that, when a young child comes to school, "learning" to read is presented as an orderly, linear, hierarchical sequence of tasks. How a child measures up to this "theory of instruction" becomes the benchmark of his or her early reading development. When an individual child's learning does not fit the instructional training program, "problems" are diagnosed and "remediated," using more intensive doses of linearly sequenced decoding skills. Children are labeled and pigeonholed, and their own learning is denied. (Taylor 1989, p. 186)

This sounds familiar to many parents whose children have experienced such treatment within our educational system. Significantly, Taylor points out that it is not only our practices but our theories that are at fault:

> What researchers and educators who support such "methods" fail to appreciate is that the "errors" that they mark on workbook pages are not aberrations in the learning abilities of young children but are merely reflections of their own aberrant theories and pedagogical practices. They have learned not to see that children's early literacy behaviors are disorderly, seemingly erratic, and incomprehensibly chaotic. (Taylor 1989, p. 186)

Among other things, this means educators have learned not to see that reading and writing don't actually develop one skill at a time or in completely predictable and invariant ways, even when these processes are taught that way. Nor have such researchers and educators come to realize that through engagement in these untidy and even chaotic behaviors, children not only learn to read and write, but develop surprisingly sophisticated concepts of the functions, uses, and forms of written language. Educators have been so busy "teaching" and "remediating" children according to their preconceived theories and notions that they have not paused to document how and what children actually learn when their learning is facilitated but not controlled.

Unfortunately, millions of students are no more fortunate than the aforementioned Tom in the instructional methods and expectations they encounter. As a society, we seem to tolerate increasingly greater numbers of "learning disabled" students, rarely stopping to consider that

❝As a society, we seem to tolerate increasingly greater numbers of "learning disabled" students, rarely stopping to consider that the problem may be more with our educational model than with the students.❞

the problem may be more with our educational model than with the students. As indicated in Chapter 2, our schools seem to create many of the less competent readers and writers, as well as many of the so-called disabled learners, by adopting an inappropriate model of education.

HOW THE TRANSMISSION MODEL BREEDS FAILURE

There are several ways in which our educational model, materials, and methods breed failure—both for the individual and for the system. Because instruction is not aligned with our broad educational goals, we subvert those goals and label as failures the youth we desperately want to have succeed. This section focuses on the observation that what we teach is what we get, with an emphasis on basal reading programs as promoting a limited concept of literacy, and remedial instruction for less competent readers as, ironically, serving to keep such students from becoming more competent.

What We Teach Is What We Get

Educators are increasingly recognizing that what we teach is what we get. As Judith Langer, co-author of several NAEP reports, has said:

> Results such as those from the National Assessment of Educational Progress (NAEP 1985) continue to suggest that schools are successful in teaching what they have set out to teach. Whether by accident or design, school curricula and the tests that go with them have rewarded relatively simple performance, and have undervalued the attainment of more thoughtful skills. *They have been driven by a model of literacy that focuses on discrete skills and bits of information instead of big ideas and deeper understandings.* It is my argument that student performance such as reported by NAEP is no surprise, since these are the ways of thinking that are highlighted in the curriculum, supported by the instructional materials, and reinforced by the tests we use and the grades we give. (Langer 1989, p. 2; emphasis mine)

In short, our educational approach has been dominated by a transmission model of teaching and learning.

In *Crossroads in American Education*, the authors of several NAEP reports discuss the discrepancy between students' relatively successful performance in school and their relatively unsuccessful performance on NAEP tasks that require more than simplistic reasoning. One possibility, certainly, is that the students are not as engaged in taking the NAEP tests as they are in their ordinary schoolwork. There is substantial data, however—such as that discussed in the British Columbian document *Legacy for Learners* (pp. 63–64 in this book)—suggesting that few students are much engaged in most of the schoolwork they do. The hypothesis that seems supported by the widest range of evidence is that "institutional goals have tended to support and reinforce the teaching and learning of less difficult concepts and skills to the neglect of those that are more challenging. Recent reports have tended to support this last contention, and if this is so, the goals, materials, and methods of instruction may need to be reformulated" (Applebee et al. 1989, p. 26).

Commenting on the NAEP findings in the *Crossroads* report, the heads of both major teacher unions agreed that American education is at a crossroads. Mary Hatwood Futrell of the National Education Association said that "only comprehensive, systematic change will make the dramatic improvements in learning our nation needs to see." Albert Shanker of the American Federation of Teachers said, "Let's stop pretending that we have the one and only cure and start taking some risks that engage teachers in bringing about change" (National Council of Teachers of English May 1989, citing *Education Daily* February 15, 1989).

As Mary Futrell phrased it in an "opinionnaire" (*Education Week* March 15, 1989), "Unfortunately, America's schools are not structured to develop the full potential of our nation's young. Our schools are still structured on the old industrial model that treats students as 'products' coming down the assembly-line and teachers as mass production workers." This is another way of viewing a transmission model.

Basal Readers and the Transmission Model

Unfortunately, the transmission model is embodied in the majority of textbooks and programs used in the public schools, and basal reading series are no exception. In fact, the traditional basal programs may be a prototype because certainly their use within kindergarten and first grade has demonstrated to children at the outset of their schooling that they are expected to be passive, complete-the-worksheet, repeat-after-me, and find-the-right-answer kinds of learners.

Of course, neither the basal publishers nor editors and authors nor teachers nor administrators and policy-makers are alone to be blamed for the fact that traditional basal programs reflect this passive concept of learning. The basal reading programs simply reflect the transmission model of education that is unthinkingly held by most people in our society, including many of the highly educated. As a society, we *know* that we need to develop students' ability to think critically and creatively, and we *say* we want to and intend to. But then what we too often do is devise "critical thinking" and reading programs that subvert the

Basals: Part of the Problem

There is a significant gap between how reading is learned and how it is taught and assessed in the vast majority of our classrooms today. This gap is perpetuated by the basal reading series that dominate reading instruction in roughly 90 percent of the elementary classrooms in the United States. Such textbook series are often viewed as complete systems for teaching reading, for they include not only a graded series of books for the students to read but teachers' manuals telling teachers what and how to teach, workbooks and dittos for the students to complete, sets of tests to assess reading skills, and often various supplementary aids. Because of their comprehensiveness, basal reading systems leave very little room for other kinds of reading activities in the schools where they have been adopted. This is all the more unfortunate because current theory and research strongly support such conclusions as the following:

- Basal reading series typically reflect and promote the misconception that reading is necessarily learned from smaller to larger parts.
- The sequencing of skills in a basal reading series exists not because this is how children learn to read but simply because of the logistics of developing a series of lessons that can be taught sequentially, day after day, week after week, year after year.
- Students are typically tested for ability to master the bits and pieces of reading, such as phonics and other word-identification skills, and even comprehension skills. However, there is no evidence that mastering such skills in isolation guarantees the ability to comprehend connected text, or that students who cannot give evidence of such skills in isolation are necessarily unable to comprehend connected text.

Figure 3.3   Concerns about basal reading programs from "Basal Readers and the State of American Reading Instruction: A Call for Action." Position statement, Commission on Reading, National Council of Teachers of English 1988

very skills and strategies they were designed to teach. We try to teach *active* thinking and reading in a *passive* way that inhibits the development of those very abilities. Such are the programs that pervade our schools from kindergarten through high school and beyond.

In the long run, these programs will surely have far more weight than any programs geared specifically to teach the metacognitive strategies involved in reading or the HOTS (higher-order thinking skills) that are currently popular, even if some of these programs reflect a transactional rather than a transmission model of learning.

It was largely concern with this outdated model of learning as manifested in basal reading programs that led the Commission on Reading of the National Council of Teachers of English to encourage the research

- Thus for many if not most children, the typical basal reading series may actually make learning to read more difficult than it needs to be.

- So much time is typically taken up by "instructional" activities (including activities with workbooks and skill sheets) that only a very slight amount of time is spent in actual reading—despite the overwhelming evidence that extensive reading and writing are crucial to the development of literacy.

- Basal reading series typically reflect and promote the widespread misconception that the ability to verbalize an answer, orally or in writing, is evidence of understanding and learning. Thus even students who appear to be learning from a basal reading series are being severely shortchanged, for they are being systematically encouraged not to think.

- Basal reading series typically tell teachers exactly what they should do and say while teaching a lesson, thus depriving teachers of the responsibility and authority to make informed professional judgments.

- "Going through the paces" thus becomes the measure of both teaching and learning. The teachers are assumed to have taught well if and only if they have taught the lesson. Students are assumed to have learned if and only if they have given "right" answers.

- *The result of such misconceptions about learning and such rigid control of teacher and student activities is to discourage both teachers and students from thinking, and particularly to discourage students from developing and exercising critical literacy and thinking skills needed to participate fully in a technologically advanced democratic society.*

Figure 3.3   (*continued*)

that led to the publication of the *Report Card on Basal Readers* (K. Goodman et al. 1988); to develop two position statements on basal readers (Commission on Reading 1988b); and to draft a resolution on basals that was passed at the 1988 business meeting of the National Council of Teachers of English (NCTE January 1989). Figure 3.3 reproduces the Commission on Reading's concerns about basal programs, as expressed in the shorter position statement, while Appendix 3.1 reproduces the statement in its entirety, including recommended actions for local administrators and policy-makers.

As Chapters 1 and 2 indicated, the transmission model that underlies most basal programs has encouraged us as a society to conceptualize reading and literacy in fragmented and limited ways. The *Report Card on Basal Readers* expresses it succinctly: "reading is not making sense of print anymore. It is doing well on the basal tests" (K. Goodman et al.

1988, p. 108). Or, one might add, it is doing well on standardized and state-mandated tests. As the Commission on Reading's position statement suggests, the concept of "reading" is reduced to what can be taught skill by skill and measured the same way, according to a transmission concept of education. No wonder, then, that few students are learning to read, write, or think actively.

The "Poor" Get Poorer Reading Instruction

There is increasing concern about the kind of instruction offered students who are perceived to be lacking in "skills," particularly reading skills. They are often labeled "remedial" or "at risk" and given " 'lessons that are shaped by a behavioral or training perspective: lower-level skills, fragmented knowledge, or easily tested facts.' " With at-risk students, this tracking often amounts to racial and socioeconomic bias because it results in " 'restricted access of poor, racial minority students to rigorous academic work' " ("Helping Underachievers Succeed," August 1989, quoting a paper, "Access to Knowledge: Breaking Down School Barriers to Learning," prepared by Pamela Keating and Jeannie Oakes as part of the Education Commission of the States' Youth at Risk project).

Since it is the reading of authentic texts rather than skills work that has been demonstrated to enhance students' ability to read, placing students considered to be poor readers into classes with even more emphasis on skills will naturally tend to make them poorer readers, not better.

In 1985, two articles summarized various studies of the kinds of instruction received by students placed in lower reading groups, in comparison with those in higher reading groups (Shannon 1985, Hillerich 1985). Some of these differences are as follows, with the original source indicated whenever it is especially pertinent:

1. Readers in lower groups spend approximately 70–75 percent of their time in oral reading, done round robin—in trying to say the words correctly while the teacher listens and corrects. Consequently, they not only focus less on meaning but read much less than those in higher groups, who spend about 70–75 percent of their time reading silently, for meaning and enjoyment (Allington 1983).

2. When readers in higher groups make a miscue ("error"), teachers typically ignore the miscue or suggest how the surrounding text may help to clarify meaning. When readers in lower groups make

a miscue, however, teachers typically stop them and often call attention to the letter/sound cues exclusively or correct them immediately, giving the students in lower groups much less time to discover a lack of continuity in meaning and to correct themselves. Thus, the attention of readers in lower groups is directed toward getting the words rather than on constructing meaning. The frequent interruptions and corrections contribute to such readers' general hesitancy in reading, to their frequent appeals for assistance from teachers, and to their reluctance or inability to monitor their own comprehension (Shannon 1985).

3. Reading lessons for lower groups are more teacher-centered, more tightly monitored, and more likely to focus on literal interpretation of text rather than upon drawing inferences, analyzing, evaluating, and extending or relating to what has been read (Brophy and Good 1986).

4. Readers in lower groups receive much more drill on isolated words than readers in higher groups receive. It is the lower-group readers who are kept busy with workbooks and dittos, drilled on word lists and flash cards, and assigned skills work while the others read whole books and participate in creative ways of enhancing and expressing comprehension. While readers in higher groups may take home library books to read, lower-group readers are more likely to take home flash cards, vocabulary lists, and skills sheets.

Again, if such skills work were reliably demonstrated to improve students' ability to read and comprehend the variety of texts encountered in the external world, we might grudgingly approve this focus for students who appear to have difficulty with such work. Just the opposite appears to be true, however: Actual reading and writing usually do as much or more to raise ''reading-achievement'' scores, even on tests of various kinds of skills. But more important, engaging in authentic acts of reading and writing is much more effective in developing independent and lifelong readers and writers, thinkers and learners (see Chapter 6). Thus, students in lower reading groups are systematically, if inadvertently, being excluded from the kinds of experiences most likely to facilitate their literacy and their intellectual development.

Notice that I have carefully refrained from labeling such students as poor or poorer readers. Often the students assigned to the lower reading groups are merely the ones who cannot or will not complete the skills work, or those who have not yet read higher ''levels'' in the basal reading program or completed the accompanying workbooks. They are not necessarily students who cannot construct meaning from text (see pp. 189–190, Chap. 9).

❝Thus, students in lower reading groups are systematically, if inadvertently, being excluded from the kinds of experiences most likely to facilitate their literacy and their intellectual development.❞

Unfortunately, there is a growing tendency to label children as deficient, and to do so at an earlier age, even in or before kindergarten (see Durkin 1987). Instead of revamping education to meet the needs of most learners in regular classrooms, we single out individual children as unready or unable to adjust to existing curricula—and then, typically, subject them to more of what they have been unsuccessful at. Says Richard Allington of the State University of New York/Albany, "'I think we tremendously underestimate the . . . stigmatization' of children brought on by being identified as deficient in some way. . . . In several schools Allington has worked with, 'literally two-thirds of the children have been labeled as failures before the 3rd grade' by being retained or referred for special services" ("Early Identification Efforts Raise Doubts" 1989, p. 6). If these children are then dosed with low-level skills work, as is typical, inappropriate instruction will then combine with and compound their lowered self-esteem, crippling them intellectually and tending to make them failures for life.

Fortunately, there is also a countermovement. As a result of the increasing recognition that often our "remedial" efforts are actually creating less competent readers, writers, and thinkers, a movement is growing aimed at eliminating remedial classes and/or offering students who appear to be lacking in skills the kind of enriched curriculum typically offered to the so-called gifted. (See, for example, the article on Denver's elimination of remedial classes in *Education Week*, October 11, 1989, and the aforementioned articles in the Association for Supervision and Curriculum Development *Update*, August 1989.)

This shift toward treating remedial students as gifted makes considerable sense from several points of view. First, from the viewpoint of the self-fulfilling prophecy, what you teach is what you get—in this case either low-level skills work or a more sophisticated ability to read, write, and reason. Second, it makes sense from the point of view of learning strategies and styles: The vast majority of students put in remedial classes today are individuals who are less able to do isolated skills work than to think critically and creatively about a vast array of questions, issues, and phenomena (see Carbo 1987, all references).

And from a whole language viewpoint, treating *all* learners as gifted individuals capable of complex reasoning makes sense not only for the reasons just given but because constructing meaning is more than merely building from smaller parts to larger wholes. The parts have relatively little meaning in isolation, and focusing on skills rather than texts distorts the reading process and may actually confuse students as to what is required in reading connected text effectively and efficiently. Language and literacy are best learned through actual reading and writing, as explained more fully in Chapter 4 and as corroborated by research discussed in Chapter 6.

In short, the transmission model of education is not serving our students well, and most of all it is shortchanging and severely damaging those who have already demonstrated their difficulty in learning according to that model. A transactional approach to literacy and learning will better serve the needs of all learners, as well as the demands of the society in which they will find themselves as adults.

CANADA: IMPETUS AND BLUEPRINT FOR REVISION AND REFORM

Canada is significantly ahead of the United States in moving toward a transactional model of education, as reflected particularly in a whole language philosophy. Whole language education has for several years been official policy in the provinces of Alberta, Quebec, and Nova Scotia, as well as in other local school districts. The province of British Columbia adopted in the late 1980s an official model of education that can be characterized as transactional, with whole language mentioned approvingly as a more specific model for revision and reform.

The recently developed policy in British Columbia is particularly admirable, I believe, because it stems in part from interviews with students from grades 3 through 12; that is, the policy-makers sought to determine how students themselves feel about the role of formal education in their lives.

Some of the students, particularly some attending nonpublic schools, were found to receive and be motivated by academic challenge. Unfortunately, however, such students were—and are—rare. Some, the investigators found, were turned off to school; some were defeated by school; others, while not defeated, were struggling their way through. None of this will surprise people who work with students daily. What may be realized less often, however, is that many of the students who do *well* in school are hardly any more *engaged* in learning than those who do not do well. As the Royal Commission report *A Legacy for Learners* expresses it, ''While the school remains at the centre of their lives, it is apparent that their studies tend to be impediments they must endure along the way to what really matters'' (Sullivan 1988, p. 61).

Still, there appears to be hope, to the extent that we actively involve young people in their learning—that is, to the extent that our teaching reflects a transactional more than a transmission model. In their concluding discussion of students' concepts of school and learning, the researchers for *A Legacy for Learners* summarize:

> It was interesting, but not particularly startling, that the learners we interviewed approached school, generally, with a utilitarian perspective. They looked to schools for the benefits they could gain from them

> [social benefits, entry into the world of work or college], rather than wishing to pursue learning for its own sake. Yet, somehow paradoxically, the young people we interviewed held personal and social views about the importance of their own learning. For the most part, they portrayed it as an intensely personal activity which provoked the imagination and kindled a spirit of challenge when it occurred. They viewed learning also as a group activity, one to be shared with friends and classmates. Accordingly, they valued teachers who provided them with opportunities to take risks and strive for more than they thought they could achieve, but, somehow, who were also able to create that sense of belonging to a group in which all members could share in the challenge. (Sullivan 1988, p. 62)

This sounds very much like what whole language educators are trying to accomplish in their classrooms, with and among their students.

Not surprisingly, then, the Royal Commission Report on education recommends an approach to English such as that ''reflected in the Whole Language Approach and in the Writing Process. . . . Fundamental to each of these is a view of children as active participants in their learning, a view the Commission holds to be extremely important'' (Sullivan 1988, p. 96). Some of the key concepts underlying the proposed curriculum revisions in British Columbia are:

> To be useful, the curriculum must reflect a view of knowledge that connotes more than a set of predetermined facts and conclusions being transmitted untouched and unmodified from one generation to the next.
> The curriculum must be designed to involve students in critical thinking if it is to be useful. Moreover, children must be able to see this usefulness for themselves; the curriculum and its goals must engage students in their learning for it to be meaningful to them. . . .
> Teachers and schools must recognize the wide range that exists in students' abilities, interests, ambitions, beliefs, attitudes, and values. Curriculum must repsond to it by providing variety and choice.
> Achievement is often narrowly defined in terms of test scores—how much has been learned. We need to be concerned about attainment of the broader goals we espouse for our children. (Sullivan 1988, p. 79)

Such statements again suggest a transactional model and a whole language philosophy of education.

The new emphasis on learner-focused, integrative education has been further clarified in a formal address by A. J. Brummet (1989b), Minister of Education of British Columbia. (See Figure 3.4. See also Sullivan 1988, pp. 79–82 and 95–104, for statements that similarly reflect a transactional model and a whole language philosophy.)

Because this philosophy promotes the maximum rather than minimal learning of *all* students, it is perhaps not surprising that whole language has become official policy or else a philosophy/approach recommended approvingly not only in New Zealand where it is said to have originated,

. . . I see a curriculum that is focused on the learner rather than on our present subject-focused, grade-stamped curriclum. We will need to identify the specific learning outcomes we expect for our students, but we also need to move away from always specifying the textbook they have to read or country they have to study.

The individual student or class interest will play larger roles in determining the specific day-to-day learning experiences.

We will concentrate more on taking our students from where they are when they enter our class to where their potential will take them, rather than prescribing a complete set of hoops they must jump through.

We will instill in our students the love of learning and the ability to learn lifelong.

Third, we will see a teaching force that reflects the ideal of "facilitating learning" rather than the delivery of pre-packaged teaching modules that our students are expected to ingest.

Our teaching force will enhance its already high professional standards. They will truly be models of the lifelong learners we hope our children will become.

Together we will identify appropriate methods to enable our teachers to remain up-to-date with the newest methods of the profession.

In essence we will provide the teachers with greater flexibility in the classroom to do what they do best—help our children learn.

Figure 3.4   Excerpts from address to British Columbia School Trustees Association by A. J. Brummet, Minister of Education (Brummet 1989b)

but also in parts of Australia, several provinces in Canada, and a rapidly growing number of U.S. schools and school systems. Though a whole language approach to learning and teaching has spread less rapidly in the United States than elsewhere, here too the underlying transactional model of education is being increasingly advocated as more appropriate than a transmission model.

THE UNITED STATES: WIDESPREAD RECOGNITION OF THE NEED FOR A TRANSACTIONAL MODEL

Among various professionals and professional groups involved in U.S. education, there is widespread and growing recognition of the narrowness, inappropriateness, and ineffectiveness of the transmission model reflected in traditional reading programs and in many teaching materials in most disciplines.

Such recognition is demonstrated, for example, in recent statements and reports by professional organizations with a particular content focus: the National Council of Teachers of Mathematics, the American Association for the Advancement of Science, and the National Science Teachers Association; and a coalition of professional organizations concerned with the teaching of English and the language arts, whose views are expressed in *The English Coalition Conference: Democracy through Language* (Lloyd-Jones and Lunsford 1989). In each case, the organizations recommend what has been called a transactional model of education: a view of education as actively involving learners in exploring significant concepts and ideas, in part through reading, writing, and discussion, rather than passively receiving and regurgitating mere factual information.

The need for a transactional model is expressed with equal force by professional organizations that are not focused on a particular content area, such as the National Association for the Education of Young Children; Appendix 3.2 gives excerpts from its position statement, *Developmentally Appropriate Practice in Early Childhood Programs*. The principles articulated in that document are echoed in *Right from the Start* (1988), a position statement of the National Association of State Boards of Education, and in *Early Childhood and Family Education: Foundations for Success* (1988), a position statement of the Council of Chief State School Officers. An active approach to education has also been recommended by the National Research Council.

While many groups recognize the need for a transactional approach at the elementary and especially the primary-grade levels, active involvement in learning is equally critical at higher levels of education, as suggested by the recent NAEP report *Crossroads in American Education*. The authors of this report conclude from their examination of recent NAEP assessments—not only of reading and writing but of mathematics, science, history, and literature—that the current passive concept of education must be replaced by an active view:

> Discussion teams, cooperative work groups, individual learning logs, computer networking, and other activities that engage students as active learners will need to be added, and may even predominate. Using these new approaches will require teachers to move away from traditional authoritarian roles and, at the same time, require students to give up being passive recipients of learning. Instead, teachers will need to act more as guides, and students more as doers and thinkers. (Applebee et al. 1989, p. 41)

Only by more actively engaging students in their own learning are we as a society likely to create the kinds of thinkers and problem-solvers needed in the twenty-first century. As Judith Langer says, we need to conceptualize literacy ''as the ability to think and reason'' within our society (Langer 1989, p. 1), not as the ability to score well on skills tests.

Whole language educators, then, are in the mainstream of current educational thinking. What they know about how literacy develops, and how as teachers they can foster the development of literacy, is simply one particular manifestation of a broader model of learning and of teaching. Whole language is simply good education.

REFORMS IN CONFLICT?

As this movement toward providing education more suitable to children's learning strategies and development gains momentum, there is a concomitant movement to reform education by establishing national goals and standards for education. In the aftermath of the "education summit" at Charlottesville, Virginia, in the fall of 1989, national goals are being determined and national standards for education set.

In 1988, Congress established the National Assessment Governing Board and charged it with performing such functions as overseeing the National Assessment for Educational Progress and establishing appropriate achievement goals for each *age, grade,* and *subject area* to be tested under the National Assessment. Included, of course, is the area of reading—and presumably writing.

One might be tempted to assume that this mandate to establish goals and standards is, in effect, a mandate for establishing minimal performance objectives like those that typically drive a transmission-oriented model of education. However, that is apparently not the intention of the National Assessment Governing Board. The board plans to emphasize not minimal skills needed for survival but more complex skills needed for achievement and advancement in today's world. Also, "there is an underlying assumption of a developmental curriculum. That is, specific objectives span several grades as the students' capacity develops from the lower levels of the content taxonomy in the elementary grades to the highest levels at the upper grades" (National Assessment Governing Board December 8, 1989, p. 16).

Thus, the drive toward national education standards should not be interpreted as a mandate to continue or expand a transmission, skills orientation to education in general, or to reading and writing in particular. On the contrary, it appears that the National Assessment Governing Board's emphasis on more-than-minimal skills and on a developmental perspective is, if anything, encouragement to implement a transactional model of education that holds greater promise than the traditional skills model for fostering the development of literacy, as broadly conceived.

We shall turn in Chapter 4 to research on developing language and literacy: how language and literacy develop "naturally" when children

" Whole language educators, then, are in the mainstream of current educational thinking. What they know about how literacy develops, and how as teachers they can foster the development of literacy, is simply one particular manifestation of a broader model of learning and of teaching. **"**

transact with adults in an atmosphere of positive expectation and response. Though there are developmental trends in children's emergent language and literacy, we shall see that these are by no means definite enough to justify a stage theory of development. There is pattern within the chaos of children's literacy development, and yet each child's development remains, in many respects, quite idiosyncratic.

Appendix 3.1
A Statement of the Commission on Reading,
National Council of Teachers of English

BASAL READERS AND THE STATE OF AMERICAN READING INSTRUCTION: A CALL FOR ACTION

THE PROBLEM

As various national studies suggest, the problem of illiteracy, semi-literacy, and aliteracy in the United States appears to be growing, due at least in part to escalating standards of literacy in the workplace and in the civic area. And at a time when our information-age society demands increased literacy from all citizens, reading instruction is locked into a technology that is more than half a century out-of-date.

BASALS: PART OF THE PROBLEM

There is a significant gap between how reading is learned and how it is taught and assessed in the vast majority of our classrooms today. This gap is perpetuated by the basal reading series that dominate reading instruction in roughly 90 percent of the elementary classrooms in the United States. Such textbook series are often viewed as complete systems for teaching reading, for they include not only a graded series of books for the students to read but teachers' manuals telling teachers what and how to teach, workbooks and dittos for the students to complete, sets of tests to assess reading skills, and often various supplementary aids. Because of their comprehensiveness, basal reading systems leave very little room for other kinds of reading activities in the schools where they have been adopted. This is all the more unfortunate because current theory and research strongly support such conclusions as the following:

- Basal reading series typically reflect and promote the misconception that reading is necessarily learned from smaller to larger parts.
- The sequencing of skills in a basal reading series exists not because this is how children learn to read but simply because of the logistics of developing a series of lessons that can be taught sequentially, day after day, week after week, year after year.
- Students are typically tested for ability to master the bits and pieces of reading, such as phonics and other word-identification skills, and even comprehension skills. However, there is no evidence that mastering such skills in isolation guarantees the ability to comprehend connected text, or that students who cannot give evidence of such skills in isolation are necessarily unable to comprehend connected text.
- Thus for many if not most children, the typical basal reading series may actually make learning to read more difficult than it needs to be.
- So much time is typically taken up by "instructional" activities (including activities with workbooks and skill sheets) that only a very slight amount of time is spent in actual reading—despite the overwhelming evidence that extensive reading and writing are crucial to the development of literacy.

- Basal reading series typically reflect and promote the widespread misconception that the ability to verbalize an answer, orally or in writing, is evidence of understanding and learning. Thus even students who appear to be learning from a basal reading series are being severely shortchanged, for they are being systematically encouraged not to think.
- Basal reading series typically tell teachers exactly what they should do and say while teaching a lesson, thus depriving teachers of the responsibility and authority to make informed professional judgments.
- "Going through the paces" thus becomes the measure of both teaching and learning. The teachers are assumed to have taught well if and only if they have taught the lesson. Students are assumed to have learned if and only if they have given "right" answers.
- *The result of such misconceptions about learning and such rigid control of teacher and student activities is to discourage both teachers and students from thinking, and particularly to discourage students from developing and exercising critical literacy and thinking skills needed to participate fully in a technologically advanced democratic society.*

RECOMMENDED ACTIONS FOR LOCAL ADMINISTRATORS AND FOR POLICYMAKERS

For Local Administrators

- Provide continual district inservice for teachers to help them develop a solid understanding of how people read and how children learn to read and how reading is related to writing and learning to write.
- Provide time and opportunities for teachers to mentor with peers who are trying innovative materials and strategies.
- Support teachers in attending local, regional, state, and national conferences to improve their knowledge base, and support continued college coursework for teachers in reading and writing.
- Allow/encourage teachers to use alternatives to basal readers or to use basal readers flexibly, eliminating whatever their professional judgment deems unnecessary or inappropriate; for example,
  —encourage innovation at a school level, offering teachers a choice of basals, portions of basals, or no basal, using assessment measures that match their choice
  —discuss at a school level which portions of the basal need not be used, and use the time saved for reading and discussion of real literature
  —provide time for teachers to work with one another to set up innovative programs.
- Give teachers the opportunity to demonstrate that standardized test scores will generally not be adversely affected by using alternatives to basal readers, and may in fact be enhanced.
- Provide incentives for teachers to develop and use alternative methods of reading assessment, based upon their understanding of reading and learning to read.
- Allow/encourage teachers to take charge of their own reading instruction, according to their informed professional judgment.

For Policymakers

- Change laws and regulations that favor or require use of basals, so that
  —state funds may be used for non-basal materials
  —schools may use programs that do not have traditional basal components
  —teachers cannot be forced to use material they find professionally objectionable.
- Provide incentives to local districts to experiment with alternatives to basals, by
  —developing state-level policies that permit districts to use alternatives to basals
  —changing teacher education and certification requirements so as to require teachers to demonstrate an understanding of how people read, of how children learn to read, and of ways of developing a reading curriculum without as well as with basals
  —mandating periodic curriculum review and revision based upon current theory and research as to how people read and how children learn to read
  —developing, or encouraging local districts to develop, alternative means of testing and assessment that are supported by current theory and research in how people read and how children learn to read
  —funding experimental programs, research, and methods of assessment based upon current theory and research on reading and learning to read.

Prepared for the Commission on Reading of the National Council of Teachers of English by the present and immediate past directors of the Commission, Connie Weaver and Dorothy Watson, and based on the *Report Card on Basal Readers*, written by Kenneth S. Goodman, Patrick Shannon, Yvonne Freeman, and Sharon Murphy and published by Richard C. Owen, Publishers, 1988. See also the Commission on Reading's Position Statement ''Report on Basal Readers''; one copy is free upon request from the National Council of Teachers of English if a self-addressed and stamped envelope is sent with the request. Write NCTE, 1111 Kenyon Road, Urbana, IL 61801.

Appendix 3.2

National Association for the Education of Young Children

INTEGRATED COMPONENTS OF APPROPRIATE AND INAPPROPRIATE PRACTICE IN THE PRIMARY GRADES

Component	Appropriate Practice	Inappropriate Practice
Curriculum goals	• Curriculum is designed to develop children's knowledge and skills in all developmental areas—physical, social, emotional, and intellectual—and to help children learn how to learn—to establish a foundation for lifelong learning.	• Curriculum is narrowly focused on the intellectual domain with intellectual development narrowly defined as acquisition of discrete, technical academic skills, without recognition that all areas of children's development are interrelated.
	• Curriculum and instruction are designed to develop children's self-esteem, sense of competence, and positive feelings toward learning.	• Children's worth is measured by how well they conform to group expectations, such as their ability to read at grade level and their performance on standardized tests.
	• Each child is viewed as a unique person with an individual pattern and timing of growth. Curriculum and instruction are responsive to individual differences in ability and interests. Different levels of ability, development, and learning styles are expected, accepted, and used to design curriculum. Children are allowed to move at their own pace in acquiring important skills including those of writing, reading, spelling, math, social studies, science, art, music, health, and physical activity. For example, it is accepted that not every child will learn how to read at age 6; most will learn to read by 7; and some will need intensive exposure to appropriate literacy experiences to learn to read by age 8 or 9.	• Children are evaluated against a standardized group norm. All are expected to achieve the same narrowly defined, easily measured academic skills by the same predetermined time schedule typically determined by chronological age and grade level expectations.

Component	Appropriate Practice	Inappropriate Practice
Teaching strategies	• The curriculum is integrated so that children's learning in all traditional subject areas occurs primarily through projects and learning centers that teachers plan and that reflect children's interests and suggestions. Teachers guide children's involvement in projects and enrich the learning experience by extending children's ideas, responding to their questions, engaging them in conversation, and challenging their thinking.	• Curriculum is divided into separate subjects and time is carefully allotted for each with primary emphasis given each day to reading and secondary emphasis to math. Other subjects such as social studies, science, and health are covered if time permits. Art, music, and physical education are taught only once a week and only by teachers who are specialists in those areas.
	• The curriculum is integrated so that learning occurs primarily through projects, learning centers, and playful activities that reflect current interests of children. For example, a social studies project such as building and operating a store or a science project such as furnishing and caring for an aquarium provide focused opportunities for children to plan, dictate, and/or write their plans (using invented and teacher-taught spelling), to draw and write about their activity, to discuss what they are doing, to read nonfiction books for needed information, to work cooperatively with other children, to learn facts in a meaningful context, and to enjoy learning. Skills are taught as needed to accomplish projects.	• Instructional strategies revolve around teacher-directed reading groups that take up most of every morning, lecturing to the whole group, total class discussion, and paper-and-pencil practice exercises or worksheets to be completed silently by children working individually at desks. Projects, learning centers, play, and outdoor time are seen as embellishments and are only offered if time permits or as reward for good behavior.
	• Teachers use much of their planning time to prepare the environment so children can learn through active involvement with each other, with adults and older children serving as informal tutors,	• Teachers use most of their planning time to prepare and correct worksheets and other seatwork. Little time is available to prepare enriching activities, such as those recommended in the teacher's

Component	Appropriate Practice	Inappropriate Practice
Teaching strategies (*continued*)	and with materials. Many learning centers are available for children to choose from. Many centers include opportunities for writing and reading, for example a tempting library area for browsing through books, reading silently, or sharing a book with a friend; a listening station; and places to practice writing stories and to play math or language games. Teachers encourage children to evaluate their own work and to determine where improvement is needed and assist children in figuring out for themselves how to improve their work. Some work is corrected in small groups where children take turns giving feedback to one another and correcting their own papers. Errors are viewed as a natural and necessary part of learning. Teachers analyze children's errors and use the information obtained to plan curriculum and instruction.	edition of each textbook series. A few interest areas are available for children who finish their seatwork early or children are assigned to a learning center to complete a prescribed sequence of teacher-directed activities within a controlled time period.

- Individual children or small groups are expected to work and play cooperatively or alone in learning centers and on projects that they usually select themselves or are guided to by the teacher. Activity centers are changed frequently so children have new things to do. Teachers and children together select and develop projects. Frequent outings and visits from resource people are planned. Peer tutoring as well as learning from others through conversation while at work or play occurs daily.

- During most work times, children are expected to work silently and alone on worksheets or other seatwork. Children rarely are permitted to help each other at work time. Penalties for talking are imposed.

- Learning materials and activities are concrete, real, and

- Available materials are limited primarily to books,

Component	Appropriate Practice	Inappropriate Practice
Teaching strategies (*continued*)	relevant to children's lives. Objects children can manipulate and experiment with such as blocks, cards, games, woodworking tools, arts and crafts materials including paint and clay, and scientific equipment are readily accessible. Tables are used for children to work alone or in small groups. A variety of work places and spaces is provided and flexibly used.	workbooks, and pencils. Children are assigned permanent desks and desks are rarely moved. Children work in a large group most of the time and no one can participate in a playful activity until all work is finished.
Integrated curriculum	• The goals of the language and literacy program are for children to expand their ability to communicate orally and through reading and writing, and to enjoy these activities. Technical skills or subskills are taught as needed to accomplish the larger goals, not as the goal itself. Teachers provide generous amounts of time and a variety of interesting activities for children to develop language, writing, spelling, and reading ability, such as: looking through, reading, or being read high quality children's literature and nonfiction for pleasure and information; drawing, dictating, and writing about their activities or fantasies; planning and implementing projects that involve research at suitable levels of difficulty; creating teacher-made or child-written lists of steps to follow to accomplish a project; discussing what was read; preparing a weekly class newspaper; interviewing various people to obtain information for projects; making books of various kinds (riddle books, *what if* books, books about pets); listening to recordings or viewing high quality films of	• The goal of the reading program is for each child to pass the standardized tests given throughout the year at or near grade level. Reading is taught as the acquisition of skills and subskills. Teachers teach reading only as a discrete subject. When teaching other subjects, they do not feel they are teaching reading. A sign of excellent teaching is considered to be silence in the classroom and so conversation is allowed infrequently during select times. Language, writing, and spelling instruction are focused on workbooks. Writing is taught as grammar and penmanship. The focus of the reading program is the basal reader, used only in reading groups, and accompanying workbooks and worksheets. The teacher's role is to prepare and implement the reading lesson in the teacher's guidebook for each group each day and to see that other children have enough seatwork to keep them busy throughout the reading group time. Phonics instruction stresses learning rules rather than developing understanding of systematic relationships between letters

Component	Appropriate Practice	Inappropriate Practice
Integrated curriculum (*continued*)	children's books; being read at least one high quality book or part of a book each day by adults or older children; using the school library and the library area of the classroom regularly. Some children read aloud daily to the teacher, another child, or a small group of children, while others do so weekly. Subskills such as learning letters, phonics, and word recognition are taught as needed to individual children and small groups through enjoyable games and activities. Teachers use the teacher's edition of the basal reader series as a guide to plan projects and hands-on activities relevant to what is read and to structure learning situations. Teachers accept children's invented spelling with minimal reliance on teacher-prescribed spelling lists. Teachers also teach literacy as the need arises when working on science, social studies, and other content areas.	and sounds. Children are required to complete worksheets or to complete the basal reader although they are capable of reading at a higher level. Everyone knows which children are in the slowest reading group. Children's writing efforts are rejected if correct spelling and standard English are not used.

Excerpted from NAEYC's expanded edition of *Developmentally Appropriate Practice in Early Childhood Programs Serving Children from Birth through Age 8*. Ed. S. Bredekamp. © 1987 by NAEYC. Used with permission.

Developing Language and Literacy

A whole language philosophy is based on what has become a widespread view among educators: that the most productive and enduring learning is typically transactional, involving the learner in actively seeking and constructing meaning. On the other hand, such learning does not take place in a vacuum, isolated from other human beings. Quite the contrary—others play a vital role in facilitating learning.

Thus, the title of this chapter, "Developing Language and Literacy," is deliberately ambiguous. It suggests that parents and educators can—indeed, must—actively help children develop oral language and literacy: They must transact with the children. But the title also suggests that not only oral language but literacy will frequently develop or "emerge" with little direct instruction of the transmission kind, given appropriate conditions and transactions that facilitate rather than stifle development. This cornerstone of a whole language philosophy is based upon systematic ethnographic research as well as informal observation, in a wealth of naturalistic and classroom environments. Such is one of the major lines of research that gives rise to a transactional model of learning.

Drawing upon such research, this chapter discusses the development of oral language and literacy as transactional processes, then compares the transactional model seen in most homes and a growing number of classrooms with the transmission model embodied in the majority of school programs. Finally, the chapter concludes by clarifying some of the ways whole language educators draw upon the research on emergent literacy in fostering children's development of reading and writing in primary classrooms.

❝ . . . not only oral language but literacy will frequently develop or 'emerge' with little direct instruction of the transmission kind, given appropriate conditions and transactions that facilitate rather than stifle development. **❞**

LANGUAGE DEVELOPMENT AS A TRANSACTIONAL PROCESS

If you ask people how their parents taught them to talk, your question may be met by incredulous stares or comments like "I don't remember'' or ''I don't think they really *taught* me to speak.'' Usually, parents are not much more certain how they themselves ''taught'' their children to speak. They realize that they have talked to and with their children, typically in the context of daily events like feeding, diapering, and playing with the baby. They may remember naming objects (''See? This is a *book*''), and they may be aware of sometimes having simplified their vocabulary and sentence structure for the child's sake. They may be aware, too, of deliberately expanding upon their children's utterances and responding in ways that model adult forms of the language. When invited to consider how they taught their children to talk, though, most parents quickly realize that *they didn't*. The children somehow learned, with little if any of the direct instruction typical in classrooms.

How Children Develop the Rules of Language

What have children learned when they learn a language, and how have they learned it? Adults commonly assume that children have merely ''imitated'' the language they have heard, but clearly other, powerful learning strategies are at work.

Take, for example, the rule for forming the past tense of regular verbs, in the oral language. Verbs like those in the first column add a /t/ sound to form the past tense; verbs like those in the second column take a /d/ sound. As you scan the lists, see if you can figure out the *rule* that determines which sound will be added:

stop	rub
look	hug
laugh	love
unearth	seethe
miss	raise
watch	judge
finish	deluge

The key is the final sound of each verb. If the verb ends in an unvoiced consonant (with the vocal chords not vibrating), we add a /t/ sound to make the past tense. If the verb ends in a voice consonant or a vowel (vowels are all voiced), we add a /d/ sound. For regular verbs the only exceptions are those that themselves end in a /d/ or a /t/ sound.

I have yet to meet an adult who could verbalize this rule, let alone teach it to someone, unless the person had studied articulatory phonetics. Yet children master the basic application of the rule by about age 2 or 3. We can tell they are not simply imitating verb forms they have heard because, when they first unconsciously recognize that the formation of past tenses is rule-governed, children apply the rule indiscriminately to irregular verbs that do not follow the rule, as well as to regular verbs that do.

Having learned the rule for making the past tense of regular verbs, the child who formerly said "I ate it" and "Mommy bought it" (apparently having learned *ate* and *bought* through imitation) will begin to say "I eated it" or "I ated it" and "Mommy buyed it" or "Mommy boughted it," adding the regular past tense ending to either the base form or the irregular past tense form. The result is similar when the child first grasps, unconsciously, the rule for forming the plural of regular nouns: the regular endings are added to irregular nouns as well. Thus, the child who formerly said "men" to refer to more than one man will now begin saying "mans" or "mens," applying the rule to either the base or the irregular plural form (see, for example, Cazden 1972, pp. 44–45).

Clearly, these rules have not been taught directly, yet the child has "learned" them, and at a remarkably early age. Linguists studying children's acquisition of language have generally concluded that from the language children hear, they abstract the rules at an unconscious level, at first applying them to *all* verbs and nouns and later restricting their rules to words that follow the regular pattern.

One more example should help to clarify the powerful rule-generating capacity of young children's minds: this time not a rule of the phonological system but rather of the syntactic system. What I want to demonstrate is not the generation of a single rule but of increasingly sophisticated rules that gradually give way to whatever form is common in the language community surrounding the child. In spite of the fact that they may never hear such forms used, children typically generate a series of rules like the following, for making utterances negative:

Examples	Rule
No money.	Put "no" or "not" at the beginning of
No a boy bed.	the utterance (or, less often, at the end).
Wear mitten no.	
That no fish school.	Put "no" or "not" between the subject
He no bite you.	part of the utterance and the predicate
I not crying.	part.
I didn't did it.	To make a past tense utterance nega-
You didn't caught me.	tive, add "didn't" between the subject
	part of the sentence and the verb.

It is common for these unconsciously formulated rules to precede the adult rules as the child gains increasing control over the forms of the language (Klima and Bellugi-Klima 1966, pp. 192–96).

Double negatives are also the rule at a certain phase in language development, regardless of the dialect to which the child has been exposed. Furthermore, all of these various rules for negation are virtually impervious to change through direct instruction. After her mother's eight unsuccessful attempts to get her to repeat the sentence ''Nobody likes me'' instead of persisting with her own ''Nobody don't like me,'' a young child finally produced, with pride, what she thought her mother had said: ''Nobody don't likes me'' (McNeill 1966, p. 69). At that point in her language development, the girl was simply unable to replace her own grammatical rule with her mother's, and the force of her own rule was so strong that she could not even accurately imitate her mother's utterance.

What the child brings to the language-learning task, then, includes an innate ability to generate, test, and develop increasingly sophisticated hypotheses about the nature of the world in general and language in particular. This ability is activated by the child's equally strong drive to make sense of and gain control over his or her world. Humans also appear to have an innate need for acceptance and approval, which can either activate or retard a child's ability and drive to make sense of the world, depending upon how the child's efforts are received by others. Learning the language to which they are exposed is a transactional process that depends not only upon the nature of children's abilities and actions but also upon the response and nurturing children receive from the environment.

How Adults Facilitate the Development of Language

If we cannot directly *teach* children to talk, how can we facilitate their *learning* to talk? In effect, we address their cognitive, affective, and social abilities and needs by demonstrating the forms and functions of language, by holding and communicating positive expectations for their success, and by responding in ways that foster rather than inhibit language development. Somewhat more specifically, we encourage children to learn the language to which they are exposed by such means as these:

1. We model (demonstrate) adult language structure and how meanings can be mapped onto words. Though we simplify our sentence structure and our vocabulary, focusing on the here-and-how, we do not usually speak in unnatural kinds of language

patterns. (When people deliberately imitate children's own "baby talk," children's growth in developing adult language patterns does seem to be retarded.)

2. We illustrate (demonstrate) a variety of language functions incidentally, by using language for various purposes. We surround children with a language-rich environment, using language as a natural part of such everyday activities as feeding, diapering, and playing with the baby; reciting nursery rhymes and reading books to the child; and talking with others within the young child's hearing. The activities vary somewhat according to the individual child's circumstances, but most children are exposed to a rich variety of oral language functions.

3. We expect success and demonstrate that expectation consistently. We assume that children will eventually learn to talk like adults, and we rarely try to accelerate their language development by direct instruction (at least until they begin school). We do not expect failure, nor do we penalize children for not being "on schedule."

4. We respond to the meaningfulness of children's utterances, focusing on meaning rather than on form. Adults correct children for inappropriate meanings (calling a horse a dog), but we rarely correct young children for immature grammar ("That no fish school") or for immature phonology ("Dass gweat" for "That's great").

5. Similarly, we respond to the expressive or communicative function and intent of children's utterances rather than to the form, intuitively realizing that their grammar and pronunciation will gradually approach adult conventionality. Only rarely is this expectation not fulfilled.

6. We respond positively to children's efforts to use and control language, rewarding successive approximations to adult language rather than demanding correctness. Because we realize that learning to talk is both a natural and a gradual process, we do not expect adult language from the moment a child utters a sound that might optimistically be construed as a real word. Children receive enthusiastic response for what they *can* do rather than repeated criticism for what they cannot do.

Thus, adults facilitate children's learning of language in several ways. They activate children's ability to formulate rules about language itself by providing a language-rich environment: that is, by modeling numerous and varied examples of *whole language* (not sounds and words isolated from language use). They activate children's innate drive to make sense of and gain control of their world by demonstrating various functions of language: that is, by using language for a variety of real-life purposes. And they provide the acceptance and approval children need in order to take the risks necessary to learn and grow, without fear of negative consequences. In short, adults facilitate children's ability to *engage*, or to invest themselves, in the language-learning task. The abilities and conditions that appear to be necessary for such engagement are given in Figure 4.1. (I am particularly indebted to Brian Cambourne for his articulation of conditions necessary for engagement in learning; Cambourne 1988.)

Thus, as parents encouraging our children's language growth, we intuitively adopt a transactional model of learning and teaching, somehow knowing that we cannot directly teach children to talk but only facilitate their language development. Through very similar means, many parents foster their children's development of literacy.

	Cognitive	Affective	Social
What the child brings to the language learning task	Innate ability to generate, test, and develop increasingly sophisticated hypotheses	Innate need for acceptance, approval	Innate drive to make sense of and to gain control of his/her world
Conditions necessary for child to engage in the language learning process	Recognition that language is meaningful and structured; it *can* be grasped	Recognition that attempting to learn the language will gain the child approval and acceptance	Recognition that learning the language will further the purposes of the child's life in the here-and-now
What adults do to facilitate the child's learning of the language	Model (demonstrate) adult language structure, and how meanings can be mapped onto words	Expect success, and demonstrate that expectation consistently	Illustrate (demonstrate) a variety of language functions incidentally, by using language for various purposes
	Respond to the meaningfulness of child's utterances, focusing on meaning rather than form	Respond positively to the child's efforts to use and control language, rewarding successive approximations to adult language rather than demanding correctness	Respond to the function and intent of the child's utterances, focusing on these rather than on form

Figure 4.1   **Language development as a transactional process**

LITERACY DEVELOPMENT AS A TRANSACTIONAL PROCESS

As language develops when children are actively engaged in formulating and reformulating hypotheses about the language, so literacy develops most readily when children are actively engaged in formulating concepts about print rather than passively completing skills work. For many children, a great deal of this kind of intellectual work occurs before formal schooling, facilitated by parents and others in the child's environment. In order to formulate concepts about print, children need to engage repeatedly in authentic acts of reading and writing and to receive the kinds of demonstrations, response, and assistance that they were given as they learned to talk.

This section explores the nature of print-rich environments, gives examples of children's emergent writing and reading, and then contrasts the transactional model that facilitates development of literacy with the transmission model that all too often thwarts or skews the development of literacy.

> **"**As language develops when children are actively engaged in formulating and reformulating hypotheses about the language, so literacy develops most readily when children are actively engaged in formulating concepts about print rather than passively completing skills work.**"**

Facilitating Literacy through a Print-Rich Environment

A print-rich environment is one in which reading and writing are used for a wide variety of authentic, everyday purposes. Just as most homes provide a language-rich environment for the learning of language, so most provide a print-rich environment for the learning of literacy. This point needs emphasis because of the common assumption that lower-class families, especially those living in poverty, do not model literacy for their children.

It is true, of course, that the kinds of literacy will vary and that there are some fairly characteristic differences in the nature and range of literacy activities modeled in different kinds of environments. This point is corroborated, for example, by the pioneering study of Shirley Bryce Heath in *Ways with Words* (1983), which documents similarities and differences in the kinds of literacy demonstrated and valued in the homes of a white working-class community, a black working-class community, and a ''mainstream'' community of both white and black families. Most significant, however, is that adults in *all* of these communities modeled literacy in a variety of forms.

Equally significant is the study by Denny Taylor and Catherine Dorsey-Gaines, *Growing Up Literate* (1988), which challenges our blithe tendency to equate poverty with illiteracy. In this study, the authors examined the literacy environments of children whose parents considered them to be successfully learning to read and write. The subjects of the study were six urban black families living in poverty.

Taylor and Dorsey-Gaines found that the adults in these households read a wide variety of materials for various purposes and also modeled the use of writing for many purposes. Figure 4.2 lists the types and uses of reading and writing documented in their Shay Avenue neighborhood study; most of these kinds of reading and writing were also documented by Heath in the three communities she studied. Clearly, it would be a mistake to assume that *books* are the only or even the major demonstrations of literacy in most homes—including the homes of many of our nation's poor. It would also be a mistake to assume categorically that children in poor families do not grow up in literate environments. Indeed, these environments may be more print-rich than many primary classrooms, particularly in the range and variety of print available. Figure 4.3, for example, offers specific examples of six of the ten kinds of reading and writing documented in the Shay Avenue study. Most if not all of these are visible to children in the household as models or demonstrations of what literacy is, and adults in the household clearly demonstrate in various ways what a literate person does.

The Development of Writing

In many homes and an increasing number of primary classrooms, learning to read and write are fostered in much the same way as oral language development: by providing a print-rich environment in which reading and writing are used for a variety of real-life purposes, by encouraging and responding positively to children's emergent reading and writing, and by providing informational demonstrations and assistance as needed. This approach enables children to develop increasingly sophisticated hypotheses about the nature of reading and writing.

There are no rigid sequences or stages through which children develop as readers and writers, but there are some general trends. For example, children's earliest "writings" do not yet reflect an understanding that there is a relation between the letters and sounds of English. Once they have grasped the phonemic principle, their writings still progress gradually toward adult conventionality, revealing an attempt to reflect more and more of the sounds of the words. As children gain experience reading books and other printed matter, they increasingly try to spell words by using patterns they have seen in print—spelling long vowels with two letters, for example, even though the "correct" spelling might call for only one ("mie" for *my*). These changes in spelling strategies reflect increasingly sophisticated hypotheses about the structure of written language.

Instrumental: reading to gain information for meeting practical needs, dealing with public agencies, and scheduling daily life

Social–interactional: reading to gain information pertinent to building and maintaining social relationships

Recreational: reading [books, magazines, newspapers, etc.] during leisure time or in planning recreational events

Critical/Educational: reading to fulfill educational requirements of school and college courses; reading to increase one's abilities to consider and/or discuss political, social, aesthetic, or religious knowledge; reading to educate oneself

Financial: reading to consider (and sometimes to make changes in) the economic circumstances of one's everyday life; reading to fulfill practical (financial) needs of everyday life

Environmental: reading the print in the environment

News-related: reading to gain information about third parties or distant events or to gain information about local, state, and national events

Confirmational: reading to check or confirm facts or beliefs, often from archival material stored and retrieved only on special occasions

Instrumental: writing to meet practical needs and manage/organize everyday life; writing to gain access to social institutions or helping agency

Social–interactional: writing to establish, build, and maintain social relationships; writing to negotiate family responsibilities

Recreational: writing during leisure time for the enjoyment of the activity

Educational: writing to educate oneself; writing to fulfill college assignments

Financial: writing to record numerals and amounts and purposes of expenditures, and for signatures

Environmental: writing in public places for others to read

Reinforcement or substitute for oral message: writing when oral communication is not possible or a written message is needed for legal purposes

Memory aids: writing to serve as a memory aid for both the writer and others

Autobiographical: writing to understand oneself, to record one's life history, to share life with others

Creative: writing as a means of self-expression

Figure 4.2 Types and uses of reading and writing documented in the Shay Avenue neighborhood study by Taylor and Dorsey-Gaines (1988)

Instrumental: Directions on toys, watches, and radios sold in the street or bought in stores; labels, telephone dials, clocks; addresses in address books; telephone numbers in address books and written on old envelopes or scraps of paper; *T.V. Guide;* recipes; notes left on refrigerator of items to buy at the store, to be read and acted upon by another family member; applications for food stamps, AFDC, WICS; reminders of obligations to report changes of circumstances to welfare board; notice on assignment of support rights; and so forth

Instrumental: Writing out schedules; keeping calendars and appointments; planning a Thanksgiving dinner; keeping telephone and address books; signing name on visitors' pass to gain access to school; filling out application for day care; school forms; forms for summer programs; health checkup forms, hospital forms, forms for social agencies, form for "Existing Housing Assistance Program: Preliminary Application for Tenant Eligibility," and applications for counseling by Urban League

Social–interactional: Letters from friends; letters from children away for the summer; letters received from prisoners (some of whom one has never met, others one has visited, many of whom are serving life sentences); greeting cards; flyers; newspaper features; notices of local events, births, and deaths; storybooks shared with young children

Social–interactional: Letters to family members and friends (many families do not have a phone); letters to children ("I love you" letters, informational letters, "clean up your room" letters); thank-you letters; cards sent at Christmas, Valentine's Day, and birthdays; writing and drawing with young children; helping with homework assignments

Figure 4.3 Specific examples of types and uses of reading and writing documented in the Shay Avenue neighborhood study by Taylor and Dorsey-Gaines (1988)

The more we look for stages in development, however, the more we see the individuality that defies stage theory (see Harste, Woodward, and Burke 1984). Therefore, I have chosen to illustrate children's early writing not in order of increasingly sophisticated stages—of spelling or of anything else—but generally in the order in which functions of language were presented in Figure 4.3, except that the children's writings that were highly adult-directed are placed at the end.

Of course, the writings of young children are usually produced spontaneously and not necessarily for an audience: They are what James

Recreational: Local and national newspapers and magazines (*Time, Newsweek, Ebony, Essence, Jet, Black Enterprise*); books; poetry written by friends or cut from the newspaper; unknown child's school journal found in the street; clues to crossword puzzles and conundrums; comics and cartoons

Confirmational: Birth certificates; social security cards; school report cards; honor roll cards; facts about law; personal attendance records for work; letters of recommendation; children's letters, poems, and drawings; food stamp certificates; newspaper cuttings

Financial: "Keeping an eye on the economy" (with the view to establishing a small silk-screening business); reading stock market reports; reading prices of cars and appliances; reading apartment ads (paying particular attention to prices); reading forms, including statements about one's financial status; reading "money-off" coupons; reading prices in stores

Recreational: Crossword puzzles; conundrums; doodling; letters

Creative: Writing poetry; painting with children, experimenting with letter formation; writing names of family members in different scripts; playing with configurations of letters in names

Memory-aids: Writing college schedules; bathroom schedule for potty-training a child; monthly planner; list of postnatal exercises; menu for Thanksgiving dinner; lists of food for a party; notes on refrigerator; lists of books read and books to read; and so forth

Autobiographical: Letters written to oneself in difficult times; writing prose to oneself; writing a journal; writing names of family members; writing names of new babies, trying different names and writing different forms of script; when new babies are born, writing names, weight, dates of birth, and times of delivery

Figure 4.3 *(continued)*

Britton called "expressive" writings (1970). Even writings meant to be shared with someone are more expressive of self than *transactional* (written to inform or persuade) or what Britton called *poetic* (intended as an aesthetic object). Thus, it may be somewhat inappropriate to label these using the adult categories found in the Shay Avenue study. Perhaps the children's writings are best considered as precursors of these types—and even then, some may fit into more than one category.

With this caveat, then, I have chosen to present samples or precursors of only the six writing functions presented in Figure 4.3, plus one other—the informational or "all about" writing that is common among children.

Whether the writings are entirely spontaneous or elicited by an adult, the underlying model of learning is clearly a *transactional* one (see Chap. 1, pp. 8–11). The emphasis is not on teaching but on the child's learning: The child's development of concepts about print is facilitated by adults but not taught according to an artificially determined sequence or schedule. Learning moves from whole to part, from the child's global intent to mean, to increasingly greater control of the conventions of writing. There is no risk of failure because the adults respond positively to whatever the child is able to do. Such positive response is vital to the child's learning.

Instrumental. First, then, is an example of writing that seems to exemplify the instrumental function (Figure 4.4). This is a Christmas list from Michael, age 3 years 11 months (Hill 1989, p. 56). When Mary Hill asked Michael about this writing, he pointed to the first line of print, drew a line under it, and said that it was Santa's name. Then he followed the same procedure for the other four lines of print, while saying the words *ball, wagon, spacesuit,* and *doctor's kit*. The large circular lines were to indicate how big he wanted the ball to be. When Hill asked Michael what the lines he'd drawn meant, he said they didn't mean

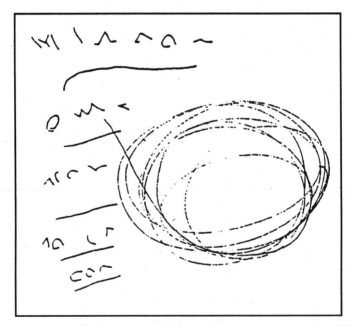

Santa Claus
Ball
Wagon
Spacesuit
Doctor's Kit

Figure 4.4   Christmas list of Michael, age 3 years 11 months (Hill 1989, p. 56)

anything, but his mother puts them on her shopping list. As Hill points out, Michael's comment is clear evidence that his mother "had provided him with a demonstration each time she wrote her shopping list" (Hill 1989, p. 57).

Social–Interactional. An example of writing that seems to have been done more as social interaction than as a solitary act is a journal entry written by Shawn, age 6 (Figure 4.5). This seems social–interactional because the child and his teacher regularly engaged in such written conversations, so Shawn would have anticipated a written response, to which he in turn would respond.

In *The Craft of Children's Writing*, Newman (1984) discusses Shawn's writing development over the course of his first-grade year. This journal entry was written in January. When Shawn entered first grade, he was not reading much environmental print (such as the writing on signs, food packages, TV, and so forth), nor was he reading from books. Though he was able to copy, he refused to write anything independently: Thus his writing looked "correct," but this was a correctness not his own. With a supportive teacher who responded only to the meaning of the children's writing and not to the form, Shawn began to develop as a writer. This meant abandoning someone else's correctness in order to engage in his own cognitive processes of learning.

The journal entry itself reads as follows:

I hope my father catches
a deer for us.
There was lots of noise in
our classroom.
(Who was making all the noise
in our classroom?) Them guys.

Newman discusses this entry as follows:

This journal entry, written in early January, is interesting for several reasons. The percent of conventional spelling is the lowest of any in Shawn's journal entries (21%). Yet at the same time we can see him experimenting with several new conventions. In addition to beginning each new sentence on a separate line (which he seems to have been doing consistently up to this point), he is now using periods to mark the end of some of his sentences. He also demonstrates an awareness of digraphs: chr for *there*, chm for *them*. In this entry Shawn edits for meaning in the process of writing (an indication that he is reading his own text): ni (*in*) is written over an erased a (the start of awr for *our*). The spelling of *in* (ni), of (af) and *our* (awr) are also of interest; they reveal that, in addition to his other spelling strategies, Shawn is "spelling the way it looks." (Newman 1984, p. 53)

I hope my father catches
a deer for us.
There was lots of noise in
our classroom.
(Who was making all the noise
in our classroom?) Them guys.

Figure 4.5   Written conversation between Shawn, age 6, and his teacher (Newman 1984, p. 52)

Newman continues documenting Shawn's progress as a writer through the remainder of the school year. By the end of the year, his writing looks much more correct by adult standards. Most important, however, Shawn is no longer copying someone else's writing. By reading and writing a lot and receiving positive response from his teacher, Shawn himself has developed increasingly sophisticated concepts about print and strategies for spelling. He has become a learner.

Recreational. Much of young children's writing might be considered recreational, if by that term we simply mean writing for the sheer pleasure of it. Annabrook's writing/drawing in Figure 4.6 particularly reminds me, however, of some of the kinds of recreational writing done by the adults in the Shay Avenue study: the deliberate playing around with print. Note the comment ''writing backwards was easy for her'' (Temple, Nathan, and Burris 1988, p. 37). Early in their writing development, children have not necessarily developed a firm grasp of the principle that writing in English proceeds from left to right and top to bottom. Furthermore, they often enjoy experimenting with conventions of print, such as directionality. This is an exceedingly common phenomenon among young children and should *not* be viewed as evidence of dyslexia, however that may be defined. The vast majority of children develop adult concepts of directionality with no difficulty, given time and the freedom to experiment in writing as well as frequent opportunities to view how print is read.

Memory Aids. This example of a reminder is a note from a 5-year-old boy to his sister. He had offered her some of his french fries, and she responded with more enthusiasm than he expected. Figure 4.7 shows his spontaneous drawing of the incident, with a written reminder ac-

Figure 4.6   Annabrook, age 5 (Temple, Nathan, and Burris 1988, p. 37)

Figure 4.7 Five-year-old boy's note to his sister (Goodnow 1977)

companying the drawing. Like many examples of children's early "writing," this sample indicates that much of the meaning is initially conveyed by the child's drawing rather than by the print itself. Clearly, though, this first-grader demonstrates awareness of directionality and of the principle that drawn-out sounds (typically long vowels) are often represented by two letters. He has noticed that words start with a capital letter, but has not yet refined this observation to limit initial capitals to only *some* words (the beginnings of sentences, the pronoun *I*, and proper names). This process is analogous to overgeneralizing the rule for forming the past tense of verbs, as the young child typically does in learning to speak the language.

Creative. Figure 4.8 presents part of a ghost story written by Jane (age 3½) one day while she was visiting researcher Judith Newman. To entertain the child, Newman handed her some paper and crayons for drawing. But Jane wanted to "'make a book'" instead. She took Newman's pencil and proceeded to write the story herself, composing aloud. While Jane wrote, Newman transcribed the story word for word. To her surprise, Jane "read" the text almost verbatim, and even two weeks later still approximated the text very closely when again reading her "ghost book" to Newman.

Newman's comments are insightful and instructive. She observes that as Jane wrote, she moved from left to right, top to bottom. She distinguished between drawing (the two ghosts on the left) and writing: the drawings are circular, the writing linear. Furthermore, Jane had some sense of what a sentence is—each complete idea in her story was represented by a continuous mark. The story also shows Jane's sophisticiated

Mary Kate and Jane were playing outside.
Then they went inside to watch TV.
Then when they were watching TV
they saw a scary thing—a ghost.
So they hided under their covers.
Then the ghost couldn't see them.
The ghost felt sad
and he wrecked up the place.
Then the ghost finally leaved.
Then the girls lived happily ever after.

Figure 4.8   Part of a ghost story by Jane, age 3½ (Newman 1984, p. 13)

grasp of story structure: It opens with an introduction to the characters, who are placed in a setting; it proceeds with a series of events involving an antagonist, the ghost; and it ends with a resolution, in which the ghost finally leaves—and, of course, the girls live happily ever after (Newman 1984, p. 14).

Figure 4.9 is another example of what the teacher, at least, intended as creative writing. It was written by a first-grader in October of the school year. The children had listened to a story about a dragon, made their own dragons out of clay, talked one-on-one with a preservice teacher about fun things they'd do with their pet dragons, and now were to write a story. Interestingly, though Brett is in some ways clearly a more

Bob and Ashley kissed and mommy had a baby.
Mommy had her baby, happy day.
Mommy had a pet dragon, Bob. Bob is a born baby, he cries.
Today is Halloween. Heidi is the baby.

Figure 4.9   Dragon story by Brett, a first-grader

advanced writer than 3-year-old Jane, either he has much less of a sense of story or he has chosen not to exercise his story sense in this writing activity. Present concerns—the new baby in his family, and Halloween—overshadow his interest in the pet dragon. Indeed, the dragon and the baby converge: Brett sees this as *Mommy's* pet dragon, not his. One suspects that the dragon is of more interest to the teacher than to Brett. This is the kind of activity traditionally initiated by energetic and enthusiastic teachers, and I must confess that ten years ago this is an activity that I myself engineered.

Informative. Much of the spontaneous writing of young children involves telling "all about" something, and this is a kind of writing sometimes required by primary teachers as well. But what to call it? Is its purpose informative? or merely expressive? Or if teacher-assigned, is it "educational"? In any case, children's writings abound with print that appears informative in nature, if not in function. Figure 4.10 is an

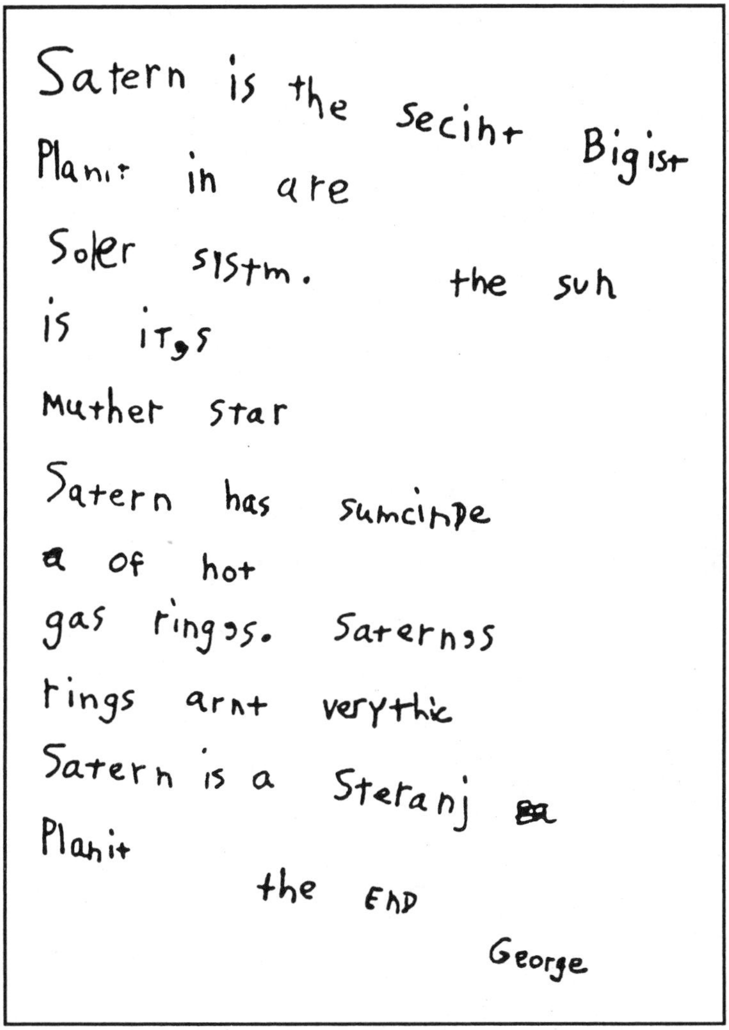

Satern is the seciht Bigist Planit in are Soler sistm. the suh is it,s Muther star Satern has sumcinpe a of hot gas ringɔs. Saternɔs rings arnt veryᵗhic Satern is a Steranj Planit the ENP George

Saturn is the second biggest
planet in our
solar system. The sun
is its
mother star.
Saturn has some kind
a of hot
gas rings. Saturn's
rings aren't very thick.
Saturn is a strange
planet.
The end
George

Figure 4.10   Science report of George, a first-grader (Chomsky 1979, p. 60)

example of a first-grader's science report on Saturn (Chomsky 1979, p. 60). One feature of George's spelling that has always fascinated me is <u>cinde</u> for *kind* (in <u>sumcinde</u>). This spelling reflects sophisticated knowledge on the writer's part: He knows that an initial /k/ sound may be represented by the letter *c*, and he knows that the letter *e* is often added to the end of a word to indicate a long vowel sound. As this example demonstrates, sometimes the strangest-looking spellings are indications of the most sophisticated spelling strategies!

Autobiographical. The last example is autobiographical in content (Figure 4.11): It tells what the child likes to do on his favorite holiday, Easter. But with this writing, as well as the dragon story (and maybe the Saturn report), one again wonders: Is this "authentic" writing, furthering some purpose of the child's—other than the obvious purpose of complying with the teacher's request? This last piece is my son's, so when I asked him, now age 19, what he thought the purpose of the writing was, he blurted out, "Boring. It was just another one of those boring assignments." In other words, the writer's purpose may simply have been to meet the teacher's expectation rather than to express or share something about himself (see Edelsky and Smith, "Is That Writing—or Are Those Marks Just a Figment of Your Curriculum?" 1984). So we may well

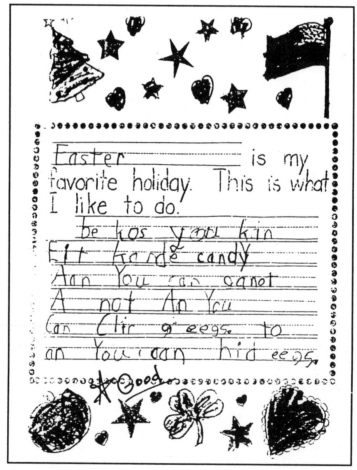

Easter [is my
favorite holiday. This is what
I like to do.]
because you can
eat candy, candy.
And you can [?]
[?] And you
can color eggs too.
And you can hide eggs.

Figure 4.11   Autobiographical assignment by John, age 6 years 7 months

question whether the writing had an autobiographical function for the writer, despite its obviously autobiographical content.

Commentary upon the Writings. These several examples reflect a sample of early writings from children of varying ages, illustrating a variety of functions and purposes. What, then, might be said about the writing development of these children? Several things, I think. Clearly, the children have already learned a great deal about the various functions and conventions of print and even about the conventions of various genres (story structure). The children are becoming increasingly literate by engaging in the acts of literate adults—composing and constructing meaning through print, for a variety of purposes.

Taken together, these writing samples clarify what was indicated at the outset: that there is no definable sequence according to which concepts about print and written language are or should be learned. Obviously, older children are not necessarily more sophisticated writers than younger ones, and certainly not all children of the same age or grade have learned about the conventions of writing to the same degree.

What all these children have in common is that their writing development has been fostered in much the same way as their oral language development. Though adults have demonstrated adult writing forms and functions through daily use, the adults have not attempted to *teach* the children how to write—certainly not in part-to-whole fashion, focusing first on correct letter formation and spelling. Rather, adults have simply encouraged the children to write and have responded positively to the children's writings, focusing on content and intent rather than form or correctness. The adults have not responded as if the children were failures or would become failures at writing simply because these early writings were not "correct." Rather, the adults have responded enthusiastically to whatever the child did and was able to do.

Such are essentially the ways in which adults foster oral language development in young children: through demonstrating language use, by offering positive response to the children rather than negative or punitive response, and by treating the children as competent and developing rather than as incompetent and deficient. As a consequence, these children are well on their way to becoming competent and independent writers.

The Development of Reading

In the home and in an increasing number of whole language classrooms, the development of reading is fostered in essentially the same positive ways.

> **"**The children are becoming increasingly literate by engaging in the acts of literate adults—composing and constructing meaning through print, for a variety of purposes.**"**

Even children with little exposure to books before they enter school typically see a rich variety of print in their homes and neighborhoods. In homes, there is usually print on boxes, cans of food, and various other containers; there are phone books and TV guides; adults write and read lists, memos, letters, cards; and even television demonstrates the use of print in commercials, program credits, and so forth. In neighborhoods, there are signs on stores and within stores, as well as on merchandise itself, such as candy wrappers and T-shirts. There are road signs and billboards. And many children attend church or synagogue, where other forms of print are encountered and their uses demonstrated.

Much of this print is what has come to be characterized as *environmental*, because the environment or context in which it occurs plays a significant role in clarifying its meaning. When asked what the label on a tube of toothpaste says, for example, young children may say ''toothpaste'' instead of giving the brand name; the context has clarified the general meaning, if not the specific word. More specifically, the octagonal red sign at an intersection provides the context for *Stop*, the golden arches provide a context for *McDonald's*, and a red-and-white can provides the context for *chicken noodle*.

Because environmental print is highly contextualized, children readily develop an understanding that print is meaningful, simply by seeing some of the purposes it serves: often to name something, or to give warnings or directions. From environmental print, children also learn specific words and phrases, which can serve as part of a data bank for developing their own concepts about print. Thus, most children begin school as emergent readers, already understanding the uses of some kinds of print and able to construct an appropriate if overgeneralized meaning for many words and phrases they have encountered in print. Just as the child learning language will initially overgeneralize the use of naming words—for example, at first calling all four-legged animals *dog*—the emergent reader will overgeneralize, saying *toothpaste* for the names on various brands of toothpaste or *chicken noodle* for the names of all soups printed on the familiar red-and-white can.

Even more significant, emergent readers have learned that a strategy important in making sense of oral language is just as important in making sense of print: namely, use everything you know.

This strategy serves emergent readers well, not only in reading environmental print but in reading books. In many homes, a love of books is instilled early, perhaps literally from birth. Children often learn to read before even attending school. How? Partly from environmental print, of course, but often just as much or more from reading literature, particularly picture books (books in which pictures and text work together to facilitate the construction of meaning). The process varies somewhat from child to child, of course, but generally children first engage in what has already been alluded to as reading-like or *emergent reading* behavior. That is, the children begin to act like readers, even though they cannot yet read new texts independently.

These young readers often begin by attempting to reconstruct the meaning of picture books, based upon their recollection of the text, the pictures, and often their own language patterns and experiences. One example is Sean's rendition of part of Eric Carle's *The Very Hungry Caterpillar*, as reported in Doake (1988, p. 37). Italic type indicates the parts that Sean (age 2 years 11 months) changed:

Text	Sean
The day was Sunday again. The caterpillar ate through one *nice* green leaf and then he *felt* much better.	But Tuesday (self-corrects) . . . on Tuesday, he ate through one green leaf and then he feeled much better.

This example reflects both Sean's language structure (overgeneralization of the past tense rule, in *feeled*) and his real-world concepts: every day of the week was Tuesday, for Sean! Clearly, he was not reciting the story verbatim. Rather, he was reconstructing the story.

A similar example is presented in McKenzie (1986, p. 36). The rendition is by Shelley, 5 years 4 months, as she read (reconstructed) Arnold Lobel's *Prince Bertram the Bad*:

	Text	Shelley
p. 7	The royal cook would not speak to Prince Bertram. He had thrown four spiders into the chicken noodle soup.	He even used to throw four spiders in the royal cook's soup.
p. 8	The swans in the royal lake would not swim near Prince Bertram. He made terrible noises and horrible faces to frighten them.	He even used to make faces at the swans and frighten them. The swans never came near Prince Bertram.
p. 9	"If only a spanking would do some good," the King sighed. His hands were red and sore because he had to spank Prince Bertram every day.	His dad smacked him every day. He had a raw red hand.

Text	*Shelley*
p. 10 Of all the children in the whole kingdom there was not one who was as wicked and as nasty as Prince Bertram. Everyone called him Bertram the Bad.	All the children in . . . . . . the classroom called Prince Bertram, Prince Bertram the bad.
p. 11 One morning Prince Bertram sat in the highest castle tower hitting the birds with stones with his catapult.	One day he sat up (in) the tall palace shooting with his parashooter, stones at the birds.
p. 12 He saw a large, long-nosed blackbird in the sky and hit it, too.	He thought . . . . A long-nosed blackbird he thought was coming by. He hit that too.
p. 13 It was not a long-nosed blackbird at all but a witch, who was passing by on her broomstick.	But it was only a witch passing by . . . on her broomstick.
p. 14 The witch was very angry with Prince Bertram. She pointed a finger at him and shouted, ''ALAGABIM.'' Prince Bertram was quickly changed into a small scaly dragon. ''That will teach you to throw stones at me,'' said the witch as she flew away.	She shout . . . . She pointed a finger at him and shouted . . . . Alacaboo. He turned into a sl . . . . . spotted white dragon. There was nothing left but the gold crown on his head. She said, ''That will teach you to throw stones at me.''

Obviously, Shelley has drawn upon her life knowledge and the illustrations as well as upon the text as she remembers it. McKenzie comments: ''From these few pages we can see how Shelley is handling written language, how she can transform direct speech in the text into reported speech, making all the correct grammatical agreements, and how the changed language is unmistakably written language'' (1986, p. 36). Shelley, like Sean, is engaging in sophisticated language processing as she reconstructs the text.

At some point in such children's developing literacy, they become aware that reading is supposed to be tied to the print on the page. Their fluent renditions of texts may then become halting and nonfluent, as they try to make what they say match the words of the text. Doake (1988) gives several examples of how emergent readers begin to move from whole (the meaning) to part (the words) as they develop in ability to coordinate language cues and reading strategies. The following is one of Doake's examples. Gillian, age 5 years 11 months, is reading from Maurice Sendak's *Where the Wild Things Are*. Doake reports that he had helped Gillian select the book from the public library and had read it to her twice. At her request, they began to read it a third time, with Gillian reading along and sometimes taking the lead. Suddenly, Doake reports, she interrupted him and, in her most authoritative tone, said, " 'You've got to let me read now!' " Below is a transcript of part of her reading (Doake 1988, with corrections supplied by Doake). Her deviations from the original text are given in italics whenever possible.

Text	*Gillian*
The night Max wore his wolf suit	The night *when* Max (pauses and self-corrects) . . . the night Max wore his wolf suit
and made mischief of one kind and another,	*making a* mischief of one kind and another,
his mother called him wild thing.	his mother called him *the* wild thing.
And Max said, "I'll eat you up!"	And Max said, "*I'm going to* eat you up!" (Read with tremendous emphasis.)
So he was sent to bed without eating anything.	So *Max went* (self-corrects) . . . so he *went* to bed without eating anything.
That night in Max's room a forest grew.	That *very* (points to *night* and asks "What does that say?" but before she can be told, she rereads, self-corrects, and begins to "voice point.") . . . that night—in—Max's—room—a—*jungle*—grew (pauses and self-corrects)—a—forest—grew. (When asked how she knew that the word was *forest* and not *jungle*, she pointed to the *f* in *forest* and said, "That's not a 'juh,' it's a 'fuh.' ")

One thing that intrigued me about Gillian's reading, as I typed this, was the way she initially began to read the last sentence: "That *very* night in

Max's room a forest grew.'' That's the way I remembered it too—and sure enough, in my copy of the book, that's the way it reads.

Doake reports and comments:

> Gillian read the rest of the book in this manner, pausing occasionally to ask what a word was and then, before I could respond, saying it correctly herself, frequently after rereading the part of the text just before the word. What miscues [conventionally called ''errors''] she made were almost always of high quality. She read confidently, expressively and fluently, occasionally reverting to arhythmic reading to run a more careful check on the visual information. Since this was only the third time the book had been read with her, it was not possible for her to have memorized all the words. In a very real sense, she was now using all the strategies employed by competent, adult readers, despite the fact that her graphophonic [letter/sound] knowledge was not fully developed. *Most significantly, she was in control of her own learning, monitoring her performance and self-correcting when she felt it was necessary.* (1988, p. 67; emphasis mine)

Thus Gillian—and Shelley and Sean, too—were well on their way to becoming competent and independent readers.

These examples, particularly of Gillian, illustrate some of the parallels between how children learn their native language and how they develop literacy. The children do not merely imitate adults but rather generate, test, and develop increasingly sophisticated hypotheses about the nature and demands of the reading task. This is particularly evident with the more proficient reader, Gillian, who is abandoning her earlier concept of reading as reconstructing meaning from pictures and memory in favor of a concept of reading that involves processing the words on the page, in the task of constructing meaning. As with oral language learners, we see Gillian's strong drive to make sense of and develop control over her world: in this case, the world of reading and books. In learning to read, Gillian has taken advantage of adult demonstrations of what reading is, but she is essentially learning the process and developing the strategies herself—with feedback when requested, but without direct instruction.

Among the factors that similarly facilitate the development of literacy in the classroom are those Jane Hansen discusses in *When Writers Read* (1987): ample—indeed, lots—of *time* to engage in authentic acts of reading and writing; considerable *choice* in what students read and write; *response* and encouragement to develop *responsibility* for their own learning and for helping their peers learn; *structure* that, paradoxically, facilitates flexibility and freedom; and a supportive *community* of learners and teachers within and beyond the classroom. Clearly, these are factors that facilitate the development of literacy in individuals of all ages. And they resemble the conditions under which literacy is fostered in the home.

DEFINITIONS AND MODELS OF LITERACY REVISITED

In many respects, then, the learning and teaching that take place in whole language classrooms resemble what occurs in most homes, especially those in which literacy is actively valued and fostered. Of paramount importance is that in both environments, adults respond positively to what children can do instead of constantly emphasizing what they cannot do, or cannot do well. Children are not taught according to an artificially determined scope and sequence chart but are expected to develop literacy gradually and are given appropriate assistance as needed. They are immersed in written language, just as they were immersed in oral language while learning to talk.

The earlier model of "Language Development as a Transactional Process" (Figure 4.1) can become a model of literacy development, with only slight changes in wording. Here, I contrast "What adults usually do to facilitate the child's learning of the language" with "What teachers using traditional reading and writing programs may often do" in the hope of teaching literacy. The contrast is striking:

❝Children are not taught according to an artificially determined scope and sequence chart but are expected to develop literacy gradually and are given appropriate assistance as needed.❞

What Parents Usually Do to Facilitate the Child's Learning of the Language	*What Teachers Using Traditional Programs May Do in Teaching Literacy*
Model (demonstrate) adult language structure and illustrate a variety of language functions by using language for various purposes.	Model unnaturally simplified language and a severely limited range of language functions (in the basal reading program).
Respond to the meaningfulness and to the function and intent of the child's utterances, rather than to form.	Respond to the form of the child's writing and the accuracy of the child's reading, rather than to meaning or function and intent.
Expect success and demonstrate that expectation consistently.	Expect and set children up for varying degrees of failure.
Respond positively to the child's efforts to use and control language, rewarding suc-	Respond negatively to the child's independent efforts to read and write, rewarding

What Parents Usually Do to Facilitate the Child's Learning of the Language	*What Teachers Using Traditional Programs May Do in Teaching Literacy*
cessive approximations to adult language rather than demanding correctness.	only those behaviors that are deemed "right" by the program; expecting a degree of correctness exceeding even that attained by most adults.

Under circumstances such as those on the right—and they are far more common than most of us would like to think—it is not difficult to understand why relatively few students genuinely *engage* in their schoolwork, including the tasks that are set for them in the name of teaching literacy. This kind of teaching does not meet the conditions needed for children to engage in learning. What children are asked to do often does not seem meaningful, nor do the texts they are offered in the beginning levels of traditional basal reading programs seem very meaningful; certainly such texts are far from interesting. Furthermore, the oversimplified language of these beginning-level texts thwarts rather than facilitates children's strategies for making sense of print. The texts they are given to read and the skills tasks they are given to complete do not exactly contribute to children's recognition that learning to read and write will fulfill the purposes of their lives in the here-and-now. And finally, too many children receive repeated confirmation that attempting to learn to read and write will *not* gain them approval and acceptance: They receive far more powerful criticism for what they cannot do than positive response for what they can do.

Is it any wonder that many children develop a concept of literacy similar to the one attributed to the transmission model in Chapter 2? And is it any wonder that many caring teachers have already adopted the more productive transactional model in their classrooms?

DEVELOPING LITERACY IN THE CLASSROOM

Drawing upon research into how language and literacy are fostered in the home, a growing number of whole language educators are creating similar environments and conditions for classroom learning (see, for example, the starter bibliography of books on emergent literacy, Figure 4.12). Following are some characteristics of these educators' classrooms, materials, methods, and expectations. The emphasis here is on fostering emergent literacy among young children, but similar conditions apply to stimulating literacy development among older students.

Introductions for parents and others

Clay, Marie M. 1987. *Writing Begins at Home.* Portsmouth, N.H.: Heinemann.

Doake, David. 1988. *Reading Begins at Birth.* Richmond Hill, Ontario: Scholastic.

Gentry, J. Richard. 1987. *Spel. . . Is a Four-Letter Word.* Richmond Hill, Ontario: Scholastic. Available in the U.S. from Heinemann.

Hill, Mary W. 1989. *Home: Where Reading and Writing Begin.* Portsmouth, N.H.: Heinemann.

Newman, Judith. 1984. *The Craft of Children's Writing.* Richmond Hill, Ontario: Scholastic. Available in the U.S. from Heinemann.

Taylor, Denny, and Dorothy S. Strickland. 1986. *Family Storybook Reading.* Portsmouth, N.H.: Heinemann.

Emergent literacy in the classroom

Cambourne, Brian. 1988. *The Whole Story: Natural Learning and the Acquisition of Literacy in the Classroom.* Auckland, New Zealand: Ashton Scholastic.

Jensen, Julie M. 1989. *Stories to Grow On: Demonstrations of Language Learning in K–8 Classrooms.* Portsmouth, N.H.: Heinemann.

Routman, Regie. 1988. *Transitions: From Literature to Literacy.* Portsmouth, N.H.: Heinemann.

Schwartz, Judith I. 1988. *Encouraging Early Literacy: An Integrated Approach to Reading and Writing in N–3.* Portsmouth, N.H.: Heinemann.

Strickland, Dorothy S., and Leslie Mandel Morrow, eds. 1989. *Emerging Literacy: Young Children Learn to Read and Write.* Newark, Del.: International Reading Association.

Emphasis on research

Allen, JoBeth, and Jana M. Mason, eds. 1989. *Risk Makers, Risk Takers, Risk Breakers: Reducing the Risks for Young Literacy Learners.* Portsmouth, N.H.: Heinemann.

Hall, Nigel. 1987. *The Emergence of Literacy.* Portsmouth, N.H.: Heinemann.

Harste, Jerome C., Virginia A. Woodward, and Carolyn L. Burke. 1984. *Language Stories and Literacy Lessons.* Portsmouth, N.H.: Heinemann.

Taylor, Denny, and Catherine Dorsey-Gaines. 1988. *Growing Up Literate: Learning from Inner-City Families.* Portsmouth, N.H.: Heinemann.

Wells, Gordon. 1986. *The Meaning Makers: Children Learning Language and Using Language to Learn.* Portsmouth, N.H.: Heinemann.

Figure 4.12   Starter bibliography of books on emergent literacy

1. The classrooms are "littered with literacy": that is, they offer a rich variety of environmental print as well as books, magazines, and newspapers. They are print-rich environments.

2. Even the most rudimentary books for emergent readers are interesting and meaningful. The language is not stilted and artificially repetitive, as in most basal reading programs, but natural and predictable. Often, the language of emergent reading materials is rhythmical, even rhymed, and it offers plenty of repetition, but at the stanza and sentence levels (contrast, in Figures 4.13 and 4.14, the language typical of the beginning levels of a basal reading series with the language typical of more holistic programs).

3. Children are expected to learn, and given assistance in learning, from whole-to-part rather than the other way around. Instead of

---

Play!

Can I play?

Yes, you can play.

I can play!

Can I play?

Yes, you can play.

I can play too!

Can I play?

No, you cannot play.

I am not happy.
I can not play.

The spaces between lines indicate a change of speakers, which would ordinarily be cued with different faces in the text. Note how impoverished the print is, without any accompanying pictures. This "story" exemplifies the stilted language typical of the beginning levels of basal reading programs in the mid to late 1980s.

Figure 4.13   Language typical of beginning levels of basal programs

Greedy Cat
by Joy Cowley

Mum went shopping
and got some sausages.
Along came Greedy Cat.
He looked in the shopping bag.
Gobble, gobble, gobble,
and that was the end of that.

The episodes repeat, with Mum buying, and Greedy Cat eating, a
different item of food each time. Finally, Mum solves the problem by
buying a pot of pepper!

—From the *Ready to Read* program,
distributed by Richard C. Owen Publishers

In a Dark Dark Wood
traditional rhyme adapted by
June Melser and Joy Cowley

In a dark dark wood, there was a dark dark path.
And up that dark dark path, there was a dark dark house.
And in that dark dark house, there was a dark dark stair.
And up that dark dark stair, there was a dark dark room.
And in that dark dark room, there was a dark dark cupboard.
And in that dark dark cupboard, there was a dark dark box.
And in that dark dark box, there was a . . . ghost!

—From *The Story Box* program, distributed by the Wright Group

Figure 4.14   Language typical of holistic programs

beginning with letter/sound correspondences or sight words,
they read and reread highly predictable texts, reconstruct less pat-
terned texts, and gradually learn to attend to words and to letter/
sound relations. In writing, they construct their own texts, again
with initial emphasis on content and meaning rather than first
and foremost on correct letter formation, correct spelling, or other
conventions: a whole-to-part approach.

4. Children are expected and encouraged to approach adult standards and models of correctness gradually, as they did in learning
to talk—and they are given appropriate and timely assistance in
doing so. They are praised for growth and successive approximations rather than penalized for what they have not mastered.

5. Given these and other conditions that are conducive to success,
whole language educators naturally expect that children will
learn to read and write—and virtually all are well on their way to
becoming independent readers and writers by the end of first
grade.

> ❝Their development is facilitated by teachers and peers, of course, yet the children are (and always have been) in control of their own learning.❞

Children in such whole language classrooms early learn to think of themselves as readers and writers. And because they engage frequently and fearlessly in authentic acts of reading and writing, most children readily develop increasingly sophisticated concepts about print and strategies for reading and writing. Their development is facilitated by teachers and peers, of course, yet the children are (and always have been) in control of their own learning. And being in control of their own learning, they tend to learn considerably more than they do in more traditional classrooms. Specifically, they develop a far more productive concept of reading, writing, and literacy and of themselves as literacy learners.

We shall examine the relative effectiveness of whole language in the following two chapters, which discuss research comparing the effects of instructional practices: Chapter 5 from a part-to-whole perspective and Chapter 6 from a whole-to-part perspective.

C H A P T E R 5

What Does the Research Say? Research in Support of Part-to-Whole

In our schools, instruction is often part-to-whole: We teach first the smaller and then increasingly larger "parts" of a discipline. For example, reading instruction typically begins with a focus on letters and sounds, then on words—first with attention to "literal" comprehension, then on inference, analysis, synthesis, evaluation. A whole language approach moves in the opposite direction, from meaningful wholes toward the parts—for example, from enjoying and memorizing or reconstructing a repetitive and predictable story, song, or poem to gaining increased control over the words and the letter/sound associations. This approach is based on the observation that mastery of written language, like oral language, develops gradually toward adult conventionality through frequent engagement in reading and writing.

The question naturally arises, which approach is "better"? What does "the research" say? Chapter 4 has already indicated how research on language acquisition and emergent literacy supports a whole language approach. This chapter and the next will discuss classroom research. As we shall see, determining which approach is better depends at least partly upon what we are trying to accomplish, as reflected in what gets measured and how the results are interpreted and reported.

LIMITING WHAT WE MEASURE

Conventional means of assessment severely limit what is measured. Reading is measured as if it were a collection of skills and subskills rather than the ability to make sense of coherent and connected text. As the authors of the *Report Card on Basal Readers* point out, this reduction-

109

ism is inherent in the basal reading materials typically used for reading instruction. Original stories and other texts are rarely found intact and in their entirety; instead, students typically read synthetic, contrived texts at the beginning levels and adapted or abridged texts at subsequent levels. Reading is "taught" through round-robin reading, comprehension questions included with the selection, and workbook pages and skills sheets, all orchestrated by the teacher's manual. Ultimately, reading is assessed by the unit tests (K. Goodman et al. 1988, p. 85). "So reading is not making sense of print any more. It is doing well on the basal tests" (p. 108).

More globally, of course, "reading" means doing well not only on the basal tests but on standardized and state-mandated tests. Testmakers know that they had better test what is taught; that way, the schools can document the "success" of their program, even when there is clear evidence that many of our youth are not learning to read thoughtfully and critically. So, reading is reduced to bits and pieces of skills: phonics and other skills for identifying words, plus vocabulary skills and comprehension skills, such as locating information presented in the text (literal recall, or recognition), perceiving cause/effect relationships (recognition, or inference), and determining the "main idea" of a paragraph or short selection (inference). When researchers talk about students' "reading achievement," they are describing performance on such tests of skills, not students' ability to construct meaning for and by themselves from authentic texts in a variety of natural reading situations. The well-documented inability of many of our high school graduates to read and write adequately on the job attests all too poignantly to the fact that genuine reading ability is not the same as "reading achievement."

Thus, "reading achievement" is a severely limited concept, and often there is not a strong correlation between reading achievement scores and ability or inability to meet the literacy demands of everyday life. Almost by definition, I think, we can say that standardized tests assess only "reading achievement"—the ability to perform on skills items like those taught in virtually all of our commercially prepared reading programs. As discussed in Chapter 9, even the few large-scale tests that attempt to assess a more sophisticated concept of reading are not necessarily valid measures of actual reading ability; they too can claim only to assess "reading achievement."

It should also be noted that what counts as "reading achievement" changes over time. At the lower grade levels, there are proportionately more items that test word identification and other discrete skills, while at upper levels there are proportionately more questions designed to assess students' comprehension of passages that are at least a paragraph

" . . . 'reading achievement' is a severely limited concept, and often there is not a strong correlation between reading achievement scores and ability or inability to meet the literacy demands of everyday life.**"**

or more in length. Thus, the tests themselves reflect a part-to-whole concept of reading and learning to read, and therefore of "reading achievement." That concept, however, is simply not valid (see Chapters 4 and 10).

But since "reading achievement" scores are currently a reality with which teachers and administrators must cope, it seems imperative to discuss the effect of contrasting approaches upon such scores as well as to discuss alternative kinds of assessments that come closer to documenting students' real reading ability.

"PHONICS-FIRST": A PART-TO-WHOLE PERSPECTIVE

A part-to-whole approach involves skills for identifying words, then what are thought to be increasingly sophisticated skills for comprehension. Much of the part-to-whole research focuses on the teaching of phonics: letter/sound relationships, patterns, and rules. Proponents of phonics-first typically argue that children get off to a better start in reading if they first learn to "break the code" of our language, so they can sound out unfamiliar words. As Jeanne Chall expressed it in her landmark book *Learning to Read: The Great Debate*, proponents of a "code-emphasis" approach believe "that the initial stage in reading instruction should emphasize teaching children to master a code—the alphabetic code" (Chall 1967, p. 75). In practice, this most often means an early emphasis on phonics.

Since a considerable body of research focuses on the efficacy of phonics, and since letters and sounds are among the smallest significant parts of our language, it seems appropriate to focus on phonics research as typifying a part-to-whole approach.

Research purporting to demonstrate the superiority of an early emphasis on the direct teaching of phonics skills has been popularized lately, as in "What We Know About Phonics," a 1988 Research in Brief document from the offices of William Bennett and Chester Finn, and in *What Works*, a 1987 booklet also from the U.S. Department of Education. The research base is primarily that cited in Chall (1967), with relatively little updating.

In *Learning to Read*, Chall attempted to synthesize the results of reading research from the beginning of the century through the early 1960s, contrasting the effects of a "code-emphasis" approach (most typically phonics) with those of a "meaning-emphasis" approach (typically a sight word approach, which focuses on only slightly larger though more meaningful parts than a code-emphasis approach). She classified as "systematic phonics" those programs that "taught phonics early and systematically—usually, but not always, before sight (whole) words." Chall classified as "intrinsic phonics" programs that "stressed sight or thought reading, introduced phonics later, and taught a more moderate amount of it—all *intrinsic* to meaningful reading, which was the supreme consideration" (Chall 1967, pp. 102, 103). In short, "systematic phonics" is a part-to-whole approach, while "intrinsic phonics" is a whole-to-part approach. *Worth noting, I think, is that today's whole language approach is not a no-phonics approach but by Chall's definition an "intrinsic phonics" approach.*

We shall consider, then, summaries of the evidence for a systematic phonics approach, the flaws in that research evidence, and the lack of a theoretical base for that approach. We shall then examine more recent evidence supporting an intrinsic phonics approach, ultimately suggesting the limitations and inappropriateness of research and assessment focused narrowly on "reading achievement" rather than upon the development of literacy as broadly conceived and characterized.

Systematic versus Intrinsic Phonics

At the outset of her study, Chall admitted that "One of the most important things, if not *the* most important thing, I learned from studying the existing research on beginning reading is that it says nothing consistently. . . . Taken as a whole, the research on beginning reading is strongly inconclusive" (Chall 1967, pp. 87, 88). Nevertheless, guided by her theoretical perspective, Chall attempted to create order out of the chaos of conflicting data (Chall March 1989, pp. 524–28).

Because they are often oversimplified and then cited as definitive, Chall's early conclusions are worth listing in detail:

> In summary, judging from the studies comparing systematic with intrinsic phonics, we can say that systematic phonics at the very beginning tends to produce generally better reading and spelling achievement than intrinsic phonics, at least through grade 3.
>
> More specifically, the child who begins with systematic phonics achieves early superiority in word recognition. This superior ability may not always show up on standardized silent reading (comprehension and vocabulary) tests in the first grade. But by the second and third grades, greater facility in recognizing words probably increases his ability to read for meaning, as measured by standardized silent reading tests of vocabulary and comprehension.
>
> As for rate, systematic phonics may produce slower readers in grades 1 and 2 because it develops greater concern for working out the words. However, by the middle grades, rate seems to be about equal to that produced by intrinsic phonics.

> Finally, there is probably a limit to the advantage that early facility with the code gives on comprehension tested after grade 4. After this point, intelligence, experience, and language maturity probably become more important factors in success than ability to recognize words. (Chall 1967, p. 114)

Thus, according to this early synthesis, systematic phonics produces higher scores on tests of reading and spelling "achievement," though only through the primary grades.

Bond and Dykstra's 1967 summary of the 27 USOE cooperative first grade studies conducted during 1965–1966 has also been influential in promoting systematic phonics. In a later summary of his conclusion favoring phonics, Dykstra says:

> The evidence clearly demonstrates that children who receive early intensive instruction in phonics develop superior word recognition skills in the early stages of reading and tend to maintain their superiority at least through the third grade. These same pupils tend to do somewhat better than pupils enrolled in meaning-emphasis (delayed gradual phonics) programs in reading comprehension at the end of the first grade. (1974, p. 397)

Thus, these studies would seem to favor systematic phonics over intrinsic phonics: at least for grades 1 through 3, and at least according to standardized measures of reading achievement that emphasize phonics and other word recognition skills at those grade levels. What we teach is often what we get, it seems.

Post-1967 Research Conclusions

In her 1983 update of *Learning to Read: The Great Debate*, Chall reports that between 1967 and 1981 there was scarcely any research either to support or challenge her earlier conclusion: "The hope that coordinated studies would avoid uncertainties in [earlier] results did not materialize" (Chall 1983, p. 7).

Nevertheless, on the basis of very little research evidence beyond that synthesized in these studies, the authors of *Becoming a Nation of Readers* echo Chall's early conclusion, only extending it by referring to the scanty research on long-term effects of phonics instruction:

> Data on the long-term effects of phonics instruction are scanty. In one of the few longitudinal studies, children who had received intensive phonics instruction in kindergarten or first grade performed better in the third grade than a comparison group of children on both a word identification test and a comprehension test. By the sixth grade, the group that years earlier had received intensive phonics instruction still

> did better than the comparison group on a word identification test but the advantage in comprehension had vanished. (Anderson et al. 1985; they cite Becker and Gersten 1982)

More recently, Marilyn Jager Adams has completed a study originally titled "Phonics and Beginning Reading Instruction," the purpose being to provide guidance as to how we might maximize the quality of phonics instruction in beginning reading programs. As a prelude to this discussion, she describes the studies which together suggest "that programs including systematic instruction on letter-to-sound correspondences generally lead to higher achievement in both word recognition and spelling at least in the early grades" (Adams 1990a). She does not, however, provide any convincing new evidence that phonics should be taught intensively or first, before students engage in meaningful reading.

The two studies cited as showing the effects of early intensive phonics instruction upon later achievement are the Becker and Gersten (1982) study mentioned by Anderson et al. (1985) and another by Gersten and Keating (1987). In these studies, the Follow Through program used with the experimental group placed heavy emphasis upon phonics. However, the conclusion that heavy phonics instruction leads to improved reading is highly suspect. Examination of Becker and Gersten's article reveals that although those fifth- and sixth-graders who had been in the Follow Through program in the primary grades scored much higher than comparison groups on a test of decoding skills, they did not maintain their early advantage in reading comprehension, as measured on the Metropolitan Achievement Test of reading. The comparative scores on the MAT comprehension test were not given by Becker and Gersten. They wrote, however, that in fifth- and sixth-grade, "there is evidence [for the Follow Through students] of significant and enduring effects in all domains [except the reading comprehension test]. Probably taking her cue from a table in the article itself, Adams reports this simply as an overall difference in favor of the Follow Through group. Similarly, careful examination of Gersten and Keating's article (1987) comparing high school seniors does not clearly demonstrate that either intensive phonics or direct instruction can be credited with the various kinds of superiority the Follow Through seniors demonstrated, in comparison with peers. Indeed, from their article, one may reasonably infer that the students' enhanced self-esteem from being treated as "successful" was probably far more responsible for the positive effects than either phonics or direct instruction per se.

In fact, from Adams' report (1990a) and the much briefer summary of it (1990b), it would appear that Adams does not necessarily believe that research supports the teaching of phonics either first or intensively, despite the confusing language that is sometimes used—especially in the summary undertaken by Stahl, Osborn, and Lehr (Adams 1990b). For example, Adams begins her discussion of phonics by saying studies show that "something about that large and general class of programs that purport to teach phonics is of genuine and lasting value. In particular, each of these classes of evidence suggests that, to become proficient readers, students must appreciate the alphabetic principle: they must acquire a sense of the correspondences between letters and sounds upon which it is based" (Adams 1990a). Perhaps no educator would disagree with such a cautiously worded conclusion. However, it is a far cry from this observation to the frequently made statements that the research supports "intensive, explicit [or systematic] phonics" (Adams 1989b, p. 13), which is generally taken to mean phonics *first*.

In any case, Adams' report provides no *new* evidence that phonics instruction produces better reading achievement scores in the primary grades, and no *convincing* evidence that it produces longer-lasting gains.

What, then, of other kinds of evidence for direct, systematic phonics? Describing some more recent research from various disciplines, Chall (1989) argues in responding to a critique of her earlier research syntheses that this varied research justifies her conviction that "Segmenting and blending phonemes (separating the sounds in words and putting them together again) are considered to be the sine qua non of early reading development. Moreover, when students are trained through tasks designed to develop their awareness of phonemes, their reading achievement improves" (Chall 1989, p. 529). Once again, of course, it is "reading achievement" that is measured—not the ability to constuct meaning from authentic texts in a variety of real-life situations.

VIEWING THE RESEARCH IN PERSPECTIVE

One concern with the research purporting to demonstrate the superiority of phonics-first is that the standardized tests used in such studies typically lack construct validity. That is, they do not test what they seemingly purport to test, namely, the ability to read; rather, they test the ability to respond to items dealing with the alleged skills of reading. Research does not support, however, the underlying assumption that together those skills add up to the ability to construct meaning from coherent and connected text (see Chapter 9). Or to put it another way, the standardized tests both reflect and promote a severely limited, even erroneous, concept of reading.

Another concern is that a great deal of what promotes literacy may be sacrificed in pursuing this narrow goal of higher scores on tests of word identification, vocabulary, and comprehension skills. Traditionally, this

❝Another concern is that a great deal of what promotes literacy may be sacrificed in pursuing this narrow goal of higher scores on tests of word identification, vocabulary, and comprehension skills.**❞**

aim has been pursued mainly by having students complete worksheet after worksheet, workbook after workbook, covering the so-called skills of reading. With such an instructional program geared toward the same kind of testing, students are less likely to develop a flexible repertoire of reading strategies, less likely to feel good about themselves as readers, and less likely to read for enjoyment, or even meaning. Thus, the tests themselves promote a severely limited concept not only of reading itself, but of literacy.

For the present, however, I want to focus not upon the tests that purportedly show the superiority of systematic phonics but upon the research itself. Let us consider the following questions:

1. How reliable is Chall's synthesis of the early research?
2. What accounts for and justifies Chall's theoretical base, other than this research?
3. What body of research are Chall and others considering—and what are they not considering—when they conclude that "the research" supports a phonics-first approach?
4. What are they implicitly assuming about the relationship between reading achievement scores and the actual ability to read and construct meaning from authentic and coherent texts?

The Reliability of Conclusions Based on the Oft-cited Research

First, then, we shall examine the question of reliability, in the popular rather than the technical sense: Are Chall's conclusions based on a solid synthesizing of, and justifiable inferencing from, equally solid research studies?

In a 1988 critique of Chall's research synthesis in *Learning to Read: The Great Debate* (1967, updated 1983), Marie Carbo points out what Chall admitted in her original attempt to synthesize the results of the experimental research studies: many of them had serious design flaws. Carbo's further analysis of the data from 16 of 31 studies discussed by Chall reveals some additional flaws in Chall's own analysis and reporting of these studies. In several ways, Chall tended to skew the data as being more favorable to phonics instruction than the data seem to warrant. Carbo (November 1988, October 1989) demonstrates that this criticism applies not only to the studies reviewed and to the conclusions in Chall's original, 1967 edition of *The Great Debate* but also to the post-1967 studies that Chall discusses (Chall 1983).

In Chall's defense, her own concern about the reliability of the research data should be quoted:

> Since previous summaries based on practically the same body of experimental evidence had arrived at conflicting conclusions, I knew before starting that a major problem was how to read the research. . . .
>
> As I had suspected beforehand, practically none of the studies specified all these [aforementioned] conditions. Most did not indicate how the experimental and control groups were selected, how much time was allotted to various aspects of reading, how the teachers were selected, whether the quality of the teaching was comparable in both groups, or even whether the teachers followed the methods under study. Even more important, most studies did not specify clearly what a "method" involved, but instead merely assigned labels (e.g., "phonics"), expecting the reader to understand what was meant. (Chall 1967, pp. 100–101)

At the outset of her 1967 synthesis, then, Chall openly and admirably admitted her own concerns about the research she was attempting to synthesize.

But in response to Carbo's article, Chall defended this inadequate research base largely by downplaying it, claiming that her conclusions had been based as much upon her "theoretical base" as upon the allegedly flawed research, or her allegedly skewed interpretation of it: "Working from a theoretical base, as well as from a synthesis of the experimental, correlational, and clinical findings of the research base, I recommended an earlier and more systematic emphasis on phonics in beginning reading programs, as well as reading for understanding" (Chall 1989, p. 525).

What Supported the Theoretical Base?

The problem is, *it is difficult to determine what supported the theoretical base other than these research studies.* Chall does not make this clear either in her 1967 book or in her 1989 article, suggesting that her syntheses of the research reflect the imposition of her a priori convictions upon the data.

Of course, one can scarcely fault Chall for interpreting the data through the lenses of her own theoretical glasses. As I have discussed elsewhere, it is now widely recognized that external reality cannot be understood objectively, as it *really* is, but only as it is observed, assessed, and interpreted through a particular theoretical perspective or world view (Weaver 1985, 1988, 1989). One wonders, then, what data or beliefs gave rise to the theory that seems to have guided Chall's interpretation of these research studies? And what justifies and supports this belief system?

The inference I draw from Chall's original, 1967 book is that her theory and theoretical base stemmed mainly from: (1) the a priori assumption that in order to use a knowledge of letter/sound relations in reading, one must study those relations *explicitly* (an assumption implicitly questioned in Chapter 4 and explicitly challenged in Chapter 7); and (2) the observation that, according to various critics, the sight word method of teaching reading that was popular from the 1940s to the 1960s was not successful in teaching everyone to read. Putting together the assumption with the observation, one might logically develop a *hypothesis* to the effect that systematic phonics would be a more effective approach than the sight word approach. *However: showing that one method is inadequate does not prove that a competing method is necessarily any better, much less the best possible method or approach. Both methods might be inappropriate or inadequate, each being in its own way less than optimal.*

The question remains, then: from whence came the theoretical base that justified Chall in her 1967 book in creating "out of chaos" the particular "order" she did (Chall 1989, p. 528) when others have created a far different order (as admitted in Chall 1983, p. 6) or seen no consistent patterns at all within that same chaos (see Corder 1971)? What research supports the theoretical base itself, other than the research studies that are interpreted from the vantage point of that base?

Selective Narrowing of the Research Base

True, Chall in her 1989 article cites much more recent research of differing sorts: not merely the aforementioned research comparing approaches to instruction but related research from cognitive psychology, psycholinguistics, developmental psychology, and the study of learning disabilities. The research cited does *appear* to support Chall's contention that an early emphasis on decoding facilitates reading, but what is measured is typically "reading achievement": scores on standardized tests, which—particularly in the early grades—typically put a heavy premium upon the ability to identify words in isolation (see Figure 5.1), even when purporting to test comprehension. Of course, ability to recognize words will generally facilitate comprehension. *However, that does not mean that getting higher scores on standardized tests in the primary grades necessarily makes a child a better reader.* As we shall see in Chapter 6, this implicit assumption is severely challenged by research from a broader perspective.

Though drawing upon research from several disciplines to justify the theory that is—at best—weakly supported by the experimental research

It is hot.

It tastes good.

The cat is

    ○ running   ○ flying   ○ jumping

The cat is in a box on the floor.

We like to play in the

    ○ ripe   ○ rope   ○ rain   ○ risk

The children wanted to have a party for Billy. Sally made cookies.
Jimmy got some ice cream. Mother had milk for them to drink. The party
was fun!

Who made cookies?	Who got some ice cream?	What else did they have?
○ Billy	○ Sally	○ cookies
○ Sally	○ Jimmy	○ cake
○ Mother	○ Billy	○ milk

**Figure 5.1 Some kinds of reading comprehension questions found at the
earliest levels of standardized tests (directions are given orally)**

she cites, Chall unfortunately ignores, or is ignorant of, much of that research: for example, the research demonstrating that emergent literacy can effectively be fostered in much the same way as emergent language (Chapter 4), as well as a growing body of experimental and quasi-experimental studies that lead to conclusions different from Chall's (Chapter 6). Thus, Chall's audacious claim that "the research" supports her position is simply untrue. A broadened research base invites significantly different conclusions.

Unfortunately, however, researchers with a part-to-whole perspective have tended to narrow or distort the research base, as well as to make clearly unwarranted claims about research on the effectiveness of a whole language approach.

The Treatment of Whole Language

Though the authors of *Becoming a Nation of Readers* (Anderson et al. 1985) are known more for a whole-to-part perspective than a part-to-whole perspective, their discussion of phonics and whole language reflects the latter perspective—perhaps because of the influence of Jeanne Chall, who was a member of the commission that prepared the report. In any case, what the authors say about the effectiveness of a whole language approach is simply invalid. It is invalid not only because the research is severely outdated, but because a whole language "approach" was not used in any of the studies from which conclusions were drawn about whole language practices in the United States:

> It is noteworthy that these [whole language] approaches are used to teach children to read in New Zealand, the most literate country in the world, a country that experiences very low rates of reading failure. However, studies of whole language approaches in the United States have produced results that are best characterized as inconsistent. In the hands of very skillful teachers, the results can be excellent. But the average result is indifferent when compared to approaches typical in American classrooms, at least as gauged by performance on first- and second-grade standardized reading achievement tests. (Anderson et al 1985, p. 45)

At least the authors note that the effectiveness of a whole language approach is being measured only by children's performance on standardized reading achievement tests, though one wonders what the authors mean by saying the average result is "indifferent": as good as the result from any other approach?

At any rate, what the authors do not *explicitly* tell their readers is even more significant. Those who read the footnotes should be immediately suspicious, because the *only* reference cited in support of the conclusion that whole language produced "indifferent" results in the United States is Bond and Dykstra's 1967 summary of the 27 USOE cooperative first grade studies, which were undertaken twenty years before *Becoming a Nation of Readers* was published. Surely the authors of the latter do not expect anyone to conclude that in the past twenty years there has been no other research that might provide insights into the effects of a whole language approach? And surely such reputable scholars as the authors of *Becoming a Nation of Readers* ought themselves to have been suspicious of a twenty-year-old source.

What further invalidates their conclusion is that a whole language approach per se was scarcely even known in the United States (if at all)—much less researched here—during 1965 and 1966, when the cited research was undertaken. What came closest to being a whole language approach was the language experience approach, but it represents only a small part—at most only one activity—of what constitutes whole language. How, then, could the authors of *Becoming a Nation of Readers* presume to draw conclusions about the efficacy of a whole language approach in comparison with approaches more typical in American classrooms? They claimed to know what "the research" said while citing twenty-year-old studies that did not even deal with the approach in question.

Perhaps one can empathize with their misconception that whole language is essentially the same as language experience, since whole language was less well understood among scholars a few years ago, when *Becoming a Nation of Readers* was written. But Steven Stahl and Patricia Miller (1989) cannot so readily be excused for lumping together whole language and language experience approaches in their more recent statistical meta-analysis ("quantitative research synthesis") of data from various studies. Clearly, these authors understand not only the philosophical similarities between the two approaches but also the fact that language experience is only one kind of *activity* within whole language classrooms. I would suppose that these researchers combined the two whole-to-part approaches mainly in order to have enough studies to compare them with the effectiveness of a basal reader approach, which is generally skills-oriented, proceeding from part-to-whole.

Given this confounding methodology, Stahl and Miller (1989) conclude from their statistical analysis that "overall, whole language/language experience approaches are approximately equal in their effects," but with several exceptions. For example, they note that whole language/language experience approaches may be most effective for developing concepts about print, while more direct approaches might be better at helping students master word recognition skills (Stahl and Miller 1989, p. 87).

Because of their methodological approach, however, it scarcely matters what they concluded about whole language. Language experience is at most only one instructional activity within a much more comprehensive whole language approach, so treating the two as if they were the same invalidates any and all conclusions about their relative effectiveness, or lack thereof.

Summary of Concerns About This Research Base

It should not be surprising, then, that many scholars are concerned about the widespread credibility granted to the research purporting to demonstrate the superiority of a phonics-first approach. There is legitimate reason to question the reliability of both the research studies themselves and the syntheses and summaries of these studies. Yet publications like *What Works* and even *Becoming a Nation of Readers* typically quote as gospel Chall's early research summary or a variant thereof, offered without the original admissions that the research was inconclusive or flawed, without Chall's frank admission that other researchers have interpreted the same evidence differently, without any suggestion that the ''evidence'' might reflect the interpreter's biases as much as the data, and without any admission that there might be other research that supports different conclusions. The latter objection is extremely important. While conflicting and contradictory evidence has increasingly proliferated, some phonics-first advocates such as Chall and more recently Marilyn Adams continue to offer their research studies and evidence as if these were all that existed, or all that have bearing on how reading might best be fostered in the schools.

❝ Perhaps most damaging, however, is the unquestioned assumption of phonics-first advocates that test scores on standardized tests tell us everything we need to know about children's development of the ability to read. **❞**

Perhaps most damaging, however, is the unquestioned assumption of phonics-first advocates that test scores on standardized tests tell us everything we need to know about children's development of the ability to read. Equally dangerous is the related assumption that it is important for children to score higher on standardized tests in the primary grades, even though the alleged advantage of phonics-first does not seem to be maintained beyond the early elementary years.

MOVING BEYOND ''THE GREAT DEBATE''

In Chapter 6, we shall see that a part-to-whole approach is not necessarily more effective than a whole-to-part approach, not even in the primary grades and not even when measured by standardized tests that emphasize word analysis skills and identifying words in isolation. Whole language educators, however, are convinced that the profession needs to move beyond the "great debate" over which produces better test scores, a part-to-whole or whole-to-part approach.

This conviction is expressed also by assessment expert Richard Turner, who with a strong background in assessment but no particular stance from which to defend a perspective on reading education, evaluated Chall's and Carbo's contrasting claims about the research originally analyzed and summarized by Chall. At the outset, Turner decided to consider only "the best evidence" from carefully designed research. Thus, he rejected both laboratory experiments, which inevitably distort the nature of the normal reading process, and "patched-up program evaluations," which constituted the vast majority of articles cited by Chall and criticized by Carbo.

This left nine randomized field experiments that compared a systematic phonics approach with either an intrinsic phonics approach or a "no-phonics" approach, in which students were left to develop, over time, their own methods for figuring out sounds in unrecognized words. Turner suggests that the latter strategy would be characteristic of a whole language approach, but in practice most whole language teachers combine this expectation with various kinds of direct and indirect teaching of phonics (see Chapter 7). As far as one can tell, none of the studies compared systematic phonics with a whole language approach that begins with whole, predictable, and repetitive text, moving gradually toward developing a stock of sight words as well as letter/sound associations. In other words, it appears that none of the studies compared systematic phonics with whole language.

What the studies did compare is systematic phonics with differing variants of a whole word approach. Systematic phonics is a part-to-whole approach, while relative to that, whole word is a whole-to-part approach (though from the viewpoint of whole language, whole word is also a part-to-whole approach). Turner hypothesized that any initial advantages one approach might have over the other would appear early in the primary grades and then disappear. The data generally supported this hypothesis, leading Turner to the following summary statement.

> My overall conclusion from reviewing the randomized field studies is that systematic phonics falls into that vast category of weak instructional treatments with which education is perennially plagued. Systematic phonics appears to have a slight and early advantage over a basal-reader/whole-word approach as a method of beginning reading instruction. . . . However, this difference does not last long and has no clear meaning for the acquisition of literacy in the sense of enhancing vocabulary and improving comprehension. Moreover, learning theory offers little reason to believe that it should do so. (Turner 1989, p. 283)

❝Thus, in effect, Turner seems to be suggesting that we turn away from the question of how to achieve higher scores on standardized tests in the primary grades, to the question of what best develops literacy as more broadly conceived and assessed.**❞**

Thus, in effect, Turner seems to be suggesting that we turn away from the question of how to achieve higher scores on standardized tests in the primary grades, to the question of what best develops literacy as more broadly conceived and assessed.

From the perspective of an ethnographer who has meticulously documented children's literacy development in contexts where children have been allowed to explore reading and writing rather than assigned skills lessons, Denny Taylor goes even farther, concluding:

> When viewed against the broader context of the past 20 years of research into the ways in which young children learn to read and write, the "Great Debate" can be seen as little more than a trivial argument over an issue that has no scientific relevance. (1989, p. 185)

Somewhat similarly, Turner concludes his analysis of the randomized field experiments by suggesting the inappropriateness of continuing the "great debate" over the importance of systematic phonics:

> Perhaps it is time for reading experts to turn away from the debate over systematic phonics in search of more powerful instructional treatments for beginning reading that will influence the development of literacy in the middle grades and beyond.

As we shall see in Chapter 6, classroom research is beginning to confirm that whole language is a much more powerful "treatment." And while most of the current research on the effectiveness of whole language has focused on the primary grades, researchers are beginning to document the efficacy of this philosophy and approach throughout the educational system, and even with adult learners (see Stephens' [1990] bibliography). Though such research is still in its infancy, the early results are highly encouraging.

CHAPTER 6

What Does the Research Say? Research in Support of Whole-to-Part

WITH DIANE STEPHENS

Chapter 5 indicates that research supporting a part-to-whole approach typically examines mastery of the alleged "parts" of reading, more than the whole. In the primary grades, for instance, such research may assess "reading achievement" by determining students' ability to recognize letters and make letter/sound correlations, to choose one of four words that best fits the blank in a given sentence, to find a sentence or phrase in a brief paragraph that provides the best answer to a question about content, and so forth. Beyond the primary grades, standardized assessment instruments demand somewhat greater ability to construct meaning, yet they still typically focus on "skills," such as identifying what the test-maker thought was the main idea, determining cause-effect relationships, and drawing inferences from sentences in the text. In traditional classrooms, there is usually a good match between what is taught and what is assessed on standardized tests: namely, skills.

however, we should not be teaching to standardized tests.

What we teach and test is too often what we get—at best, an ability to do well on tests of skills; at worst, low scores that seem to suggest failure. As we shall see in Chapter 9, there is not necessarily a strong correlation between the ability to do well on skills tests and the ability to construct meaning when reading authentic texts for real purposes. But even if the two were strongly correlated, such scores certainly tell very little of what we ought to know about students as developing readers and writers.

Whole language educators are among those who realize that "reading achievement" scores on such standardized tests are not appropriate

125

measures of literacy. Nor are such scores even appropriate as measures of "the basics," because other kinds of abilities, attitudes, and habits are far more basic to the development of literacy. The kinds of questions we should be asking, in our research as well as in our classrooms, include but are not limited to the following:

1. Do the students view themselves as good readers and writers?
2. Do they consider meaning of prime importance when explaining what makes someone a good reader or writer?
3. Do they demonstrate interest in reading and writing outside school?
4. Do they exhibit flexibility in solving the problems they encounter as readers and writers?
5. Do they take risks as learners?
6. Are they learning to construct meaning from a variety of texts, written for differing purposes?
7. Are they learning to convey meaning through writing, for a variety of purposes and audiences?
8. Are they developing a flexible repertoire of reading strategies, including the ability to orchestrate the language cue systems (meaning, structure, letters and letter/sound relations) in order to construct meaning, and the ability to monitor their own comprehension?
9. Are they developing a flexible repertoire of strategies for generating, drafting, revising, and editing their writing, including strategies for developing and organizing their ideas as well as strategies for learning the conventions of written language?
10. Are they developing strategies for analyzing, synthesizing, and evaluating what they read—and write?
11. Are they developing the ability to think not only critically but creatively, through language?
12. Are they developing the attitudes and habits of independent, self-motivated, lifelong readers and writers, thinkers and learners?

These are the kinds of factors emphasized in whole language classrooms and therefore deemed most significant in assessing the efficacy of whole language teaching.

The heart of this chapter will focus, then, on research that has sought to determine which is more effective in promoting these abilities and attributes, a part-to-whole approach or a whole-to-part approach. Most of these studies, however, also deal with how "skills" have fared in the contrasting approaches.

Before turning to these matters, though, it is important to emphasize that research comparing the effects of different instructional approaches is not the only kind of research supporting whole language teaching and a whole-to-part approach.

TYPES OF RESEARCH SUPPORTING WHOLE-TO-PART

Basically there are *two* significantly different research bases that support a whole-to-part approach. The first consists of work conducted in fields such as language acquisition and emergent literacy, psycholinguistics and sociolinguistics, cognitive and developmental psychology, anthropology, and neurology as related to reading and reading "disabilities." Work in these fields has provided many of the understandings discussed in earlier chapters: that reading and writing are more than collections of skills; that teaching and assessing reading and writing as skills may actually mitigate against the development of effective reading and writing strategies; and that literacy develops naturally in much the same way that language is acquired, and under similar conditions.

Much of the research providing the theoretical foundation for a whole literacy philosophy and approach to teaching is not experimental in nature but "naturalistic." That is, it stems from observation and analysis of how children learn language and develop an increasingly sophisticated understanding of their world, how they learn to read and write in relatively natural settings, and how readers process text to construct meanings. Rather than attempt to isolate one variable for comparison while holding others constant (as in experimental research), naturalistic research focuses on the complexities of real-life events—learning to talk, to read, to write. Because the subject of naturalistic research is broadly defined, the results allow researchers to draw at least tentative hypotheses about a wide range of phenomena. Indeed, anything can be observed, recorded, and analyzed that seems to have bearing on what is being investigated. As the study progresses, new hypotheses may emerge which are then tested by further observation and collection of data.

In naturalistic literacy research, the development of skills is assessed within the broader context of literacy development, and literacy development is often examined within the authentic reading and writing that children do as they engage in the processes of making and sharing meaning with and from print. Products are thus assessed within the context of processes.

It is predominantly naturalistic research that has provided the theoretical basis for a whole language philosophy. When teachers began to

❝In naturalistic literacy research, the development of skills is assessed within the broader context of literacy development, and literacy development is often examined within the authentic reading and writing that children do as they engage in the processes of making and sharing meaning with and from print.**❞**

make curricular decisions from a whole language perspective, often researchers also chose naturalistic methods to understand what came to be called whole language classrooms. Naturalistic methods provide researchers the means to understand and document the complexities of teaching and learning in the classroom. Experimental and quasi-experimental approaches, used less often, help researchers understand particular parts or aspects of whole language classrooms. Both naturalistic and experimental methods have been used to compare traditional (skills-based) classrooms with whole language classrooms (sometimes also referred to as *literacy based, integrated, process oriented, literature based,* or *immersion*).

Weaver (1988, pp. 213–16) discusses some of the early experimental attempts to determine how implementing a whole language philosophy affects the acquisition of skills; one of these studies is discussed here. Stephens has recently compiled a much more extensive bibliography of research on whole language (1990). She defines the subject of her bibliography as research conducted in classrooms in which language was used to meet the learner's purpose and in which reading, writing, speaking, and listening were integral parts of language in use. Thirty-six studies are annotated in that bibliography (28 classroom studies and 8 case studies of children). The bibliography is not exhaustive, of course, *nor is the research necessarily any less flawed than that synthesized by Chall* in what is considered her landmark book, *Learning to Read: The Great Debate* (Chall 1967, 1983). Such studies as these, however, form only *part* of the research base that supports whole language learning and teaching.

In this chapter, we discuss seven studies at length. About half of these are studies so recent that they have not yet appeared in journals or books. These particular studies were selected to contrast with those discussed in Chapter 5; therefore, they include measures of children's "reading achievement," usually as determined by one or more skills-oriented standardized tests. However, the studies also document some aspects of literacy development mentioned in the preceding section—aspects that one might logically expect would fare better in a whole-to-part approach.

NATURALISTIC STUDIES

Naturalistic studies of whole language classrooms describe the classroom experience, report the curricular decisions made, and examine the learning that occurs. They are sometimes conducted solely by educators from university settings; occasionally, the classroom teacher and the university educator collaborate on a study. Recently, more and more teachers have been conducting their own research in their own classrooms.

Avery, 1985

Avery, Carol S. 1985. Lori "figures it out": A young writer learns to read. In Jane Hansen, Thomas Newkirk, and Donald Graves, eds. *Breaking Ground: Teachers Relate Reading and Writing in the Elementary School.* Portsmouth, N.H.: Heinemann.

Avery (1985) describes the growth of a child and her classmates in her first-grade "learning process classroom." She documents the literacy activities that comprised her curriculum and explains how she planned lessons, organized the classroom, and assessed the children's growth. Avery focuses her discussion on Lori, a child she describes as average, anxious, and apprehensive at the beginning of the year. Using examples from Lori's work and comments from interviews and journals, Avery follows Lori throughout the year, documenting her growth as reader, writer, and learner.

Avery provides statistical data from basal and standardized tests to illustrate the progress of the class:

> In mid-December the class took the Level 2 test of the district reading program [the 1986 Scott, Foresman Reading Unlimited Program]. A score of 45 was considered passing. The range in the classroom was 46 to 50, and nine students, including Lori, scored a perfect 50. (p. 24)

Avery notes that never in her previous years of teaching had she administered the test so early in the year, yet previous scores had occasionally "dipped to the low 40's" (ibid.). On the California Achievement Test (CAT) administered in May, the students' scores ranged from the 76th to the 99th percentile; Lori scored at the 93rd (p. 27).

The basal and standardized test scores reassured Avery and the school administrators that the children's reading "achievement" was not suffering from her integrative process approach, in which the children's own writing was "the beginning impetus and primary instrument for their instruction in learning to read," and in which reading and writing were "allowed to flow in an interactive process, each supporting and enhancing the other" (p. 16).

During the late winter months, Avery notes, both writing and reading flourished in her classroom. Whereas earlier in the year the children often read only parts of stories, by late winter they were reading entire paperback books, an assortment of basal readers, and, especially, peer-authored materials. Avery comments: "I noticed a difference in the reading approach of this class which I had not seen in previous nonwriting first graders. As readers, they were far more aggressive and critical, striving continuously for content'' (p. 25).

Thus, as Avery explains, the most important feedback about the children's reading progress came not from the standardized tests—reassuring though they were—but from her daily interactions with the children's reading process (p. 24).

As for the timid and anxious Lori, she became an ''avid reader'' who had ''assumed responsibility for and control of her own learning processes'' (p. 27). One day during the last week of school, Lori commented to Avery, ''I really like to read *Charlotte's Web*. I can read it now, the whole way through, without any struggling'' (p. 27).

Gunderson and Shapiro, 1987

Gunderson, Lee, and Jon Shapiro. Spring 1987. Some findings on whole language instruction. *Reading-Canada-Lecture* 5:22–26.

Gunderson and Shapiro (1987) took the more traditional research approach: As university educators they conducted literacy research in public school classrooms.

Indicating that the term ''whole language'' has nearly as many definitions as it has advocates, these researchers characterize whole language classrooms as ones in which reading and writing are not taught separately, and in which both oral and written language are employed for personal and functional use. They cite M. Hall's (1986) recommendations for language-centered classrooms:

> (1) initial exposure to written language should precede formal reading instruction; (2) students should be immersed in meaningful print; (3) students should be allowed to experiment with print; (4) invented spellings should be encouraged rather than discouraged; (5) language experience should be part of the program; (6) extensive writing should be encouraged at all levels; (7) extensive literature experiences must be available; and (8) mechanics of writing should be downplayed. (p. 23)

The authors then describe whole language instruction in two first-grade classrooms. The analyzed data included copies of everything the children wrote over the period of a year, including log books, draft books, cooperative stories written by the whole class, and individual skill-related assignments dealing with phonics. The activities involved reading and/or dramatizing literature; shared reading, in which children practiced individually, in pairs, or in small groups; whole group instruction in basic sight words through games; instruction in spelling; and whole group and individual experiences with phonics-oriented tasks. Each session

> began with the teacher introducing words beginning, for instance, with /č/. Students provided examples which were written on wordcards. Each glued his word on the first page of the community book, for example, *chirp, check, cheddar, chowmein*. Pages had room at the top for illustrations and lines at the bottom for writing. Each student contributed a story that contained /č/ words. (p. 24)

Analyzing the children's writings at length, the authors drew the general conclusion that neither the children's development of basic vocabulary nor their development of phonics skills suffered from the emphasis on authentic literacy rather than skills. Regarding the vocabulary, they noted:

> How does vocabulary generated by students writing their own material differ from that encountered in the basal? Three points are to be made. First, the 52 students generated nearly eighteen times the number of words they would be exposed to in the first five levels of Ginn 720 (9,857 versus 549 word types). Secondly, the low frequency items generated by students are more current, for example, *disaster, astronauts*, and *gobots*. Thirdly, the high frequency vocabulary is remarkably similar in both cases. (p. 25)

Thus, the students used in their writing not only the high-frequency words presented in the commonly used basal but also numerous words that would not have been encountered in the basal.

The development of phonics skills was also assessed through the children's writings, by examining their invented spellings—that is, their phonic misspellings rather than the conventional adult spellings:

> Students revealed that they understood phonics relationships quite well by producing such misspellings as tri(*try*), tew(*two*), wuz(*was*), werking(*working*), sine(*sign*), rane(*rain*), rany(*rainy*), mowse(*mouse*), merder(*murder*), lizrd(*lizard*), jiump(*jump*), evre(*every*), chasd(*chased*), and byootifl(*beautiful*). They produced a great number of misspellings that showed they were overgeneralizing phonic relationships to instances of words that did not follow the rule. (p. 24)

As the authors further comment, such overgeneralizations are a natural development in language acquisition as children develop increasingly

> **"**Thus, the students used in their writing not only the high-frequency words presented in the commonly used basal but also numerous words that would not have been encountered in the basal.**"**

more sophisticated hypotheses about the rules and systems of language (p. 25).

The investigators concluded:

> Findings of this study suggest, then, that contrary to critics' warnings, whole language programs result in students' learning phonics relationships and mastering high frequency vocabulary which is presented in basal readers. Further study must be undertaken to measure other areas of achievement of students involved in whole language programs compared with those in other initial literacy programs. (p. 26)

Pierce, 1984

Pierce, V. 1984. Bridging the gap between language research/theory and practice: A case study. Unpublished doctoral dissertation, Texas Women's University, Denton, Tex.

Pierce (1984) collaborated with two second-grade teachers who were interested in moving toward an integrated approach to literacy learning. Using field notes, interviews, materials gathered on site, and DeFord's Theoretical Orientation to Reading Profile (DeFord 1985), Pierce examined both teacher and student change. Her study suggests that over the year, the teachers assumed more control of the curriculum and began to see themselves as capable decision-makers. They made substantial changes in their curriculum, altered their teaching style, evidenced an appreciation of the children's developing reading and writing skills and strategies, and altered their perspective on literacy and teaching.

As the teachers made these changes, the students became more interested in and involved with reading and writing tasks. They became so enthusiastic that one teacher suggested that when the students were working on reading and writing, "it's like they are having art." The students also assumed greater responsibility for working independently and often chose literacy activities they wanted to do—not only during the school day but after school and during the summer. Examples of student work demonstrated their growth as readers and writers. Both classes also showed a two-year gain on standardized achievement test scores. In comparing scores on end-of-year standardized tests, Pierce found that these students also scored above the school and district mean as well as above the mean of students from a school with a similar population.

Obviously, these students grew in a multiplicity of ways: not only in showing an average of two years' gain on standardized achievement tests, but in developing an interest in reading and writing and an ability to take responsibility for their own learning.

EXPERIMENTAL AND
QUASI-EXPERIMENTAL STUDIES

In the experimental or quasi-experimental studies examined here, similar classes of students were exposed to different instructional "treatments" in an attempt to determine the differing effects of the two approaches. These studies provide an interesting contrast to those emphasized by phonics-first scholars like Chall: not because the studies are necessarily more rigorously designed and carried out, but because most are designed to measure a much wider range of factors than studies focusing only on "reading achievement" scores as measures of reading and literacy.

Elley and Mangubhai, 1983

Elley, Warwick B., and Francis Mangubhai. 1983. The impact of reading on second language learning. *Reading Research Quarterly* 19:53–67.

One of the first such studies was undertaken by Warwick Elley and Francis Mangubhai in the Fiji Islands of the South Pacific. Working with 9- to 11-year-old Class 4 and Class 5 students who did not speak English as their native language, they hypothesized that exposing these children to a wealth of storybooks written in English would stimulate not only their growth in reading but their growth in the acquisition of spoken English. The children in these grades were exposed to instruction in English only, but until that time they had been typically exposed to English through oral drills rather than genuine communication, with errors being viewed as wrong responses rather than as necessary to natural language growth. As the investigators put it, "Exposure to the second language [English] is normally planned, restricted, gradual, and largely artificial" (Elley and Mangubhai 1983, p. 55). In short, the program in English as a second language fit squarely into what was characterized in Chapter 2 as a transmission model of teaching and learning.

To test the above hypothesis that reading storybooks written in English would stimulate growth not only in reading but in the acquisition of oral language, the investigators randomly assigned the 380 children in the study to one of three "treatment" groups: (1) the Shared Book Experience group, where the teacher and children read together from

"Big Books" and did other reading and reading-related activities, including reading in small groups and pairs and individually, along with role-playing, word study, artwork, and writing; (2) a Sustained Silent Reading group, in which the children simply read silently; and (3) a control group using the traditional English-language course mentioned earlier. While the control group spent 20–30 minutes a day with the prescribed English-language curriculum, the other two groups spent that amount of time with Shared Book or Silent Reading activities. Each of the two experimental classes was provided with 250 high-interest storybooks for the children to read.

The results on standardized tests demonstrated that after eight months of differential instruction, the experimental groups exposed to numerous stories progressed in reading and listening comprehension at twice the normal rate. The students were also tested on their ability to complete sentences calling for the use of grammatical structures explicitly taught to the control group but not directly taught to the Shared Book or Sustained Silent Reading group. While the differences were great enough to be statistically significant only with the Class 4 children, those differences favored the experimental group. That is, the children who showed greatest command of these grammatical structures were the ones who read a lot, not those to whom the structures were directly taught.

This study contrasts two approaches to developing oral fluency in English, a direct teaching approach compared with an *immersion* approach through books. Though the study does not directly compare alternative methods of *reading* instruction, it does in general suggest the greater efficacy of a whole language or immersion approach in fostering both language and literacy.

Ribowsky, 1985

Ribowsky, Helene. 1985. *The Effects of a Code Emphasis Approach and a Whole Language Approach Upon Emergent Literacy of Kindergarten Children.* Alexandria, Va.: Educational Document Reproduction Service, ED 269 720. (Report developed more fully in Ribowsky's unpublished doctoral dissertation [same title], New York University, New York, 1986.)

According to the ERIC abstract, this "year-long, quasi-experimental study investigated the comparative effects of a whole language approach and a code emphasis approach upon the emergent literacy of 53 girls in two kindergarten classes in an all girls' parochial school in the Northeast" (Ribowsky 1985, abstract page). Ribowsky claims "This study represents the first quantitative exploration of a whole language approach in comparison with a code emphasis approach" (p. 6).

Subjects in the experimental class received experience in Holdaway's Shared Book Experience program. Ribowsky (pp. 15–16) explains that the daily program of Shared Book Experiences used the following format, from Holdaway (1979, pp. 72–73):

1. *Welcoming activity*: reading aloud of poem, chant, or song; use of enlarged material (printed matter large enough for group viewing).
2. *Favorite stories*: rereading of stories, usually by request; unison participation; discussion of syntax.
3. *Language activity*: exploration of language through games, riddles, puzzles.
4. *New story*: introduction of new story for the day; words pointed to as they are read aloud; language experiences shared.
5. *Independent reading*: self-selection of old favorites to read; engagement in literary activities of choice.
6. *Expression*: art and writing activities; group drama.

Ribowsky explains this approach further, then contrasts it with the code-emphasis approach that was taught through Lippincott's Beginning to Read, Write, and Listen program:

This [code emphasis] approach to beginning reading consists of a highly structured teacher-directed program of alphabetic instruction within a multisensory format. Children receive their own sets of 24 letterbooks which contain activities related to the letters and reading skills emphasized. The focus is upon auditory segmentation, grapheme-phoneme analysis and reinforcement of one or more traditional readiness areas such as colors, shapes, or directionality. A teacher's guide for each letterbook specifies the precise tasks to be accomplished as well as the exact words that must be used as stimuli for each letter. (p.15)

Clearly, this code emphasis reflects not only a part-to-whole approach but a transmission model of teaching. The whole language approach, on the other hand, reflects a whole-to-part orientation and a transactional model of learning.

In order to be fair to both approaches, Ribowsky assessed the children's growth not only with a Book Handling Knowledge Task (BHKT) developed by Y. Goodman and Altwerger (1981), but several standardized tests of skills: the five principal subtests of the Test of Language Development–Primary (TOLD-P), and the Letter Recognition and Phoneme/Grapheme subtests of the Metropolitan Achievement Test (MAT). The BHKT, which measures concepts about books and print, might be expected to favor the whole language group, since these students focused on books and other whole texts. The tests of letter recognition and phoneme/grapheme correspondence (consonants only) might be expected to favor the code-emphasis group, since these students focused on parts of language, particularly letters and letter/sound relations.

Ribowsky reports that the children in the two groups were remarkably similar on the pretest measures. Here is our summary of Ribowsky's concluding data:

	Gain from Beginning of Year to End	
	Whole language group	*Code-emphasis group*
Development of "linguistic literacy set" (as measured by the TOLD–P)	33.1	14.2
Development of "orthographic literacy set" (concepts about print, as measured by the BHKT)	9.7	5.4
Development of "grapho-phonemic literacy set" (as measured by the MAT Letter Recognition test and the Phoneme/Grapheme test for consonants)	*19.19*	*16.77*

Note that the italicized scores for the Phoneme/Grapheme test (consonants) do not represent gains from the beginning to the end of the year; they are post-test scores only. The consonants test was given only at the end of the year because it was considered too frustrating for children just entering kindergarten.

" . . . in each case the differences are statistically significant, in favor of the whole language group. This group did significantly better even on the tests of letter recognition and knowledge of consonant letter/sound relationships."

Ribowsky's statistical analysis of the data indicates that in each case the differences are statistically significant, in favor of the whole language group. This group did significantly better even on the tests of letter recognition and knowledge of consonant letter/sound relationships. Overall, "a whole language approach used with kindergarten children in this study had a significantly greater effect upon emergent literacy than did a code emphasis approach" (p. 19).

Freppon, 1988

Freppon, Penny. 1988. An investigation of children's concepts of the purpose and nature of reading in different instructional settings. Unpublished doctoral dissertation, University of Cincinnati, Ohio. (Children's concepts of the purpose and nature of reading in different instructional settings. Paper presented at the National Reading Conference, Austin, Texas, November 28–December 2, 1989. Submitted to the NRC/Yearbook.)

For her investigation, Freppon identified four first-grade classrooms: two "literature-based" and two "skills-based." Controlling for socioeconomic status, gender, reading ability, and reading instruction, Freppon randomly selected twenty-four average readers and used structured interviews, altered passages, and in-process oral reading behaviors to access the students' beliefs and understandings about reading. The results of her study suggest that there were significant differences between the two groups and that the differences correlated with instruction. For example, 97 percent of the literature-based group, but only 42 percent of the skills-based group, rejected sentences with scrambled word order as not being languagelike.

Results from the interview data also suggest differences between the two groups: "92% in the literature-based group said that understanding the story or both understanding and getting the words right is more important in reading . . . in the skills-based group, only 50% talked about both . . . as important in reading." Forty-two percent mentioned just getting the words right, while 8 percent could not answer the question (p. 95).

Freppon notes that the two groups also differed in the variety of strategies they used as readers, in their self-monitoring and in their understanding of a "good reader," and in their view of themselves as readers. For example, children in the literature-based group reported using more strategies, and were observed to do so; also, they more often discussed using meaning to self-monitor. While children in both groups said that they were good readers, those in the literature-based groups explained that they were good readers because they read a lot of books, while children in the skills group said they were good readers because they knew a lot of words.

Observational data suggest that the skills group "attempted to sound words out more than twice as often as did the literature group, but, when attempting to sound out, the literature group did so more successfully than did the skills group (success rates of 53% and 32% respectively)." Students' substitutions of one word for another also showed significant differences. Those in the literature-based group more often used a balance of cueing systems—meaning, structure, and visual cues together—than those in the skills-based group.

As Freppon concludes, the results of this study suggest that the

> literature-based groups were more actively involved as readers in the process of constructing meaning in the reading process . . . [they] appeared to have understood the relationship between the parts of reading (the words and word decoding) and the purpose of the whole (to communicate meaningfully). Simply put, these children seemed to have grasped the notion that reading is a language process. (p. 142)

She adds, "They seemed to have acquired some of their understandings about the importance of words and sounding out words without traditional, sequenced instruction in vocabulary building and phonics."

In contrast, Freppon notes that in the skills-based group, "the nature of the relationship of word-level aspects within the global, communicative purpose of reading did not seem well understood" (p. 165).

Analysis of the quantifiable data gathered by Freppon consistently demonstrates that the literature-based group had a better understanding of the reading process and of how to read efficiently. These students were even more successful at "sounding out" unfamiliar words than the skills-based group, since they used their letter/sound knowledge in combination with other language cues.

Stice and Bertrand, 1989

Stice, Carole, and Nancy Bertrand. 1989. The texts and textures of literacy learning in whole language versus traditional/skills classrooms. Unpublished manuscript submitted to National Reading Conference 1989 Yearbook.

The investigators begin their paper by observing: "Recent investigation indicates that poor, minority children are not becoming literate, in the fullest sense of that word, sufficiently to allow them to achieve social and economic parity." They cite Neisser (1986) as demonstrating that neither the traditional approaches to literacy instruction (phonics/skills, or traditional basal) nor the decoding, subskills approaches (or behavioral/mastery learning) have proved successful in the case of poor, minority children. Thus, their study focused on the effects of a whole language approach on the literacy development of at-risk first- and second-graders, in comparison with a traditional/skills approach.

The study involved fifty children, averaging five each in five whole language classrooms, grades 1 and 2, and their matches from traditional/skills classrooms. The study included both rural and inner-city children who were deemed to be "at risk," according to certain factors.

Several quantitative and qualitative measures were used to compare the two groups, including scores on the reading portion of the Stanford Achievement Test (Primary I and II), responses to a concepts about print survey, analysis of an oral reading and retelling, writing samples, and individual interviews.

On the Stanford Achievement Test, the whole language children showed slightly greater gains than the traditionally taught children, but the gains were too slight to be statistically significant. While the children in the whole language groups scored lower on the Concepts About Print test (CAP) to begin with, they scored significantly higher on the posttest. The children in whole language classrooms did as well on traditional spelling as their counterparts, while also using more invented spellings. Whole language children offered significantly longer, more complete versions of the stories they retold, suggesting that their comprehension might have been better.

Data from the reading and writing interviews revealed several interesting trends, similar to those in the Freppon study previously cited. Stice and Bertrand note the following:

1. Children in whole language classrooms had a greater awareness of alternative strategies for dealing with problems. For example, when asked, "When you are reading and you come to something you don't know, what do you do?", whole language children suggested six strategies, while traditional children suggested only three.
2. Whole language children appear to feel better about themselves as readers and writers. *Ninety-five percent* of the whole language children report "me" when asked, "Who do you know who is a good reader?" *Only five percent* of the traditional children reported themselves. [emphasis ours]
3. Whole language children appear to focus more on meaning and the communicative nature of language. For example, when asked, "What makes a good reader?", they report that good readers read a great deal and that they can read any book in the room. Traditional children tend to focus on words and the correctness of surface features when asked what makes a good reader. They report that good readers read big words, they know all the words, and they don't miss any words.
4. Fourth, whole language children appear to be developing greater independence in both reading and writing. Traditional children seem to be more dependent on the teacher if their initial strategy fails.

Again, the standardized test scores of the children in the whole language classrooms are slightly (though not significantly) better than the scores of children in the traditional classrooms. Other measures suggest, however, that they are far ahead of their counterparts in developing the understanding, strategies, and attitudes of readers, writers, and thinkers. As Stice and Bertrand conclude, "Whole language poses no threats to performance on mandated tests, yet children in whole language classes are more independent, more self-directed, and more motivated" (p. 9).

EXPANDING WHAT WE MEASURE

Of course, not all the research on whole language draws the same conclusions about performance on standardized tests. One hears, for example, that at such-and-such a school comprehension scores have gone up, while phonics scores have gone down. Mosenthal reports that he and his colleagues, using a more holistic approach, found their students receiving lower test scores than their colleagues' students (Mosenthal 1989). Lumping together whole language and language experience as if there were not major differences (language experience is only one limited activity within whole language classrooms), Stahl and Miller compared this alleged approach with the results of basal reader programs, performing a statistical meta-analysis upon the data from various studies. The authors found that ''overall, whole language/language experience approaches appear approximately equal to basal reader approaches in their effectiveness'' (p. 94), and that these approaches, lumped together, are clearly *more* effective than basals in kindergarten, for developing concepts about print and expectations about reading. However, comparison of data from first-grade studies led the authors to speculate that ''more direct approaches might be better at helping students master word recognition skills'' (p. 87).

Of course, lumping together whole language with the much more limited language experience means that the results can't be taken as saying anything significant about either approach, in comparison with basal readers; the methodological tactic renders any conclusions about whole language simply invalid. Still, it would not be entirely surprising if ''more direct approaches might be better at helping students master word recognition skills,'' particularly if these are tested more or less in isolation, and as early as first grade. After all, with basal reading programs there is a much closer match between instruction and test. What *should* perhaps be surprising is that in so many studies, such as the ones discussed in this chapter, children in whole language classrooms have typically scored as well or better on skills tests as those whose instruction much more closely matched the test instruments.

We have given considerable attention to the research from a whole-to-part perspective that includes standardized measures of achievement, not because we are convinced that these are valid measures of reading or reading ability, but to allay the concerns of those who fear that standardized test scores will plummet if they, or their teachers, implement a whole language philosophy in the classroom. It's possible, of course, but recent research suggests that it's unlikely. At most, the scores may decline slightly, or decline on some measures, such as phonics, while remaining the same or rising on other measures, such as comprehension. Overall, though, an emerging body of research suggests that for maintaining or raising standardized test scores, a whole-to-part approach may be as good as or better than a part-to-whole approach.

More important for the development of literacy, however, is the fact that a whole-to-part approach appears to be *considerably* better for developing in children a positive concept of themselves as readers and writers; for helping them develop a range of strategies, and flexibility in using them to solve problems as readers and writers; for encouraging

❝ More important for the development of literacy, however, is the fact that a whole-to-part approach appears to be *considerably* better for developing in children a positive concept of themselves as readers and writers; for helping them develop a range of strategies, and flexibility in using them to solve problems as readers and writers; for encouraging them to participate willingly, even eagerly, in a wide range of authentic literacy events; and for developing independent thinkers and learners.**❞**

them to participate willingly, even eagerly, in a wide range of authentic literacy events; and for developing independent thinkers and learners.

In short, when we expand what we measure to include the kinds of factors listed near the beginning of this chapter, we find that whole language teaching seems to promote not only acceptable scores on tests of "reading achievement," but an understanding of the reading and writing processes, a love of reading and writing and books, critical and creative thinking, and significant progress toward becoming independent, self-motivated, lifelong learners. If we continue to expand what we measure, along the lines of these questions suggested earlier, future research on the efficacy of a whole-to-part approach seems likely to further substantiate these conclusions.

To clarify the nature of the whole language classrooms in which such understanding, abilities, and attitudes are developed, Chapter 7 discusses some of the ways whole language teachers foster the acquisition of phonics knowledge and know-how, while Chapter 8 describes a classroom in which comprehension is developed naturally, through reading, discussion, and analysis. Returning to the subject of assessment, Chapter 9 further clarifies *why*, instead of reducing reading to skills that are isolated and tested and then glorified as measures of "reading achievement," we need to expand what we assess if we genuinely want not only to assess but to *promote* children's development of literacy. Chapter 10 examines *how* we can develop a much broader and more valid basis for assessment and educational decision-making.

C H A P T E R 7

Developing Phonics Knowledge in Whole Language Classrooms

Since English is to some extent an alphabetic language, educators may be universally agreed that children need to develop understanding of the most basic letter/sound relationships. However, it is emphatically not true, as the authors of *Becoming a Nation of Readers* claim, that teachers and educational leaders now agree that "children should be taught phonics" (Anderson et al. 1985, p. 37). Or at least, it depends upon what is meant by "phonics," and what is meant by "teach."

This chapter explores common misunderstandings about how much and what kinds of phonics knowledge and instruction are needed, then focuses on how an understanding of the alphabetic principle and basic letter/sound relations and patterns can be developed within whole language classrooms. The chapter is intended, in part, to offset the widespread myths that whole language teachers do not engage in direct instruction and that children in whole language classrooms do not learn phonics. Also, this chapter and the next offer examples of how, more generally, skills can be developed in whole language classrooms.

A key point is that in whole language classrooms, phonics is "taught" in a variety of ways and assessed continuously, rather than tested as an isolated skill. What whole language teachers assess is whether and how well children use letter/sound knowledge in conjunction with other cues *as they read*, not how well students complete worksheets. Of course, in preparing students for standardized skills tests, teachers can always give students a "crash" course in doing phonics and other skills activities. Whole language teachers know, however, that what makes a difference in the development of literacy is whether or not students can *use* letter/sound knowledge appropriately as they read.

KNOWING HOW IS NOT THE SAME AS *KNOWING ABOUT*

Phonics *knowledge* may be characterized as an awareness—conscious or unconscious—that there is a relationship between letters and sounds in English, and an awareness of some of these basic relations and patterns. To read English proficiently, readers need to have developed at least rudimentary phonics *knowledge* and an ability to use that knowledge in reading: that is, *functional know-how*. This does not necessarily mean, however, that most readers need direct phonics instruction of the sort that is commonly offered in our schools. Nor does it mean that the acquisition of phonics knowledge and the development of practical know-how should be emphasized *first* in helping children develop into proficient readers.

True, some children may need relatively direct help in developing and using phonics knowledge; such are the children who would flounder in a pure sight word approach, with no explicit attention given to the relationships between letters and sounds. On the other hand, a much larger number of children are simply frustrated, and even inappropriately labeled ''disabled'' readers, as a result of the insistence that they master the phonics that has been widely taught in recent years. Furthermore, though a majority of children can probably survive direct phonics instruction as commonly provided, they do not need it in order to become good readers. They develop phonics knowledge by inducing or absorbing many of the patterns unconsciously, much as they learned the patterns of their native language in learning to talk.

It is the ability to induce patterns unconsciously that gives children a *functional* command of what I call phonics knowledge: that is, they learn, without direct instruction, enough about letter/sound relations to make *as good or better use* of that knowledge while reading as those students who have explicitly studied phonics. For example, millions upon millions of middle-generation Americans have learned to read without phonics instruction, yet the majority of us can *use* phonics knowledge as well as our phonics-instructed children. Why? Because *knowing how* is not the same as *knowing about*. To be functionally useful, one's knowledge does not have to be explicit.

In this regard, research on the acquisition of language is particularly instructive, and to emphasize the point an example from Chapter 4 is worth repeating. The rule for forming the past tense of regular verbs is ''add a /t/ sound to verbs that end in an unvoiced consonant and add a /d/ sound to all other regular verbs, except those that end in /t/ or /d/.'' Most children master this basic rule by about the age of 5 (Berko 1958), yet only an infinitesimally small number of adults can verbalize the rule. And even if adults could verbalize the rule, how could they teach it to children? Or how could children consciously apply it? This would be something like trying to teach the centipede to become aware of how it moves all its legs; functional *dyspedagogia* (pun intended) would surely be the result.

Of course, many school-age children could probably learn to recognize the rule on multiple choice or matching tests, and indeed this is too often the kind of response that is taken as evidence that children have learned something. But, on the one hand, recognition or even intellectual understanding of the rule would not necessarily enable anyone to use it, while, on the other hand, children begin to show evidence of developing the rule long before the age of 5, when they have virtually mastered it.

So it is with phonics: *knowing about* phonics patterns does not guarantee the ability to use that knowledge while reading, whereas *knowing how* to use letter/sound knowledge does not require a conscious ability to explain it (see my argument in Weaver versus Groff 1989, p. 16). Despite educators' probable intentions, too much phonics instruction is directed toward teaching and testing knowledge *about* phonics, on the mistaken assumption that this is the only way to develop phonics knowledge and the ability to use it. As we shall see in later sections, whole language teachers concentrate instead on helping students develop practical phonics know-how.

Using Phonics Knowledge in Context

Probably one reason people mistakenly think children need to master an extensive body of phonics knowledge is that the adults do not realize how much of the information needed to construct meaning from a text is provided by the context and by prior knowledge. Try, for example, to read the following introduction to a take-off on ''Little Red Riding Hood'' (Weaver 1988, p. 63):

```
-nc- -p-n - t-m- th-r- w-s - h-nds-m- y--ng w-lf n-m-d
L-b-. L-b- l-v-d w-th h-s m-th-r -nd f-th-r -t th- -dg-
-f - d--p, d-rk w--ds. -v-r- d-- L-b- w-nt t- h-nt -t
th- -dg- -f th- w--ds, n--r th- l-ttl- v-ll-g- -f C-l--s.
```

Once you accustomed yourself to the strange-looking print, you were probably able to read the selection, even word-for-word, except perhaps for the proper names: *Lobo* (which means ''wolf'' in Spanish) and *Calais*. How were you able to do this when all the vowel letters were missing?

You used your knowledge of the Red Riding Hood story and wolves, your intuitive knowledge of grammar, and your grasp of the story as it began to evolve. By using all of these cues, you were able to read the text using only part of the visual information normally available to us as readers. (For an extensive discussion of the role of letter/sound knowledge in reading, see my *Reading Process and Practice* 1988, Chaps. 2–4, especially Chap. 3. See Smith, *Reading without Nonsense*, 1985, and *Understanding Reading*, 1988.)

What children need, then, is not extensive instruction in phonics patterns and rules, and certainly not extensive work with the vowels, since words are often identifiable in context without conscious attention to the vowels anyway. Rather, what they need is help in using minimal letter cues *in the context of real reading*, where they are encourage to use everything they know to construct meaning from print. This means that by minimally sampling the visual information they will sometimes misidentify words, but that is what *good* readers—the best comprehenders— often do: They predict from prior knowledge and context, and therefore sometimes misidentify words, as in the following example:

older
The other seals knew better.

When such miscues make sense in context, as this one did, good readers rarely correct them. In contrast to poorer readers, however, good readers normally correct, or try to correct, misreadings that do not make sense.

Too much phonics instruction in isolation can actually help to create poor readers, particularly readers who struggle to sound out words but do not succeed because they are not using meaning *along with* their letter/sound knowledge (see K. Goodman 1973 and Weaver 1988, Chaps. 4, 5, and 10).

PHONICS IN PERSPECTIVE

Children learning to read, then, must learn to use letter/sound knowledge in conjunction with context and prior knowledge. If they are always thinking, at least unconsciously, "What would make sense here?" they can make much more efficient and effective use of letter/ sound knowledge to get words and construct meaning. And because they are not using letter/sound cues exclusively, they do not need to study such relationships extensively. Furthermore, most children find actual reading easier than learning phonics patterns in isolation.

" Too much phonics instruction in isolation can actually help to create poor readers, particularly readers who struggle to sound out words but do not succeed because they are not using meaning *along with* their letter/ sound knowledge. **"**

In *Reading Process and Practice* (Weaver 1988), I have discussed research from several fields, all of which points to the advisability of developing phonics knowledge in context rather than in isolation. Hence, Figure 7.1 offers ''Fifteen reasons not to teach numerous phonics

---

1. It's not necessary. Most children will unconsciously induce the common patterns, given ample opportunity to read environmental print in context; listen to and read predictable stories, rhymes, and songs; and write using functional, "phonetic" spelling.
2. There are too many rules, especially for vowel patterns; there are too many exceptions to the rules; and even if a rule applies to a given word, it's not always possible to know which rule applies, unless you know the word.
3. It's not necessary.
4. Phonics cues provide only approximations of words, anyway. Using phonics cues *only*, readers often cannot say the word right, even with simple words (for example, *love, wind*).
5. It's not necessary.
6. Saying the word doesn't guarantee getting the meaning, anyway. And getting the meaning of a word doesn't guarantee that it's the right meaning, in context.
7. It's not necessary.
8. Too much emphasis on phonics encourages children to use "sound it out" as their first and possibly only strategy for getting words and meaning, other than asking someone.
9. It's not necessary.
10. Effective and efficient readers first use context and prior knowledge to predict what would make sense. Using context first, they then need only *sample* the visual cues. If the word is in their listening vocabulary, context plus consonants are often enough.
11. It's not necessary.
12. Overemphasizing phonics may encourage readers to focus too much upon identifying words and too little upon getting meaning.
13. It's not necessary.
14. Teaching numerous phonics patterns or rules may result in many children being labeled early as reading failures or slow readers, since for many children it's harder to learn phonics than to learn to read.
15. IT'S NOT NECESSARY!!!!!!! Just as we don't teach babies and toddlers rules for putting together sounds to make words or words to make sentences, so we don't need to teach rules for sounding out words. Most children will learn the patterns through repeated exposure, with a minimum of direct instruction. (See #1.)

Figure 7.1 Fifteen reasons not to teach numerous phonics patterns or rules

patterns or rules.'' As will be illustrated in a subsequent section, it is easiest for most children to develop the requisite knowledge and know-how while reading and rereading predictable and meaningful stories, poems, and songs. They absorb the needed letter/sound knowledge and learn to use it along with meaning, more or less simultaneously.

At this point, we consider some of the ways whole language teachers help children develop the phonics knowledge and know-how they need, both indirectly and through more direct teaching. The sections are divided into developing phonics know-how through reading, writing, activities, and conferencing. But the divisions are rather arbitrary, and so, to some extent, are the divisions between direct and indirect teaching. There is often no clear distinction between the two, since direct teaching in whole language classrooms does not follow the typical teach/practice/test format. In addition, in whole language classrooms both kinds of teaching are directed toward developing phonics know-how rather than the ability to complete worksheets or parrot back what has been taught.

DEVELOPING PHONICS KNOW-HOW THROUGH READING

In whole language classrooms, it is axiomatic that children learn to read by reading. But the logical question is, how can children learn to read by reading if they don't yet know how to read?

Various Means and Materials

Several related means/methods/materials facilitate reading, even among children who are not yet full-fledged readers—that is, not yet able to coordinate meaning (prior knowledge and context) with letter/sound knowledge to construct meaning from unfamiliar texts. The most common methods are listed here, with only brief comments. Figure 7.2 suggests some resources that offer teachers further understanding and practical suggestions.

1. Read and reread favorite books to the children. Encourage them to read and reread the stories as best they can, even if at first they are only turning the pages and ''reading'' the pictures. That is, treat the children as emergent readers rather than nonreaders, and they will more readily become independent readers.

Understanding emergent literacy

Clay, Marie M. 1987. *Writing Begins at Home*. Portsmouth, N.H.: Heinemann.

Doake, David. 1988. *Reading Begins at Birth*. Richmond Hill, Ontario: Scholastic.

Gentry, J. Richard. 1987. *Spel. . . Is a Four-Letter Word*. Richmond Hill, Ontario: Scholastic. Available in the U.S. from Heinemann.

Hill, Mary W. 1989. *Home: Where Reading and Writing Begin*. Portsmouth, N.H.: Heinemann.

Newman, Judith. 1984. *The Craft of Children's Writing*. Richmond Hill, Ontario: Scholastic. Available in the U.S. from Heinemann.

Taylor, Denny, and Dorothy S. Strickland. 1986. *Family Storybook Reading*. Portsmouth, N.H.: Heinemann.

Encouraging emergent literacy in the classroom: Focus on particular activities

The following are all relatively short books (about 32 pages) from Scholastic–TAB of Canada, available from Scholastic in the United States. There are also other useful books in this New Directions series.

Barrett, F. L. 1982. *A Teacher's Guide to Shared Reading*.

Lynch, Priscilla. 1986. *Using Big Books and Predictable Books*.

Peetoom, Adrian. 1986. *Shared Reading: Safe Risks with Whole Books*.

Emergent literacy: From theory to practice

To accompany some of their educational materials, Rigby Publishing Company offers several valuable teacher resources, including "Whole Language: A Framework for Thinking," "The Elements of the Whole Language Program," "Language, Learning and Literacy," "Shared Book Experience," and "Evaluation: A Perspective for Change."

See also Figure 4.12 for a somewhat different bibliography of books on emergent literacy; Figure 10.9 for a bibliography on spelling and spelling development; Figure 10.13 for a bibliography on reading, writing, and literacy in the classroom; and Figure 11.1 for a bibliography of instructional materials that are more holistic than traditional basal reading programs.

Figure 7.2   Starter bibliography on emergent literacy

2. Provide lots of environmental print (signs, labels, menus, notes, and so forth) that the children can ''read,'' initially by using prior knowledge and context. The classroom environment should be ''littered with literacy.''

3. Provide lots of books with accompanying tape recordings, and lots of time for children to listen to, read, and reread their favorites.

4. Develop language experience charts based on common class experiences—for example, take dictation from the children to develop a class recipe, account of a field trip, observations of an experiment, or whatever. Read and reread these with the children and provide individual copies for each child to read again and again.

5. Encourage children to write for themselves, however unsophisticated their efforts might be, and to read back what they have written. (Even if the writings aren't decipherable by an adult, these experiences help convince children that they *are* writers and readers.)

6. Introduce children to predictable books, and provide lots of time for the children to read and reread these individually and in pairs.

7. Using stories, rhymes, and songs, as well as language experience dictations, engage children in Shared Book Experiences. Such experiences can give children the confidence to read and reread favorite selections independently and eventually develop their ability to read unfamiliar materials independently.

Shared Book Experience

The so-called Shared Book Experience was first developed in 1965 in New Zealand by Don Holdaway and a team of experienced teachers and consultants. They based their teaching procedures on observation of how children learn to read as a result of the bedtime story experience in the home (Holdaway 1979).

The teacher uses a ''Big Book'' that all the children in the group can see: a commercially published Big Book, a child/teacher-authored Big Book, or simply a chart of some sort, written in large print. The steps are essentially those described in Chapter 6 in the section on Ribowsky's research, but the characterization here is derived from ''Shared Book Experience'' by Andrea Butler (n.d.):

1. *Rereading favorites*: first rhymes, songs, and poems, then stories. During these rereadings, the teacher points to the words while reading.
   Teaching pre-determined concepts or strategies: Before using the selection, the teacher will have determined what aspects of print or what reading strategies she/he might want to emphasize: for example, using prior knowledge and context plus the initial consonant of a word to *predict* what the word might be.
   Capturing the teachable moment: In addition, the teacher capitalizes upon the children's needs, to take advantage of the teachable moment.

2. *Introducing a new story*: At least once a week, a new story is introduced in Big Book format. The primary aim upon a first reading is simply to enjoy the story. The teacher *introduces* the book by mentioning and perhaps commenting upon the author, title, and cover illustrations; *invites* children to predict, from this information, what the story will be about; *reads* the story; *engages the children* in discussing the story; and *reads it again*. The initial emphasis is simply upon reading the story for enjoyment.

3. *Rereading the story independently*: Though the children may engage in related arts, crafts, drama, music, writing, and other activities, the most important follow-up to the Shared Book Experience is independent rereading. As many children as possible read a small version of the Big Book. Often, six or eight small books can be purchased as a set, along with a commercially-prepared Big Book. Particularly with teacher-made and class-developed materials, ideally each child will have his/her own individual copy to read and reread.

Many things can be learned through the Shared Book Experience. The following list is adapted from Andrea Butler, *The Story Box in the Classroom*, Stage 1 (1984); see also Elfant (in progress). What can be learned includes:

1. Conventions of print, such as:
   —we read pages top to bottom, left to right
   —we read words, not the pictures
   —what a word is
   —what a letter is
   —what punctuation does

2. Strategies, such as:
   —using meaning as the first and most important clue to getting words
   —predicting
   —self-correcting

3. Sight vocabulary

4. Letter/sound relationships

Children will typically learn most of the concepts of print simply by observing how the teacher turns the pages of books, how the teacher's hand or pointer moves across and down the page, and how the teacher correlates the spoken word with the written word by the use of hand or pointer. The concepts of *word* and *letter* can likewise be learned incidentally as the teacher points to words and letters while talking about them.

The teacher will usually be more direct in teaching other important concepts, such as effective reading strategies. By inviting students to predict what will happen next, for example, the teacher encourages them to adopt as their own the strategy of predicting. Sight vocabulary and letter/sound relationships are learned in part incidentally and in part as the teacher directs attention to particular words and letter/sound relationships or patterns within the reading selections (see "Developing Phonics Know-How through Activities" later in this chapter).

Thus, within the Shared Book Experience, the phonics knowledge needed for reading is "taught" in two ways: indirectly, by exposing children to literature from which they can absorb letter/sound knowledge, and directly, by focusing children's attention on particular letter/sound associations. Usually much of the literature chosen is highly predictable, often containing rhythm and sometimes rhyme, as well as repetition. Many selections contain alliteration and other sound features that lend themselves to direct teaching of phonics relationships. Thus, such predictable literature is often valuable for facilitating the development of phonics knowledge both indirectly and directly.

The direct teaching of letter/sound associations will be further illustrated in the sections on teaching phonics through writing and activities. For now, suffice it to note that such activities reflect a whole language philosophy in significant ways. While offering the children an opportunity to take advantage of whatever instruction they can benefit from, such activities do not implicitly assume that all children should learn the same things or in the same ways, much less that they should learn the same things at the same time. During the group readings in Shared Book Experience, for example, less able readers simply read along as best they can, gaining support from the teacher and the more able readers. Teachers record individual students' progress, mainly by observing them in daily activities (Chap. 10). They do not, however, continually test the children to ferret out weaknesses that will then be "remediated." Based upon their observations, whole language teachers provide appropriate help as needed, in the context of reading and rereading favorite selections. But they do not test the learning of skills in isolation, nor do they isolate less competent readers from their more competent classmates. The approach succeeds in large part simply because children are treated as if they *will* learn to read, in their own unique way and in their own good time, given lots of opportunities to read, appropriate help and feedback as needed, a supportive environment, and a wealth of books and other reading materials that they can appreciate and enjoy. This positive expectation rests upon a solid foundation of research in emergent literacy and how it can be fostered (Chapter 4).

> ❝Thus, within the Shared Book Experience, the phonics knowledge needed for reading is 'taught' in two ways: indirectly, by exposing children to literature from which they can absorb letter/sound knowledge, and directly, by focusing children's attention on particular letter/sound associations.❞

DEVELOPING PHONICS KNOW-HOW THROUGH WRITING

In whole language classrooms, regardless of grade level, children usually begin writing from the very first day—individual writing, not a word or sentence dictated to a scribe or a language experience "story" developed as a group. The children begin writing even if their writing looks more like drawings or scribbles or figures that vaguely resemble letters, because treating children as emergent writers gives them confidence that they are authors, that writing is something they can do.

When some of the children are beginning to use letters and letter-like symbols in their writing, even though there may be no correspondence between their letters and the words represented, the teacher may begin to demonstrate relations between letters and sounds. The teacher can do this initially by modeling with the class or a group who seem ready for such help (whether preschoolers, kindergarteners, or first-graders) how to "spell" a word, using only the sounds the children themselves hear. At first, children will probably focus on just one sound per word, usually the initial sound. The teacher can elicit the children's recognition of these initial sounds and write the letters that represent the sounds. For "I like you," the result would probably be "I L U," which emergent writers often write spontaneously to represent "I love you."

As the children become more sophisticated in segmenting words into sounds, they will represent more sounds, but at first mainly the consonants. Helping children "sound out" words and represent the sounds with letters as best they can will go a long way toward helping them develop basic letter/sound knowledge. It is fortunate that recognition of consonant sounds comes earliest, because consonants are far more important than vowels: We can often read a coherent text with the vowels missing (see p. 144), but texts with consonants missing are normally unintelligible.

Research suggests that children who develop phonics knowledge through writing may soon begin to demonstrate more sophisticated phonics knowledge than that required by the phonics skills sheets that many children seemingly cannot do (Harste, Woodward, and Burke 1984b).

Sounding Words Out

Two examples may further illustrate how teachers can actively help children develop letter/sound awareness through writing. In an early book dealing with how to foster children's writing development, Cramer gives this example of how one teacher helped a first-grader spell, as best she could, given her rudimentary letter/sound knowledge but perhaps little experience with print (Cramer 1978, p. 105). In the process, the teacher reinforced the child's developing grasp of letter/sound associations:

JENNY:	Mrs. Nicholas, how do you spell *hospital*?
MRS. NICHOLAS:	Spell it as best you can, Jenny.
JENNY:	I don't know how to spell it.
MRS. NICHOLAS:	I know you don't know how to spell it, honey. I just want you to write as much of the word as you can.
JENNY:	I don't know any of it.
MRS. NICHOLAS:	Yes, you do, Jenny. How do you think *hospital* starts? (*Mrs. Nicholas pronounced* hospital *distinctly with a slight emphasis on the first sound, but she deliberately avoided grossly distorting the pronunciation.*)
JENNY:	(*very tentatively*): h–s.
MRS. NICHOLAS:	Good! Write the *hs*. What do you hear next in *hospital*? (*Again, Mrs. Nicholas pronounced the word* hospital *distinctly, this time with a slight emphasis on the second part.*)
JENNY:	(*still tentatively*): p–t.
MRS. NICHOLAS:	Yes! Write the *pt*. Now, what's the last sound you hear in *hospital*? (*While pronouncing the word* hospital *for the last time Mrs. Nicholas emphasized the last part without exaggerating it unduly.*)
JENNY:	(*with some assurance*): l.
MRS. NICHOLAS:	Excellent, Jenny, *h-s-p-t-l* is a fine way to spell *hospital*. There is another way to spell *hospital*, but for now I want you to spell words you don't know just as we did this one.

This is an interesting example of direct and indirect teaching combined. Mrs. Nicholas elicited from Jenny what she knew and then reinforced it, in the process of directly modeling a procedure she wanted Jenny to use.

Learning from Each Other

More recently, whole language educators and others emphasizing writing as a process have focused on the social nature of learning, upon the fact that children are often one another's best teachers; thus, this second example, from Kamii and Randazzo (1985). In their article "Social Interaction and Invented Spelling," the authors explain and illustrate how children can be encouraged to compare their invented spellings for the same word, then cooperatively decide on the best spelling. The following is but one example of how one of the authors encouraged social interaction about invented spelling among the 5- and 6-year-olds in her classroom:

> The first opportunity came when we made our Thanksgiving soup. Each child brought a vegetable the day before Thanksgiving to put in the soup. . . . At group time, I clipped a large piece of paper to the easel and suggested that we make a list of all the things we had put into the soup. . . . I chose a child to start because she had been engaging in a great deal of invented spelling, often with the help of a playmate.
>   She began sounding out "cucumber," the ingredient she had brought. She said, "*cu,cu*, a 'Q.'" A few children began yelling, "No! Not 'Q,' 'K!'" She thought a moment and then wrote "KU." Her friend said "'K'" again. She began to sound out the word some more, saying "*uh-uh-uh*." She wrote an "A" after "KUK." Finally, she said "*ber-ber-ber*," and there was a chime of "B!" Some children yelled, "Now, 'R.'" Someone protested saying, "No, 'E.'" The result was "KUKABER." (Kamii and Randazzo 1985, p. 127)

The process continued until each child had written the vegetable he or she had added to the soup. The point, of course, was not to get the word "right"—though typically the final product might be better than most children's individual work. What mattered was the critical thinking that took place as the children compared ideas, explained their reasons, and thereby often grew in their understanding of letter/sound associations.

One purpose of encouraging invented spelling is to enable children to *write*—that is, to compose independently—before they are able to spell many, or any, words correctly. However, an equally significant purpose is to encourage children to develop increasingly sophisticated strategies for spelling, just as they developed increasingly sophisticated rules for speaking when initially learning their native language. Thus, the kind of critical thinking illustrated in the example just given is crucial to the development of spelling as a cognitive process rather than as a process of mere memorization. While there is no guarantee that all children will become excellent spellers through this approach (any more than through any other approach), certainly there is evidence that children develop more of an interest in spelling, more of a concern for ultimately correct spelling in their writing, and a greater repertoire of strategies for spelling correctly (see Wilde 1989).

A good starting point for further understanding the patterns of invented spelling is Temple et al. (1988), while Gentry's (1987) *Spel . . . Is a Four-Letter Word* is a valuable and readily accessible introduction to why and how whole language educators might teach spelling.

Teaching and Learning

The activities considered in this section on phonics and writing illustrate how whole language teachers demonstrate and model behavior they want children to emulate, how such teaching can occur in the context of authentic literacy events (such as writing about topics of genuine interest to the children), and how teachers can engage children in mini-lessons that in effect add ideas to the "class pot," to be drawn upon when relevant. Such examples also show how teachers capitalize upon the teachable moment, as when Mrs. Nicholas gave Jenny a *strategy* for spelling rather than telling her the spelling of a single word.

This pattern is typical of whole language teachers: Whenever possible, they offer the children generalizable strategies rather than one-time correct answers. Thus, besides gaining a firmer grasp of letter/ sound associations and strategies for spelling words they were not sure of, the children in these situations were learning valuable problem-solving strategies: "When you need advice, ask your classmates and/or do the best you can; don't wait for an adult to give you the 'correct' answer whenever you encounter problems in reading or writing." There will be time enough for adult help later, to refine reading strategies while clarifying meaning, or to refine writing strategies while revising and polishing pieces of writing for "publication." Such an approach to independent problem-solving does far more to develop independent readers and writers than all the phonics worksheets that are supposed to enable children to read independently or the spelling lists that are supposed to enable them to write independently.

For the most part, children's functional knowledge of phonics can and should be developed through authentic reading and writing activities like these, in which they are personally engaged. As leading whole language educators have expressed it, "Students must have time to read. . . . We suggest that 70–80% of the time allotted to reading instruction be devoted to real reading and writing, with 20–30% of the time spent in working on instructional strategy lessons that include thinking and talking about reading and writing" (Y. Goodman, Watson, and Burke 1987).

❝This pattern is typical of whole language teachers: Whenever possible, they offer the children generalizable strategies rather than one-time correct answers.**❞**

DEVELOPING PHONICS KNOW-HOW THROUGH LITERATURE AND ACTIVITIES

In whole language classrooms, many activities that promote the acquisition of phonics know-how may occur within the context of the Shared Book Experience (described earlier in this chapter) or during similar shared reading experiences of whatever sort. Such activities involve direct teaching, and yet they also contain an element of indirectness: The activities evolve from the reading selection and thus seem incidental to it. This indirectness is in sharp contrast to that of some activities and materials currently touted as literature-based materials for teaching reading (see, for example, Freeman 1989). In the latter lessons or programs, the literature seems to exist for the sake of teaching skills. Whole language teachers know that teaching skills in isolation, or twisting, mangling, and bastardizing literature in order to develop skills work from it, is both unnecessary and counterproductive. The skills and strategies that children need to develop can be fostered more naturally, without debasing the literature and without destroying children's appreciation of it.

With respect to developing phonics know-how in particular, whole language teachers in the primary grades make sure their reading materials include a generous selection of readings that contain *alliteration*, for teaching initial consonant sounds; *rhyme*, for teaching vowel and consonant patterns that commonly occur in the middles-plus-ends of words; and *onomatopoeia* (words that "make" the sounds they designate), for emphasizing these and other aspects of letter/sound associations. Most of these selections are likely also to be valuable for encouraging children to think what would make sense when coming to a problem word and to use letter/sound cues within that context rather than to sound it out as if the word stood in isolation.

The developers of the major alternatives to basals (Chap. 11, p. 265) have included such materials in their programs, but of course teachers need not limit themselves to commercial programs or instructional materials. The reading materials used in teaching and those available for children to read independently should include a wide variety of children's literature, with sound-oriented materials among them: Dr. Seuss books, such as *Green Eggs and Ham* (1960); Mother Goose and other books of traditional rhymes; original nursery rhymes like Dennis Lee's in *Jelly Belly* (1983); poetry books like *Edward Lear's ABC: Alphabet Rhymes for Children* (Lear 1986), the *Noisy Poems* collected by Jill Bennett (1987), and the poetry of such writers as Jack Prelutsky and Shel Silverstein; and a variety of stories that emphasize sounds, such as *Whiff, Sniff, Nibble, and Chew: The Gingerbread Boy Retold*, by Charlotte Pomerantz (1984). In addition, the classroom should abound with reading materials created by the teacher and the children, including those in which sound is prominent. Such materials may sometimes, at least, be modeled upon familiar songs or published poems or stories.

The following sections briefly indicate only a few of the ways whole language teachers may facilitate the acquisition of phonics know-how using such materials as these for shared reading.

Focusing on Initial Sounds

After children have enjoyed and become familiar with a rhyme or other poem, a song, or a story that contains *alliteration*, the teacher may call attention to key words that begin alike; or the teacher may invite the children to locate words that begin with the same consonant sound(s) as a certain word in the selection. Young children will enjoy not only simple rhymes but more challenging poems like the following, which contains several interesting words beginning with *t*, and several beginning with *s* (Prelutsky 1983):

Alphabet Stew

Words can be stuffy, as sticky as glue,
but words can be tutored to tickle you too,
to rumble and tumble and tingle and sing,
to buzz like a bumblebee, coil like a spring.

Juggle their letters and jumble their sounds,
swirl them in circles and stack them in mounds,
twist them and tease them and turn them about,
teach them to dance upside down, inside out.

Make mighty words whisper and tiny words roar
in ways no one ever had thought of before;
cook an improbable alphabet stew,
and words will reveal little secrets to you.

—JACK PRELUTSKY

Other poems with alliteration can be found in a variety of sources, including those mentioned above. David McCord's "Song of the Train" emphasizes the *cl* blend, for instance, while Dahlov Ipcar's "Fishes' Evening Song" and Jack Prelutsky's "The Yak" emphasize several initial consonant sounds or blends (all in *Noisy Poems*, Bennett 1987).

Focusing on Medial-Plus-Final Sounds

Again in the context of shared reading experiences, teachers can call attention to patterns that often occur in the middles-plus-ends of words, particularly one-syllable words, by sharing traditional and familiar songs and poems and stories with *rhyming* elements. The teacher can call attention to the rhymes—words that "end the same"—and/or invite children to find a word that ends the same as a given one from the reading selection. Such rhyming materials need not be sing-songy or trivial and boring in content, as illustrated by these two poems reprinted in *Jelly on the Plate*, a Big Book of poems collected by June Factor (1987):

The Pines

Hear the rumble,
Oh, hear the crash.
The great trees tumble
The strong boughs smash.

Men with saws
Are cutting the pines—
That marched like soldiers
In straight green lines.

Seventy years
Have made them tall.
It takes ten minutes
To make them fall.

And, breaking free
With never a care,
The pine cones leap
Through the clear, bright air.
—MARGARET MAHY

Mist

Mist crept
while I slept
        seemed to swallow
        every hollow
gray-white over every tree
gray cloak falling over me
        misty fingers reaching out
        misty fingers all about.
Mist crept
while I slept.
—SARAH KELLY

Since rhyming words are often easy to predict, such materials can be useful in encouraging children to use prior knowledge plus context and initial consonants to *predict* words that would make sense, before looking at more of the letter cues (as good readers intuitively do). For example, in ''The Pines'':

Seventy years
Have made them tall.
It takes ten minutes
To make them f____.

Focusing on Predicting

Onomatopoetic words—words that ''make'' the sounds they designate—often alliterate or rhyme with other words in the same poem. Thus, they frequently offer opportunities for focusing on initial letter/sounds and/or on the medial-plus-final sounds. But here I shall illustrate the use of onomatopoetic words in predicting: that is, in encouraging children to use prior knowledge and context *in combination with* letter/sound cues to make sense of what they are reading. See if you can supply appropriate onomatopoetic words for this poem, creating suitable ''sound'' words if necessary:

The Noisy Lunch

''I can't stand it any longer,''
        cried the weary cafeteria.

''On Mondays,
    the spaghetti goes sl____, sl____,
    into children's cavernous mouths.

''On Tuesdays,
    the ketchup goes gl____, gl____,
    lurching onto children's hamburgers.

''On Wednesdays,
    the tacos go cr____, cr____,
    teasing the children's mouths with hot sauce.

''On Thursdays, the apples go ch____, ch____,
    tearing out loose teeth for the tooth fairy.

''On Fridays, the children's feet go st____, st____,
    protesting the eternal fish.

''I can't stand it any longer,''
    cried the weary cafeteria.
        ''I quit.''

                —CONNIE WEAVER

The point, of course, is not to ''get the right answer'' but to predict alternatives that will fit—perhaps in one or two cases even to create onomatopoetic nonsense words. (For the curious, though, the words in my original poem are *slurp, glub, crunch, chomp,* and *stomp*.)

Follow-up Activities

This calling-attention-to-patterns that occurs during shared reading experiences can, of course, be followed by a variety of phonics-oriented activities, as needed: listing words that begin the same way or end the same way, for example, or writing interesting words on word cards and later having the children sort the cards into categories that make sense to them, including letter/sound categories. For instance, the names of vegetables brought for vegetable soup might be written on strips of tagboard for children to organize into whatever categories they consider important. One category will surely be words that begin the same (*carrot, cucumber, celery,* and so forth; *beans, broccoli*—why not *bananas*?). The children's categorizing, and miscategorizing, offer further opportunities for learning. The discussions will also offer many other teachable moments. For example, if some children spell *carrot* with an initial *k* and other spell it with an initial *c*, this is a good opportunity to elicit words the children know that begin with an initial /k/ sound and compare their spellings, showing how the initial /k/ sound can be spelled *c* or *k* (or sometimes *ch*, as in *Christmas*).

> **❝** . . . if some children spell *carrot* with an initial *k* and others with an initial *c*, this is a good opportunity to elicit words the children know that begin with an initial /k/ sound and compare their spellings, . . . **❞**

It may be worth emphasizing again that in whole language classrooms, such skills-oriented activities will take only a small amount of time. The poems given as examples offer numerous opportunities for choral reading and drama, visualization, writing activities, discussion, and—with most of them—integration with content area topics, such as basic food groups or environmental studies. Such varied and worthwhile activities, including repeated rereading of favorite selections and independent and group writing, can and should engage children's interest as well as most of their ''instructional'' time.

DEVELOPING PHONICS KNOW-HOW THROUGH CONFERENCING

Previously, I indicated that most children can learn to read through extensive Shared Book Experiences, largely because children are treated as if they *will* learn to read, in their own way and in their own good time, given lots of reading opportunities, appropriate help and feedback as needed, a supportive environment, and a wealth of reading materials they can appreciate and enjoy. In other words, the expectation that ''of course'' children will learn to read plays a major part in making it so.

Nevertheless, whole language teachers do not just wait around for this to happen, as the preceding sections surely illustrate: They provide opportunities for children to engage in many and varied authentic literacy events, and they directly model and teach strategies and skills that, sooner or later, the children will need to develop. They also help children individually.

Considering Miscues

Often, whole language teachers help individual children during brief mini-conferences that occur while children are engaged in daily reading and writing activities. Roving among the students, the teacher stops to ask a question, make a comment, provide help as needed. But whole language teachers also teach during more extensive and periodic one-on-one conferences, during which assessment and instruction are often combined.

Knowing that ability grouping and round-robin reading are more harmful than helpful to children, the whole language teacher assesses children's ability to coordinate the use of prior knowledge and context with letter/sound cues by having the child read aloud during at least some of these periodic individual conferences. Depending on the grade level and the child, the teacher may look for several things:

1. Does the child "read" mainly by looking at the pictures and retelling the story, suggesting that he/she is not yet ready to attend to letter/sound associations? (This impression would be confirmed if the child is not yet representing sounds with letters in independent writing.)

2. Does the child make miscues (departures from what the text says) that suggest he or she is appropriately coordinating the language cue systems to construct meaning?

3. Do the child's miscues suggest that he/she is making good use of letter/sound cues but not attending adequately to meaning—in effect, overusing letter/sound cues while underutilizing other cues?

4. Do the child's miscues suggest that he/she is making inadequate use of both meaning and letter/sound cues when encountering problem words?

"Miscues and Miscue Analysis," in Chapter 10, further extends this discussion of what can be learned by examining readers' miscues. Such assessment can then lead to teaching that helps the student develop needed strategies or effectively integrate existing strategies.

Developing Strategies

While the child reads, the teacher listens for various strengths and needs, then plans instructional situations as appropriate. Sometimes the teacher will provide "instruction" during the same individual conference—for example, by inviting the student to reconsider something that does not make sense (when the child has not self-corrected), then helping the child to generalize about the strategies used. Or the teacher may tape record the child reading and then play the tape back, encouraging *the child* to notice when something doesn't make sense, and helping the child use meaning *and* letter/sound knowledge to get problem words that are important to the overall meaning of the selection.

When working with the child at any given time, the teacher focuses just on those miscues that will help the child understand and begin to use one particular strategy, such as using meaning plus initial consonants to predict something that would make sense. The teacher waits until the reader shows proficiency with a basic strategy such as predicting before she/he focuses on other strategies the child may need to develop, such as self-correcting miscues that don't make sense with the following context.

For teachers wanting to develop their ability to analyze miscues and use that knowledge to work with children, or for others interested in this process, an excellent resource is the *Reading Miscue Inventory: Alternative Procedures* (Y. Goodman, Watson, and Burke 1987). Particularly for understanding and analyzing miscues, my *Reading Process and Practice* (Weaver 1988) is also helpful.

Chapter 10, ''Reconceptualizing and Reclaiming Assessment,'' indicates other aspects of a young child's literacy growth that a teacher might find valuable to assess during individual conferences or day-to-day classroom activities, as appropriate. However, even from this somewhat brief discussion of conferencing, several points can be made:

1. Regarding phonics know-how, the teacher is assessing what's really important: How well does the student coordinate letter/sound knowledge with other cues to construct meaning?

2. By listening to students read in individual conferences rather than during round-robin reading, the teacher can provide immediate feedback in the form of individual ''strategy lessons.''

3. This teaching of strategies on a needs basis is much more valuable than the simple correction of miscues that typically occurs during round-robin reading.

4. Thus, there is no sharp separation between assessment and instruction; the two go hand-in-hand.

STUDENTS WHO APPEAR TO NEED MORE PHONICS

Sometimes teachers assume that students need more phonics work or a more conscious grasp of letter/sound relations in order to read effectively. They may assume this if the student has difficulty completing phonics worksheets and skills activities, or, on the other hand, if the child appears to have strong analytic and auditory skills (see Carbo 1987, all references). That is, depending upon whether teachers are inclined to direct their instruction toward students' apparent weaknesses or to their strengths, the teachers may in either case assume that a child needs more phonics work, on the basis of activities and/or tests that do not assess actual reading.

Before basing instruction upon such an assumption, however, teachers should test the assumption against the student's ability to use letter/sound knowledge in actual reading. One way is to analyze, through miscue analysis, the student's use of letter/sound knowledge while reading an ordinary text. That way the teacher can determine whether the reader is using letter/sound knowledge in appropriate balance with other language cues. However, the teacher may also consider more focused analysis of miscues on words that reflect selected letter/sound patterns.

Determining Lesson

Thus, teachers may sometimes engage students in a "determining lesson": to determine for themselves, more than for the students, that real reading does not require the ability to do phonics activities, or that students readily able to do phonics activities are, nevertheless, beyond the point of profiting from them.

An example of such a lesson is provided by Dorothy Watson and Paul Crowley in their chapter on whole language in *Reading Process and Practice* (Weaver 1988). Consider the case of Jan, a fourth-grader who was a good student and who considered herself a good reader, as did her teacher and her parents. Given a worksheet on the three main sounds of *ea*, Jan completed less than half of the 72 items, and missed nearly half of the 31 items she attempted. Frustrated by this failure, Jan cried herself to sleep.

Equally frustrated and concerned, her parents consulted a reading teacher who prepared for Jan a passage containing several words exemplifying four *ea* sounds. Here is the passage, with the *ea* italicized in those words.

> When hunting s*ea*son comes Uncle Bill is almost as *ea*ger to h*ea*d for the woods as Babe and Bingo are. Babe and Bingo are b*ea*utiful b*ea*gles, but Uncle Bill calls them *ea*ger b*ea*vers when it comes to ph*ea*sant hunting.
> When Uncle Bill rel*ea*ses those dogs from their st*ea*dy l*ea*sh, you should see them str*ea*k across the m*ea*dow at br*ea*kneck speed. They can r*ea*lly work up a sw*ea*t!
> Aunt Joan dr*ea*ds hunting s*ea*son. Babe and Bingo's st*ea*dy str*ea*m of barking is d*ea*fening and gives her h*ea*daches. She can't b*ea*r to think of one f*ea*ther on a bird being harmed. Uncle Bill gives the ph*ea*sants to a neighbor. Babe and Bingo howl. (Watson and Crowley 1988, pp. 263–65)

In context, Jan was able to read three of the words, or variants thereof, that she had not been able to get in isolation: *sweat, pheasants,* and *steadier*. In fact, she had trouble with only two of the *ea* words, one of which she read correctly the second time it occurred, in a more predictable context.

"Though they cannot succeed at phonics skills work, students may be able to read without difficulty materials that contain the very phonics elements emphasized in the skills work.**"**

This example illustrates what experienced whole language teachers know: that there is not necessarily a correlation between being able to do skills work and being able to read. Though they cannot succeed at phonics skills work, students may be able to read without difficulty materials that contain the very phonics elements emphasized in the skills work. The converse is also true, however: Students may be able to do isolated skills work without difficulty, yet not be able to construct meaning effectively. Or they may be able to do phonics skills work, yet clearly not need such work because they already make sufficient use of phonics knowledge in conjunction with other language cues. Analysis of the reader's miscues, with a "determining lesson" or a less controlled text, is important for deciding whether a student does or does not need more help in developing practical phonics know-how.

Whole language teachers have found that most children develop an adequate working knowledge of phonics through authentic literacy events and the kinds of activities and instructional assistance previously discussed. There is no need for, or value in, the usual kinds of phonics worksheets and activities, most of which can be completed either mindlessly, or only with inordinate difficulty.

Reading Recovery

But what of those children whose reading and writing suggest they have not developed even a rudimentary sense of letter/sound relationships, even though they have engaged repeatedly in sustained reading experiences of various sorts, received instruction during activities and conferences, and frequently written as best they can? Such children may simply need more such experiences, and more time. On the other hand, teachers and schools must be prepared to offer more help, as needed. Brill (1985) offers some excellent ideas for the classroom teacher or reading specialist. Others have developed much more extensive programs.

In the early 1960s, New Zealand educator Marie Clay observed while investigating emergent reading behavior that after a year of reading instruction—by age 6, in New Zealand—children could be identified as progressing normally, or as being "at risk" with regard to reading. Those considered at risk were the children who had developed inappropriate reading strategies, those who had not yet developed some of the most important reading strategies, or simply those who had not yet learned to coordinate different strategies and cues into a system for reading effectively. To assist such children, Clay developed a Reading Recovery program for training teachers and tutoring students.

The steps of the tutoring program closely resemble those of the Shared Book Experience:

Rereading of two or more familiar books

Rereading of previous day's new book (while the tutor does a running tabulation and analysis of the reader's miscues)

Working with the particular skills or strategies the reader needs to develop

Writing a story

Introducing a new book, which the reader attempts to read

Notice that whatever skills or strategies the student needs to develop are highlighted within the context of reading real books and writing something of interest to the students. Within twelve to twenty weeks of daily half-hour lessons of this sort, all but a small percentage of students are able to succeed within the regular classroom programs (see Clay 1986).

This Reading Recovery program has been successful not only in New Zealand but also in Australia and in the United States. For example, teacher educators at Ohio State University were so successful in developing the program with teachers and students locally that it has been extended to the entire state of Ohio, with educators from across the nation coming to Ohio State to receive training that will enable them to establish similar programs in their own locales. Clay's assessment and teaching procedures and results are described in *The Early Detection of Reading Difficulties* (1988), now in its fourth edition. For more information on the Ohio State program and its success, see Pinnell 1985, 1988, and 1989, as well as various documents available from Ohio State University's Department of Educational Theory and Practice. I have briefly described the Reading Recovery program as well as similar programs for older, less successful readers in Chapter 11 of my *Reading Process and Practice* (Weaver 1988).

Whether the student needs to develop a rudimentary grasp of basic letter/sound associations, an ability to coordinate letter/sound cues with meaning, or some other strategy or skill, what all these special-assistance programs have in common is that they focus on the needed skill or strategy within the context of authentic literacy events. And these programs appear to be much more successful than traditional kinds of compensatory programs in helping children learn to read more effectively (see sources just cited).

PHONICS IN A WHOLE LANGUAGE CONTEXT

What, then, of the advice regarding phonics as offered in *Becoming a Nation of Readers* (Anderson et al. 1985), namely, ''Do it early'' and ''Keep it simple''? This advice seems generally sensible. However, drawing upon the various kinds of evidence and research described in previous chapters, I and most whole language educators would interpret these maxims far differently than the authors of *Becoming a Nation of Readers*.

1. Engage children in a variety of shared reading and other authentic reading experiences, as briefly described in this chapter. Call children's attention to major letter/sound associations (initial consonants, middles-plus-ends of words) within the context of some of those shared reading experiences. Offer follow-up activities if or as appropriate.

2. Offer children numerous opportunities to write independently, and encourage and help them learn to represent sounds with letters, as they become increasingly able.

3. Listen to children read in individual conferences, and help them use letter/sound cues and coordinate these with meaning cues *during the reading of authentic texts*, as the children demonstrate readiness and need.

4. Begin all of this early: in kindergarten, if not preschool.

5. But *do not test children's grasp of letter/sound associations in isolation from real reading*; instead, provide a supportive environment in which children are free to take risks without being penalized for what they cannot do.

6. Recognizing that not all students who may eventually benefit from phonics assistance can do so at an early age, be alert for students beyond the primary grades who genuinely have not acquired even the minimal amount of letter/sound knowledge needed to write words phonetically or make sufficient use of letter/sound cues in reading.

7. Provide additional help for such students by building upon their strengths and minimizing their weaknesses. A few readers may never be able to recognize many words on sight, while a few others may never be very good at using letter/sound cues, even along with context (Boder 1973). It is important to help these students succeed at what they can do and try to help them develop other strategies, while not making them feel like failures for what they cannot do well.

Based upon various lines of research, then, as well as day-to-day observations in their own classrooms, whole language teachers have a different concept than that expressed in *Becoming a Nation of Readers* as to what and how much phonics needs to be taught, and rather different procedures for teaching phonics, both indirectly and directly. Whole language teaching practices are based upon *what works* most effectively to help children become efficient, independent readers and writers.

As this discussion indicates, in whole language classrooms there is no sharp separation between reading and writing, nor between reading and reading instruction nor writing and writing instruction. Skills and strategies are developed more effectively within the context of authentic literacy events—some of which may involve both reading and writing. This natural learning of skills and strategies is further illustrated in Chapter 8, which describes in some detail a whole language classroom wherein comprehension and thinking skills are developed as children read, discuss, and analyze literature.

CHAPTER 8

Developing Comprehension and Thinking in Whole Language Classrooms

JANET VANCE

As Chapter 7 described how phonics knowledge and know-how may be developed in whole language classrooms, so this chapter deals with how comprehension and thinking can be fostered in such classrooms. The approach here is much different, however; instead of discussing a wealth of activities for developing comprehension, the chapter characterizes the kind of classroom environment in which comprehension and thinking develop naturally. Though it begins with brief reference to aspects of comprehension as traditionally defined, the heart of the chapter offers glimpses as to how comprehension and thinking develop without such artificial separations.

To achieve this aim, I describe a day's visit to one first-grade whole language classroom, with particular attention to a story mapping activity and how it enhances comprehension and encourages thinking. In the context of this activity, the first-graders "naturally" engage not only in recall but in interpretation (inference, analysis, synthesis) and critical evaluation. The description of this classroom and the story mapping activity is followed by brief discussion of other activities that foster comprehension and thinking in whole language classrooms: namely, literature groups, journals, and other forms of writing. In describing these activities, as well as the day in a first-grade classroom, the aim is actually to go beyond what the title of the chapter suggests: to give some sense of the flavor of whole language classrooms, thus clarifying how whole language teachers create positive environments and climates for learning.

COMPREHENSION DESCRIBED

The comprehension that whole language educators strive to develop in children includes thinking skills such as recognizing main ideas, making predictions, relating cause and effect, and identifying patterns. It also includes what some people inappropriately call "levels" of thinking. Figure 8.1 suggests commonalities among the familiar taxonomies of Bloom and others, combining and reducing them to four major aspects of comprehension.

Literal comprehension refers to recall, to remembering or recognizing what was read or heard—though it is often questionable whether recall and recognition involve more than simple manipulation of language (see Chap. 9, p. 196). Most basal reading workbooks and classroom worksheets include many questions requiring only such recall or recognition. Interpretive comprehension includes drawing inferences and understanding implied information, as well as analysis, synthesis, and application. Critical comprehension involves the ability to evaluate what

Relating Taxonomies to Aspects of Comprehension

Aspects of Comprehension	Taxonomies		
	Bloom	Saunders	Barrett
Literal	Knowledge Comprehension	Memory Translation	Recognition Recall
Interpretive (Inferential)	Application Analysis Synthesis	Interpretation Application Analysis Synthesis	Inference
Critical	Evaluation	Evaluation	Evaluation
Creative		Appreciation	

Figure 8.1   Aspects of comprehension (adapted from "Comprehending Comprehension" 1989)

was read and provide support for one's conclusions. And creative comprehension includes emotional response, such as an appreciation for what was read or heard and an ability to relate it to one's own life.

In traditional classrooms, literal comprehension is too often taught as if it were a prelude to the supposedly more sophisticated kinds of comprehension, as well as taught and tested as if it were an end in itself. However, traditional methods of assessing literal comprehension often require little more than the manipulation of language.

Take, for example, some literal comprehension questions based upon the first stanza of Lewis Carroll's poem ''Jabberwocky'':

> 'Twas brillig, and the slithy toves
> Did gyre and gimble in the wabe:
> All mimsy were the borogroves,
> And the mome raths outgrabe.

After reading the first stanza, a student can easily answer traditional kinds of comprehension questions: ''What did the slithy toves do in the wabe?'' ''The borogroves were _____?'' and ''What things were outgrabing?'' But even if the student answers all of the questions correctly, he or she has not necessarily demonstrated an integrated or useful understanding of the material.

My 4-year-old daughter Naomi provides an example of the difference between literal (recall) comprehension and genuine understanding. Asked where she went on vacation, Naomi will promptly reply, ''Missouri, North Carolina, and across the Mississippi River.'' But we can be ten minutes from our home in Michigan and she will ask, ''Is this Missouri?'' or, ''Is that the Mississippi River?'' With a 4-year-old, such misunderstanding can be amusing, even charming. But the traditional emphasis on parroting back answers with no underlying comprehension (see the example of a ''transmission'' lesson in Chapter 1) is not encouraged in whole language classrooms. Whole language teachers don't teach comprehension or thinking skills apart from authentic reading, writing, and discussing or apart from exploring concepts and ideas across the curriculum. Reading comprehension not only involves but essentially *is* thinking, and thinking pervades everything done in the classroom.

Instead of teaching comprehension and thinking as skills, then, whole language teachers create environments, both physical and emotional, that encourage comprehension and thinking in virtually everything children do. In such environments, children naturally learn to analyze and synthesize information; to compare and contrast, to draw inferences, and to hypothesize; to apply concepts; to evaluate and critique; and, of course, to relate what they're studying to their own

❝Instead of teaching comprehension and thinking as skills, then, whole language teachers create environments, both physical and emotional, that encourage comprehension and thinking in virtually everything children do.❞

lives. The categories or aspects of comprehension blend and become virtually meaningless as comprehension develops through day-to-day activities.

Comprehension is not, then, linear or hierarchical, proceeding from literal toward higher levels. Nor does one aspect of comprehension normally occur separate from others. Rather, these aspects of comprehension interrelate and intertwine as people strive to make sense of what they hear and read and experience.

This should not be surprising, since—as mentioned in Chapter 3—children's development of literacy is neither hierarchical nor linear, nor does their learning proceed skill-by-skill, even if it is taught that way. Observation and careful documentation of individual children's learning in whole language classrooms clearly demonstrate that their learning is not neatly sequential, tidy, or predictable. They learn best when they have daily opportunities to make meaning for themselves, just as they did in learning for themselves, albeit unconsciously, the rules for producing oral language. Such self-regulation is essential to thinking. We do not usually consider someone to be thinking when someone else "calls the plays" at every step (Palincsar and Brown 1989). Though there are many ways in which whole language teachers foster comprehension and thinking, most crucially they create environments and provide a variety of integrative experiences that enable and encourage children to comprehend and think.

Thus, the following sections offer examples of how whole language teachers create such environments and provide experiences that encourage comprehension and thinking to emerge and develop gradually, with constant use.

CREATING ENVIRONMENTS THAT FOSTER COMPREHENSION AND THINKING

The development of comprehension and thinking takes place naturally in whole language classrooms because the teacher provides an environment that is not only "littered with literacy," but that is emotionally safe and conducive to the growth of the whole child. As we saw in Chapter 4, whole language teachers create in the classroom many of the conditions that successfully foster the learning of language and literacy in the home.

Comprehension development begins naturally enough in the home. Very early in life, the child comprehends "Mama," "Daddy," and "bottle." Comprehension soon expands to include the infamous "no-no." And what toddler doesn't comprehend "Go get your coat and we'll go bye-bye''? Comprehension is not taught to babies and toddlers; it develops naturally because parents respond to their child's successes, encourage when the child misunderstands or ''fails,'' and nudge gently foward when the time seems appropriate. Learning is risk-free because adults do not penalize the young child for not having mastered certain skills.

Whole language teachers carry the safe learning environment of the home into the classroom and allow comprehension to continue its natural development. They foster this development in many ways. Mrs. Kim Doele and her first-grade class at Wealthy Elementary School in East Grand Rapids, Michigan, provide a wonderful example of the continued natural development of comprehension in a whole language classroom. Mrs. Doele and her students are depicted on the cover.

I spent a delightful day in Mrs. Doele's class in May, near the end of their school year. My specific purpose was to observe her use of story mapping and how it promoted the natural development of comprehension in the children. And it did, as I will describe later in the chapter. But I came away with the feeling that I had spent a day in an almost sacred place. Doele has provided these children with a safe and special place to come each day where they can grow and learn. She has created a physical and emotional environment in which comprehension is free to develop naturally—and, yes, idiosyncratically.

The Physical Environment

I arrived at Wealthy School, an old, two-story brick building, on a gray, rainy morning and was let into the building by a smiling little girl in a raincoat. I wandered down the hall to the stairs, finally finding my way to Mrs. Doele's classroom. She welcomed me personally; her (I should say ''their'') classroom welcomed me as well. I felt pulled to come inside and look around. I wanted to browse, to read, to stare, and to stay. This was a ''literate'' environment. Interest centers offered me choices: poetry, caterpillars and butterflies, plants, seeds, and Jack in the Beanstalk. Behind the interest centers, the cupboard doors boasted tulip artwork and accompanying original poetry. The adjacent small bulletin board displayed interesting facts about Chris Van Allsburg, famous author/illustrator from the surrounding Grand Rapids area.

Moving around the room to the window sill, I saw cups bearing the name of each student and showing plants in various stages of health or nonhealth, an observational experiment in progress. The children later informed me that they had been testing the importance of sunlight on plant growth.

Hanging from the window blinds was a large, illustrated story map of *If You Give a Mouse a Cookie*, by Laura Joffe. On a small table sat an easel filled with Big Books, both commercial and class-produced: a delightful record of the year's work. The corner was filled with bright, comfortable pillows for reading—either alone or with a friend. Also in this corner of the room was a revolving paperback book holder. Labeled with a child's name, each section contained the published writings of that child, complete with cover, title page, and text, readily available for use by the entire class.

Now at the back wall of the room, I noticed that underneath a large bulletin board proclaiming ''Life Cycles'' and ''Chickens Aren't the Only Ones'' were small plastic cups (with tops and name tags) containing caterpillars. And next to the caterpillars, in an aquarium-turned-birdcage, was a young quail that the children had been observing since before it hatched.

As I moved down the back wall, I stopped at a basketful of readers theatre scripts, carton after carton of math manipulatives, a box of delightful and intriguing puppets, and book after book about dinosaurs. Rounding the last corner, I found the publishing center, complete with typewriter, paper and cover materials, and a dictionary. Overhead, above the chalkboard, twenty-six alphabetized lists contained ''Words Authors Use,'' a gentle nudge on the bridge between invented spelling and publication. In front of the chalkboard was the reading rug, banked on one side by the writing conference table and on the other by a flipchart containing stories, poems, and songs from previous lessons. Below the chalkboard, lining the wall, were seven more baskets, full of books.

In the center of the room, the children's desks were grouped in fours. And in the middle of the desk tops, a basket contained a writing folder for each child. The room was small and full, but not at all cluttered, and not crowded: just personal and welcoming.

The Emotional Environment

About five minutes after my arrival, the children (including my rain-coated door holder) began entering the room, each with a cheerful ''Hi, Mrs. Doele!'' and more than a few hugs! With curious smiles directed toward me, they began their day.

The first forty-five minutes of the day were spent in writing workshop. The children worked intently, though not silently, on their various projects, often conferring quietly with a friend. They eagerly shared their work with me, explaining such things as where they got the idea for their writing, or the particular genre they were using, or the fact that they were revising, or doing the final editing before publication.

The overriding emotions in the classroom were mutual trust and respect between teacher and students. This respect also carried over into the students' dealings with one another. Doele's curriculum and attention were not centered around maintaining control and order in the classroom. Her attention was focused on the children as individuals. She had provided stimulating opportunities for the mental, emotional, and social growth of her students, and they responded with a delightful mixture of contentment, curiosity, and creativity.

Doele dismissed her class of first-graders to go to music class with a quiet reminder to walk quickly and quietly in the hallway. Assuring them she would arrive shortly, she continued our conversation. Children needing her attention stood quietly at her side until recognized, obviously confident that their turn was coming, and respectful of the needs of others.

As the class moved from activity to activity, they greeted each new "subject" with fresh anticipation and enthusiasm. The all-too-familiar student boredom was totally nonexistent. Children who finished early on a given task chose a book to read or opened their writing folders, eagerly illustrating or revising works already in progress.

The children worked beautifully together in ever-changing groups and pairs. The classroom was void of the normal childish, but often vicious, put-downs and insults. Here again, Doele's belief in the precious individuality of each student was evident. She spoke with pride of Josh (not his real name). Josh was not a strong reader, but he completed artistic story maps in such great detail that he often had to be reminded to move on to the next step. It was also Josh, with his especially gentle way with animals, who was called upon to calm the baby quail after it was accidentally dropped by another child. Josh would be a stifled, frustrated learner in a traditional, skills-oriented classroom. But here, where the "whole Josh" is recognized and honored, he is flourishing.

Another child I'll call Philip had been retained in first grade because "he couldn't read." About two weeks into the new school year, Philip was reading. Doele talked with the child's mother and was informed that Philip could read at home last year—he just couldn't read at school! Obviously, it didn't take Philip long to realize that Doele's classroom was a safe and comfortable place in which to learn and grow and be himself.

FOSTERING AND ASSESSING COMPREHENSION

Whole language teachers not only provide a safe and nurturing environment in which children learn and continue to develop increased comprehension, they also use a great variety of means and methods to foster comprehension and thinking—although any method, separated from the whole-child attitude, becomes simply another activity.

Whole language teachers begin with a belief in the power of applying and integrating prior knowledge with new learning. Readers make meanings, using their knowledge of the world and cues supplied by the text. As *Becoming a Nation of Readers* puts it, ''Reading is a process in which information from the text and the knowledge possessed by the reader act together to produce meaning'' (Anderson et al. 1985, p. 8). Each child enters the classroom with his or her own unique bank of prior knowledge and experience. This prior knowledge profoundly influences the meaning a child makes from a text, or what he or she ''comprehends.'' More important than a ''correct'' answer is the thought process employed by the child to reach his or her conclusion.

The influence of prior knowledge is exemplified by the following situation involving 7-year-old Joy. While reading for a miscue analysis (see Chap. 10) the story ''I Should Have Stayed in Bed,'' by Joan M. Lexau, Joy made a miscue that can be understood only in light of her prior knowledge. In the story, Sam has been having a very difficult day. At the point where Joy made such a revealing miscue, Sam had just been scolded by the nurse and his teacher, who were angry with him for getting dizzy. Then the text reads: ''She told me to open my reader and read.'' Joy read, ''She *held* me to open my reader and read.'' While obviously Joy's reading of the text was ''wrong,'' consideration of prior knowledge sheds light on the miscue. Because Joy is my daughter, I know that in our home, after a child ''gets into trouble,'' as Sam did, he or she is held by the correcting parent. This is the kind of miscue that is not obviously rational to a teacher. But it serves as a clear reminder that every child brings into the classroom a lifetime of prior knowledge that the teacher knows nothing about.

The whole language teacher brings to each student a deep respect for his or her existing prior knowledge as well as a strong desire to expand that child's wealth of knowledge and experience, and therefore his or her power to truly comprehend. Respect for each child's prior knowledge and experience provides a basis for encouraging and fostering comprehension.

From this base, however, there is no single, sequenced, or best way to foster comprehension development in children. Even a straightforward listing of methods actually distorts the nature of the learning

❝. . . there is no single, sequenced, or best way to foster comprehension development in children. Even a straightforward listing of methods actually distorts the nature of the learning process, for whole language and whole children do not function in neat, orderly segments.**❞**

process, for whole language and whole children do not function in neat, orderly segments. Reading and writing—when children are allowed to engage in real reading and writing—provide marvelous opportunities for simultaneous learning, teaching, and assessing to take place. Discussion enhances everything.

To highlight some of the kinds of activities that foster comprehension, however, I will first describe the story-mapping activity observed in Doele's classroom, then briefly touch upon literature groups, journals, and other forms of writing as means of fostering comprehension and thinking.

Story Mapping

Doele's use of story mapping is a prime example of how comprehension and thinking are fostered through reading, writing, and discussion in which the children are actively engaged.

For this particular story map, she chose to read to the children *The Tiny Seed*, by Eric Carle. With the children gathered on the story rug, Doele began by eliciting their prior knowledge. These first-graders recalled, with delight, other Eric Carle stories they knew and remembered. They discussed the illustrations and techniques used by illustrators—comparing their styles. One child commented that it looked as though Carle had made the sun from little pieces of paper. The children were adept at observing and analyzing.

As the story told of the tiny seed, its travels, growth, and life cycle, the children quickly recognized this as a ''circle story,'' and promptly predicted that the end of the story would be just like the beginning. Doele followed up on their observations and the class proved their hypothesis. The children also compared the tiny seed to their own plants growing on the classroom window sill. One child remarked, ''Remember how our plants in the closet didn't grow because there wasn't any sun?''

At the story's completion, Doele presented the children with a large piece of brown paper, about five feet square. A circle in the middle read, ''*The Tiny Seed* by Eric Carle.'' Doele then explained her idea of using flower petals because the story was about a flower; the circular petal arrangement would represent the circle story. As she modeled her thinking, the children joined in, sharing their thoughts. Doele also told the children that this was a new idea, one she hadn't tried before, but she was confident that together they could work out any problems which might arise. Step by step, the class retold *The Tiny Seed* as Doele passed out large yellow flower petals on which to illustrate a specific scene in the story. The children's ability to retell the story was remarkable, obviously having been fortified by their comprehension of the story. They had been truly engaged—not just listening, but constructing meaning as they listened.

When a disagreement arose over the sequence of events, the children quickly solved the problem by agreeing to return to the text and investigate. As we gathered later to assemble the story map, Doele had each child tell what part of the story his or her illustrations told about. Soon a very proud group of children had a beautiful wall hanging for their classroom, after experiencing, discussing, and analyzing a piece of literature. Furthermore, their teacher had ample opportunity to observe and assess the understanding of each child (see Chap. 10 for some ways of recording such observations). Doele explained that as children work on individual story maps, she can easily observe just where a problem is occurring with a particular child. A word of advice, a suggested consultation with the text, or pairing the child with a partner are all proven methods of help. Doele commented that discussing and comparing their work with others often spurs children to try harder.

Story mapping can take varying forms to fit the needs of different ages, story forms, and teacher intentions. Making a story map offers great opportunities for stimulating comprehension of likenesses and differences, event cycles, cause-effect relationships, character development, and story grammars. When making story maps, children inevitably engage in the so-called higher levels of thinking and comprehension.

Literature Groups and Journals

Whole language teachers find that when children are engaged in a text, comprehension development follows naturally. Literature groups are one way to foster this development. Students are divided into groups based not on ability but on interest in a particular book. Each group reads and discusses its chosen book, over several days or even weeks. As students read individually in preparation for discussion, they may, if they or the teacher chooses, keep a journal of problem words, strong feelings or related experiences evoked by the text, comments, questions, predictions they wish to share with the group—in short, anything of interest.

Literature groups are vastly different from traditional reading groups, not only because the book is chosen by the students but because the teacher engages the students in conversations about the book instead of grilling them on what they comprehended. For genuine discussion to take place, there must be a receptivity to different and even opposing points of view. The teacher attempts to model this receptivity and to be more of a discussion participant than an authority figure. Indeed, once the students have established the habit of dialoguing with each other, the teacher need not always participate in the group discussions. Thus the literature groups become "grand conversations" about literature, rather than modern-day exemplars of the Grand Inquisition (see Eeds and Wells 1989; see Chap. 10, pp. 245–47, for more details).

When the literature groups meet for discussion, then, individuals share opinions, knowledge, ideas, and suggestions related to their readings. This reflects the understanding that reading is a transaction— that is, that readers bring to as well as take from the text (see Chap. 9, pp. 199–202). Clearly, this understanding derived from cognitive and psycholinguistic research is in direct opposition to the traditional theory that text contains a single meaning which every reader must strive to discover, as the teacher stands in final judgment. Literature discussion groups, in contrast, expand and extend understanding for all involved, through interaction and the continual construction and reconstruction of meaning. The students naturally review events and details from the text (recall), while analyzing, synthesizing, drawing inferences and making hypotheses, interpreting, and, of course, responding critically and personally (see Eeds and Wells 1989).

To encourage comprehension and thinking, whole language teachers may have students keep literary journals not only to prepare for literature discussion groups but also (or alternatively) in response to independent reading that they may or may not discuss in class. Through such journals, students and teacher "talk" to each other about literature. Such literary conversations provide the teacher with opportunities for assessment and challenge: The teacher can determine a student's likes and dislikes, reactions to a particular work of literature, depth of understanding attained, grasp of literary conventions and genres, and so forth—and, in addition, the teacher can raise questions, offer alternative interpretations, suggest other books the student might like, and in general extend and stimulate the student's learning. In effect, teacher and student become literary buddies, and similarly the students can become literary buddies with one another. Or as Nancie Atwell describes it, her students' reading workshop journals are a means of "building a dining room table" across which readers share with other readers (*In the Middle*, 1987).

Another way that whole language teachers encourage comprehension and thinking, then, is by encouraging students to choose books for themselves and to discuss what they are reading through literary journals. Both writing about the literature and reading someone else's response serve to deepen understanding and insight.

Talking and writing about books are both important, whether in formally structured literature groups or in informal conversations, through journals or letters or some other form of personal response. As my fifth-grade son put it when asked what made his friend Irving a good reader, ''He likes to talk about books.'' Children talking and writing about what they enjoyed reading encourage other children to read. But first and foremost, of course, children need to be given time to read—not the formulated ''comprehension lessons'' or the basalized versions of good literature but pure unadulterated literature that, when consumed, continues the natural development of comprehension and creates an addiction to reading. As indicated in Chapter 2, reading and writing authentic texts does more to promote comprehension than lessons on comprehension and thinking skills.

Writing

Another way whole language teachers foster thinking is by engaging their students in the process of writing: rehearsing, drafting, revising, editing, and ultimately ''publishing'' some of their best works. Writers become critical readers, not only of their own and their classmates' works but of the trade books they read (see Avery 1985, Hansen 1987).

Writing both fosters understanding and expresses it. For example, sequencing and cause-effect relationships became clearer as the children in Doele's classroom faithfully recorded, in individual booklets, both words and pictures chronicling the development of their caterpillar into a chrysallis and eventually into a butterfly. Also included in the students' writing folders were original stories and poems, some modeled after favorite stories they had read: for example, Jenny's rabbit story in which Mother Rabbit faced dilemmas similar to those of the Little Red Hen. Earlier in the year, the class had done an extended story map comparing eight versions of *The Little Red Hen*. The discussion obviously involved analytic thinking and comparison and contrast, which led to Jenny's being able to write a similarly structured story.

Writing conferences provide teachers with the opportunity to teach each child at his or her personal teachable moment. A child struggling with the use of dialogue may be ready to absorb the use of quotation marks, while another, interested in poetry, may be ready for instruction in the use of similes and metaphors. The child is able to recall the instruction because it is taught in the context of its application—and in the context of the child's personal ''whole,'' or need.

Whole language teachers also provide their writers with an audience, which in turn stimulates them to think through, and about, their writing. Regardless of whether the audience is the teacher, other students, the custodian or the principal, or parents, writers benefit from sharing their work. They learn the value of producing readable work, of supporting their ideas, of providing a logical sequence of events, of being humorous, or of being persuasive. The list could go on and on. Or as one third-grader aptly stated, ''When I write a story, I always look back over it to make sure it has a problem, and a solution, and an ending so it doesn't get boring.''

As children learn to critique the writing of others, they begin to comprehend their own writing as others will hear or read it. At this point, we have children who are thinking, rethinking, and understanding—comprehending—as they read and write. In short, providing an audience for students' writing encourages them to think in ways not necessarily reducible to identifiable thinking skills, but in ways that will serve them well as adults.

COMPREHENSION AND THINKING IN A WHOLE LANGUAGE CONTEXT

The principles of whole language education foster the natural development of comprehension and thinking, in a variety of ways. Most crucially, perhaps, whole language classrooms provide the safe environment necessary for the mental, emotional, and social growth of children.

Children in whole language classrooms are free to be individuals with different needs and strengths, and this freedom encourages them all to learn and progress. For such children, comprehension and thinking continue the natural development begun at birth, because they are actively engaged in meaningful activities. They learn skills, but they learn them in a meaningful context. For example, Doele's students deepened their understanding of sequencing and cause-and-effect and sharpened their analytical skills, not by doing worksheets on these skills but by observing, identifying, and investigating the life cycle of a caterpillar. Furthermore, the active development of skills in one context facilitated their active use in others. Thus, the hypothesizing, data collecting, observing, and comparing that Doele's students did in their seed projects helped them analyze and comprehend *The Tiny Seed*. The thinking they did in the science project enhanced their ability to comprehend the literature.

Likewise, the literature discussion groups of both younger and older children relate text (fiction or nonfiction, traditional or classical) to personal feelings, events, or situations in the students' lives, thereby enhancing their construction of meaning and developing an ever-broaden-

❝ For such children, comprehension and thinking continue the natural development begun at birth, because they are actively engaged in meaningful activities. They learn skills, but they learn them in a meaningful context. **❞**

ing scope of comprehension. The integration of skills, subject matter, and thought processes, in an open and accepting environment, promotes a very natural and continual development of comprehension.

Whole language also provides teachers with the opportunity to see and appreciate the unique, idiosyncratic thinking processes of their students. Assessment is not limited to determining whether a right or wrong word is written in the blank, but is expanded to include conversation, written and oral; the application of skills in contextual settings; and observation of the students' ability to discuss, learn from others, draw meaning from various activities and sources, and exercise problem-solving skills. Because the teacher has many opportunities to see each student's personal development, she or he is much more able to seize those precious teachable moments. When the teacher is able to make use of these moments, understanding occurs—and comprehension develops.

The foregoing suggests, then, not only the fact that comprehension and thinking skills are inextricably intertwined and developed throughout a variety of daily activities across the curriculum, but the fact that assessment and instruction are likewise intertwined in whole language classrooms. This is a topic to which we shall return in Chapter 10, after considering many of the reasons why standardized tests are inadequate and even invalid as a basis for individual assessment and educational decision-making.

C H A P T E R 9

Reconsidering Standardized Tests for Assessment and Accountability

Whole language educators firmly believe that teachers and schools must be "accountable." But to whom, and for what? These are crucial questions, intertwined with the questions of how assessment should be carried out and accountability determined.

A growing number of educators and parents are alarmed about the increase in state-mandated and standardized testing demanded by those who would hold schools accountable. Two assumptions underlie this increase in testing: the assumption that teachers will teach better, and that students will learn more. But as Frank Smith notes in *Insult to Intelligence*, both assumptions are flawed. As a consequence of incessant testing, teachers learn not to teach, and children learn not to learn (1988a, p. 129). It is becoming increasingly evident that this current "testmania" serves politicians' need to be accountable for the expenditure of public funds better than it does the needs of students, teachers, or even of the society as a whole.

One problem with standardized tests is that they obscure a crucial difference between *evaluation* and *assessment*. Evaluation involves judging merit, achievement, or value. Assessment, as many people define it, is the gathering of data prior to evaluation. As Stokes puts it, "This is worth repeating: assessment is necessarily prior to evaluation and assessment entails the gathering of all available information which may support sensitive and accurate judgments" (Stokes 1989, p. 10). Standardized tests provide simplistic measures of evaluation, without adequate assessment: that is, they constitute judgments on the basis of inadequate evidence. No single score can provide an adequate measure of learning (see International Reading Association and the National Council of Teachers of English 1989, p. 24).

This chapter discusses some of the widespread concerns about standardized tests, considers some of the research demonstrating the inap-

> **"**Standardized tests provide simplistic measures of evaluation, without adequate assessment: that is, they constitute judgments on the basis of inadequate evidence. No single score can provide an adequate measure of learning.**"**

propriateness of such tests of reading, and describes and raises some concerns about the new reading tests being developed by the states of Michigan and Illinois. Thus, this chapter sets the stage for the next, which describes some of the kinds of assessment in whole language classrooms that provide a broader and more appropriate basis for evaluation and accountability.

The focus here is on standardized, norm-referenced tests, but many of the criticisms apply equally to state-mandated competency tests and basal tests, which are usually criterion-referenced (see, for example, the critique of basal tests in K. Goodman et al. 1988, pp. 104–122). Most of the criticisms of standardized tests apply to those kinds of tests in general, not just to tests of reading and writing.

With regard to the latter, however, this chapter emphasizes the assessment and evaluation of reading, more than writing—not because I believe that writing is any less important than reading but simply because tests of reading have become so central to educational decision-making. Students are often promoted or retained on the basis of their scores on reading tests, whether standardized or basal-supplied. Thus, inadequate and inappropriate tests have tremendous potential for educational harm, as suggested in many published critiques of such tests (see the starter bibliography in Figure 9.1).

CRITICISMS OF STANDARDIZED TESTS AND TESTING

At a 1987 conference on basal readers, Jerome Harste commented that basal reading programs should be labeled ''Warning! May be harmful to children's educational health.'' (This is the way I remember it, anyhow.) If anything, this warning is even more applicable to standardized tests: they are harmful to students, teachers, administrators, schools—and ultimately, of course, to our society. There are several reasons why standardized, state-mandated, and basal reading tests are more detrimental to education than beneficial. For a list of some of these reasons, see Figure 9.2.

1. *The purpose of standardized tests, by their very nature, is to rank-order students, teachers, and schools, and thereby label some as less successful than others, or even as failures—not to improve education.* Such norm-referenced tests are set up so that half the children will, *by definition*, be below average. ''Below average'' is a statistical concept: below the arithmetic mean. But within education, it has taken on judgmental connotations, meaning something like

Articles

Carbo, Marie. October 1988. What reading achievement tests should measure to increase literacy in the U.S. Phi Delta Kappa *Research Bulletin*, No. 7.

Corbett, Marlene. June 1989. *The Testing Dilemma.* SLATE Starter Sheet. Urbana, Ill.: National Council of Teachers of English.

Edelsky, Carole, and Susan Harman. October 1988. One more critique of reading tests—with two differences. *English Education* 20:157–70.

Madaus, George F. May 1985. Test scores as administrative mechanisms in educational policy. *Phi Delta Kappan* 66:611–17.

Neill, D. Monty, and Noe J. Medina. May 1989. Standardized testing: Harmful to educational health. *Phi Delta Kappan* 70:688–97.

Richards, T. S. March 1989. Testmania: The school under siege. *Learning 89* 17:64–66.

Sternberg, Robert J. March 1989. The tyranny of testing. *Learning 89* 17:60–63.

Wiggins, Grant. May 1989. A true test: Toward more authentic and equitable assessment. *Phi Delta Kappan* 70:703–13.

Books

Hoffman, Banesh. 1962. *The Tyranny of Testing.* New York: Crowell-Collier Press.

Medina, Noe, and D. Monty Neill. 1988. *Fallout from the Testing Explosion: How 100 Million Standardized Exams Undermine Equity and Excellence in America's Public Schools.* Cambridge, Mass.: Fair Test.

Owen, D. 1985. *None of the Above: Behind the Myth of Scholastic Aptitude.* Boston: Houghton Mifflin.

Smith, Frank. 1988. *Insult to Intelligence: The Bureaucratic Invasion of Our Classrooms.* Portsmouth, N.H.: Heinemann.

Figure 9.1 Starter bibliography of critiques of standardized tests and testing

"not good enough." If substantially more than half the students taking a standardized test begin scoring significantly above the mean or average, the test will eventually be revised so that once again it predicts that literally half the students who take the revised test will be "below average." As Wiggins puts it, "such scoring insures that, *by design*, at least half of the student population is always made to feel inept and discouraged about their work, while the other half often has a feeling of achievement that is illusory" (Wiggins 1989, p. 710).

Wiggins points out another reason why the design of norm-referenced tests should concern educators. Designing them so that the distribution of scores resembles a bell-shaped "normal"

1. The purpose of standardized tests, by their very nature, is to rank-order students, teachers, and schools, and thereby label some as less successful than others, or even as failures—not to improve education.
2. Standardized tests are inherently discriminatory.
3. Standardized tests are administered discriminately as well: that is, not administered equally to all segments of the population.
4. Standardized tests tend to perpetuate class differences and educational inequality.
5. Standardized tests give a false impression of objectivity and consequently of equal opportunity and fairness.
6. For many young children, standardized testing results in "death at an early age"—or at least to a life sentence.
7. Standardized tests are biased against those whose intellectual strengths are not in verbal and logical-mathematical areas and whose strongest learning style is not analytic, sequential, part-to-whole.
8. Standardized tests do not reflect current models of child development, or of cognitive development and learning.
9. Standardized tests tend to focus educators' attention on what students do not understand, do not know, or cannot do, in situations that are unlike the learning opportunities encountered in daily life.
10. Standardized tests tend to discourage effective teaching and engaged learning; in fact, their widespread use actively encourages poor teaching and merely going through the motions of learning.
11. Standardized tests discourage much-needed educational reforms.
12. Standardized tests undermine and deny the professionalism of teachers.
13. Standardized tests frequently are not valid; specifically, they may not meet appropriate criteria for content or construct validity.
14. Thus, scores on standardized tests may either overestimate or underestimate students' ability to engage in the intellectual tasks that are supposedly assessed.
15. Standardized tests do not tell educators what they really need to know about children's developing literacy in order to facilitate their development as readers and writers, thinkers and learners.

Figure 9.2 Criticisms of standardized tests and testing

curve not only condemns half the students to being "below average," but also implies that education has no effect, or only a random effect, upon learning! Wiggins quotes Bloom et al. (1981, pp. 52–53):

> There is nothing sacred about the normal curve. It is the distribution most appropriate to chance and random activity.

> Education is a purposeful activity, and we seek to have the students learn what we have to teach. . . . [W]e may even insist that our efforts are unsuccessful to the extent that the distribution of achievement approximates the normal distribution.

Thus norm-referenced tests have nothing to do with promoting good education. Indeed, because they condemn half of our children to being considered "below average," such tests contribute to lowered self-esteem that in turn discourages learning. By their very nature, the primary purpose of such tests is to rank order children, teachers, and schools, and to render negative and usually pernicious judgments on the basis of such rank ordering.

2. *Standardized tests are inherently discriminatory*—not necessarily because anyone wants them to be, but because it is literally impossible for them to be equally fair to children from diverse backgrounds. Tests tend, almost inevitably, to reflect the test-makers' background as to social class, culture, ethnicity, region, gender, age, and life experience, and thus to discriminate against children whose lives and backgrounds are significantly different. Consider the following examples from Edelsky and Harman (1988):

> 1. [Shows map of playground.] In walking from the teetertotter directly to the door, which of these would you pass first?
> picnic table   bike   slide

Edelsky and Harman note that in Arizona, for example, children play on "see-saws" rather than *teetertotters*, and many second-graders walk "straight" to a door, not *directly*. Thus the test question may be confusing because of language differences.

> 2. [Teacher reads aloud.] Mark the word with the same vowel sound as in *for*.
> wart   drop   roll   farther

The authors comment that "In parts of Texas and New Mexico, *for* is /far/. What then is *farther* or *wart* in that dialect?" (Edelsky and Harman 1988, p. 162). Are they both pronounced with an /ar/ sound, with the result that there are *two* correct answers rather than just one? I confess I don't know. But in my own dialect, *none* of the suggested answers would be correct.

Another source of test bias is found in questions that assume a cultural experience or perspective that is not shared by all children. Take this example from Neill and Medina's "Standardized Testing: Harmful to Educational Health" (1989, p. 692):

> The WISC-R . . . asks, "What is the thing to do when you cut your finger?" According to the test makers, the best response is, "Put a Band-Aid on it." They give partial credit for the response, "Go to the hospital," but they award no credit for "Cry," "Bleed," or "Suck on it."
>
> Minority children usually perform poorly on this item. A few years ago, a Baltimore sociologist asked several inner-city youths why they answered the question in the way they did. She found that many of these youngsters selected "Go to the hospital," because they thought that *cut* meant a big cut. Or they thought that *cut* meant a small cut—so they answered "Suck on it," since they didn't have Band-Aids in their homes. [This study was described in "The 'Culture Fair' WISC-R I.Q. Test," *The Testing Digest* Spring 1981, p. 21]

Neill and Medina point out that giving such "wrong" answers to just a few questions can cause a student's "I.Q." (or "achievement") to be severely underestimated, "with possibly life-scarring results" (1989, p. 692).

Ironically, these same authors note, attempts to create "culture-free" tests have also been found to work against minority youths and those from low-income families. Why? Possibly because adults in those households rarely ask children the kinds of questions found on such tests: questions removed from real-life context and questions to which the examiner already knows the answer (Heath 1983). In contrast, middle-class children are more likely to be accustomed "simply through cultural immersion" to respond to such questions (Neill and Medina 1989, p. 692).

3. *Standardized tests are administered discriminately as well: that is, not administered equally to all segments of the population.* In a recent survey by the National Center for Fair and Open Testing, it was found that standardized testing is most prevalent in the southern states, and in large urban school systems—"locales that tend to serve higher-than-average proportions of minority students and students from low-income families" (Neill and Medina 1989, p. 689; see also Medina and Neill 1988). The intent may not be discriminatory, but the result is: Children from minority and low-income families have a greater-than-average chance of suffering from the harmful effects of standardized testing.

4. *Standardized tests tend to perpetuate class differences and educational inequality.* It should not be surprising that standardized test

scores correlate strongly with socioeconomic status (Ramist and Arbeiter 1984, cited in Owen 1985, p. 206), since the ability to do well on such tests requires an ability to think like the test-makers. Therefore, children from lower socioeconomic families have a better-than-even chance of scoring below the mean of the norming population. Standardized tests help perpetuate the lower socioeconomic status of families across the generations because test scores are often used to assign children to reading groups and remedial or "gifted" classes. The children in lower reading groups and remedial classes receive a relatively impoverished education, in comparison with their peers (for example, more skills work, less actual reading), which in turn decreases the likelihood of their pursuing education beyond high school (or even until graduation). And their lower level of education contributes to maintaining their lower socioeconomic status and to raising their own children in environments that will perpetuate the cycle. Thus, whether deliberately or inadvertently, standardized tests contribute to "keeping the poor in their place." Irrespective of our political or moral philosophy, this is a luxury our country can ill afford. (Sources for this line of reasoning include Edelsky and Harman 1988; Wiggins 1989; Neill and Medina 1989; Corbett 1989; "Helping Underachievers Succeed" 1989; Shannon 1985; and Hillerich 1985.)

> **"**Thus, whether deliberately or inadvertently, standardized tests contribute to "keeping the poor in their place." Irrespective of our political or moral philosophy, this is a luxury our country can ill afford.**"**

5. *Standardized tests give a false impression of objectivity and consequently of equal opportunity and fairness.* One of the original aims in developing standardized tests was to avoid inequality and partiality, through "objectivity": It was assumed that if all teachers evaluated all of their students with the same evaluative instruments, objectivity and thus fairness would be guaranteed. The preceding criticisms of standardized tests certainly indicate that sameness does not guarantee equality, but neither does it guarantee "objectivity." Citing Hoffman (1962, pp. 60–61), Neill and Medina put it this way: "*objective* merely means that the tests can be scored by machines, not by subjective human scorers." The questions, the testing situation, the format and requirements of the test: all can still reflect bias, even inadvertently and despite significant efforts to avoid bias. To do well on the tests, part of what test-takers must do is consciously try to think like the test-makers: Success in test-taking requires both an ability and a willingness to "play the game," something that not all children are equally prepared to do. Thus, "the purported objectivity of tests is often no more than the standardization of bias. The replacement of the potential bias of individual judg-

ment with the numerical bias of an 'objective' test is not progress'' (Neill and Medina 1989, p. 692).

6. *For many young children, standardized testing results in ''death at an early age''—or at least in a life sentence.* Once assigned to a lower reading group on the basis of some standardized or basal test, few children are ever moved to higher groups, despite evidence that they are reading well. Take, for example, the case of Adam:

> When Adam was 9 years old he moved to a new school in another district. In his old school he'd been in the top reading group. In his new school, he was put in the bottom group. Why? Not because of a difference in the schools. In fact, both schools were quite similar in socio-economic makeup and in their expectations of students. No, Adam was misplaced because he did poorly on the reading test administered by the new school. And why did he do poorly? Test anxiety.
>
> Even so, it was soon evident that Adam could read better than the other students in the bottom group. Was he put into a higher group? No. Nothing that simple. Instead, he was retested. This time he wasn't so anxious, so he did a little better. That got him transferred into the middle group.
>
> After a while, because he was doing extremely well in the middle reading group, Adam was tested yet again. By now he felt quite comfortable at school and taking the test didn't make him anxious at all. As a result his test scores showed what had been true all along: He should be in the top reading group. Was he put in that group? No. Nothing as logical as that. Instead, noting that the children in the top group were a full book ahead of him by now, Adam's teacher said he was too far behind to join them. (Sternberg 1989, p. 62)

Perhaps Adam should be considered lucky: He at least moved to the middle reading group. Various studies document the fact that children tend to remain in assigned ''ability'' groups throughout a school year, and across grade levels (Shannon 1985 refers to several studies documenting this). And children may be assigned to low-ability groups or classes as young as kindergarten age (Durkin 1987). Thus, even if no other factors operated to keep children in these groups, their lowered self-esteem might make the implicit prediction of incompetence a self-fulfilling prophecy, thanks to placements based largely on standardized and basal tests (see Corbett 1989, citing Tyler and Wolf 1974).

The likelihood of children remaining in such groups ''for life'' is compounded, however, by the kind of instruction they typically receive. Research suggests the devastating long-term effects of being assigned to lower-ability reading groups: Year after year, students in those groups receive less appropriate and less effective instruction and experience fewer genuine learning opportunities than their classmates. They receive more "instruction" and more skills work, with significantly fewer opportunities to read; they read aloud more, and spend less time reading silently; and they receive more instruction to "sound out" troublesome words and less advice to try to determine meaning from context. They also receive more corrections of their miscues, and consequently have less opportunity to develop effective strategies for reading independently; more questions on the literal meaning of texts and less encouragement to interpret or evaluate or relate to the text; and more drill and flashcards, with fewer opportunities to read and engage in creative activities relating to books (see summaries in Hillerich 1985 and Shannon 1985).

The use of standardized tests to rank order students encourages the assignment of students to ability groups and thus inadvertently encourages differential treatment. Too often, then, scores on standardized tests result in "death at an early age": Many children are assigned to a lower-ability group that becomes self-perpetuating, and from which they can rarely escape.

7. *Standardized tests are biased against those whose intellectual strengths are not in the verbal and logical-mathematical areas and whose strongest learning style is not analytic, sequential, part-to-whole.* Because the vast majority of young children are global, whole-to-part learners more than part-to-whole learners, it is no wonder that standardized tests (and all the skills activities that resemble them) are difficult and often meaningless for most young children. However, the nature of standardized tests penalizes students of any age if their strengths are in areas other than those limited ones assessed by most standardized tests, or if their learning style is more global than analytic, or more practical than abstract. Thus, incredible numbers of our youth are judged to be deficient when we might better view them as having *different* intellectual strengths and learning styles from those traditionally recognized and rewarded by society (see Gregorc 1986; Dunn and Dunn 1978; K. Butler 1988; Carbo 1984 and October 1988; Gardner 1985, 1987; Sternberg 1989). Reflecting our own ignorance and failure to appreciate diversity, standardized tests are one means by which we condemn many children to defeat.

And "diversity" raises another issue: If it is true, as many researchers have concluded, that certain minority groups tend to be more global in learning style than mainstream America, then in this respect also standardized tests are inherently discriminatory against those minorities. (See, for example, Janice Hale-Benson's *Black Children: Their Roots, Culture, and Learning Styles*, 1986.)

8. *Standardized tests do not reflect current models of child development, or of cognitive development and learning.* We know that though there are developmental trends, children do not all develop in the same way at the same time, nor do they all develop the same intellectual and learning strengths. Standardized tests, however, reflect the implicit assumption that all children—or at least the ones we are willing to consider "successful"—will be roughly *the same* in development and strengths. Furthermore, standardized tests promote the conviction that there are single right answers to most questions, thus thwarting rather than encouraging children to reason and to deal with complex problems and issues. Such tests also reflect the notion that complex processes and abilities can be learned if they are broken down into small pieces that are then taught and tested—and often retaught and retested. This reflects the concepts of learning popular in the 1920s rather than current learning theory developed in the past two decades. We now know that even successful test performance is no guarantee of successful performance in the complex process itself—let us say, a process such as reading. *Successful test performance is evidence only of successful test performance.* (See, for example, Neill and Medina 1989; Edelsky and Harman 1988; Wiggins 1989; and the discussion of reading in "Reading and Reading Assessment" later in this chapter.)

9. *Standardized tests tend to focus educators' attention on what students do not understand, do not know, or cannot do, in situations that are unlike the learning opportunities encountered in daily life.* Though ostensibly the tests may exist to determine students' strengths, in fact, the tests do not give children the opportunity to demonstrate the full range of what they understand, know, and can do. Such an emphasis on weaknesses rather than strengths is a logical manifestation of the transmission concept of learning, according to which every child should learn the same things at the same time, in the same way—or be deemed less than fully successful. *Thus, in a very real sense, standardized tests are failure-oriented.*

10. *Standardized tests tend to discourage effective teaching and engaged learning; in fact, their widespread use actively encourages poor teaching and merely going through the motions of learning.* The tests do this in a variety of ways, and by various means, as previous and subsequent sections will suggest. One major reason, though, is that the mania for testing is currently so severe that "teaching to the test" has become an obsession in many schools and classrooms, crowding out other, more meaningful and more beneficial kinds of activities.

This is documented, for the teaching of writing, by Charles Suhor, who gathered both research data and personal opinion, the latter from a polling of 350 state and local supervisors of English and language arts. From his informal polling, Suhor concluded: "With few exceptions the testimony on objective tests was consistent and damning: both standardized, norm-referenced and criterion-referenced competency tests discourage writing instruction. . . . By contrast, praise was abundant for writing samples. . . . " (Suhor 1985, p. 636, as cited in Haney and Madaus 1989, p. 686).

The current "testmania" is documented by T. S. Richards (a pseudonym), whose school district mounted a concerted effort to raise test scores. Richards shares the comments of teachers he interviewed:

> Nan, a 3rd-grade teacher, complained about how the writing section of a statewide test takes away from teaching kids to write: "The lion's share of the test is multiple-choice questions on capitalization, punctuation, and usage. They call that writing? All the creative things—the 'thinking' things—suffer."

> Ginny, a 4th-grade teacher, was aghast at the extraordinary amount of drill and worksheet material the central office was sending her. She was supposed to use it to raise state test scores. "Don't ask about the effects of test-preparation and testing on the curriculum," she exclaimed. "The tests *are* the curriculum." (Richards 1989, p. 66)

According to the teachers, the author notes, "learning is down, and so is their morale." But as a fifth-grade teacher said, "What suffers most is the *kids*" (Richards 1989, pp. 65–66).

Unfortunately, this school district is not an isolated example. For example, Madaus cites two articles from the *Newark Star Ledger*, according to which the New Jersey state department of education admitted that not only do New Jersey teachers teach to the state test, but the department provides local school districts with copies of tests from previous years, and some teachers use these to drill students for weeks and even months (Madaus 1985, p. 616). It's possible that the situation has changed since 1981 when the articles were published, but that seems not particularly likely, given the *increased* national emphasis upon testing and accountability. In short, *standardized testing has a stranglehold on too many of our nation's schools.*

11. *Standardized tests discourage much-needed educational reforms.* By their very nature, standardized tests promote a damaging and dysfunctional concept of education, and their use damages countless children in innumerable ways: yet they not only persist, they flourish. One unfortunate consequence of the misplaced faith in standardized testing is that schools and school systems are afraid to engage in educational reform, afraid to encourage or even allow teachers to involve children in activities significantly different from what will be included on the standardized tests. Furthermore, the very cost of such tests and testing makes educational reform more difficult. The schools' limited funding must be spent on destructive kinds of evaluation rather than on books for children to read, paper and writing utensils for them to write, and extensive staff development efforts for teachers to grow in their understanding of how children learn and how they themselves can foster language, literacy, and learning. As Farr puts it, "The focus on getting better test scores will drive real instructional reform right out of the schools" (1987, p. 22).

12. *Standardized tests undermine and deny the professionalism of teachers.* Encouraging teaching to the test is, of course, one major way standardized tests undermine teachers' professionalism. Whole language educators and others grounded in a transactional philosophy of learning know that the commonly tested skills are likely to flourish if genuine literacy is fostered, but even they may sometimes get caught up in pressures to teach extensively to the test. True, many whole language teachers find that a relatively short time spent helping children learn test-taking skills is sufficient to produce scores that are comparable to, if not better than, the scores of other classes in their schools. But though this may solve the problem of the test scores, it undermines the teachers' integrity as it denies the validity of their professional judgment about the children's growth and needs.

Standardized tests, in fact, may not only distress and demoralize teachers but encourage disillusionment and cynicism, even dishonesty. The same can happen to administrators at all levels, as T. S. Richards' article describes and documents:

> I've heard numerous stories of teachers writing the correct answers on the chalkboard, suggesting that students change wrong answers while they're still taking the test, even changing answers themselves after students have turned in their tests. Further, I have direct evidence that the answer sheets of the students who scored lowest on our district tests are being removed before they are sent to the central office, where district averages are computed. (Richards 1989, p. 66)

Obviously these—and countless other—teachers and administrators are succumbing to the relentless and ridiculous pressure to produce high test scores. Oddly enough, they are responding to irrational demands in rational, if dishonest, ways.

But teachers and administrators should not have to engage in such dishonesty in order to gain approval, promotion, or funding—*especially when high test scores may reflect* poor *educational practices: namely, teaching to the test instead of teaching in ways that foster engaged learning.*

13. *Standardized tests frequently are not valid; specifically, they may not meet appropriate criteria for content or construct validity.* Content validity depends upon the match between the test items and what has been emphasized in the curriculum or classroom—whether the test assesses what was "taught" or what the students were expected to learn. Construct validity examines how well a test actually correlates with what it purports to measure—for example, how well results on a "reading" test actually correlate with ability to read authentic texts in daily life situations (my interpretation and elaboration of Farr and Carey 1986, p. 148). Standardized tests may reflect neither—particularly in whole language classrooms, where children engage in learning experiences far different from the experience of taking standard tests.

In more traditional classrooms, though, standardized tests may correlate with or predict success in school tasks—particularly since standardized tests tend to resemble typical school tasks and tests, and vice versa. This, of course, is no accident. Both teaching and evaluation often reflect Edward Thorndike's behavioral laws of learning from the 1920s, which lead to the teaching, practice, and testing of isolated skills: What is tested is not the ability to read a variety of materials for various purposes, for example, but the ability to perform on skills tests that closely resemble the worksheets assigned. Indeed, one of Thorndike's laws states that the learning of a particular skill (stimulus–

response connection) should be tested separately, and under the same conditions as it was learned. Since Thorndike's outmoded laws of learning underlie both the typical basal reader worksheets and tests and what is often assessed on standardized tests, the results of these may well resemble one another.

On the other hand, there is not necessarily a strong correlation between the abilities that standardized tests *purport* to measure and the *actual* development of those abilities, or the exercise of them in appropriate situations. For example: ''A study of 1000 children showed no particular relationship between their actual reading and their scores on the California Test of Basic Skills. Some children scored high but read poorly; others scored high and read well; some low scorers read well and others didn't'' (Altwerger and Resta 1986, as summarized in Edelsky and Harman 1988, p. 159). It should not be surprising that there is not necessarily much correlation between ability to perform on standardized tests of reading, on the one hand, and ability to read and construct meaning from authentic texts, on the other: The actual ability to construct meaning from normal kinds of texts is not what the standardized tests are measuring. They commonly measure the skills taught in basal reading programs.

In such basal programs, authentic texts are typically ''reduced'' to stilted, artificial texts for beginning readers, and often to abridged and adapted texts for older students. But reading is reduced even further, to the bits and pieces of skills taught during reading groups and practiced in workbooks. It is these skills, isolated from normal reading, that are then tested and ''reified'': that is, treated as if they were *real* reading (K. Goodman et al. 1988, pp. 85 and 108; see also Neill and Medina 1989 and Shannon 1989). Such isolated skills—including comprehension skills—are commonly what has been tested on standardized tests. The tests do not genuinely assess students' ability to construct meaning from a variety of real-life texts, much less their ability to do so in various real-life situations.

Standardized tests thus reflect but also promote an inappropriate and damaging concept of literacy: Learning to read and write and reason are thought of as merely a matter of mastering reading, writing, and thinking ''skills.'' Nothing could be much further from the truth.

14. *Thus, scores on standardized tests may either overestimate or underestimate students' ability to engage in the intellectual tasks that are supposedly assessed.* For example, it is possible for students to read well yet do poorly on tests of reading achievement, for all of the reasons previously mentioned in this discussion of standardized

> **''**On the other hand, there is not necessarily a strong correlation between the abilities that standardized tests *purport* to measure and the *actual* development of those abilities, or the exercise of them in appropriate situations.**''**

tests—and more. What may not be so obvious is how it is possible to do well on such tests, yet not have developed effective strategies for reading many of the kinds of texts encountered in everyday life. Often, what the test questions require is little more than the ability to locate the "correct" answer within the passage, and/or an ability to manipulate language. Consider, for example, this nonsense passage and the common kinds of "comprehension" questions that follow (Weaver 1988, pp. 36 and 51):

> The blonke was maily, like all the others. Unlike the other blonkes, however, it had spiss crinet completely covering its fairney cloots and concealing, just below one of them, a small wam.
> This particular blonke was quite drumly—lennow, in fact, and almost samded. When yerden, it did not quetch like the other blonkes, or even blore. The others blored very readily.
> It was probably his bellytimber that had made the one blonke so drumly. The bellytimber was quite kexy, had a strong shawk, and was apparently venenated. There was only one thing to do with the venenated bellytimber: givel it in the flosh. This would be much better than to sparple it in the wong, since the blonkes that were not drumly could icchen in the wong, but not in the flosh.

> *Comprehension questions*
>
> 1. *Literal:* Where was the small wam?
> 2. *Translation:* What is "drumly"?
> 3. *Inference:* Why weren't the other blonkes drumly?
> 4. *Reorganization:* In what way(s) was the drumly blonke like/unlike the others?
> 5. *Evaluation:* If bellytimber is venenated, is it wise to givel it in the flosh? Why or why not?

With careful attention to the passage and a little thought, but not necessarily any real comprehension, it is possible to "correctly" answer even the inference and evaluation questions—and without a set of multiple choice answers from which to choose. Thus, students can often score high on tests of "reading comprehension" while comprehending very little. Perhaps this is partly what accounts for the fact that our students are doing well on the National Assessment of Educational Progress test questions that assess "basic" skills, while performing miserably on questions that genuinely require an ability to construct meaning from texts, and to draw upon their own knowledge and experience to reason about ideas encountered in print.

Valencia et al. nicely summarize some of the problems stemming from this lack of correlation between "reading achievement'' as measured on standardized tests and actual ability to construct meaning from a variety of texts:

> if we equate high scores on existing tests with good reading, we may be led to a false sense of security. Conversely, low scores may lead us to believe that students are not reading well when, by a more valid set of criteria, they are. . . . In short, tests may be insensitive to growth in the abilities we most want to foster and may be misguiding instruction. (Valencia et al. 1989, p. 57)

15. *Standardized tests do not tell educators what they really need to know about children's developing literacy in order to facilitate their development as readers and writers, thinkers and learners.* What reading tests measure is not really reading but a variety of other factors. What writing tests measure is not really writing, if they are like the aforementioned state assessment; and even tests that involve a writing sample are inadequate to provide a representative and fair sampling of the writer's abilities. Similarly, tests of thinking skills rarely test the ability to reason about problems and issues as complex as those that students, even children, often face in their daily lives. In order to assess children's developing literacy and learning in ways that are both fair to the child and useful to the teacher and informative to parents, educators need to develop a broad repertoire of assessment measures. Only such a multifaceted approach to assessment is likely to provide sufficient data for evaluation and for educational decision-making.

STANDARDIZED TESTS, VALIDITY, AND ACCOUNTABILITY

What too few educators and parents realize is that standardized tests of reading do not reflect construct validity—that is, ''reading is not what reading tests test'' (Farr and Carey 1986, p. 16). Furthermore, the test scores are typically used in a variety of ways that further invalidate the test results: uses such as assigning children to alleged ability groups and, worse yet, determining promotion or retention, and even denying high school graduation.

Testing experts repeatedly point out the inappropriateness of using a single test score, or even a collection of such invalid test scores, as the sole means for making educational decisions. Such use further invalidates tests that are already invalid, in that they measure both more and less than, or things other than, what they purport to measure. As Johnston says, ''invalidity lies as much in the claims which we make about what we have measured as in the instrument itself'' (1983, p. 50). And Farr and Carey repeatedly emphasize that "the validity of any test must be determined in relation to the use that will be made of the results" (1986, p. 2). The many objections to standardized tests stem as much from the uses made of test results as from the tests themselves.

In their concern for "accountability," it is typically politicians and others far removed from the schools and from children who demand that standardized and state-mandated tests be conducted. It is time, I think, for the tables to be turned—time to hold bureaucrats and politicians accountable for what their demand for test results does to children and, inevitably, to schools and to society. But others closer to the educational enterprise are also responsible for how the test results are interpreted and the uses to which the results are put. Educators face a major challenge in educating first themselves and second parents, the public, and the politicians about the misleading and invalid results of standardized tests, not to mention the pernicious effects of the ways in which test results are often used. Thus de-emphasizing the influence of standardized tests will require, I think, both intense educational effort and concerted political effort.

At the same time as we inform and then mobilize ourselves for such action, however, we as educators can do other things to encourage the development, implementation, and acceptance of more appropriate means of assessment and evaluation. One is to develop better standardized and state-mandated tests. The following section of this chapter discusses recent insights into the nature of the reading process itself and then examines efforts to incorporate some of these insights into current state assessments of reading, specifically in Michigan and Illinois. However, these tests are subject to many of the same objections as traditional standardized tests (and some objections unique to them as well). Clearly, such tests—no matter how improved—can never be as valid or as valuable as a combination of informal assessment means and measures.

Thus, we as educators cannot expect to rely on the newer state assessment tests as more valid measures of reading. We must assess reading—and writing, and literacy—through a variety of informal and semiformal means, collecting performance samples and making observations of literacy events in a variety of situations and contexts, and supplementing these with data from interviews, questionnaires, and student self-evaluations. In short, we must make assessment an ongoing activity in our classrooms, through a variety of means. This is an area in which whole language educators have made significant progress (see, for instance, *The Whole Language Evaluation Book*, edited by K. Goodman, Goodman, and Hood 1989). Chapter 10 will explore such varied and informal means of assessment, for as various reading and assessment experts have concluded, informal assessment has the greatest potential to be valid (see Farr and Carey 1986, p. 151).

READING AND READING ASSESSMENT

In the past two decades, our understanding of the reading and writing processes has burgeoned, along with our understanding of how people learn. The most recent National Assessment of Educational Progress tests reflect an attempt to take account of this understanding, as do assessment tests being developed in several states. This section first explores some of what has been learned about reading, to help clarify why new kinds of assessments are necessary. Then we consider the new assessment tests developed in Michigan and Illinois, two states that are pioneering in the effort to make assessment reflect the new knowledge.

Reading as Constructing Meaning

It has been common for educators as well as the uninformed public to assume that reading is a matter of identifying words and getting their meaning, and that learning to read is therefore a matter of developing skills for identifying words. This view, however, is now understood to be simply *wrong*. Reading, even for beginners, involves far more. We saw this in Chapter 4 with Gillian, as she read *Where the Wild Things Are*: Quite naturally, she had learned to predict what was coming next, and she was in the process of learning to match her predictions with what was on the page. As she continued to read, she confirmed or corrected what she had just said—changing her original ''jungle'' to ''forest,'' for example, by using the word's initial letter/sound in conjunction with context and her prior knowledge of the story. Thus, Gillian had learned strategies for constructing meaning, not merely skills for identifying words. In fact, her effort to construct meaning enabled her to ''get'' many of the words she otherwise could not yet have identified.

Still, contemporary research into the reading process tells us that as educators, we have overemphasized the identification of words while underemphasizing the construction of meaning. Both points could be developed and supported in considerable detail (see Smith's *Understanding Reading*, first published in 1971; K. Goodman 1973; Pearson 1986; Weaver 1988), but for brevity I shall simply invite you to engage in two activities that should help clarify the concern about overemphasizing words while underemphasizing the construction of meaning.

> **❝** Still, contemporary research into the reading process tells us that as educators, we have overemphasized the identification of words while underemphasizing the construction of meaning. **❞**

First, read the following passage through *once* at normal speed, then look away and write down the sentences verbatim:

> The young men and women walked round and round the plaza in the hot electric night: the men one way, the girls another, never speaking to each other. In the northern sky the lightning flapped. It was like a religious ceremony which had lost all meaning, but at which they still wore their best clothes. (Graham Greene, *The Power and the Glory* 1940, p. 139)

If you compare your version with the original, you will probably find that though you preserved most of the essential content, you made some changes in the wording—just a minute or two later, you could no longer remember the exact words. This experience is, of course, typical: Research shows that within half a second, we begin forgetting the exact words we've read (see Weaver 1988, pp. 120–121, for further discussion). Why, then, have educators put such a premium on saying or identifying all the words correctly?

Certainly it is easy to demonstrate that identifying all the words will not necessarily result in grasping the meaning. Take the following passage from a textbook on literary criticism; this is the second paragraph (easier than the first) from "Metacommentary," an essay by Fredric Jameson. Try to read the passage word for word:

> What is felt to be content varies, of course, with the historical situation: thus the concept of a symbol once served a negative, critical function, as a wedge against an older Victorian moralizing criticism. Now, however, along with the other basic components of the new-critical ideology such as irony and point of view, it all too often encourages the most irresponsible interpretation of an ethical or mythical and religious character. To name a symbol is to turn it into an allegory, to pronounce the word irony is to find that the thing itself, with all its impossible lived tension, has vanished into thin air. No wonder we feel symbolism in the novel to be such a lie: no wonder Williams' attack on metaphor came as a liberation to a whole generation of American poets! (Jameson 1986)

Typically my undergraduate students, preservice teachers, find that they can read this passage almost flawlessly; they can identify the words in the sense of saying them, and they even know what most of the individual words supposedly mean. But they get virtually no meaning from the passage. Identifying the words is not sufficient for constructing meaning when a person lacks background knowledge and experience in what is being discussed or described.

What we have learned about reading, then, is that our commonsense notions are much too simplistic, indeed downright erroneous. To summarize briefly, what we have learned includes the following:

1. Reading is a cognitive act, an active process of making meaning.

2. Reading is an individual act, influenced by a variety of social and situational factors: The meaning constructed from a text will, of necessity, be influenced by the reader's prior knowledge, background, and life experiences; perception of the situation and the demands of the reading task; reading strategies or lack of them; and engagement or lack of engagement in the reading act.

3. Thus, meaning does not reside in the text; it is constructed from the text by each reader, to some degree uniquely. The author–reader communication is never a perfect one.

4. Recall is virtually inseparable from interpretation.

5. Identifying words and getting meaning are by no means the same: Readers can identify words without getting much meaning; and conversely, they can get the essence of a passage without identifying all the words.

6. Good readers do not read flawlessly (either aloud or silently), but they tend to notice when meaning goes awry; they focus on constructing meaning more than on identifying words correctly.

7. Good readers continually monitor their own comprehension and call upon a variety of ''fix-it'' strategies as needed to help in constructing meaning.

8. Good readers are often *consciously aware* of the reading strategies at their disposal. (Strategies of which readers are consciously aware are now often called *metacognitive strategies*.)

Valencia et al. offer a typical description of good readers, based on the current understanding of reading and what good readers do:

> From this perspective, we no longer define good readers as those who are able to decode precisely all the words on the page but rather as those who can build meaning by integrating their own knowledge with information presented by an author. Good readers are not those who demonstrate mastery of a series of isolated skills, but those who can apply important skills flexibly for a variety of purposes in a variety of authentic reading situations. Good readers are not those who can read short pieces of text and answer literal interpretation questions, but those who can read longer, more complete, authentic texts about a variety of topics and respond to them thoughtfully and critically. Finally, good readers are not those who simply read on demand in school, but those who have developed a disposition for reading and a commitment to its lifelong pursuit. (Valencia et al. 1989, p. 58)

What researchers from various disciplines have also concluded is that a part-to-whole approach emphasizing word identification skills *may actually operate to prevent many children from becoming good readers*, as defined above. They never quite learn that identifying all the words isn't the purpose of reading, nor do they develop a sufficiently large or flexible range of strategies for constructing meaning. Typically a whole-to-part approach, focusing on the use of word identification strategies within the context of meaningful reading, is more effective. *Thus, one major implication for educators is that skills/strategies for identifying words should be used and practiced while constructing meaning from authentic texts, not separately.*

Together, the newer insights into reading and learning to read have led educators to develop definitions of reading that focus on the active construction of meaning rather than on the paper-and-pencil mastery of reading skills. For example:

> Reading is the process of constructing meaning from written texts. . . . A text is not so much a vessel containing meaning as it is a source of partial information that enables the reader to use already-possessed knowledge to determine the intended meaning. (Anderson et al. 1985, pp. 7–8)

> Reading is the process of constructing meaning through the dynamic interaction among the reader's existing knowledge, the information suggested by the written language, and the context of the reading situation. ("Reading Redefined," 1984)

These definitions, and the elaboration of them, emphasize the newer understanding that meaning is not *in* the text itself but rather is constructed as the reader transacts with the text (see Rosenblatt 1978). Thus, reading *is* comprehension. Comprehension is a process of constructing meaning.

New Assessments of Reading: Michigan and Illinois

As a broad spectrum of educators are aware, most standardized and state assessments of reading do not adequately or appropriately test reading. They tend, for example, to focus on isolated skills, including comprehension skills, when this in reality is not what good readers do. Thus, they encourage instruction that is not only not maximally beneficial but downright harmful to many children.

Figure 9.3, from Valencia and Pearson 1987, contrasts what we know from current reading theory with what most formalized assessment tests do and don't do. In developing new assessment tests in Michigan and Illinois, these scholars and others have attempted to avoid the pitfalls of most reading assessment tests, while incorporating new elements that reflect our current understanding of reading (see Valencia et al. 1989;

Current views of reading suggest...	Yet reading assessments...
prior knowledge is an important determinant of reading comprehension.	fail to assess its impact on comprehension and try to mask its effects by using many short passages about unfamiliar topics.
naturally occurring texts have topical and structural integrity.	use short pieces of texts that do not approximate the integrity found in most authentic texts.
inferential and critical reading are essential for constructing meaning.	rely predominantly on literal and sentence-level inferential comprehension items.
reading requires the orchestration of many reading skills.	often fragment reading into isolated skills for item development and reporting.
skilled readers apply metacognitive strategies to monitor and comprehend a variety of texts for a variety of purposes.	seldom assess metacognitive strategies.
positive habits and attitudes affect reading achievement and are important goals of reading instruction.	rarely include measures of these literacy experiences.
skilled readers are fluent.	fail to assess fluency.

Figure 9.3   Contrasts between reading theory and reading assessments (Valencia and Pearson 1987, as reproduced in Valencia et al. 1989, p. 58)

Peters and Wixson 1989; Roeber and Dutcher 1989; and several articles in the April 1987 issue of *The Reading Teacher*).

Though there are differences between the Michigan and Illinois tests, both stem from a view of reading as involving the construction of meaning, and both reflect a concerted effort to select authentic texts: full-length stories or articles (500–2,000 words) that are taken from classroom materials such as children's magazines, literature, and content area texts.

Both tests consist of a primary test component, *constructing meaning* (or, "Comprehension"), and three supporting components *that are to be used in deciding how to interpret the score on the "constructing meaning" section*. In effect, these three supporting components are designed to help teachers and parents decide how valid the score on the constructing meaning component might be.

All three of these supporting sections are constructed with reference to the particular passages in the *constructing meaning* section. The *topic familiarity* section is designed to determine how familiar the student is with each topic about which he or she will subsequently read, in order to assess the positive or negative effect of prior knowledge upon the student's ability to construct meaning. The *metacognitive knowledge* section is designed to assess the reader's understanding of strategies and aspects of the text itself that would help in constructing meaning from each passage in the test. The *attitudes and self-perception* section is designed to assess the student's degree of interest in each passage read, his or her ability to understand it, and how hard he or she worked to read it and answer the questions. Thus, the scores on these three passages are not meant to stand alone, but rather to help teachers and parents understand why the student did well or poorly in constructing meaning from a particular passage.

Figure 9.4 offers ''a preview of the new reading tests'' (Peters and Wixson 1989, p. 53). The aforementioned articles on the Michigan and Illinois reading assessments further clarify and exemplify the nature of the tests, as well as the rationale.

Some Concerns About the New Assessments

Perhaps the greatest asset of such tests is that they focus exclusively on comprehension, not on word identification skills. Thus, instead of encouraging the teaching of word identification skills as ends in themselves, the tests implicitly encourage teachers to attend more to constructing meaning from authentic texts. Furthermore, the tests at least imply, by their very construction, that a single, unexamined score on a reading test (for example, the *constructing meaning* score) can never, by itself, be an adequate measure of reading ability.

Unfortunately, however, these tests are also fraught with problems, as even casual inspection of a ''preview of the new reading tests'' suggests (Figure 9.4). For example, the true–false nature of the topic familiarity questions renders them of dubious validity, even without reference to the questions themselves. Correctly answering questions about metacognitive strategies and text features is not the same as actually using these strategies and features. And we surely cannot assume that students will necessarily be honest in responding to questions designed to determine their degree of interest in each passage read and how hard they worked to read and answer questions about it. Initial administration of the test in Michigan indicates that these are only some of the issues legitimately raised with regard to the assessment test's validity and value.

Some of these problems may, of course, be alleviated in subsequent modifications of the test(s). But more important in the long run is the fact that such assessment tests are still subject to many of the same objections as the more typical standardized tests. For example:

1. The purpose of these criterion-referenced tests is not to rank order students, teachers, and schools—but they will almost certainly be used that way.

2. These tests still have the potential for discrimination and bias of various sorts, though that may be minimized somewhat by the greater length of the passages and the supporting sections designed to ferret out characteristics of the reader, with respect to each passage.

3. "Better" questions requiring more than simple recall and simplistic inferencing usually generate a wider range of well-reasoned responses, only one of which is considered right. Therefore, on multiple choice tests, the better the comprehension questions, the greater the likelihood that critical and creative thinkers will give "wrong" answers (see Johnston 1983, p. 45). This practice decreases the construct validity of the test as well as penalizes the best readers and thinkers.

4. While the texts selected for the test may be authentic, still the tests themselves are artificial and unlike the kinds of tasks that readers and writers normally engage in. Furthermore, the texts reflect a severely limited range of genres and functions of print, compared with those that people encounter and need to deal with in daily life.

5. The tests may still be used to focus attention on what students do not know and cannot do, rather than on the reader's strengths. Thus, they can still contribute to "death at an early age."

6. The tests could lead to instruction that is as trivialized as the instruction promoted by standardized tests—for example, instruction focusing on getting students to give right answers to questions about metacognitive strategies rather than on developing the use of those strategies through reading authentic texts.

7. These tests still do not tell educators what they really need to know about children's developing literacy, in order to facilitate their development as readers and writers, thinkers and learners.

8. Ultimately, perhaps most damaging of all, these new and clearly improved tests might lull educators into complacency, encourag-

> **"**Ultimately, perhaps most damaging of all, these new and clearly improved tests might lull educators into complacency, encouraging them to think that 'now we're finally assessing reading the way we ought to be.'**"**

A preview of the new reading tests

"The Dip" is a narrative fiction selection used in Michigan's new reading tests at the 7th-grade level. The story, included in full (1,200 words) on the test, is summarized below. The sample questions are modeled on those that appear on the test.

Comprehension questions for narrative texts such as "The Dip" are written to reflect the key structural elements of stories: theme, setting, character, problem, resolution, conflict, and events. Questions for informational articles reflect nonfiction organizational techniques. Questions for selections at other grade levels reflect developmental differences—for example, finer distinctions about the importance of various story elements are required of upper-grade students than of lower-grade students.

Summary of "The Dip"

A boy named Tick has a private place, the dip, where he likes to go to be alone. However, his privacy—and consequently his special place—is spoiled when another boy intrudes. Tick fights to protect his turf, but is forced to declare a truce. Then something unexpected happens: The boys notice an injured duck and work together to try and save it. The duck dies, but the cooperative experience makes Tick willing to share the dip with the other boy.

Typical questions for "The Dip" (correct answers are starred; rationale for questions is in italics)

• *Constructing Meaning*

Tick and the other kid learned an important lesson about

- A. how to care for an injured animal
- B. how to be alone
- C. sharing with others*
- D. getting their own way

To answer this question students must identify a story theme by using what they know about people in general. The word "sharing" is not used in the story.

What did the other kid make Tick do?

- A. examine his beliefs about sharing the dip*
- B. take care of the injured duck
- C. leave the dip for another place
- D. examine his beliefs about fighting

Students must draw on their own knowledge to decide which character traits are most important to the story. They must be aware of the importance of plot structure to the story.

• *Knowledge About Reading*

Which of these experiences would best help you understand the story?

- A. caring for animals
- B. making a new friend*
- C. playing with others
- D. fighting with others

Students must know how their own experiences relate to understanding a story.

Figure 9.4   A preview of the new reading tests (Peters and Wixson 1989)

The purpose of the first two sections of this story is to

- A. give the main idea of the story
- B. hint at the outcome of the story
- C. outline the story events
- D. describe the setting and the characters*

Students must understand how the different elements of a story interact.

Why does the author write "a look passed between them" in two places in the story?

- A. It tells you that Tick and the other kid cannot get along.
- B. It helps you to understand the setting.
- C. It tells you that Tick will never give up the dip.
- D. It gives you a clue about how the story will end.*

Students must understand how the organizational device of foreshadowing is used.

What would be the best way to find out what the other kid looked like?

- A. Guess from what you know about the other kids.
- B. Make a prediction from the title.
- C. Search the story·for specific information.*
- D. Think about the main idea of the story.

Students must know how to choose a strategy to find information.

• Topic Familiarity

Does being alone help to tell about privacy?

yes _____ no _____

Is keeping your bedroom door closed an example of privacy?

yes _____ no _____

Students must be able to identify the key concept of the story and to demonstrate a range of understanding about it.

• Attitudes and Self-Perception

It was easy for me to answer the questions for "The Dip."

- A. strongly agree
- B. agree
- C. disagree
- D. strongly disagree

I worked carefully to understand so I would do well on "The Dip."

- A. strongly agree
- B. agree
- C. disagree
- D. strongly disagree

I would like to tell my family or friends about "The Dip."

- A. strongly agree
- B. agree
- C. disagree
- D. strongly disagree

Students' answers to these questions provide information about their ability, effort, and interest.

Figure 9.4 (*continued*)

ing them to think that ''now we're finally assessing reading the way we ought to be.'' But no single measure, no matter how improved, is adequate. A reading test simply cannot provide assessment information that is adequate for evaluation and educational decision-making.

Despite their improvements, then, these tests may produce results that are as invalid as those produced by traditional standardized tests, or nearly so. And the test results are similarly subject to misuse that further invalidates those results.

TOWARD INFORMAL ASSESSMENT

The authors of the new reading tests themselves point out that while large-scale assessment can provide data for "agencies charged with monitoring large numbers of students," such data alone do not serve as valid assessments of *individual* progress:

> To be valid, assessments should provide students with multiple opportunities to apply their reading skills to a variety of real-life texts and tasks. Therefore, we advocate moving assessment away from traditional quantifiable tests to a portfolio system. This portfolio system should incorporate multiple indicators of expertise (e.g., comprehension, uses of literacy, metacognitive strategies), multiple measures in various contexts (e.g., reading different genres, reading for different purposes), and ongoing measures of this evolving expertise (e.g., repeated measures over time). Assessment must also take advantage of the many classroom indicators of achievement that cannot easily be reduced to paper-and-pencil measures. (Valencia et al. 1989, p. 59)

In order to provide more valid measures for assessment, these and other scholars are developing a "portfolio" approach to assessment that has far more potential than standardized or state-mandated machine-scorable tests. What I have seen so far, however—a preliminary version of the Michigan Interactive Reading Portfolio—reminds me of a grab bag of assessment instruments that could all too easily be imposed upon the teaching/learning enterprise instead of evolving from it. The underlying reading theory may be contradicted, or at least undermined, by the learning theory implicit in some of the recommendations for instruction and assessment, which reflect a concept of learning as predetermined by the teacher, rather than focusing on the needs and idiosyncratic development of the learners.

With similar aims but a different concept of learning, whole language educators have developed various means and assessment measures that provide a broader, more appropriate, and more valid basis for evaluation than standardized, state-mandated, and basal tests. Such means put the learner at the forefront of accountability: They reflect a conviction that first and foremost, teachers and schools must be accountable to the children for facilitating their learning. Those who have adopted a transactional model of learning are convinced that this focus better enables them to promote literacy and learning, and therefore enables them to be more appropriately accountable to society.

Chapter 10 deals, then, with reconceptualizing and reclaiming assessment and accountability.

C H A P T E R   1 0

Reconceptualizing and Reclaiming Assessment and Accountability

❝Thus, in order to reclaim their classrooms as places where genuine learning and teaching can take place, teachers must reclaim assessment and accountability.**❞**

As Frank Smith points out in *Insult to Intelligence: The Bureaucratic Invasion of Our Classrooms* (1988a), whoever controls assessment in effect controls education. Thus, in order to reclaim their classrooms as places where genuine learning and teaching can take place, teachers must reclaim assessment and accountability. By developing alternative means of documenting students' progress, they can demonstrate the inadequacy and inappropriateness of making educational decisions on the basis of standardized, state-mandated, and end-of-book or unit tests. Although such tests are not likely to fade into oblivion, their harmful effects upon children and society can be minimized as the beneficial effects of a broader range of assessment measures are realized. This effort is crucial: Education must be controlled by knowledgeable professionals in the field rather than by politicians or bureaucrats or by psychometricians who know statistics and test design, but do not know children.

Whole language teachers and administrators are at the forefront of those developing alternative means of assessment and documentation that are clearly more appropriate for educational decision-making than the scores on standardized and state-mandated or basal tests. Such broadly based assessment serves several aims. It enables educators to consider the overall effectiveness of the teaching/learning environment in achieving long-range educational goals. It also serves to document individual students' progress and determine ways in which we as educators can support and encourage students' continued growth. Thus, a broadened assessment base will provide for more appropriate evaluation of students, teachers, administrators, and schools. It will also help educators demonstrate their accountability for fostering children's learning.

210

This chapter begins, then, by discussing the nature of assessment as an evolving process of observation, analysis, and documentation, emphasizing the importance of aligning assessment with educational goals as well as the importance of self-evaluation. A brief section follows on ways of recording data and reporting the results of assessment.

The heart of the chapter focuses on many of the means teachers can use and sources of data they can draw upon to determine and document student progress, with particular emphasis on documenting student growth in literacy. Teachers can elicit and analyze *periodic performance samples* of children's work, concentrating on their reading and writing; elicit *think-aloud protocols* that reveal children's reading and writing processes; accumulate *recorded observations*, both systematic and unplanned, interactive or merely interpretive; hold *conferences and interviews* with both students and parents; solicit data via *inventories and questionnaires*; draw upon students' notes and responses in their *dialogue journals and learning logs*; and derive information from *student-kept records*. In contrast with standardized and state-mandated and unit tests developed by persons far removed from the classroom, such teacher-developed forms of assessment may be characterized as ''informal''—though, in fact, they may be used quite systematically, most in a relatively formal way. Still, they are informal in the sense that they evolve from classroom learning and teaching instead of being imposed or supplied from without; they are not prepackaged or immutable.

Whole language assessment, unlike standardized tests, only rarely focuses on reading and writing isolated from one another or from the rest of the curriculum: Thus, several assessment strategies are illustrated with examples of learning across the curriculum. Furthermore, these categories are not all-inclusive, nor are they mutually exclusive. For example, data for periodic assessment of literacy can be gathered and interviews conducted during conferences; questionnaires can form the basis for response in dialogue journals; and reflective observation and self-evaluation constitute the heart of all informal assessment (see Figure 10.1). These divisions are simply convenient ways of approaching the discussion of assessment, but assessment itself is both inevitable and indivisible: a seamless fabric reflecting and permeating everything that teachers and learners do.

Illustrative of this seamless fabric, class activities and projects typically offer rich opportunities not only for learning but for many of the kinds of assessment mentioned earlier. Therefore, a substantial section of the chapter will suggest some activities and projects that can serve this dual role, thus illustrating more concretely some of the kinds of information that can be valuable in assessment. This section will include a discussion of semantic mapping and story graphing, informal drama, cross-genre writing, and the Quest design for projects.

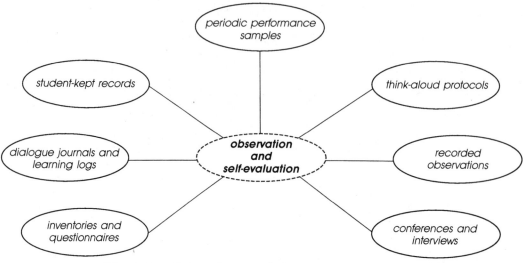

Figure 10.1 Informal means of assessment

The purpose here is to offer enough information for teachers and administrators to decide what they might consider and explore in developing a broad base for assessment in their schools. Of course, teachers need not use all of the means discussed and illustrated. They must select and develop assessment measures to suit their own and their students' needs, perhaps starting with just a few and adding others as they become more confident with the nature and value of what they are doing.

For those wanting more information on holistic kinds and methods of assessment, I particularly recommend the *Whole Language Evaluation Book* (K. Goodman, Goodman, and Hood 1989), because the personal narratives of educators in this collection offer a rich sense of the promise and possibility of assessment. *The Primary Language Record* developed by educators in London (Barrs et al. 1989) offers an excellent example of how and why an entire school system can adopt a broad basis for assessment and evaluation. See Figure 10.2 for these and other resources.

RECONCEPTUALIZING ASSESSMENT

Developing a broad base for assessment involves reconceptualizing assessment data not as test scores but as any recordable data from which inferences about learning and teaching can be drawn. Teachers every-

Articles on Reconceptualizing Assessment

Durkin, Dolores. April 1987. Testing in the kindergarten. *The Reading Teacher* 40:766–70.

Goodman, Yetta. June 1978. Kid watching: An alternative to testing. *National Elementary School Principal* 57:41–45.

Johnston, Peter. April 1987. Teachers as evaluation experts. *The Reading Teacher* 40:744–48.

Teale, William H., Elfrieda H. Hiebert, and Edward A. Chittenden. April 1987. Assessing young children's literacy development. *The Reading Teacher* 40:772–77.

Articles and Books with Assessment Instruments and Forms

Barrs, Myra, Sue Ellis, Hilary Tester, and Anne Thomas [Centre for Language in Primary Education]. 1989. *The Primary Language Record: A Handbook for Teachers.* Portsmouth, N.H.: Heinemann.

Baskwill, Jane, and Paulette Whitman. 1988. *Evaluation: Whole Language, Whole Child.* Richmond Hill, Ontario: Scholastic-TAB. Available in U.S. from Scholastic.

Clay, Marie M. 1988. *The Early Detection of Reading Difficulties.* 4th ed. Portsmouth, N.H.: Heinemann. Describes procedures for "running records" and Concepts About Print test.

Glazer, Susan Mandel, Lyndon W. Searfoss, and Lance M. Gentile. 1988. *Reexamining Reading Diagnosis: New Trends and Procedures.* Newark, Del.: International Reading Association.

Goodman, Kenneth S., Yetta M. Goodman, and Wendy J. Hood, eds. 1989. *The Whole Language Evaluation Book.* Portsmouth, N.H.: Heinemann.

Goodman, Yetta, and Bess Altwerger. n. d. Pre-schoolers' book handling knowledge. University of Arizona, Tucson. Included in the Stage 1 Teacher's Resource Manual for the *Bookshelf* Program: New York: Scholastic.

Goodman, Yetta M., Dorothy J. Watson, and Carolyn L. Burke. 1987. *Reading Miscue Inventory: Alternative Procedures.* Katonah, N.Y.: Richard C. Owen Publishers.

Johnson, Terry, Robert Anthony, Jim Field, Norma Mickelson, and Alison Preece. 1988. *Evaluation: A Perspective for Change.* Crystal Lake, Ill.: Rigby.

Weaver, Constance. 1988. *Reading Process and Practice: From Socio-psycholinguistics to Whole Language.* Portsmouth, N.H.: Heinemann. Chapter 10 focuses on assessment, particularly miscue analysis.

Figure 10.2   Starter bibliography on assessment

where know intuitively that assessment occurs day-to-day, minute-by-minute in their classrooms. They are continually observing and interpreting children's appearance and actions, their overt behavior as well as their written work. What is new in whole language classrooms is that such observations are recorded and interpreted so that they can serve as an important facet of assessment.

In whole language classrooms, assessment is ongoing and inseparable from instruction: The teacher is a participant–observer or "kid-watcher," as Yetta Goodman put it (1978), all the while learning from children and developing in ability to understand and interpret what is observed. Goodman explains further: "As teachers interact with students, they are not just discovering what students know about any particular learning but are also using the moments of interaction to question the student, to encourage, to stimulate, and to challenge." They *teach*, in other words, at the same time as they assess students' learning. This interactive or *transactional* observation is grounded in the work of various scholars in education, ethnography, psycholinguistics, and sociolinguistics (Y. Goodman 1989, p. 11).

The following list reflects these and other important aspects of assessment in whole language classrooms:

1. Assessment is mostly ongoing, occurring in the natural ebb and flow of the classroom. Learning activities typically offer opportunities for assessment, not only by the teacher but also by the student(s). Assessment, particularly that stemming from self-evaluation or interactive observation, will in turn stimulate learning.

2. Assessment emphasizes what children know and can do rather than what they do not know and cannot do. Teachers build upon the successes of learners, thus helping them develop the self-confidence and motivation to want to *engage* or invest themselves in learning.

3. Literacy development is fostered and therefore assessed throughout the curriculum, not merely by means and measures focusing specifically on reading or writing.

4. Assessment focuses on progress toward long-term goals rather than the achievement of short-term, easily measurable objectives that may in fact deter progress toward long-term goals. (Alternatively, short-term goals and/or objectives are written to be congruent with, and to promote, long-term goals.)

5. Self-evaluation (whether by students, teachers, or administrators) is considered the most significant kind of evaluation. As Crowley puts it, "When students are actively involved in planning, executing, and evaluating their own learning, they have the opportunity to become self-directed, independent learners" (Crowley 1989, p. 239). This is one of the major goals of whole language education.

ASSESSMENT AND SELF-EVALUATION

First and foremost, I believe, assessment must lead to and stem from self-evaluation on the part of administrators and teachers. We must consider what is known about children's learning and the development of literacy, compare this with careful observation of what stimulates children's growth in self-concept and learning, determine what we want our students to be and do as adults, and then evaluate our curriculum goals, our programs and teaching procedures, and our assessment instruments accordingly.

For example, if we want our students as adults to become avid readers and prolific writers, critical and creative thinkers, independent and lifelong learners, we need to establish a climate that fosters such development. We need to make certain that our shorter-term goals and objectives are designed to measure progress toward these long-term goals, to redirect our teaching efforts as necessary, and to align assessment with what we are trying to achieve.

Self-evaluation on the part of students is equally important. As Johnson et al. put it, "Students should be given frequent opportunities to monitor, reflect upon, and evaluate their own progress, learning strategies, work habits, products, and achievements" (1988, p. 25).

As an example, take Anna, whose ability to read a story word perfectly is, in this case, a result of her increasing ability to coordinate language cue systems in her quest for meaning. Jane Hansen describes Anna's self-evaluation and her "evidence" for it:

> In December 1987 I said to Anna, "You've been in second grade for three months now. What have you learned about yourself as a reader?"
> "I'm better," she said through her sideways smile.
> "Prove it," I grinned, knowing she could.
> "Listen." Anna took *Bread and Jam* by Josephine Wright from her reading folder and . . . read the old (1947) paperback's fourteen pages perfectly. She had finally started on the road to becoming a reader [having started first grade three years before], knew she was on her way, and knew how to prove her competence. In other words, Anna could evaluate herself and provide convincing evidence about her progress to others. (Hansen 1989, p. 19)

The self-evaluation and progress of Anna, and others in the class, also provided data for assessing the appropriateness of the learning environment provided by her teacher.

When teachers and students assess not only their own growth and progress but one another's, each kind of evaluation supports and facilitates their mutual growth. Students too can assess the appropriateness of teaching/learning activities and can suggest means of assessment that are congruent with agreed-upon goals.

> **❝**We need to make certain that our shorter-term goals and objectives are designed to measure progress toward these long-term goals, to redirect our teaching efforts as necessary, and to align assessment with what we are trying to achieve.**❞**

RECORDING DATA AND REPORTING RESULTS

It is not necessarily obvious how best to record and organize the various kinds of data collected. There is no "right" way, and most whole language educators find themselves continually experimenting with new methods that might simplify their record keeping while at the same time facilitating insightful assessment and evaluation.

To capture the unplanned observations that occur daily, almost minute-to-minute, teachers need some means of recording that is quick and simple, but ideally also easy to transfer to more permanent record files. Some teachers record anecdotal observations on stickers, then later affix these to each student's record sheet(s) as appropriate. Others use post-its or index cards for the same purpose. Double-spaced copies of the class list (one for each school day) will work too, for recording raw, anecdotal data that can later be analyzed and transcribed as appropriate to individual students' files. Checklists and forms for recording classroom observations, and checklists of work in progress or completed, may also be valuable; again the data can be transferred to students' individual records.

Some teachers find it valuable to keep a journal or log in which they not only record anecdotal information but also reflect upon their observations, consider ways to support the students' learning (collectively and individually), and evaluate their own teaching. Such journal-keeping may be particularly valuable for teachers just beginning to experiment with new means of assessment. Comments particularly relevant to individual students can later be transferred to the students' folders or files.

Individual student records can be organized in looseleaf notebooks, individual student folders, accordion files—in fact, whatever works. Teachers within a school or school system may together devise reporting forms and procedures, such as those in *The Primary Record Book* (Barrs et al. 1989; see also Barrs 1990).

From the accumulated data, some ambitious teachers develop *literacy biographies* or *literacy profiles* for each student. Such profiles, constructed periodically throughout the school year, provide an incredibly detailed and personal record of each student's literacy behavior and development (Taylor 1990). Here, for example, is part of the first paragraph of the first profile that third-grade teacher Kathy Matthews developed for one student:

> "I don't know what's different," Rob told me one day. "Last year I thought reading was, you know, just okay. But this year I *love* reading! It's my best thing!" Rob's enthusiasm for reading also appears in his reading journal: "I feel like I read a million pages. It's a wonderful

book.'' Rob generally chooses reading as an independent activity, sometimes bemoaning the fact that he has to stop reading to participate in other activities. Rob often talks about books and how he feels about the stories he reads. He is attentive to his peers' opinions about books and their reading choices and frequently becomes involved in lively, spontaneous discussions. (pp. 188–89)

This and other examples are included in Denny Taylor's ''Toward a Unified Theory of Literacy Learning and Instructional Practices'' (1989).

A brief word about reporting the results of assessment may be in order, as most teachers are obviously confronted with the reality of report cards and/or grades. In some schools, concerned educators have developed and implemented the use of report cards that carry written comments *instead of* numerical or letter grades. Some educators have managed, too, to develop report forms that do not fragment learning into small pieces called ''spelling,'' ''handwriting,'' ''reading,'' ''writing,'' and ''language.'' Kathy Matthews' literacy profiles are a wonderful, if rather atypical, example. Other educators have involved both students and parents in the preparation of periodic reports (see Johnson et al. 1988). Even under the most adverse conditions, whole language educators have often managed to develop various means of assigning grades that do not seriously compromise the integrity of their teaching or the integrated nature of students' learning. John and Carol Woodley describe one such teacher's method of handling the grading problem in ''Whole Language, Texas Style'' (1989, pp. 69–75).

Holistic assessment need not be confined to the elementary school. For my undergraduate reading-process course at the university, for example, I am currently specifying seven interrelated factors to be considered in determining students' course grades: consistent attendance and participation in class activities, plus evidence of significant effort, professionalism, understanding of concepts explored, ability to apply new knowledge to practical situations, and growth as learners and teachers. I attempt to assess these through various means, including observation, analysis, interactive teaching/learning, and students' self-evaluations. Though I frequently share my evaluative responses with the students and note these on individual record sheets, I resist reducing the complexity of learning to the simplistic assignment of grades until the last possible moment—sometimes the very day that grades are due in the registrar's office. Thus, the final grade reflects not an average of numerical scores but a more holistic assessment based solidly upon a variety of assessment means and measures.

In summary, teachers can record and organize their observations and other assessment data in a variety of ways, gradually evolving a system that suits them—at least for the moment. There are also various ways they can handle the difficulties posed by grading systems and report cards that violate their philosophy of learning and teaching. Eventually, they may even change those grading systems and report cards.

PERIODIC PERFORMANCE SAMPLES: EMPHASIS ON READING

In order to assess children's reading and writing appropriately, teachers need a thorough understanding of the reading and writing processes, of developmental patterns and trends in literacy development, of current perspectives on learning theory, and of assessment techniques that are congruent with such understanding. Such understanding cannot be developed overnight, particularly since it often requires a "paradigm shift"—a shift from an implicit commitment to a transmission concept of learning to an explicit commitment to a transactional concept. The following discussion only begins to suggest what kind of understanding teachers need to develop, with substantive and long-term support from administrators.

Period assessments can, of course, be undertaken in any area or combination of areas in which it is deemed important: not only reading and writing, but oral language, math, science, social studies. The focus here, however, is on analyzing and assessing reading and writing, with an emphasis on *performance samples* and data that can be elicited along with them.

More particularly, this section focuses on obtaining and analyzing performance samples of reading. Though not all of the other informal assessment means will be explicitly discussed here, further reflection may suggest how eliciting periodic reading samples can at the same time involve collecting and analyzing data from reading protocols (think-alouds), recorded observations, conferences and interviews, inventories and questionnaires, dialogue journals and learning logs, and student-kept records. Of course, such data gathering analysis should also involve self-evaluation on the part of both students and teachers. Furthermore, the assessment of reading need not be entirely separated from the assessment of writing, nor from the assessment of other aspects of learning and growth.

Emergent Literacy Assessment: Emphasis on Reading

To assess the literacy development of young children who cannot yet read and write independently, teachers need to know enough about emergent literacy to recognize signs of growth. And with emergent literacy especially, the child's writing will indicate growth in under-standing of reading, and vice versa. Therefore, the emergence of literacy is often assessed all-of-a-piece, along with children's development of oral language.

For example, Chittenden and Courtney (1989) describe a current project to develop ways of documenting teachers' observations of chil-dren's progress in natural classroom situations and settings. Story time, when the teacher reads to the children, is one such opportunity. While reading, teachers note many things about children's understanding and development, just by observing the children's nonverbal behavior and verbal comments. Figure 10.3 presents an observation form educators have developed for describing each child's work and behavior for various classroom contexts; a parallel form is used for rating each child's interest/investment in different classroom contexts. One major advan-tage of such forms is that they help teachers document children's growth and strengths instead of pinpointing minute skills the children might not have mastered in isolation. They focus attention on the child's overall pattern of development.

To give some idea of the kinds of understanding that teachers need to develop in order to assess emergent literacy effectively, Figure 10.4 presents "Signs of Progress in the Emergent Reading Stage" from Moira McKenzie's *Journeys into Literacy* (1986, p. 61). Other teacher/researchers have developed similar lists or descriptions; see, for exam-ple, Cochrane et al. 1984, and Hall 1987. For teachers' use in assessing emergent reading, the developers of *The Primary Language Record* (Barrs et al. 1989) have included a beginning reading scale to document chil-dren's movement from dependence to independence as readers; see Figure 10.5. Obviously, there is a world of difference between such a scale that encourages teachers to view children as capable and develop-ing and, on the other hand, the typical "reading readiness" tests that encourage teachers to view children as deficient.

Other assessment instruments that can be used with young children include Marie Clay's Concepts about Print test (see Clay 1988) and Yetta Goodman and Bess Altwerger's related technique for assessing book-handling knowledge and print (their assessment instrument can be found in the *Bookshelf* Stage 1 Teacher's Resource Book, from Scholastic Inc.). The advantage of Goodman and Altwerger's procedure over Clay's is that their procedure better elicits what children know about books and print: children's practical, functional knowledge, irrespec-tive of whether or not they can verbalize that knowledge (see Hall 1987, pp. 33 and 64–66; and Y. Goodman 1981).

Other aspects of emergent literacy—especially the development and analysis of spelling—will be briefly discussed in the section on periodic analysis of writing samples, where it may become even clearer that the

**Description of child's work and behavior for each context
(cite specific indications of skills or knowledge)**

Settings and Activities	Examples of Child's Activities
Story Time: Teacher reads to class (responses to story line; child's comments, questions, elaborations)	
Independent Reading: Book Time (nature of books child chooses or brings in; process of selecting; quiet or social reading)	
Writing (journal stories, alphabet, dictation)	
Reading Group/Individual (oral reading strategies: discussion of text, responses to instruction)	
Reading Related Activities Tasks (responses to assignments or discussion focusing on word/letter pro-perties, word games/ experience charts)	
Informal Settings (use of language in play, jokes, story-telling, conversation)	
Books and Print as Resource (use of books for projects; attention to signs, labels, names; locating information)	
Other	

Figure 10.3 Form for assessing emergent literacy in classroom contexts (Chittenden and Courtney 1989, p. 110)

development of reading and writing are intertwined. Useful for offering a perspective on early literacy assessment is Morrow and Smith (1990), *Assessment for Instruction in Early Literacy*.

Miscues and Miscue Analysis

Teachers implicitly or explicitly operating from a word identification concept of reading need to investigate the nature of the reading process in order to better understand, analyze, and respond to the miscues that students make while reading. A *miscue*, as Kenneth Goodman defined it, is simply any departure from what the text says. Unlike "error," the term "miscue" is judgmentally neutral, leaving open the possibility that many miscues may be *good*.

If reading is constructing meaning, then miscues that preserve or at least do not seriously disrupt meaning are among those that may be considered "good" miscues. They reflect readers' active use of their background knowledge (including their intuitive grasp of language structure, or syntax) as well as attention to the print and the evolving meaning of the text itself, while engaging in the process of constructing meaning.

For example, if I were to begin a sentence "Our means of assessment must be consistent with our educational . . . ," you as an efficient reader would automatically draw upon your knowledge of syntax, your background as an educator, and your understanding of this book to predict a word like *aims, goals, intentions,* or *purposes*. If you were reading this example sentence aloud and the word *educational* occurred at the end of a line, you might "read" the next words as *aims*, let us say, only to find out that the text actually said *goals*. This would be an example of a good miscue, since it does not distort the essential meaning of the text. Good readers—children as well as adults—automatically predict text on the basis of their background knowledge and experience, in conjunction with their understanding and their sampling of the evolving text.

Teachers with little understanding of the reading process have typically "corrected" children's miscues as they read aloud and/or suggested the use of predominantly one strategy: "sound it out." But with an understanding of reading and of reading miscues, teachers can analyze the strategies behind the miscues and can then help students develop more effective strategies or enlarge their repertoire and integrate their use of effective strategies.

Such teachers would realize, for example, that with miscues like those in Figure 10.6, a child like Tony may not understand that what he reads should sound like language and should make sense. In reading this

❝But with an understanding of reading and of reading miscues, teachers can analyze the strategies behind the miscues and can then help students develop more effective strategies or enlarge their repertoire and integrate their use of effective strategies.❞

Significant Behaviours 1

- 'reads' and re-reads stories, poems, rhymes, using reading-like behavior.
- 'reads' by approximating to the text, taking on the author's language or making the author's meaning with own language.
- reads with little or no attention to the text on the page.
- writes messages—imitates writing form, using any letters, or letter-like shapes known.
- spelling (pre-literate: pre-phonemic).

Examples

Reading

from 'Meg and Mog'—Aziz (5)

Text

They all stirred the cauldron as they chanted their spell.

Re-enactment

They whispered the magic word.

Writing

Mary

Razia
writing like Alice
(her sister) does.

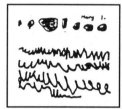

Significant Behaviours 2

- reads Big Books (and others) following a line of print, knows where a particular part begins and ends.
- attempts and learns one-to-one correspondence.
- has good idea of using left-right direction.
- monitors reading—knows where there is a mismatch and tries to correct.
- knows there is a message in the print that remains the same, and tries to get it.
- can recognize particular words in text, or can locate them by reading along the line or sentence.
- begins to use initial consonants as cues, or checking strategies.
- writing moves towards sound-letter correspondence.
- spelling strategies (early phonemic: letter-name strategies).

Examples

Reading

from 'The Tiger who came to Tea'—Joanne (5.5)

Text

Sophie's mummy said, "I wonder who that can be. It can't be the milkman because he came this morning. And it can't be the boy from the grocer because this isn't the day he comes."

Re-enactment

Sophie's mummy said, "I wonder what that can be. It can't be the milkman 'cos he came this morning. Can't be the boy from the grocer."

Writing   John

I qP It s Qa t is
F P HS
(I play hop scotch and Jt is fun
playing hop scotch)

Leanne

I Like cims Dai I
Hav loos of Pess
my Bro hav lots
of Pess And I hav
my cins Tev Up
(I like christmas day I have lots of
presents.my brother have lots of presents
and I have my christmas tree up.)

Figure 10.4   Signs of progress in emergent reading (McKenzie 1986, p. 61)

Significant Behaviours 3	**Examples**
• has developed one-to-one correspondence.	**Reading**
• uses directional rules appropriately.	Reads well-known texts with a high degree of accuracy.
• makes appropriate predictions in new material in terms of expectation of meaning and language.	Tackles new texts with support.
• knows some words and most letter-names.	**Writing**
• writing shows growing knowledge of sound-symbol correspondence—can spell a few words, is beginning to leave spaces.	Wes Rashida
• spelling (early phonemic: uses some letter-name strategies).	

Figure 10.4 (*continued*)

passage, his primary strategy seems to have been "sound it out," with little concern for meaning. Before drawing such a conclusion, however, a knowledgeable teacher would invite Tony to retell the story and then ask him questions to further elicit understanding; readers often understand *far* more than their miscues would lead a listener to believe. Ideally, the teacher would also discuss some of Tony's miscues with him to see if he is aware (or to help him become aware) that the miscues don't make sense. The teacher would also see if he is aware of using any strategy other than "sound it out" (or "wait for the teacher to tell me") when confronted with problem words, and perhaps begin helping him consciously *use* meaning in order to construct meaning from a text. Alternatively, the discussion between Tony and his teacher might lead them to conclude that Tony simply didn't have the background knowledge to construct meaning from this text.

Miscue analysis, then, involves more than the mere recording and analysis of miscues. Typically the teacher invites a student to read something in its entirety: a story, article, or other suitable selection the reader will find challenging but not inordinately difficult. The student is told beforehand that he or she will be asked afterward to retell what was read; usually the student is also told he or she will not be given help, so that the teacher can see how the reader deals with problem words when reading independently. Afterward, the student is asked to tell about the reading, and the teacher will then ask questions to further learn what the

Reading Scale 1

DEPENDENCE

↑

Beginner reader 1	Does not have enough successful strategies for tackling print independently. Relies on having another person read the text aloud. May still be unaware that text carries meaning.
Non-fluent reader 2	Tackling known and predictable texts with growing confidence but still needing support with new and unfamiliar ones. Growing ability to predict meanings and developing strategies to check predictions against other cues such as the illustrations and the print itself.
Moderately fluent reader 3	Well-launched on reading but still needing to return to a familiar range of texts. At the same time beginning to explore new kinds of texts independently. Beginning to read silently.
Fluent reader 4	A capable reader who now approaches familiar texts with confidence but still needs support with unfamiliar materials. Beginning to draw inferences from books and stories read independently. Chooses to read silently.
Exceptionally fluent reader 5	An avid and independent reader, who is making choices from a wide range of material. Able to appreciate nuances and subtleties in text.

↓

INDEPENDENCE

Figure 10.5 Becoming a reader: From dependence to independence (Barrs et al., *The Primary Language Record: A Handbook for Teachers*, CLPE 1989, p. 26)

expert *Molda*
Every day except Friday, Mohamed went to school with the

nother vi'ner
other village boys. The class was outdoors, and the children

beaches frose *shape*
sat on little benches in front of the teacher in the shade

of a tall palm tree. They did not have books, so the boys

ramped
repeated everything the teacher said, over and over, until

other classrooms hurt *vengil*
they knew their lessons by heart. The girls of the village

did not go to school, for the people thought that school was

imprentice *to*
not as important for girls as it was for boys.

Figure 10.6 A sample of miscues from Tony, grade 3 (analyzed and discussed in Weaver 1988, pp. 349–52)

reader remembered and understood, and how the reader interpreted and responded to the selection. If the selection was a story, for example, the teacher might ask questions to find out what inferences the reader drew about key characters or events or theme, how the reader might have reacted under similar circumstances, if or how the reader related to the story, what the reader thought of the story—in short, whatever seems appropriate in order to elicit not only recall but understanding and evaluation, involvement and appreciation.

In the same session, the teacher may also interview the student to learn more about what the student thinks reading is, how the student views himself or herself as a reader (self-concept), what the reader thinks he or she does well as a reader, what the student wants to work on, and so forth. The session is tape-recorded so that the teacher can later record, analyze, and reflect upon the data (though some teachers do record miscues and other data during the session). In later sessions, the teacher may further determine how the reader handles different genres (textbooks, let us say) and/or how the reader handles the same genre, at other levels of difficulty.

The example of Tony and this further sketch of miscue analysis procedures briefly illustrate how assessment and instruction can be intertwined and how student self-evaluation can likewise blend with the teacher's evaluation. The procedure includes analysis of a *performance sample*: the student reads, and the teacher tries to determine not just how well, but *how* the student reads. But clearly there is far more than can be learned during and from the reading/discussion/interview session. For example, the teacher can invite the student to explain where in the text he or she had problems, and together they can discuss strategies the student used and might have used to try to resolve the difficulty. Through such discussions, a great deal can be learned by both the teacher and the student.

The original miscue analysis procedures and later adaptations are discussed in the *Reading Miscue Inventory: Alternative Procedures* (Y. Goodman, Watson, and Burke 1987). Other adaptations may be evaluated in accordance with how well they preserve the principles and philosophy of miscue analysis. For example, the *Reading Miscue Inventory* indicates the importance for analysis of using passages of about 500 words or more, long enough to give the reader an opportunity to use his or her developing understanding of the selection as aid in constructing meaning; often, readers' miscues will reflect better strategies when they are a little farther into a text (Menosky 1971). *The Primary Language Record* suggests an adaptation of this procedure, namely, that teachers choose a passage of about 150–300 words for the child to read aloud. The authors point out, however, that this selected passage "should not be too near the beginning in order that the child has time to get into the text" (Barrs et al. 1989, p. 61). By having the student read a sizable portion of text silently before reading a subsequent portion aloud, this adaptation preserves the basic miscue analysis principle of giving the reader an opportunity to demonstrate his or her reading strategies at their best.

Another adaptation in *The Primary Language Record* may, in fact, reflect the philosophy of miscue analysis even better than the original procedure itself. At the very least, it seems to be a valuable alternative to the standard operating procedure first developed for teachers in the original *Reading Miscue Inventory Manual* (Y. Goodman and Burke 1972). The adaptation is this: the reader reads the text silently, retells or describes the text, and *only then* reads the text aloud (afterward discussing it with the teacher, who may then ask more probing questions). The authors of *The Primary Language Record* suggest these advantages of having children read silently before reading aloud:

> This will offer children an opportunity to demonstrate their growing ability to read silently as well as read aloud even if they are still

operating at the very early stages of silent reading (sub-vocalising). It will also convey to children that the ultimate aim in learning to read is to be able to do so silently, where pace and enjoyment are in control of the reader. This sense of control means that they can organise the ways in which they come to understand texts without being over-concerned about the element of performance in reading aloud. (Barrs et al. 1989, p. 61)

These concerns reflect basic principles of miscue analysis within a whole language philosophy.

For an introduction to the reading process and the concepts of miscues and miscue analysis, many teachers have found my *Reading Process and Practice* (Weaver 1988) to be helpful. Though already I would make some changes in the miscue analysis form and procedures recommended in Chapter 10, the form there seems particularly valuable in that it encourages sufficiently detailed analysis to enable teachers to consider such questions as ''Do the miscues suggest that the reader is making adequate use of prior context to *predict* what might be coming next?'' ''Do the miscues suggest that the reader is making appropriate use of following context to *correct* miscues that don't make sense with what follows?'' In other words, the analysis of data is clearly directed toward interpretation and instruction.

Another adaptation of the original miscue analysis procedures is what has come to be known as *retrospective miscue analysis*, or RMA (Marek 1989). This procedure is actually a strategy that merges self-evaluation with instruction. The strategy involves leading readers to assess their own miscues, with the result that they learn from this evaluation. The student's reading is tape-recorded, and at first the teacher guides the student in evaluating the miscues. Tony (Figure 10.6), for example, might be led to notice and evaluate his miscues that do not make sense. The instructional message, of course, would be something like ''Reading is supposed to make sense.'' Further sessions could refine this understanding and help Tony develop and integrate strategies for constructing meaning from texts.

Marek herself has developed the strategy with adults who were convinced that they were poor readers. These readers had in common not only the conviction that they could not read adequately but the conviction that reading better would involve learning to pay closer attention to the letters and the sounds within words. They held a word identification concept of reading. Thus, the primary question Marek led these women to ask of selected miscues was ''Does the miscue make sense?'' She wanted the women to realize that often their miscues did make sense in context, that they were using some effective reading strategies, and that constructing meaning from a text is more important than getting all the words "right" (Marek 1989). Again, assessment is intertwined with instruction.

In one of two co-published papers on retrospective miscue analysis, Y. Goodman describes the history, procedures, and prospects for such analysis, mentioning studies that have used this teaching strategy with students from upper elementary school through college. In her paper, Marek describes in detail the use of retrospective miscue analysis with two adult readers (Y. Goodman and Marek 1989). Both papers should be useful to teachers interested in using miscue analysis for instruction.

Readers of this book may well wonder how teachers can find the time to do miscue analysis with all their students even once a year, much less near the beginning and once or twice later to assess progress. But most teachers have found that a solid understanding of the reading process and some experience with miscue analysis enables them to analyze the patterns of students' miscues much more readily, simply by listening. They can then use very simple forms—perhaps as simple as that in Figure 10.7—for assessing the reading strategies of most children, while reserving more detailed analysis for working with children whose strategies are not so readily apparent. In other words, immersion in miscue analysis is essential for teachers' own learning because it helps them understand the reading process as well as how to analyze miscues. Once they have developed such understanding, however, teachers can adopt, adapt, or devise simpler procedures for class use.

Running Records

Marie Clay's procedure for making *running records* of miscues has gained popularity with the spread of her Reading Recovery Program (see Clay 1988 for a detailed description of her procedures). The procedure differs from miscue analysis most crucially in that the teacher marks the reader's miscues while listening to the reading, not afterward. The teacher does not even need a typescript or photocopy of the reading selection for recording the miscues, since every word read correctly is indicated with a check mark, or simply a slanted line. Thus, if written on another piece of paper rather than on a copy of the reading selection, a running record of Tony's reading would consist mostly of check or slanted marks, as indicated in Figure 10.8.

This procedure has the advantage of enabling teachers to record miscues "on the run": without preplanning, and without tape-recording the reading or making a typescript or copy of the material read. Obviously, the procedure saves time and facilitates spontaneity. However, initially recording the miscues out of context (as in Figure 10.7) can encourage teachers to analyze them that way also, and to consider

MISCUE ANALYSIS PROCEDURE IV INDIVIDUAL CONFERENCE FORM

READER _____ DATE _____

TEACHER _____ AGE/GRADE _____

SELECTION _____

Does the sentence, as the reader left it, make sense within the context of the story?

Yes _____ Total _____

No_____ Total _____

Number of Sentences _____ Comprehending Score _____

Divide total Yes by Total number of sentences for Comprehending Score

Retelling Information

Comments

Figure 10.7 Simplified miscue analysis form (Y. Goodman, Watson, and Burke 1987, Appendix C)

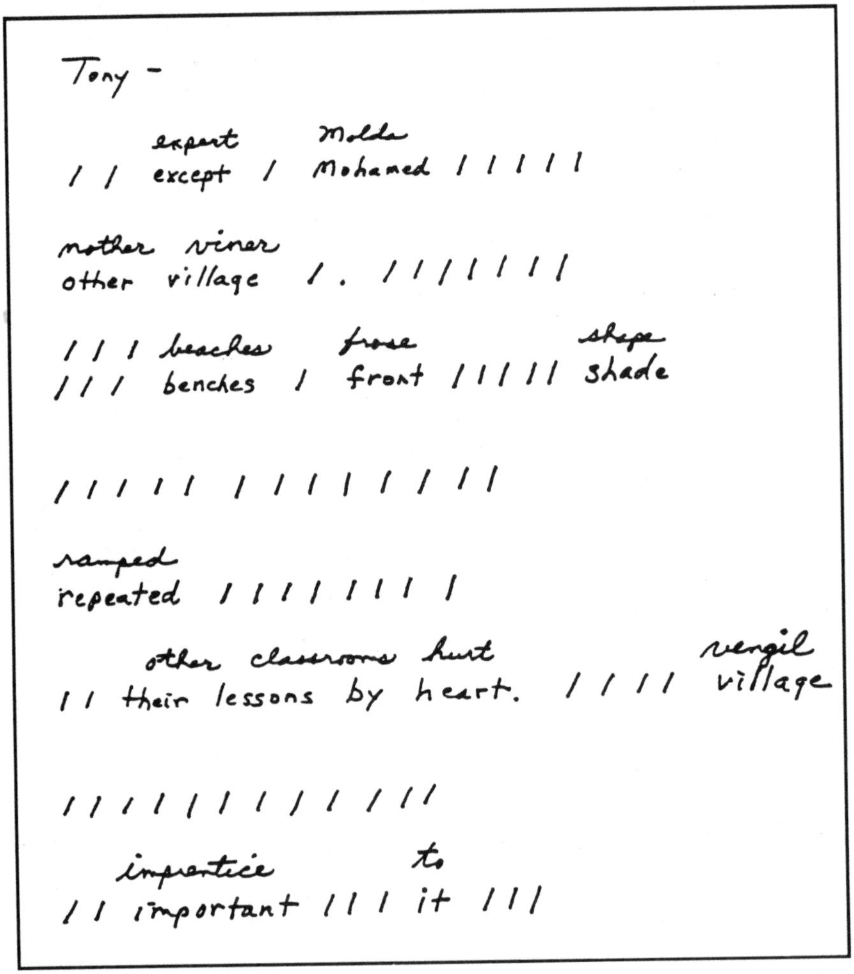

Tony –

	expert	Molda	
/ /	except	/ Mohamed	/ / / / /

	mother	viner	
other	village	/ . / / / / / / /

	/ / /	beaches	frose		shape
/ / /	benches	/ front	/ / / / /	shade

/ / / / / / / / / / / / /

	ramped
repeated	/ / / / / / / /

	other classrooms	hurt		vengil
/ /	their lessons by heart.	/ / / /	village

/ / / / / / / / / / /

	imprentice		to	
/ /	important	/ / /	it / / /

Figure 10.8   Running record of Tony's miscues (compare with Figure 10.6)

the quantity of miscues more than the quality. Thus, the major advantage of the ''running record'' procedure can also become its major disadvantage.

Informal Analysis

While listening to a child read and discuss the reading afterward, the teacher can often informally assess the child's reading strategies, based upon careful listening and informed observation, rather than detailed analysis. The teacher might devise a form for recording and summarizing evidence bearing on such strategies as the following:

—whether the child uses pictures along with prior knowledge of the story to "read" a familiar text

—whether the child uses prior knowledge and context to predict

—whether the child integrates use of grapho/phonemic cues with meaning and syntactic cues

—whether the child has developed a flexible repertoire of strategies for dealing with problem words, or relies on only one or two (for example, "sound it out" or "ask the teacher")

—whether the child monitors his or her comprehension and attempts to resolve difficulties in constructing meaning

—whether the child is developing strategies for reading informational text

See *The Primary Language Record* (Barrs et al. 1989, p. 28) for a related list of strategies that are particularly relevant for the primary grades.

Teachers can develop their own simplified forms for recording information such as this. Once teachers have developed some understanding of the reading process and of effective reading strategies, they rarely need to engage in detailed analysis or to use complex forms for recording observations and conclusions.

PERIODIC PERFORMANCE SAMPLES: EMPHASIS ON WRITING

As with reading, the analysis and assessment of children's writing may require a "paradigm shift" on the part of teachers. They need to conceptualize writing not as a one-shot opportunity for students to demonstrate the correctness of their writing skills but as a multidimensional process involving rehearsal, drafting, revision, editing, and often "publication"—that is, some form of sharing with an audience beyond the writer. Teachers and parents and administrators need to appreciate the fact that when students have extensive opportunities to engage in the writing process, correctness of form develops gradually, over time: through the years, as children develop greater awareness of the conventions of print and writing, and through a series of drafts with any given piece. As with oral language, writers attend first to the purpose, function, and content of the writing, then gradually to form. Thus, to assess writing appropriately, teachers need an understanding of the writing process and of developmental patterns and trends in children's writing, as well as an appreciation for each writer's uniqueness.

> **"**They need to conceptualize writing not as a one-shot opportunity for students to demonstrate the correctness of their writing skills but as a multidimensional process involving rehearsal, drafting, revision, editing, and often 'publication' . . .**"**

Many teachers keep two separate folders of writing samples for each child: one, a folder of writings completed or abandoned, and another of works currently in progress. Multiple drafts of a single piece are often stapled together to facilitate assessment by both the teacher and the student. As often as once a month, many teachers select a writing sample to analyze and assess the writer's development. Often, the child and the teacher together select a representative piece, or what they agree is the child's ''best'' during the time period, using criteria that have evolved as children have shared their writing and have received responses from other children as well as from their teacher. The teacher may involve the student in evaluating his or her own writing strengths, strategies, and growth, as well as encourage the student to establish a goal to work on as a writer. Thus, the selection, analysis, and assessment of writing samples can involve the student in evaluation and goal setting. A simple, evolving form for record keeping might include columns for ''What I can do as a writer'' and ''What I want to work on,'' along with the date (see, for example, Hansen 1987, pp. 89–100).

From the writing samples themselves, teachers and students can learn many things, which will be discussed under five headings:

Emergent literacy: Emphasis on writing

Development of a growing range of purposes

Development of an understanding of literary genres

Development of understanding of the writing process and of writing strategies

Development in control of various aspects of the written product

Clearly there is overlap among these sections; the division is partly a matter of convenience. Assessment itself is far less divisible into categories than such divisions would suggest. (For assessment of writing portfolios on a larger scale, see Simmons 1990.)

Emergent Literacy: Emphasis on Writing

Because it's obvious to us as literate adults that books are read from front to back, that print in English goes from left to right and top to bottom, and that words are separated by spaces, we tend to assume that these aspects of books and print are equally obvious to the emergent reader and writer. They are not. Thus, some of the earliest signs of emergent literacy are revealed as writers demonstrate their growing understanding of such concepts that are important to both reading and writing (see Clay 1975 and 1987). See, for example, Figure 10.4, which suggests what might constitute developmental progress in writing and reading, including spelling. This list, however, should not be taken as definitive, much less as prescriptive.

In the past decade and a half, researchers have gained considerable understanding of how spelling develops and can be taught. It is not best taught by assigning and testing twenty spelling words every week but by encouraging and responding positively to students' ''invented'' spellings while, at the same time, helping them develop a variety of strategies for correcting their spelling as they edit. The teacher also encourages spelling by making a variety of spelling resources available to students (other people, books and environmental print, class lists of frequently needed words, individual lists or word banks of ''Words I can spell,'' and so forth). In conferences, teachers can ask children about their spelling strategies and can encourage them in using other strategies. From writing samples alone, though, teachers can document children's spelling development and draw inferences about their strategies for spelling.

The examples of children's writing in Chapter 4 illustrate some of the early strategies for spelling. Without going into more detail here, I will simply recommend that educators consult some of the references in the starter bibliography on spelling development (Figure 10.9).

With young writers, samples for analyzing the development of concepts about print can be collected in at least three ways:

1. By having a child write again something earlier written from memory, allowing for comparison of the two samples. Fitzgerald (1984) reports the use of this technique with nursery rhymes and songs that kindergarteners and first-graders had first learned orally, and then learned to read.

2. By dictating something that a child wrote earlier and having the child rewrite it, again allowing for comparison of the two writing samples. (See, for example, Hull 1989.) Figure 10.10 shows an example from Cochrane et al. 1984. Between September and June of first grade, the writer clearly developed more sophisticated concepts of spelling, spacing, punctuation, and letter formation.

3. By simply keeping and filing freely generated writings. See, for instance, the writing sample and analysis in Figure 10.11, from Baskwill and Whitman 1988.

Each of these techniques allows for comparing earlier and later writing samples to determine a child's progress in developing concepts about print. Comparing freely generated writings, however, allows for comparison of other dimensions of writing growth as well.

Articles

Gentry, J. Richard. November 1982. An analysis of developmental spelling in GNYS AT WRK. *The Reading Teacher* 36:192–200.

Hall, Susan, and Chris Hall. December 1984. It takes a lot of letters to spell "erz." *Language Arts* 61:822–27.

Kamii, Constance, and Marie Randazzo. February 1985. Social interaction and invented spelling. *Language Arts* 62:124–33.

Wilde, Sandra. Looking at invented spelling: A kidwatcher's guide to spelling, Part 1, and Understanding spelling strategies: A kidwatcher's guide to spelling, Part 2. In Kenneth Goodman, Yetta Goodman, and Wendy Hood, eds. *The Whole Language Evaluation Book.* Portsmouth, N.H.: Heinemann, pp. 213–26 and 227–36.

Books

Bean, Wendy, and Christine Bouffler. 1987. *Spell by Writing.* Rozelle, Australia: Primary English Teachers Association. Available in the U.S. from Heinemann.

Gentry, J. Richard. 1987. *Spel . . . Is a Four-Letter Word.* Richmond Hill, Ontario: Scholastic-TAB. Available in the U.S. from Heinemann.

Newman, Judith. 1984. *The Craft of Children's Writing.* Richmond Hill, Ontario: Scholastic-TAB. Available in the U.S. from Heinemann.

Temple, Charles, Ruth Nathan, Nancy Burris, and Frances Temple. 1988. *The Beginnings of Writing.* 2nd ed. Boston: Allyn & Bacon.

Books: In-depth Studies

Bissex, Glenda. 1980. *Gnyx at Wrk: A Child Learns to Write and Read.* Cambridge, Mass.: Harvard University Press.

Ferreiro, Emilia, and Ana Teberosky. 1982. *Literacy Before Schooling.* Translated by Karen Goodman Castro. Portsmouth, N.H.: Heinemann.

Henderson, Edmund H., and James W. Beers, eds. 1980. *Developmental and Cognitive Aspects of Spelling.* Newark, Del.: International Reading Association.

Figure 10.9   Starter bibliography on spelling and spelling development

Development of a Growing Range of Purposes and Functions in Writing

Many of the functions of writing in everyday life are catalogued in ethnographic studies of family literacy (see Heath 1983, Taylor 1983, Taylor and Dorsey-Gaines 1988; see Chap. 4 here). If the classroom is also a print-rich environment in which children are encouraged to write for various purposes and functions, then it is natural for children to continue expanding the forms of writing they employ, as well as their control of these forms. Thus, one sign of development as a writer is simply an expanding repertoire of functions and genres. As Newkirk

In September, a first grader wrote this story about her Barbie doll:

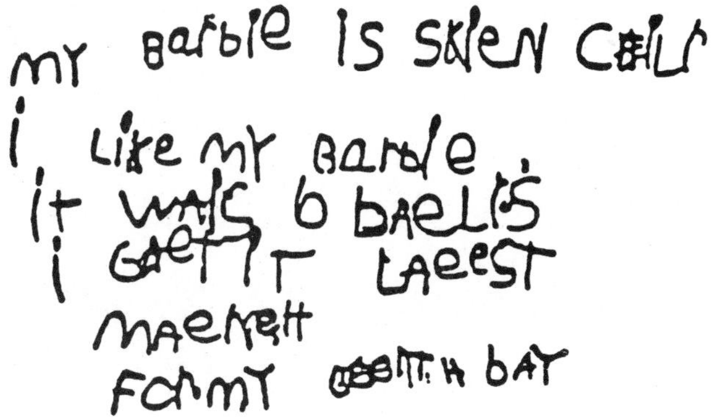

> my Barbie IS SkleN C#Lr
> i Like my Barbie
> It was 6 baelES
> i Get iT Laeest
> maeket
> FormY gent h bay

When the same story was dictated to her in June, she wrote this:

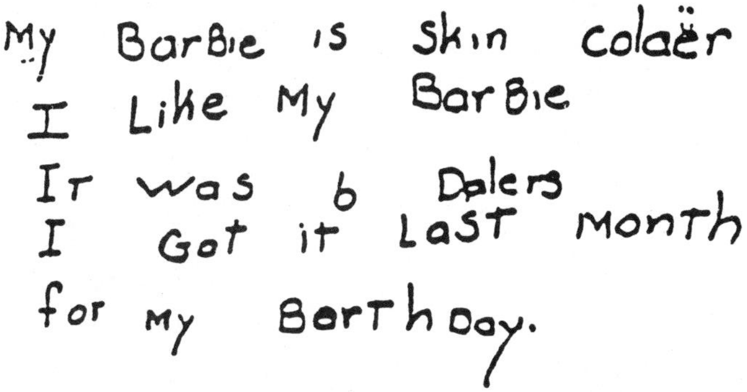

> My Barbie is Skin colaër
> I Like My Barbie
> It was 6 Dalers
> I Got it Last month
> for my BerThoay.

Figure 10.10   Original writing and later dictation (Cochrane et al. 1984, p. 108)

documents, even very young children can write lists, labels, signs, letters, menus, captions, descriptions, arguments, dialogues, complaints, invitations, and much more (Newkirk 1989). Documentation of students' writing development can include, then, notes on their increasing repertoire.

Development of an Understanding of Literary Genres

The focus here is on children's understanding of the nature and conventions of various genres of writing, which can be determined partly by the increasing command they demonstrate as writers.

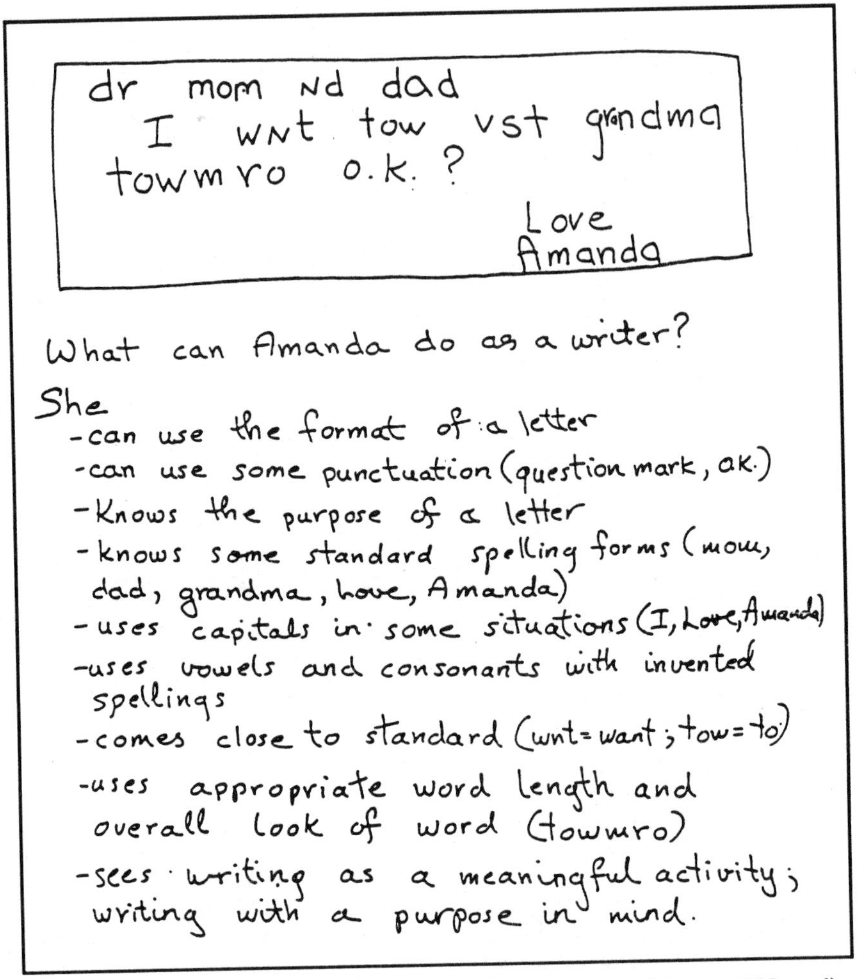

dr   mom   nd dad
   I   wnt   tow   vst   grndma
towmro   o.k. ?
                Love
                Amanda

What can Amanda do as a writer?

She
- can use the format of a letter
- can use some punctuation (question mark, ok.)
- Knows the purpose of a letter
- knows some standard spelling forms (mom, dad, grandma, love, Amanda)
- uses capitals in some situations (I, Love, Amanda)
- uses vowels and consonants with invented spellings
- comes close to standard (wnt = want ; tow = to)
- uses appropriate word length and overall look of word (towmro)
- sees writing as a meaningful activity; writing with a purpose in mind.

Figure 10.11   Writing sample and analysis (Baskwill and Whitman 1988, p. 6)

Take, for example, a sense of story. At a rudimentary level, young readers and writers may be aware that stories have a beginning, middle, and end and/or that many stories (fairy tales, folktales) begin with "Once upon a time" and end with "They lived happily ever after." Even young children whose "writing" consists of scribbles or drawings can exhibit a strong sense of story: consider the ghost story written/dictated by Jane (Chap. 4, Figure 4.8) and the book "Baby," by 5-year-old Marisol (Figure 10.12). The captions under Marisol's drawings were dictated to a scribe. Note that this elemental story has a beginning, rising action, climax, and resolution.

"The lady is going to have a baby."

"They drove to the hospital."

"And she had the baby. They were so happy and they loved the baby so much . . .

". . .they decided to get married!"

Figure 10.12   Story by Marisol, age 5 (Calkins 1986, p. 43)

Teachers can assist children in developing story graphs not only of published stories (Chap. 8) but also, occasionally, of their own stories. Again, there is opportunity to merge instruction, assessment, and evaluation by both teacher and student.

Development of Understanding of the Writing Process and of Writing Strategies

Young writers typically conceptualize writing as a one-draft process. Indeed, the difficulty in transcribing their ideas onto paper militates against their producing more than one draft, but initially their understanding inhibits this as well. It takes a while for young writers to become aware of the needs of an audience, whether the needs are those of content (for example, more detail) or form (for example, spaces between words, more letters to represent a word). Such development is gradual and can be documented through analysis of children's writing samples, as well as through discussion with the child.

Lucy Calkins (1986) discusses a variety of these developmental trends in understanding the writing process and control of strategies for writing. For example:

> For young children (in the K–1 range especially), drawing is an important form of rehearsal for writing; indeed, a story may be told more through pictures than writing, as Marisol's "Baby" story suggests. Drawing tends to give way to talking (with peers perhaps more than with the teacher) as a more important form of rehearsal. Later, the child becomes more able to try out ideas on paper (writing several "leads" for example, before choosing one). Still later, children become better able to weigh options mentally, without recourse to talking or writing. What they once did in revision, writers may now be able to do in rehearsal. (p. 96)

> As writers begin to understand the need for including more information in their writing, they may still be unable to sustain or even attempt the writing of a second draft. Early "revision" strategies may consist of writing more on a separate page and stapling it to the original, or of adding and clarifying details during discussion. Later, children may write more than one draft of a story, but without looking back at previous drafts with a concern for making improvements. Revision is a concept that evolves gradually. (passim)

> When young children write personal narratives, at first they seem unable to select or focus upon important details; they tell everything surrounding an important event, from the time they got up in the morning until they went to bed at night. For this reason, Donald Graves has dubbed such narratives "Bed-to-bed" stories. The events seem to be in control rather than the writer, and children are concerned to "tell it like it was." With more experience in writing and in reading published literature and each others' narratives, however, children often learn that their writing is more effective when it focuses on essentials. They may even discover "that sometimes the Truth of an event can best be conveyed by skipping some parts and taking poetic license with others." (p. 98)

Calkins' *The Art of Teaching Writing* documents in greater depth children's growing understanding of the writing process and of strategies for effective writing. These topics are explored more thoroughly also in some of the books on writing in the starter bibliography on reading, writing, and literacy in the classroom (Figure 10.13).

Development in Control of Various Aspects of the Written Product

As the foregoing discussion of writing development suggests, there is much to be learned from children's writing samples besides the degree to which the children can write "correctly." Correctness of form develops gradually, and children's development of the conventions of print should constitute only one of several factors considered in analyzing children's writing samples as products. Depending upon the maturity and experience of the writer, teachers might consider what a comparison of periodic writing samples shows about growth in such areas as these:

Effective leads: has the writer increased his or her repertoire of effective ways for beginning a piece?

Detail: has the writer developed in ability to employ detail effectively?

Focus: has the writer developed in ability to focus a piece of writing?

Voice: has the writer developed a clearer "voice," or developed in ability to modify voice according to the audience and purpose and topic?

Sequencing, organization: has the writer developed in ability to sequence or organize his or her writing?

Conventions: has the writer developed in control of any of the conventions of writing?

Considering conventions of language as only one of several aspects of the writing helps keep a concern for "correctness" in appropriate perspective.

Periodic Writing Samples: In Conclusion

As suggested above, writing samples can be analyzed and assessed not just by teachers alone, but with students during conferences. Such conferences enable teachers to better understand both the students and their writing. They also provide an opportunity for teachers to encourage students' metacognitive awareness of the writing process and their writing strategies, their self-evaluation, and the setting of goals for themselves as writers.

When writing is taught and assessed first and foremost as a process, the products can become truly amazing. So can the range of concerns exhibited by even rather young writers. For instance, Calkins in *Lessons from a Child* documents how Susie went from a concern merely for *information* (what to say next?) and *convention* (is this right?) at the

Atwell, Nancie. 1987. *In the Middle: Writing, Reading, and Learning with Adolescents*. Portsmouth, N.H.: Boynton/Cook.

Calkins, Lucy McCormick. 1986. *The Art of Teaching Writing*. Portsmouth, N.H.: Heinemann.

Calkins, Lucy McCormick, and Shelley Harwayne. 1987. *The Writing Workshop: A World of Difference*. Portsmouth, N.H.: Heinemann.

Cambourne, Brian. 1988. *The Whole Story: Natural Learning and the Acquisition of Literacy in the Classroom*. Auckland, New Zealand: Ashton Scholastic. Available in the U.S. from Scholastic.

Cochrane, Orin, Donna Cochrane, Sharen Scalena, and Ethel Buchanan. 1984. *Reading, Writing and Caring*. Winnipeg: Whole Language Consultants. Available in the U.S. from Richard C. Owen Publishers.

Enright, D. S., and M. L. McCloskey. 1988. *Integrating English: Developing English Language and Literacy in the Multilingual Classroom*. Reading, Mass.: Addison-Wesley.

Gilles, Carol, Mary Bixby, Paul Crowley, Shirley R. Crenshaw, Margaret Heinrichs, Frances E. Reynolds, and Donelle Pyle, eds. 1988. *Whole Language Strategies for Secondary Students*. Katonah, N.Y.: Richard C. Owen Publishers.

Graves, Donald. 1983. *Writing: Teachers & Children at Work*. Portsmouth, N.H.: Heinemann.

Hansen, Jane. 1987. *When Writers Read*. Portsmouth, N.H.: Heinemann.

Hansen, Jane, Thomas Newkirk, and Donald M. Graves, eds. 1985. *Breaking Ground: Teachers Relate Reading and Writing in the Elementary School*. Portsmouth, N.H.: Heinemann.

Harste, Jerome C., Kathy G. Short, and Carolyn Burke. 1988. *Creating Classrooms for Authors: The Reading-Writing Connection*. Portsmouth, N.H.: Heinemann.

Jensen, Julie M., ed. 1988. *Stories to Grow On: Demonstrations of Language Learning in K–8 Classrooms*. Portsmouth, N.H.: Heinemann.

Figure 10.13   Starter bibliography on reading, writing, and literacy in the classroom

beginning of her third-grade year to a concern for numerous factors two months later (Calkins 1983, p. 66):

information (what to say next?)
convention (is this right?)
action (it has a lot of action. I like when it goes plop!)
focus (it tells a lot about just one thing)
tone (I want this part to be shorter, quicker)
organization (I don't know how this fits together)
sequence (what happened next?)
truth (I want to think back to what really, really happened . . . have it fit with the real thing)

Johnson, D., and D. Roen, eds. 1989. *Richness in Writing: Empowering ESL Students.* New York: Longman.

Nathan, Ruth, Frances Temple, Kathleen Juntunen, and Charles Temple. 1988. *Classroom Strategies That Work: An Elementary Teacher's Guide to Process Writing.* Portsmouth, N.H.: Heinemann.

Newkirk, Thomas. 1989. *More Than Stories: The Range of Children's Writing.* Portsmouth, N.H.: Heinemann.

Newkirk, Thomas, and Nancie Atwell, eds. 1988. *Understanding Writing: Ways of Observing, Learning, and Teaching,* 2nd ed. Portsmouth, N.H.: Heinemann.

Newman, Judith M., ed., 1985. *Whole Language: Theory in Use.* Portsmouth, N.H.: Heinemann.

Rhodes, Lynn K., and Curt Dudley-Marling. 1988. *Readers and Writers with a Difference: A Holistic Approach to Teaching Learning Disabled and Remedial Students.* Portsmouth, N.H.: Heinemann.

Rigg, Pat, and Virginia D. Allen, eds. 1990. *When They Don't All Speak English: Integrating the ESL Students into the Regular Classroom.* Urbana, Ill.: National Council of Teachers of English.

Romano, Tom. 1987. *Clearing the Way: Working with Teenage Writers.* Portsmouth, N.H.: Heinemann.

Routman, Regie. 1988. *Transitions: From Literature to Literacy.* Portsmouth, N.H.: Heinemann.

Schwartz, Judith I. 1988. *Encouraging Early Literacy: An Integrated Approach to Reading and Writing in N–3.* Portsmouth, N.H.: Heinemann.

Strickland, Dorothy S., and Leslie Mandel Morrow, eds. 1989. *Emerging Literacy: Young Children Learn to Read and Write.* Newark, Del.: International Reading Association.

Watson, Dorothy, ed. 1988. *Ideas and Insights: Language Arts in the Elementary School.* Urbana, Ill.: National Council of Teachers of English.

Figure 10.13   (*continued*)

audience (will they know where I am?)
ending (I don't know if the ending is too good)
detail (putting all the stuff that happened . . . I could write a big, big, book on it)

As Calkins points out, much of this expansion in focus is surely due to the teacher's adoption of a process approach to writing and the assessment of writing. With such an approach, students learn to ask themselves and one another a wide range of questions about their writings and their writing processes (see Calkins 1983, pp. 129–30 and 158). Assessment becomes an ongoing process in the classroom, engaged in by both teachers and students.

THINK-ALOUD PROTOCOLS

Protocols are simply think-aloud sessions, recorded for later analysis. To help students become more reflective about their literacy and learning processes, teachers can first model their own process of reading something or writing something or perhaps of studying something to understand it more fully. Then students can be encouraged to try the same procedure.

Thus, a student may be invited to think aloud before, while, and after engaging in the process of reading a story, textbook selection, or other kind of text. The reader can be invited to predict what will happen or what the text will contain and to explain reasons for the prediction—then, while reading, to discuss how predictions are confirmed or changed and new predictions generated. The reader can be encouraged to discuss problems encountered in dealing with specific words, as well as strategies that the reader chooses to try, or not to try. The reader may also discuss the process and development of understanding, consider problems arising when comprehension seems to be lost, explore strategies for dealing with problems in constructing meaning, and share ongoing reflections upon the content of the selection. In short, anything the reader thinks or thinks about while reading can be verbalized and tape-recorded for later analysis and discussion between teacher and student.

Much the same procedure can be followed for eliciting protocols revealing a student's writing process—or process of researching, studying for a test, or whatever process is of particular interest to the teacher.

Calkins' *Lessons from a Child* (1983) contains many anecdotal examples of students' thinking-aloud about the writing process. The use of more formal protocols is discussed and illustrated, with respect to reading, in Brown and Lytle's ''Merging Assessment and Instruction: Protocols in the Classroom'' (1988). Such protocols offer a unique view of the thinking involved in children's process of reading and constructing meaning from text as well as their process of composing written text.

RECORDED OBSERVATIONS

Observation, like self-evaluation, is at the heart of all good teaching, across all aspects of the curriculum. Teachers are constantly observing how students engage in and respond to learning experiences, then reconsidering and modifying what they themselves do accordingly. What is different for many who have become whole language teachers is that casual observation now becomes the basis for *recorded observations:*

❝Observation, like self-evaluation, is at the heart of all good teaching, across all aspects of the curriculum. Teachers are constantly observing how students engage in and respond to learning experiences, then reconsidering and modifying what they themselves do accordingly.❞

documented evidence of the learning process. Legitimatizing this normal activity as a form of assessment leads teachers to observe more, reflect more insightfully upon what they and their students are doing, and in turn become better teachers. Again, assessment and instruction blend together, but in this instance it is perhaps teachers who learn the most—not only about students' learning, but about their own teaching.

Many things can be noted as students engage in individual, pair, small-group, and whole-class activities. Such activities offer teachers many opportunities to observe and record such things as the student's interest and involvement in various kinds of activities and projects; the student's self-confidence as a reader, writer, thinker, and researcher; and, of course, anecdotes about any aspect of learning or notes on kinds of support that learners seem to need. Anything and everything can be observed and jotted down for later recall or consideration. Such observations become invaluable when preparing periodic reports or preparing for parent–teacher conferences.

For example, frequent observations would enable a teacher to determine the most appropriate characterization of a reader according to the "scale of experience" chart provided in *The Primary Language Record* (Barrs et al. 1989); and if none of the descriptions quite fit, or the student seemed on the borderline, the teacher could explain why. This is the kind of record-keeping summary that may be facilitated by recorded observations (see Figure 10.14).

For recording such observations, a variety of formats can be used. One that may be particularly helpful is a form on which teachers record children's participation in various activities associated with a thematic unit or a research project; see, for example, the section on "Middle Grade Expansions" in the *Whole Language Evaluation Book* (K. Goodman, Goodman, and Hood 1989). Class checklists can also be handy for recording data that is later synthesized for evaluation: see, for example, Dalrymple's "Basic Form Used for Science," Figure 10.15.

Checklists, however, can become impediments rather than aids to appropriate assessment when each child is rated in terms of a list of minute behaviors or skills. For example, Gail Heald-Taylor (1989) provides a checklist of over 125 listening, speaking, reading, and writing behaviors that might be observed as signs of growth in kindergarten and grade 1 ("Whole Language Behavior Inventory," pp. 128–33). This extensive list includes behaviors such as "listens to stories from books, records, films," "retells stories from literature," "holds a book and tells a story as though reading," and "composes narrative through scribble or invented letters." Such a list can be highly valuable in suggesting kinds of behaviors the teacher might anticipate as signs of language and literacy development, but devastating if used as a checklist for behaviors,

Reading Scale 2

INEXPERIENCED

Inexperienced reader 1	Experience as a reader has been limited. Generally chooses to read very easy and familiar texts where illustrations play an important part. Has difficulty with any unfamiliar material and yet may be able to read own dictated texts confidently. Needs a great deal of support with the reading demands of the classroom. Over-dependent on one strategy when reading aloud; often reads word by word. Rarely chooses to read for pleasure.
Less experienced reader 2	Developing fluency as a reader and reading certain kinds of material with confidence. Usually chooses short books with simple narrative shapes and with illustrations and may read these silently; often re-reads favorite books. Reading for pleasure often includes comics and magazines. Needs help with the reading demands of the classroom and especially with using reference and information books.
Moderately experienced reader 3	A confident reader who feels at home with books. Generally reads silently and is developing stamina as a reader. Is able to read for longer periods and cope with more demanding texts, including children's novels. Willing to reflect on reading and often uses reading in own learning. Selects books independently and can use information books and materials for straightforward reference purposes, but still needs help with unfamiliar material, particularly non-narrative prose.
Experienced reader 4	A self-motivated, confident and experienced reader who may be pursuing particular interests through reading. Capable of tackling some demanding texts and can cope well with the reading of the curriculum. Reads thoughtfully and appreciates shades of meaning. Capable of locating and drawing on a variety of sources in order to research a topic independently.
Exceptionally experienced reader 5	An enthusiastic and reflective reader who has strong established tastes in fiction and/or non-fiction. Enjoys pursuing own reading interests independently. Can handle a wide range and variety of texts, including some adult material. Recognises that different kinds of texts require different styles of reading. Able to evaluate evidence drawn from a variety of information sources. Is developing critical awareness as a reader.

EXPERIENCED

Figure 10.14 **Experience as a reader across the curriculum (Barrs et al., *The Primary Language Record: A Handbook for Teachers*, CLPE 1989, p. 27)**

Time Study Sept. '86 Science	Time Line	Described ↓ OBSERVATIONS	Design of Experiment	Record of Data	Hypothesizing ↓ generalizing	Log Entries
Mark	✓+	+	✓ soil+	—	+	—
Todd	✓	✓	✓ soil	—	+	✓
Sue	✓	—	— beans	—	—	—
Marge	✓	✓	✓ soil	✓	✓	✓ —
Carol	⑦ ✓	✓ —	— leaf	—	—	✓ —
Don	✓ —	+	— water	—	—	
Richard	✓ —	+	✓+ pre-serve	✓+	✓	✓
Scott	—	✓	✓ oil	✓	✓	✓ —
Melissa	+	+	+ aloe	✓+	✓+	✓+
Darrell	✓	✓ —	TM 1	O	O	—
Nancy	✓+	+	+ aloe	+	+	+
Tye	✓	✓	TM 5	✓	+	✓
Peter	✓+	+	✓ oil	✓	✓	✓ —
Kevin	✓ —	✓ —	— beans	—	—	✓ —
David	✓ —	✓	TM 3	✓ —	✓	✓
Derek	✓	✓	TM 3	✓ —	✓	✓
Dawn	—	✓	TM 3	✓ —	✓	✓
Maggie	⑦ ✓	✓	TM 6	✓+	✓	+
Emily	✓ —	✓	TM 4	✓	✓	✓
Darin	⑦ ✓	✓	TM 5	✓	✓	✓
Trish	✓+	✓	✓ — plants	✓ —	✓ —	✓ —
Ellen	+	+ ESSAY	O	O	+	+
Jean	✓+	✓+	✓ seeds	✓ —	✓	✓
Jane	+	✓	✓ seeds	✓ —	✓	✓

Figure 10.15 Basic form used for science (Dalrymple 1989, p. 116)

all of which the child is expected to exhibit over the course of the kindergarten and first-grade years.

As mentioned earlier, teachers need some efficient yet effective means of capturing the unplanned observations that occur daily: for example, stickers, post-its, or index cards that can be later added to each student's record sheet or file.

Observations can, of course, be recorded using video- and audio-tapes. Such means might be particularly appropriate in recording for later analysis the discussion that occurs in literature study groups as the students and teacher discuss a book the group is reading. The teacher as leader may encourage students to engage in thoughtful consideration of the text by asking questions and responding to teachable moments. But most of all the teacher is genuinely a member of the group, sharing her or his own uncertainties about what is happening, making hypotheses and predictions, and relating the book to her or his own life.

The article "Grand Conversations: An Exploration of Meaning Construction in Literature Study Groups" offers some idea of what teachers might observe as they (or in this case, teachers in training) lead literature study groups with children of middle-school age. The purpose, as the title suggests, is to have "grand conversations" about literature, not the teacher-dominated inquisitions that often stem from the questions in basal reading programs. In literature study groups, teachers deliberately minimize the asking of literal recall questions, yet the nitty-gritty of factual information necessarily emerges in the discussions; in fact, participants in the study group help one another decide what is going on in the story, if the text is not immediately clear to everyone. Talk among students helps create a better understanding of what is being read.

The authors of this article summarize from their field notes and from audiotapes of the literature study sessions, supplemented by teacher journals:

> In these study groups, which were made up of readers of varying abilities, children as young as ten participated in rich discussions of works of literature which revealed that they were capable of (1) articulating their construction of simple meaning, but also changing it as they heard alternate views; (2) sharing personal stories inspired by the reading or discussion, often in poignant and revealing ways which triggered identification by other group members; (3) participating as active readers—predicting and hypothesizing and confirming or disconfirming their predictions as they read; and (4) showing that they had attained insights about how the author had communicated her message to them and supporting their evaluations of that communication with their interpretations of the text. (Eeds and Wells 1989, p. 27)

As the authors of this study point out, "even when the teacher-leaders were making conscious efforts not to ask traditional comprehension questions, students consistently practiced the very behaviors these questions are designed to invoke" (p. 11). But obviously, they engaged also in more sophisticated kinds of thinking and responding, including the kinds of behaviors typical of proficient readers. Teachers can look for and record such evidence of reading and thinking abilities when observing literature groups in their own classrooms (see the sample form in Figure 10.16). Such observations are facilitated when students become comfortable enough with the format to engage in "grand conversations" on their own. (Useful in understanding why and how to initiate such conversations is Louise Rosenblatt's *Literature as Exploration*, a classic that

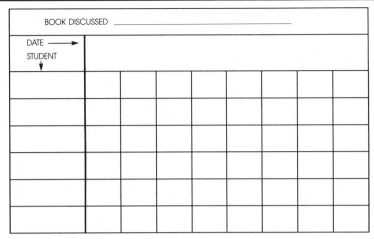

BOOK DISCUSSED _____

DATE ⟶
STUDENT ↓

RESPONSES FOCUSED ON:

U= understanding and interpreting essentials of story
S= relating to book by sharing personal stories
P= predicting, hypothesizing, confirming/disconfirming
A= commenting on and/or evaluating author's strategies,
    craft, literary devices
O= other

**Figure 10.16 Sample form for recording response types in literature study
group**

was first published in 1938; *Literature in the Classroom: Readers, Texts, and
Contexts*, edited by Ben Nelms, 1988; and *Talking About Books: Creating
Literate Communities*, Short and Mitchell-Pierce 1990.)

Of course, these examples exhaust neither the settings nor the means
nor the kinds of observations that can become a part of documentation
and assessment. Teachers can record observations of students after they
have engaged in a Shared Book Experience, while they are engaging in
group research discussions, while they are choosing a book to read
silently—anywhere and everywhere. Whatever other assessment measures teachers may adopt, ongoing observation is crucial, and written
observations are an invaluable means of record keeping, of preserving a
moment in time.

CONFERENCES AND INTERVIEWS

Like observation, conferencing is central to whole language education. In conferences, teachers can collect samples of children's reading
and select samples of their writing for analysis; interview children about
their concept of themselves as a reader and a writer and/or about their
reading and writing interests and strategies; listen to children read,

discuss the book, and help readers enlarge their repertoire of effective strategies; read children's writing, suggest writing strategies, and explain skills while helping children reconsider and revise their piece; engage students in self-evaluation and goal setting, and so forth.

One kind of conferencing that offers simultaneous opportunity for instruction and assessment is the "roving" mini-conference, perhaps as brief as a couple of minutes. While moving among students as they read or write, the teacher may stop beside a child and ask "How's it going?" "What's your book (or writing) about?" "Is there anything you need help with?" With these and similar questions, the teacher can assess children's progress and needs, provide support as necessary, and later write down observations that form part of the documentation of children's learning.

Whole language teachers sometimes conference with or interview parents and children at the beginning of the school year to gain insight into "where the child is at." For example, *The Primary Language Handbook* provides information on conducting an initial discussion with parents: what might be discussed, how the discussion might be conducted, and how parents and teacher together can decide what should be recorded as a result of the discussion. This is to become part of the child's permanent record (Barrs et al. 1989, pp. 12–13). The same document gives similar suggestions for an initial conference with the child. For example, "The child would be asked to bring to the conference a self-chosen selection of books or other texts in English and/or other community languages that s/he had read recently, and a selection of her/his writing, which might include writing in more than one language" (Barrs et al., p. 14). These would serve as a starting point for discussion during a language and literacy conference, providing data for initial assessment that could be compared with data from a conference near the end of the year.

These are illustrations of what might be considered the two extremes: mini-conferences and maxi-conferences. Various kinds of conferences offer different opportunities for data gathering, record keeping, and assessment.

INVENTORIES AND QUESTIONNAIRES

Inventories and questionnaires can be important sources of insight for teachers. Compare, for example, the responses of the two children in Figure 10.17 to questions based on Burke's Reading Inventory (Y. Goodman, Watson, and Burke 1987, pp. 219–20). Clearly, one child has a meaning-based definition of reading while the other has a word-based definition. Strategies for working with these children must surely differ.

Jenny, Grade 3

I: What do you think reading is?

J: Something that um, helps you learn words.

. . . .

I: What do people do when they read?

J: They just read the words that are in the book.

I: They read the words in the book? Anything else? No? Okay, when you're reading something and you come to a word that you don't know, what do you usually do?

J: Sound it out.

I: Sound it out? Do you ever do anything else? No? Okay. Who is a good reader that you know?

J: Shaun.

I: Who is Shaun?

J: My sister, her friend um, her brother, he keeps on reading and he tries to do jump rope when he's reading a book.

I: What do you think makes Shaun a good reader?

J: He went to speech where um, they um, teach him how to read and stuff real good.

I: Do you think Shaun ever comes to a word or something in a story that he doesn't know?

J: Sometimes.

I: Sometimes? What do you think Shaun would do if he came to a word he didn't know?

J: Sound it out.

I: You think he'd sound it out too.

. . . .

I: If you knew someone who was having trouble reading, what do you think you would do to help them?

J: Ask and see if they would sound it out and maybe that would help.

I: Sound it out? Is there anything else you might do to help them? What if they couldn't sound it out?

J: I would tell them the word.

I: Oh, you'd tell them the word.

Barbara, Grade 1

I: What do you think reading is?

B: When you read, it's um, kind of like you're just looking at a book but you're just saying the words because you think they're easy, but they're really not so easy. And, like, stuff like that.

I: That's a good answer of what you think reading is. When you're reading and you come to a word that you don't know, what do you do?

B: Kind of like I sound it out. It's kind of like you come to a word and you think, "Well, should I sound it out, or should I just ask somebody?" Then you see that all the people you want to ask are busy and you kind of sound it out.

I: Do you ever do anything else when you come to a word you don't know?

B: Um, most of the time I skip it.

I: After you skip a word, do you find it easier?

B: Yeah. Like when you skip a word and then go to the end, you can go back to it and read it.

I: Does this help more than sounding it out?

B: Yeah.

Figure 10.17 **Comparison of two children's initial reading inventories (interviews)**

Another kind of inventory or questionnaire can elicit what the student has read for enjoyment in the past three months; the kinds of books and materials the student most enjoys reading, and the authors; or other interests the teacher might draw upon in recommending books, magazines, and other materials for the student to read. Writing experience and habits might be determined, too, along with interests and topics the student might like to write about. In each case, the inventory or questionnaire can provide initial data for comparison with data gathered later in the year, to determine progress.

DIALOGUE JOURNALS AND LEARNING LOGS

Since the publication of Toby Fulwiler and Art Young's *Language Connections: Writing and Reading Across the Curriculum* (1982) and then Nancie Atwell's award-winning *In the Middle: Writing, Reading, and Learning with Adolescents* (1987), teachers at all levels have increasingly become aware of the potential for learning and assessment of such interactive (transactive) devices as *dialogue journals, written conversations,* and *learning logs.* What all these have in common is that they encourage students to dialogue with themselves—that is, to think on paper—as well as to communicate with teachers, and sometimes with other students. They offer teachers opportunities to respond to students in a variety of ways, such as by clarifying what a student has only partially understood, asking and responding to questions, affirming, challenging, and extending the student's thinking, encouraging the student to pursue other ideas and resources, and just responding human being-to-human being. Furthermore, written reflections provide both students and teachers with rich opportunities for assessment and self-evaluation.

In her book *In the Middle*, Atwell describes how she turned her eighth-grade reading class into a reading workshop, during which a brief minilesson is followed by time for reading: everyone reads silently, including the teacher. In order to enrich students' reflection upon the books they read, to create written conversations about literature that resemble the ''dining room table'' talk that she and her husband enjoyed in sharing books, Atwell initiated dialogue journals: an exchange of letters between her students and herself and between students and their peers. Here are the first two paragraphs of her first letter to students at the beginning of the school year:

> Dear Readers,
> Your notebook is a place for you, me, and your friends to talk this year about books, reading, authors, and writing. You'll be chatting about literature in letters to me and friends; we'll write letters back to you. All our letters will stay here together, arranged chronologically, as a record of the thinking, learning, and reading we did together.
> In your letters talk with us about what you've read. Tell what you noticed. Tell what you thought and felt and why. Tell what you liked and didn't and why. Tell how you read and why. Tell what these books said and meant to you. Ask questions or for help. And write back about our ideas, feelings, experiences, and questions. (Atwell 1987, p. 193)

Atwell's intention, of course, was to encourage her students to become *readers*: not just students who *could* read but young people who *chose* to read, for their own purposes and pleasure. Allowing students to choose their own books, she found, virtually ensures that everyone will "get into" books: "Each year by the end of September even the most reluctant readers have found the one good book that begins a turnaround in their attitudes toward reading and abilities as readers" (1987, p. 162). Atwell offers the following data as evidence that as a result of simply reading and responding to books, students read more, comprehend better, and value books to a greater degree:

> Last year's eighth graders, including eight special education students, read an average of thirty-five full length works, from Blume to Bronte, Strasser to Steinbeck, Voight to Verne. Their scores on standardized achievement tests averaged at the seventy-second percentile, up from an average at the fifty-fourth percentile when fully twenty-one percent scored in the bottom quartile; last year, that figure was just two percent. In June, 92 percent of my students indicated that they regularly read at home for pleasure—that they were taking home the books they read during reading workshop—and when I asked how many books they owned, the average figure they gave was 98, up from September's average of 54. (I have no way of knowing whether they did, in fact, own more books by the end of eighth grade. I do know they perceived themselves as owning more, as being the sort of people who acquire and collect libraries.) (Atwell 1987, p. 158)

This is the sort of documentation that may begin to convince those accustomed to seeking evidence of learning through numerical data. However, what was revealed through students' dialogue journals gave far richer evidence of their learning. In an appendix, Atwell lists over 100 kinds of "talk" that emerged in students' dialogue journals over the course of a year, involving not only various facets of the author's craft and concepts of genre and mode (traditionally the province of the English class) but also the reader's own reading processes and own writing, the reader's personal response to the book, book recommendations and criteria for making them, and how books are published. In short, the students evidenced engagement with books, interest in writing and writers, and increasingly sophisticated criteria for deciding what makes a book "good." The dialogue journals provided ample documentation that learning had taken place.

The term *written conversation* seems to be used mainly by primary teachers, in reference to very brief written exchanges. Galindo, for instance, provides a sample of what some educators call a written conversation, in this case between two first-grade children, one whose native language is English, the other Spanish. The bilingual conversation offers each child the opportunity to grow in understanding the other language (see Figure 10.18).

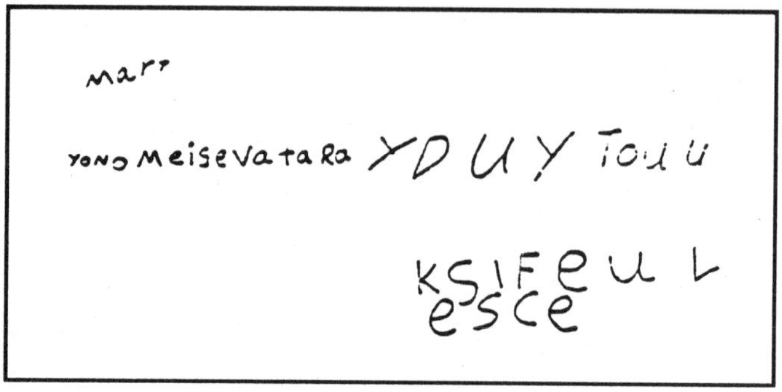

Lupe: Yo no me quise levantar en esta mañana.
(I didn't want to get up this morning.)
Luis: Why didn't you want to get up?
Lupe: Because I feel lazy.

Figure 10.18 Bilingual written conversation between two first-graders (Galindo 1989, p. 64)

The term *learning log* is sometimes used for journals in various content areas, regardless of grade level. For instance, Fulwiler and Young offer examples of how college students wrestle with concerns about the environment and with concepts such as "humanities," in what some educators would refer to as learning logs (Fulwiler and Young 1982, in their article "The Personal Connection: Journal Writing"). In such academic journals or learning logs, students can share their struggles in working math problems, brainstorm causes of World War II, record observations of experiments and speculate on the results—whatever is appropriate to the topic and field of study. And in responding, teachers can assess students' learning and modify instruction and support accordingly.

STUDENT-KEPT RECORDS

Students themselves can record a considerable amount of the data that teachers later use for assessment. This engages the students in valuable self-reflection, self-evaluation, and goal setting.

For example, even beginning readers and writers may be able to keep simple records of the books they have read: The teacher can provide a simple form on an index card, with only minimal information required. Students can also keep lists of possible topics for writing. And before engaging in exploration of a topic or theme, they may brainstorm and jot down "What I know" about the topic and "What I'd like to know," then later complete a third column, "What I learned" about the topic.

Individually and in groups, students can also evaluate their own work and their progress. One interesting example comes from a second-grade teacher, whose students in a group evaluation session compared their current journals with their journals earlier in the year. "At first Rosa did not make sense. Now her writing does," they concluded. "Chris has become a better speller." "Damon has become a better writer. He writes more now." And so forth (Woodley and Woodley 1989, p. 72). The group self-evaluation encourages appreciation of each others' strengths and growth, as well as the development of criteria for evaluation.

Perhaps most impressive, even young children can keep a record of skills they know and can use, then use this list as a benchmark against which to measure their work. For example, Giacobbe explains how her first-graders keep a cumulative list of editing skills for which they can take responsibility. The child adds a new skill to the list when both teacher and child think the child is ready. See, as an example, Figure 10.19, showing a first-grader's own cumulative list of editing skills for which she can be held accountable: everything from "Write my name" to "Use periods" and "Use a comma instead of *and*" (Giacobbe 1984). Students in whole language classrooms willingly accept a tremendous amount of responsibility for their own learning and self-evaluation.

> **❝**Students in whole language classrooms willingly accept a tremendous amount of responsibility for their own learning and self-evaluation.**❞**

ACTIVITIES AND PROJECTS: OPPORTUNITIES FOR LEARNING AND ASSESSMENT

In whole language classrooms, language and literacy are vehicles for learning throughout all the content areas. In turn, involvement in exploring literature, social studies, science, and math, for example, provides many opportunities for students to actively use oral language and reading and writing as vehicles for coming to understand and to express their understanding, thus enabling them to become more proficient in producing and comprehending language. Whether the approach is thematic or otherwise, such integrated learning provides many opportunities for assessment of various sorts, including the assessment of reading and writing.

Some activities are relatively limited in scope, while others take on dimensions that make them seem more like extensive projects. I will merely mention a few that begin to suggest ways in which assessment can evolve from learning and instruction. And while I will not belabor the point with extensive examples, it should be clear that all of the kinds of assessments mentioned earlier, and more, can occur as students

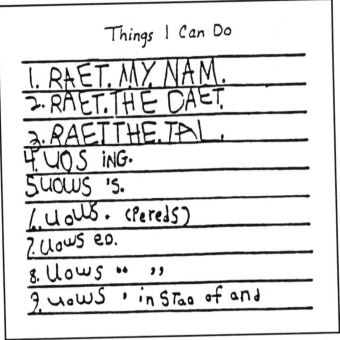

Figure 10.19 First-grader's list of editing skills (Giacobbe 1984)

engage in the varied learning experiences offered in whole language classrooms.

Semantic Mapping, Story Graphing

Part way through the writing of this chapter, I made a *semantic map* of various means of assessment other than tests, worksheets, and the like, to help clarify my thinking. The map thus served as a means of self-assessment—and three or four versions later, the map became Figure 10.20. In the classroom, teachers will sometimes invite students to make their semantic map of a concept as ''rich'' or detailed as they can, in an effort to assess the full range of the students' understanding. For example, one third-grade teacher had students do a map for ''technology'' after exploring its effects through children's books, hands-on activities, discussion, and writing. The act of producing a semantic map stimulates recall and thought, while honoring students' unique perceptions.

For more detail on the uses of semantic mapping, see Joan Heimlich and Susan Pittelman's *Semantic Mapping: Classroom Applications* (1986).

Figure 10.20 **Story map prepared by first-graders (Photograph by John D. Willison)**

Also, *graphic organizers* or ''structured overviews'' of various kinds offer similar benefits for learning and assessment. See, for instance, Wilson's chapter in my *Reading Process and Practice* (Weaver 1988), which offers not only some examples but a valuable discussion of how to facilitate reading and comprehension in the content areas; the techniques would offer many opportunities for assessment. *Story graphs or maps* can be developed, particularly with younger or less experienced readers, in order to facilitate their understanding of the structure of a story, their ability to structure stories similarly in their own writing, and, of course, for assessment (see Reutzel 1985, and Marshall 1983); see Figure 10.20.

The potential for assessment is inherent in all of these learning activities.

Informal Drama

An example described in an article by Betty J. Wagner (1983) beautifully illustrates the potential of informal drama for learning and assessment. Wagner and a colleague introduced a group of 8- and 9-year-olds to a social studies unit on Brazil and a science unit on water by having students dramatize and role play events that occurred when a team of Brazilian engineers built a dam down river from the valley that for generations had been the home of the Moqui Indian nation. The adults themselves adopted roles in the dramatic episodes, with the children playing the parts of the Moqui as well as the engineers. Together, the group worked through several imaginary dramatic episodes as the Indians were forced to leave their homeland and find somewhere else to live because of the flooding that would be caused by the dam.

First, the drama leaders led the children in activities to help them begin to feel like a Moqui tribe:

> The class was divided into small groups, each of which became a different family in the tribe, and we began the drama by improvising waking up and starting the routine tasks of the day. . . . No information was given beforehand; we were interested at this point in helping them believe they were Indians; too many facts might have taken their mind away from the focus needed for belief. Anything they imagined at this stage—unless it was a gross anachronism—was allowed to grow from inside the children. Slowly—almost at life rate—the children improvised routines of washing, building fires, hunting or fishing, preparing food, eating, or caring for the young. The movements were largely pantomime as the group concentrated on exploring what it must be like to be Indians. Only after this slow-paced building of belief were they ready to plan a group event that would symbolize the life of the tribe. (Wagner 1983, pp. 156–57)

This establishment of a tribal sense preceded the introduction of the conflict: the fact that white men had been seen down river cutting down trees with axes and throwing them into the river, to build a dam.

Children's learning was reflected and could be assessed in various ways: by their resolving of the dilemma (the needs of the Moqui in conflict with the needs of the white engineers); by their understanding of the tribal life and values, as reflected in what they wrote in their role as tribesperson; by their intellectual curiosity, as demonstrated by the questions about the Moqui that they generated and researched, after engaging in the several role-playing activities; by their ability to use more adult texts for research, as a result of their incipient knowledge and generation of their own questions; and so forth. As Wagner points out, a final activity might have been to recreate the life of the tribe in a more tangible and accurate way than was done in the initial improvisation (Wagner 1983, p. 161). This activity, too, would have been a form of assessment, stimulating and growing naturally from the students' learning.

For more ideas on how improvisational drama might be used for learning and assessment, you might consult Wagner 1976, O'Neill and Lambert 1982, and Morgan and Saxton 1987.

Cross-Genre Writing

A particularly valuable way of stimulating and assessing students' learning is to provide opportunities for them to convey factual information and understanding in a variety of written genres: stories, plays, poems, letters, advertisements, newspapers and magazines, travel brochures, or any other form that seems to accommodate the particular topic.

When my son was in the sixth grade, for example, his science/language arts teacher Louise Harvey divided the class into eight groups, one for each of the known planets, other than Earth. The groups were to serve as travel agencies, preparing a poster and possibly a brochure advertising ''their'' planet. They were to research their planet and incorporate factual information about it into their advertising. Figure 10.21 shows what John wrote for the brochure, reflecting his factual knowledge about Mars, his understanding of scientific principles (people couldn't survive in a carbon dioxide atmosphere), his recollection of the cantina scene in *Star Wars*, and an ability to suit persuasive details to his assumed audience. This was also, of course, an occasion for the teacher to guide students in rehearsal, drafting, revision, and editing, as well as ''publishing'' (creating the brochure). Again, more opportunities for assessment.

Factual knowledge and creative and sophisticated thinking can be encouraged and assessed through a variety of writings across the curriculum. For example: students who have researched the Underground Railroad could write first-person accounts of a slave who has escaped to freedom; students who have studied the Revolutionary War could write letters to the editor of the *Boston Observer* regarding various issues; students in a human development class could write and respond to each others' Dear Abby letters, drawing upon what they're learning; and so forth.

Recently, I've been very successful in encouraging ''creative'' final exams in my reading-process course. Students are encouraged to write in whatever format they wish, other than the traditional academic essay; the purpose is to demonstrate the most important things they have learned, being sure not to focus too narrowly on one or two limited topics. Writers are encouraged also to draw upon relevant personal experiences and the experiences of others they know. The ''exams'' are written outside class rather than during our two-hour exam period. I've received letters, imaginary and real; dialogues and dramas; detective and adventure and sci-fi stories; parodies of children's and adults' books (*The Wizard of Oz* seems to be a favorite); entire newspapers and magazines; journals and diaries written specifically for the exam; a lengthy

Are you tired of sitting around all winter? And not having anyplace to go or anything to do in the summer? If so, Mars is the place for you!

Since there is only carbon dioxide on Mars, you would be living in our new luxurious oxygen-filled domes enclosing the crater lakes filled with our imported water.

So when it is winter on your planet and summer on Mars, you can go swimming in the crater lakes and get a suntan nearby, and there are also places where you can go rock hunting and maybe find lots of jewels. There's a casino where you can play the slot machines, roulette, poker, and all sorts of other games. And an arcade where you can leave your children for the afternoon. Also there is a new disco where you can have your favorite drinks and try our new Martian Martini, meet all sorts of other people and space creatures from other galaxies, and dance to the music played by the Aboogle Gullipsy band. You can travel by our new rocket tram to the other cities and visit famous night clubs, and even see the Martian capital.

When it is summer on your planet and winter on Mars, at the two polar caps you can go ice skating, ice fishing, or skiing outside the dome, wearing our new jetomatic suits. Or you can go snowmobiling and sledding down Terror Hill with all of the new ten-foot-high ice jumps. And in the evening after you come back from skiing or whatever, you can watch the erupting of the red hot lava from the volcanoes Marsheverous or Olympus Mons, the biggest of the volcanoes.

On our new ship, that is guided by our guide ship Enterprise, we will take you through the asteroid belt and point out the most famous asteroid, Ceres, as we are going at the exhilarating speed of 54,000 miles per hour for a fun-filled trip of 33 days and nights.

For the average round trip of 98,000,000 miles from Earth to Mars, you pay only the low, low price of $35,000. And when your planet is closest to Mars you can get a special rate. So consult your travel agent today for the best deal ever!

Figure 10.21   Text for travel brochure advertising Mars (John, grade 6)

rhymed poem written in rap style; fairy tales and fables; and probably other genres that I don't happen to remember. Students who are convinced they aren't creative often settle for writing letters or dialogues, but in every case the attempt to personalize the writing often leads to new insights and understanding. Students comment enthusiastically about how much they learn writing these finals, and naturally their engagement contributes not only to their learning but to a persuasive, high-quality product. Every semester, I receive *several* papers that I consider of publishable quality. (See, for example, Peterson 1987; her article was an ''exam'' from the first semester I encouraged cross-genre writing.)

Experimenting with this kind of teaching/learning/assessment is well worth the effort.

Projects: The Quest Design

Classroom projects can, of course, take many forms. Here, I want to describe just one: the Quest design developed by Stephen Tchudi (1986, 1987). With appropriate modifications, the Quest approach can stimulate reading, writing, and learning across the content areas at all levels, elementary through college. In brief, students brainstorm possible topics and then choose one for investigation; brainstorm questions they might consider researching, related to the topic; and then divide into interest groups related to the questions, wherein the students can do more detailed semantic mapping (or "webbing") to explore the topic. After several sessions of question formation and discussion, each student takes a specific question related to the more general subtopic to investigate further.

One particularly noteworthy feature of the Quest design is the wide range of resources the students are encouraged to draw upon (see Figure 10.22). Resources may include people, institutions like museums, newspapers, businesses, and industries, as well as books, magazines, recordings, films, and videotapes. Students may need to write letters, interview people, or gather information by telephone; thus, research for the project involves students in using both oral and written language.

The other particularly valuable feature of Quest is the wide range of formats that students are encouraged to consider in reporting their results, depending on the nature of the Quest: fiction, drama, television reports, newscasts, position papers, children's books, posters, demonstrations, videotapes, and so forth. The projects offer many opportunities to assess students' language and literacy skills as well as their understanding of the topic. Of course, assessment can take many forms—including the response of those beyond the classroom with whom the resulting projects might be shared. Sharing their work with a broader audience is a powerful incentive to students' learning.

FROM ASSESSMENT TO ACCOUNTABILITY

Informal, teacher-developed assessment has, then, many facets. The assessment of reading, writing, and literacy should include periodic performance samples of reading and writing, but it will surely include

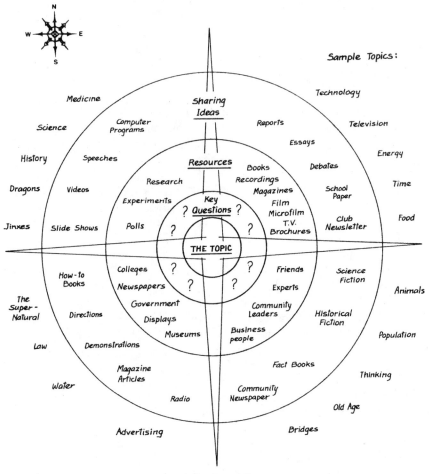

Figure 10.22   The Quest design (Tchudi 1987)

data gathered from a variety of other means and measures, such as: think-aloud protocols, recorded observations, conferences and interviews, inventories and questionnaires, dialogue journals and learning logs, and student-kept records. Observation and self-evaluation permeate all such assessments, and assessment is continuous and inextricably intertwined with instruction. Thus, children's daily involvement in activities and projects offers ample opportunities for most kinds of assessment, both of language and literacy development and of learning in other areas. Considered together, the data from several such informal means of assessment provide a far more valid and valuable basis for

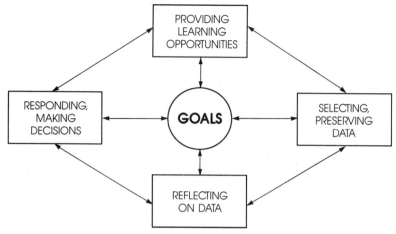

Figure 10.23 Assessment in the classroom context (based on Cameron 1990)

educational decision-making than standardized or similar kinds of tests.

While providing learning opportunities, the teacher has opportunities for selecting and then preserving data for assessment. After reflecting on the data, the teacher responds and makes educational decisions regarding subsequent opportunities—and so on. But this process is not merely unidirectional, as suggested in Figure 10.23, and the teacher can consider any aspect of this ongoing process in reference to long-term educational goals. *Reflection* is the key to using informal assessment as a basis for making decisions with regard to learning activities and data to be collected.

As teachers and administrators continue to develop a broad base for assessment and evaluation, accountability also takes on new meaning. When educators strive to align both instruction and assessment with long-range educational goals, administrators and teachers hold themselves accountable not merely or mainly for high test scores, but for facilitating students' growth as readers and writers, as thinkers and learners, and for helping them achieve their full potential as human beings. They offer parents and the public not merely number and letter grades but instead, or in support of these, detailed evidence of student growth in far more, and more significant, domains than those purportedly assessed by standardized, state-mandated, and basal tests. This documentation provides a much more adequate and appropriate basis for educational decision-making and evaluation of all involved in the educational enterprise.

❝When educators strive to align both instruction and assessment with long-range educational goals, administrators and teachers hold themselves accountable not merely or mainly for high test scores, but for facilitating students' growth as readers and writers, as thinkers and learners, and for helping them achieve their full potential as human beings.**❞**

From Understanding to Implementing a Whole Language Philosophy

In a sense, whole language is nothing more—nor less—than good education. Derived from research converging from a variety of disciplines, the underlying philosophy emphasizes the importance of viewing the learner and the learner's needs as central to education. Thus "doing whole language" means making a commitment to an active, transactional model of learning rather than to a passive, transmission model. It means valuing the ability to read and write for a variety of purposes above scoring well on tests of isolated skills—though, in fact, the former may lead to the latter. It means teachers developing the curriculum with and in response to the learners rather than someone else imposing a prepackaged curriculum upon teachers and students. It also means teachers taking primary responsibility for assessment and evaluation. It means developing language and literacy by engaging students in speaking and listening and reading and writing as they explore concepts and issues across the curriculum and beyond. And it means valuing and cultivating critical and creative thought.

The question is, of course, how can the implementation of such a salutory philosophy of education be facilitated, particularly since the transmission model of education has been incumbent for so long? There is no simple or single answer, but the experience of a growing number of administrators and other change agents—curriculum supervisors and consultants, teacher educators, and classroom teachers themselves—provides valuable observations, suggestions, and guidelines. (See Bird 1989 and Lester and Onore 1990.)

First, it may help to consider what change agents and teachers themselves have observed about how teachers come to change their instructional philosophy and practice in becoming whole language educators.

UNDERSTANDING TEACHER CHANGE

For some, becoming a whole language teacher simply involves deepening and extending their current understanding. As Linda Cameron explains it, speaking of teachers in Scarborough, Ontario:

> for many of these wonderful teachers there was not much change that had to be made. These teachers have just got a better understanding of the development of literacy and child-development; some techniques that facilitate this development; confidence that reading, writing, listening, speaking, drama and viewing support and enhance one another; more good literature; more support for their practice. (Personal correspondence, cited more fully in "Implementing Whole Language" later in this chapter)

These are the teachers who readily become advocates of whole language learning and teaching, and agents for change.

After exploring some of the research underlying a whole language philosophy and supporting whole language practice, other teachers may make almost overnight a "paradigm shift" in their thinking, and consequently in their practice: Their own experience validates what they have learned about fostering the development of literacy, and they readily modify their teaching accordingly. Kittye Copeland, described in Chapter 1, is such a teacher. But they may be relatively rare.

For most of us, change is more gradual. On the one hand, from studying the research we may readily come to recognize the validity of a transactional model of education, but then begin to implement our understanding little by little, with contradictions between our theory and our practice lessening gradually, over time. Or we may gradually change some of our practices until the success of a more active and more holistic approach eventually generates a shift in our concept of education, from a transmission to a transactional model. Either way, change in educational practice tends to be gradual, and almost always must be bolstered, if not initiated, by consideration of some of the research that gives rise to a whole language philosophy and that demonstrates its effectiveness in fostering literacy and learning in the classroom.

How can change agents foster such shifts in theory and practice? Again, there is no simple answer, but we may hope to learn from one another's successes and difficulties.

> **❝** Either way, change in educational practice tends to be gradual, and almost always must be bolstered, if not initiated, by consideration of some of the research that gives rise to a whole language philosophy and that demonstrates its effectiveness in fostering literacy and learning in the classroom. **❞**

CONSIDERING NEW MATERIALS

Because our schools have commonly treated published materials as if they themselves *were* the curriculum, it may be tempting to assume that a change to more holistic materials will effect a change in teachers' thinking and practice. And as just indicated, the adoption of more holistic, less skills-oriented materials does indeed facilitate change, for many teachers. Figure 11.1 gives some indication of the range of more holistic materials and teaching options that became available in the late 1980s; the programs toward the left of the diagram tend to provide a greater degree of structure for teachers and/or students, while the options toward the right allow more flexibility and teacher/student decision-making.

Teachers developing a whole language philosophy will generally use more and more quality literature and environmental print and student-authored books as reading material in their classrooms, but at first some may need the security of a more structured program in order to feel that they are teaching adequately. Particularly noteworthy in this regard is the 1989 *Journeys* program from Ginn of Canada, available in the United States (Hawthorne Publishers). The program provides considerable structure, yet also encourages flexibility and individual choice on the part of both teachers and students.

Though the list in Figure 11.1 may be a helpful starting point, it should not be taken as definitive: Existing programs are being expanded into other grades, these companies keep adding new materials and programs and titles to their lists, and new companies offering more holistic materials are entering the market. Most of the companies offering what I have (with some trepidation) termed whole language materials also offer teachers both resources and support: professional books and videos, and in some cases professional development seminars.

It would be a mistake, however, to assume that adopting new materials is enough to change practice. At best, new materials can encourage a change in practice, but this change is likely to be minimal or only partial, until and unless teachers understand and accept the underlying philosophy of education. Furthermore, teachers themselves need to be empowered with the knowledge to *choose* the more holistic materials. Selecting materials *for* them denies the very philosophy we are trying to implement.

COMBINING ADOPTION WITH PROFESSIONAL DEVELOPMENT

One large school system that is attempting to implement a whole language philosophy and an integrated language arts program is that of Portland, Oregon. In 1985, as the time approached for a new textbook adoption in reading, the then language arts specialist, Mary Bothwell,

More holistic basals from the mid-1980s	"Literature-based" instructional programs, like	"Whole language" basal	"Whole language" programs, like		
Impressions (Holt, Rinehart and Winston of Canada; available in the U.S.)	Bridges (K-6, Scholastic)	Journeys, 1989 ed. (Ginn of Canada, available from Hawthorne Publishers in the U.S.)	Bookshelf (K-2, Scholastic); includes materials for all areas of the curriculum	Various collections of Big Books and wordless books and predictable books for primary grades, from companies like Rigby, Wright Group, Scholastic, Modern Curriculum Press, DLM Teaching Resources	Variety of environmental print (menus, telephone books, ads, TV Guide, etc.)
Networks (Nelson Canada)			Sunshine (K-6, Wright Group); includes stories to teach math, soc. studies, science, as well as other literature		Library of student-authored books
Unicorn (McGraw-Hill of Canada)			Story Box (K-3, Wright Group)	Various collections of literature, based on age, genre, classics, favorite authors, special interests and themes, multicultural, content relating to social studies, science, math, etc.; Scholastic has a particularly wide range through high school.	Various magazines, journals, newspapers
			Ready to Read (K-2), Richard C. Owen Publishers		Free choice of a wide variety of fiction and nonfiction (not bound by organized "collections")
			Book Centre (2-6, Scholastic); collections of books with teaching resources		

Figure 11.1 Considering materials that are more holistic than traditional basals

became increasingly concerned about how elementary children were being taught. "My own training was heavily in secondary, but when I went into some elementary classrooms I was bothered by what I saw: boredom, apathy, even crying, and much strict regimentation. I felt instinctively that there was something wrong" (Hardt 1988, interview with Bothwell).

She engaged the textbook adoption committee, about three-fourths of whom were regular classroom teachers, in studying professional literature on the reading process and the teaching of reading. Ultimately, they recommended the adoption of Holt, Rinehart and Winston's *Impressions* series, an integrated reading and language arts program. This program was available only for grades K–4. Middle-school teachers were encouraged to develop their own literature-based program, but were provided with "the best basal program we could find" at that time. Teachers also could choose to use a management system called *Success in Reading and Writing*. The following year, when it came time for another adoption committee to recommend a language arts program, they were easily persuaded that no separate language arts program was needed: Reading, writing, and language skills could be developed with the materials already adopted, and by engaging children in various reading and writing experiences.

The adoption of Holt's *Impressions* was launched through a city-wide literacy conference in May 1987 (the elementary schools were closed for all teachers and administrators and the schools' specialists to attend). This conference was followed by various kinds of seminars, workshops, institutes, and meetings. Teachers were encouraged to attend the 1988 International Reading Association convention in Toronto, and at least ten attended the IRA World Congress in Australia. And teachers have been provided with resources for their own professional reading, including "Reading Alerts" that address issues of immediate concern; they also are given numerous opportunities for collaboration and peer support. Although change was initiated in part through the adoption of new, more holistic materials, it is clear that this adoption has been accompanied by a massive effort to educate teachers to the new philosophy and the need for change, as well as to offer them practical ideas and support for implementing the philosophy. It is both assumed and expected that understanding and implementation will be gradual, with some teachers bounding ahead and others progressing more slowly.

As of this writing, the Portland schools have just begun to assess the program itself: what is actually occurring in classrooms, how this relates to the teacher's understanding of a whole language philosophy, and so forth. Then, suggests the current language arts specialist Jane Braunger, we can look at the effects on students' attitudes and achievement in reading and writing (1989, personal communication).

Because of the sheer magnitude of this effort to implement a whole language philosophy (there are eight clusters of schools in the Portland district), the successful aspects of implementation may well be worth considering for adaptation elsewhere. The school system's efforts may also provide valuable evidence of what concerns and problems one might anticipate, and what may not be very effective in implementing a whole language philosophy. Meanwhile, the following section offers ''voices of experience'' as to what does and does not work well in implementing whole language.

IMPLEMENTING WHOLE LANGUAGE: VOICES OF EXPERIENCE

In order to gather data from which to draw generalizations about implementing a whole language philosophy, I solicited comments from major whole language educators and teacher support groups. Though encouraging them to respond freely from their own experience, I also posed some questions they might consider in reflecting upon that experience in implementing a whole language philosophy in a school or school system or in a district, province, or state.

The questions I posed are as follows:

1. How can an administrator, curriculum supervisor or consultant, or teacher educator foster the development and implementation of a whole language philosophy within a school or school system?

2. How can classroom teachers do the same?

3. What approaches, if any, might tend to be counterproductive in implementing a whole language philosophy?

4. To what extent can a whole language philosophy be developed by engaging in whole language kinds of activities (such as the Shared Book Experience) and/or by using more holistic kinds of materials and programs (such as the *Story Box* and *Ready to Read* programs, or *Bookshelf*)? That is, to what extent can practice affect theory, bringing about a paradigm shift in teachers, administrators, and others?

5. To what extent and in what ways is it important or necessary to involve parents? To enlighten policy-makers? (And so forth.)

Respondents' freely generated comments and their reactions to these questions proved so interesting that I decided to include a sampling, in each person's own words. Teachers, teacher educators, administrators, and curriculum supervisors echoed many of the same themes, each in her or his individual voice. Hence, the ''voices of experience.''

Jane Bartow, Teacher Department, Breck School
Minneapolis, Minnesota

In response to the request for information I sent to the Minnesota TAWL (Teachers Applying Whole Language) group, I received a letter from Jane Bartow, who teaches at a private school in Minneapolis. Her enthusiasm for what is happening at Breck school is contagious, as these excerpts show:

We are one of the main private schools in the Twin Cities, with waiting lines for admission. Grades P–4 are entirely whole language in philosophy, although each classroom differs somewhat in practice. We use process writing workshops for children as young as Kindergarten; every child has at least four, 45-minute periods to write each week. Reading classes are literature-based, with teachers choosing books to share in literature groups or with individuals, as the needs and interests arise. (We do NOT follow the practice of implementing certain books at certain grade levels and collecting worksheets and ideas for each title.) Teachers are totally free to choose and use what they would like. We have developed growing collections of literature sets, which we all share; teachers ask for certain titles, and so far we have been able to supply everyone's suggestions. Our classrooms are abuzz with activity.

Teachers are in various stages of becoming whole language teachers, and they do a lot of sharing with one another and with other schools and districts. Because our school is rather prestigious in this community, the philosophy of holistic education has gained some respect. . . .

To think that just eight years ago we were a phonicating, Lippincott-driven school simply amazes me, and it shows, I think, how quickly exciting change can happen! When I joined the staff at Breck eight years ago, I was dismayed at the academic pushing as well as at the curriculum, which was almost totally text-oriented. As I was department head for grades 1 and 2, we began to look at what was really right for children. We began to use a bit more literature and adopted Houghton Mifflin basals.

One of the teachers in our department went to the Vineyard one summer and got involved with Graves, et al. The following school year her classroom was watched by all of us as she implemented her writers' workshops. The following summer, with that teacher present to help explain things, the members of the first and second grade team read through Graves' *Writing: Teachers and Children at Work*. We discussed our responses to the readings (much as we do now with our children and their literature). When summer (and the book) was over, several of us decided to give it a try. Several others needed more time. Those of us who jumped into process writing were excited by what happened in our classrooms! And from there, we began to examine how we were teaching reading. (We had already had Math Their Way training and were well into a manipulative math approach.)

As we began to think about empowering children in reading, the members of my department took several different tracks. The teacher who had worked with Graves at the Vineyard was invited back to work on holistic reading strategies. I went to the University of Missouri to work with Dorothy Watson. Another teacher went to several local workshops. When we came together in the fall, we were so excited to share what we had learned. We have been checking out library sets of books, and we decided to use our budget monies to purchase our own literature sets. We had the absolutely delightful chore of choosing which titles to spend our money on. Our program has continued to develop, as we have all sought out more and more education through workshops and classes. We are also now asked to help others. We have formed a Breck TAWL group which welcomes others from the community.

The important thing that happened in our school was that this effort to become more holistic was always open for others to join in. No one came across as a know-it-all, so that others would be afraid to risk or wouldn't want to join. In fact, we who began this push invited others into our classrooms to watch the fun things that are going on (plays and productions are fun for guests to see, and they were a way that we could begin to talk about what else we were up to). Teachers have sponsored morning breakfasts of book sharing (B.Y.O.B. = Bring Your Own Book). We added the muffins and fruit and had some good discussions and free sharing of literature in a non-threatening way.

> **"**The important thing that happened in our school was that this effort to become more holistic was always open for others to join in. No one came across as a know-it-all, so that others would be afraid to risk or wouldn't want to join.**"**

We teachers helped to educate our already child-centered administrator by telling her about workshops we had attended, by sharing good books with her, by helping her to know which were the "big names" in our movement. We encouraged her to set up a library of books for the teachers to use, but we have also made certain that there is money in the budget for any teacher to choose and purchase his/her OWN copy of any book on the resource shelf. Many teachers have taken advantage of that and have begun to do a lot of reading. Teachers consequently share good books and ideas with one another. . . .

Our administrator has been a good model of holistic teaching, emphasizing a love of literature. She reads to classes. She gave awards to each child who successfully published a book, thereby exciting a large number of children to write—and a somewhat smaller but very significant number of teachers to get writing workshops into the academic schedule. Our administrator has been encouraging, freeing, delighting in our development as a school. She hasn't been threatened because we always included her in our plans as we were growing and changing. Indeed, she celebrated with us and encouraged our new path. . . .

When I started teaching at Breck, our parents seemed to want an academic PUSH in the old tradition. But by sharing with the parents what we are doing and WHY, we have the full support of a most joyful body of parents. They love it that their children know authors. Many wonder why they didn't know much about children's literature when they grew up. Parents love the books and magazines their children publish. They delight in the joy their children feel when they come to school. They are interested in the projects that their children are encouraged to work on, and they can see that what is happening for these youngsters is real and so meaningful. Our parents have begun a publishing company to help teachers keep up with the writing. They appreciate the growth shown in invented spellings as they develop over the year. They like the fact that children choose their own literature and are not assigned a book to read (very often). The children mix themselves up as they choose books to read; they work with different people on their projects. Collaboration is the norm, and learning to get along in a group or a pair is natural for our children.

Lee Dobson, Educational Consultant and Former Classroom Teacher, Vancouver, British Columbia

In her letter, Lee reflects upon her experience as a classroom teacher, describing how she and her colleagues, Marietta Hurst, Mayling Chow, and Joy Nucich, implemented whole language in their classrooms and shared their experiences and knowledge with other teachers. Within their school, a whole language philosophy gained momentum, thanks to these dedicated professionals.

Lee comments further concerning the role of classroom teachers in implementing a whole language philosophy:

For a time, our first school was a ''model'' school, better than any I have ever seen intentionally established as a ''showpiece.'' But such teachers and staffs must have support if their efforts are to have any wider impact. We were doing a lot of extra work—reading professionally, attending conferences, giving workshops, having visitors in to observe, etc.—and no compensation or even recognition was given from the central office staff. We were never asked to be on advisory committees, etc. . . . I think teacher empowerment is a ''big deal,'' and involves much more than making decisions in your own classroom.

Concerning the effect of practice upon theory:

While I'd like teachers to understand theory, I tend to encourage them initially to try out some of the practices, and then reflect on what's happening. But I have seen teachers who consider themselves whole language teachers using themes, and shared reading, and writing patterns, and brainstorming, all in a traditional way. . . . It makes it look as if whole language doesn't work.

Concerning the support of parents:

As for parents, I've found they understand easily when you relate learning written language to learning a spoken language. They also enjoy tracking their child's work over time. The progress they see makes a lot more sense to them than reporting reading levels or test scores.

Concerning mandated policies and programs:

Here in British Columbia we *now* have a provincial Ministry of Education who is advocating ungraded classrooms, continuous progress, child-centered programs, etc. . . . [See Chap. 2, here.] With this approval from the policy makers, teachers are in a much stronger position to make change. . . . We're hopeful that the result will be better curricula and teaching. But imposed programs are not necessarily popular with teachers, and if the support is not there for implementation, then the innovation will fail. Also, ministry policies can contradict each other; for example, a developmental stand on learning but a continuing call for standardized testing, with marks entered on a central computer.

Concerning the role of teachers and administrators:

Experienced teachers are tired of change for change's sake (it seems), initiated by people who aren't in classrooms. Many of them view whole language with a cynical eye and as just another gimmick. But they are impressed sometimes by enthusiastic teachers who enjoy their work and have orderly, but active classrooms. . . . I do think that if teachers like children and find them interesting, and like books and find them interesting, and don't think their job is to correct (eradicate) error, then they love whole language and will never return to traditional ways. That's what they tell me, and it's my own experience. . . .

Whole language, as I see it, is simply better teaching: "whole language" is only a convenient label.

Linda Cameron, English Language Arts Consultant, English Language Centre Scarborough, Ontario

Describing their experience implementing a whole language philosophy in Scarborough, Linda emphasizes the factors that help teachers make a "paradigm shift'' from the kind of philosophy reflected in a transmission approach to education to the transactional philosophy reflected in whole language classrooms:

We have witnessed teachers making the paradigm shift, one-by-one. The things that seem to be the most significant factors in this shift are:

- a desire to learn, on the part of the teacher
- a willingness to be a risk-taker
- having someone accessible to support the teacher's learning—a colleague, a consultant, an administrator
- materials to use—books, books, books
- a chance to witness the use of techniques used by responsive teachers (like conferring, observing, responding . . .)
- regular opportunities to gripe and celebrate with others who are trying some of the same things
- having someone who will listen and answer questions (that may be someone like you, with whom you can visit in the pages of a book)

The teachers in my study needed a situation that enabled them to be risk-takers, with support and a consistent and trusted administration. . . . They changed because they had many opportunities to interact, cooperate, and collaborate with others who were interested in the same things. Someone was available to help them organize and facilitate the practical aspects of a whole language program and to help them monitor their growth and development. Also important is an official language arts *policy* that reflects a whole language philosophy, and that therefore supports and encourages change.

In a subsequent letter, Linda added some significant observations about the interrelationships between teachers, students, and administrators:

There is another *very*, very significant factor that I missed initially: it is that as the teachers changed, the children responded and reinforced the teachers' change:

- the kids became more motivated as the issue of ownership shifted towards them
- they became more skilled as the opportunities for practice in meaningful contexts increased
- they became more interested in risk-taking as the notion of process was reinforced
- they became happier at school and with themselves as the teachers changed—so they behaved better!

It's interesting that if the principal/administrator is growing and learning, it seems that it's easier for him or her to support appropriately a teacher who is growing and learning, and a teacher who is a learner understands and can support appropriately his or her students in the same process. Administrators and teachers who are merely managers and technicians want different things from their students than do responsive educators.

Kitty Kaczmarek, Director of Program/Staff Development,
Glendale Elementary School District
Glendale, Arizona

Kitty focuses her response on suggestions for principals and people in positions such as hers, regarding how to elicit the support of parents:

We are trying to develop a sincere collaboration between parents, teachers, and children regarding literacy development. School has begun to look very different from when the parents were in school, so they have many questions regarding their role in the reading and writing process. We can support parents, as learners, in their understanding of literacy development by using strategies such as the following:

1. *Professional Articles.* Principals and teachers can gather a collection of professional articles that reflect recent research in literacy development. The articles should be "short and sweet," in language parents can understand. Parents do read these! These can be utilized during parent/principal conferences. If parents would like to read more about the role of invented spelling in the writing process or the use of literature in the classroom, then they can refer to the article for additional information. A professional article can be distributed at parent meetings and used as a basis for discussion.

2. *Parent Lending Libraries.* Parent lending libraries can be established as part of the school media center. Books on literacy development can be checked out by both parents and teachers. If a parent would like to know more about strategies for reading aloud to his or her child, then the principal can direct the parent to *The Read-Aloud Handbook* by Jim Trelease, or other pieces of professional/parent literature.

3. *Literacy Breakfasts.* We have been conducting literacy breakfasts where we invite parents to breakfast to discuss a specific issue, such as "Use of Predictable Books" or "The Role of Invented Spelling in Your Child's Writing." The classroom teacher usually conducts the meeting, and over coffee, she will show writing

samples on the overhead, or share literature and bibliographies. The parents enjoy the informality of the literacy breakfasts and often bring neighbors and friends to the following meeting.

Peter Krause, Director General
Lakeshore School District,
Montreal, Quebec

Peter emphasizes that administrators cannot successfully implement a whole language philosophy through autocratic methods: that is, by employing a transmission model of educational change that is contrary to the transactional model of education they are trying to implement. Peter comments:

Ken Goodman suggests that a WHOLE LANGUAGE ENVIRONMENT requires a humanistic approach to people interactions. In other words, it would be difficult to find successful applications of the WHOLE LANGUAGE philosophy in environments that are autocratic and authoritarian. I would contend that Ken's premise is very accurate. . . .

In the humanistic approach, the following principles are paramount:

- a respect for the individual
- a belief that the individual is capable of fulfilling the established requirements
- trust
- empowering individuals to take responsibilities and risks
- coaching rather than directing
- having a fundamental belief that people will succeed

At the Lakeshore School Board, we have a tradition of this type of philosophy. We have consciously nurtured this attitude in all dealings with the people making up the community of the Lakeshore School Board. . . . All conflicts are defined as problems for which solutions must be found. With that type of attitude, especially with the underlying belief that a solution can be found, the environment becomes supportive of the WHOLE LANGUAGE philosophy.

Lynn Rhodes, Associate Professor of Education,
University of Colorado
Nancy Shanklin, Assistant Professor of Education,
University of Colorado
Denver, Colorado

In her letter, Lynn Rhodes reports that when she arrived in Denver eleven years ago, she was the only person to have ''whole language'' in the title of her presentation at the Colorado affiliate of the International Reading Association.

Now, whole language is so widespread that virtually every session of the conference program deals in some way with whole language. Lynn and her colleague Nancy Shanklin have been instrumental in implementing a whole language philosophy in the Denver public schools. Lynn sent me their article "Transforming Literacy Instruction," from the March 1989 issue of Educational Leadership. *I heartily recommend the whole article, which deals with the process and challenges of staff development and with ways of transforming the evaluation of literacy (alternatives to standardized tests). Here, I shall excerpt just a few of the comments on staff development:*

Administrators may encounter challenges to their concept of, and commitment to, staff development. Joyce and Showers (1980) claim that the usual vehicle of staff development—presentations by experts— results in a 5 percent implementation rate, while a combination of presentations, demonstrations, and coaching results in a 95 percent implementation rate. . . .

To encourage teachers to transform their literacy instruction, we provided the same things that we wished them to provide students: supportive environments and opportunities for frequent reflection, sharing of ideas, and problem solving. . . .

Although teachers were required to participate in staff development, they chose their staff development option each year. Some teachers selected staff development that encouraged great change. Others opted for staff development that eased them into reconsidering literacy instruction. Reluctant teachers gradually began to take risks, their confidence bolstered by the successes of colleagues who had risked change earlier. . . .

Not until teachers enjoy the power of making decisions and solving their own problems will they encourage students to do the same. . . .

We learned to be patient and to persevere when teacher change was very slow. We have come to understand that the change process and what causes transformations are different for each teacher. . . . We have come to understand that change comes from teachers' own initiatives, some of which we spark, some of which other persons or events ignite. . . . Probably our hardest lesson has been shifting responsibility and decision making to teachers and administrators. . . .

> **❝**We have come to understand that change comes from teachers' own initiatives, some of which we spark, some of which other persons or events ignite.**❞**

Julie Kniskern, Former Consultant for English Language Arts and Gifted Education, St. Vital School Division #6 Winnipeg, Manitoba

In responding to my questions, Julie—currently a research student at the University of London Institute of Education—chose to emphasize how crucial it is that administrators be educators, rather than just managers:

I have lots of ideas on how a ''whole language'' philosophy can be developed and implemented within a school or a school system. But, in the end, it all boils down to the people at the top—the administrators in the head office and the principals in the schools. In my experience as a classroom teacher and as a curriculum developer and implementer, all the blocks come at the top. If administrators are managers rather than educators, chances are they will not be successful in either understanding or implementing whole language in their schools or school systems. But if they are truly ''curriculum leaders/educational leaders'' and not ''business managers'' working on a factory model of education, and if they listen to their teachers and understand children and how they learn, then it will happen.

Mary Snow, Assistant Professor of Education, Lesley College Graduate School Cambridge, Massachusetts

In responding to my questions, Mary described several ways that administrators could affect and effect change. One of these is by engaging teachers in evaluation:

It's important to involve teachers in longitudinal evaluation from a very early time. The question of evaluation is actually a critically important one. In Cambridge, we began an evaluation study at the Longfellow School at the beginning of the second year of the project. We have been following children's progress for five years now. We have collected dated tapes of reading and dated samples of writing from all the children, as well as much more voluminous files, including art and other samples of work from selected representative children in the study, in all the grades. The evaluation must be consonant with the theoretical base of the teaching: that is, developmental, longitudinal, and child-centered.

Administrators will learn a lot about children's progress using this form of evaluation, and should make sure that they get the feedback through some regular forms of communication. The startlingly new aspect such evaluation provides is about individual children's progress, which can be tracked and even shown in bar graph form, from year to year. Standardized tests are a slice in a moment of time, and while they yield comparative information, they tell little about the child's learning, where s/he is coming from, and how s/he is progressing. The forward movement is far more important than where s/he is at any given moment.

Mary also shared some of the ways that Don Holdaway, New Zealand originator of whole language, modeled the philosophy as he worked with teachers and teacher educators to develop the Cambridge Lesley Literacy Project of which she speaks.

The natural learning model [Holdaway 1986] holds for grownups, too. Don began with a powerful period in which he *demonstrated* shared reading with classrooms of kids, while the teachers and interested spectators were drawn in as part of the literate community. We had to be participants. We weren't allowed to sit apart and murmur to each other. We were expected to enter in.

After a time, teachers were invited to try their own hand at leading shared reading, and I remember how scared we were to enter that *participation*, but he held our collective hand, helped us get started on big books and charts of chants, songs and poems, making some of his own at home to show us that approximations were welcomed.

Then after a while, he began simply not to be always there, and we began that period of *self-regulated practice* during which we were actually glad he wasn't there, because we needed to role-play ourselves into being this new kind of teacher. As the year wore on, we began to have more and more visitors, and teachers found themselves in the position of being someone whose work was of great interest to others. We were into that fourth phase of the natural learning cycle Don calls *performance*. This had the effect not only of increasing our sense of self-respect, but also of our professionalism. . . .

We were also introduced to the Down-Under concept [from New Zealand and Australia] that evaluation is continuous, longitudinal, and occurs in the midst of things, not at the end of the process. Teachers are constantly engaging in it by closely observing their children's learning. They learn from the children what reading and writing are all about. We began to do our own mini-research: collecting tapes of children's reading and samples of their writing, and watching the interactions and the complex literate activity with which we were surrounded the minute *we* stopped setting the tasks and let *the children* do it. . . .

Voluntarism, Don insists, is at the heart of change. I think he believes this because he respects adults as learners, just as he respects children as learners. If we are not going to violate children by dictating the terms under which they will learn, we certainly shouldn't violate the adults who are responsible for them.

Ardis Tucker, Coordinator of Reading, Writing, and Language Arts, Hilton Central School District Hilton, New York

In her letter, Ardis comments on several of the questions I raised:

A paradigm shift is very difficult in a culture where instruction has been dominated by publishers and test producers. In fact, curriculum is often equated with commercial programs. There currently is a focus on accountability, and that accountability is tied to standardized test results. Again, what needs to be evaluated, how it will be evaluated, and how the data will be interpreted occurs outside the classroom. Teachers have not had opportunity or authority to make instructional decisions for so long that our effectiveness as decision makers seems atrophied. . . . We need to push for educators making educational decisions. . . .

Teacher training must be the focus of any implementation. Teachers, not the program or the test, need to be given ownership for instructional decisions. This must include support as they make these decisions. Teachers need to identify what's working in their classrooms, and why. This will mean tremendous pressure in terms of personal accountability, since problems cannot be laid to programs or curriculum schemes. This kind of shift is unlikely to occur unless the teacher, administrator, and school board are in agreement as to their understanding of the learning process and expected outcomes.

Administrators will have difficulty supporting this movement when the pressures of state and federal demands for excellence aren't aligned with learning theory and don't focus on strategies most necessary for learners in our society. Unless we can really impact on decision makers at the state and federal level, I fear leaders at the local level will be reluctant or unable to take the risks necessary to bring about real change.

New York State is unusual in that the Bureau of English and Reading has been supportive of whole language. The State Curricula are excellent. Within the last few years the department has sponsored numerous regional and one state whole language conference, with another one planned for this October. This year they have brought a staff development project from Australia. The project is called ELIC (Early Literacy Inservice Course), and currently about 60 teachers have been trained. This provides the much-needed staff development for teachers, the need for which becomes apparent after awareness conferences. In addition, the state has also made two trips to Ohio [State University] to investigate Reading Recovery. My hope is that this trend [of state support for whole language] will become more pervasive, so that it raises questions at the federal level.

You asked about how practice can affect theory. In many cases, teachers like "how to" ideas. Showing them how to use certain materials such as *Story Box*, big books, and *Ready to Read* can spark their interest. If they are supported, they can clarify their own theory about learning. So, in these cases, materials do support theory. My concern is that in many cases, people are using materials and not understanding their purpose. This leaves them with limited strategies for developing and modifying their own classroom program. When problems occur, they are not able to identify specific causes, and thus abandon the whole language perspective. Attempting to use "whole language" materials and methods without developing a theoretical perspective also allows

❝ Attempting to use 'whole language' materials and methods without developing a theoretical perspective also allows teachers to be extremely vulnerable. Often they select materials and programs that claim to be whole language, but indeed are not theoretically sound. **❞**

teachers to be extremely vulnerable. Often they select materials and programs that claim to be whole language, but indeed are not theoretically sound.

I think that theory is the foundation for any classroom program. The strength of the foundation determines the ability of the structure to withstand the pressures that it will need to deal with, in future years.

Yetta Goodman, Professor of Education, University of Arizona Tucson, Arizona

Yetta Goodman, internationally regarded as one of the key leaders in whole language education, responded concisely but thoroughly to the questions posed:

In order to foster the development and implementation of a whole language philosophy within a school or school system, the administrators and others you mention need to be knowledgeable about whole language. They need to know that whole language is a philosophy that each teacher must develop for him/herself. . . . that it cannot be cloned one classroom to another nor one teacher to another. Therefore whole language cannot be mandated in traditional ways of imposing one particular set of practices that is specified in one particular way. Certainly a school district, school, state or province can adopt a policy that is whole language in nature. But that policy must be stated in such a way that diversity is permissible and, given whole language philosophy, indeed expected. Teachers who want to do things somewhat differently than agreed upon by most whole language experts would have the opportunity to do so as long as they can justify what they are doing as intellectually stimulating for students. Also, whole language, if it's established as the ''way to go,'' must be flexible. There should be no adoption of such regulations as ''All students must do literature sets on a regular basis''; ''All students must write in dialogue journals''; or ''All teachers must hold writing conferences daily and keep anecdotal records.'' Rather, the school, district or whatever unit should come together and establish more general holistic curriculum policies but allow teachers to do a variety of things to meet the policies, not establish specific methods that must be followed. More global statements would be ''Students must read and write daily for a variety of functions and in a range of genres'' and ''Teachers must provide information about the variety of ways they evaluate students.''

The best way to foster an environment for whole language is to establish a learning community within each school: a community that would include every member of the school community involved in the development of the whole language context where dialogue and planning and discussion and development and change are all open to scrutiny and criticism.

Approaches contrary to whole language would include those mechanisms that set up dogmatism about anything, such as: "This is the way to do Big Books"; "The writing process should be taught in this manner"; "These are the steps we must follow for literature groups," etc. In other words, opportunity for dynamic growth must always be built into any development of whole language curriculum.

Ken Goodman has been saying lately that whole language practice is indeed ahead of whole language theory. I believe that this is based on his belief that when teachers are released to develop curriculum in classrooms with their students, exciting things emerge from the creativity of the whole learning community in the classroom.

I think whole language materials can support teachers who are developing a philosophy, and the materials can then add to the teachers' repertoire and expand on the teachers' philosophy. But at the same time whole language materials can be used in a skillsy way by teachers who do not really know what whole language is. I believe the teacher is the crucial element in the development of a whole language philosophy—materials can only represent such a philosophy. Like any published materials, what the users bring to the materials will be reflected in how "whole language" materials are used.

Parent support is crucial. It just makes the lives of everyone in the school community easier. When parents know why things are happening as they are, then they are more willing to accept the possibility that kids should have a different, more supportive and more problem-solving education than they did. Also, when whole language schools have an articulate and educated-about-whole-language group of parents, it is harder for anti-whole-language forces to bring to bear the kinds of nonsensical criticism that sometimes comes to whole language.

Lastly, the more any group knows about whole language, the less threatening it becomes and the more commonplace such views become in education. Then whole language can be considered good education in the most general sense. That's the political, expedient way to go—inform the public in general.

Yvonne Freeman, Director of Bilingual Education,
Fresno Pacific College
Fresno, California

After mentioning the administrators with whom she has worked and describing the schools in which she has helped to implement a whole language philosophy, Yvonne offers these generalizations:

1. Whole language cannot be forced. Not only is it against all we know about learning for children to impose whole language on teachers, but you *can't* make people be whole language teachers.

2. It must be realized that it *takes time* to implement change. Teachers who attend a whole year of inservice may seem to understand and even talk about whole language activities, but the amount of change one sees in their classroom procedures [from inservice sessions alone] is usually very small.

3. It is almost essential for teachers to visit whole language classrooms in order for them to begin to see how they can adapt ideas to their own classrooms. What they see when they visit may surprise or disappoint consultants and administrators, but teachers must be allowed to take away from their experiences what they are ready to notice.

4. The more professional reading that teachers do, the more change is usually observed—*if* it is combined by support and observations.

5. Outside consultants may make a big difference for teachers—even though the message they bring is exactly what the school inservice people have been saying. "A prophet in his own land. . . ."

6. If different outside consultants are used, it is *critical* to have their messages be consistent with a whole language philosophy of learning.

7. Consultants must be prepared to make theory *palatable*. Bringing in consultants who "spout theory" all day only turns teachers off. A mixture of theory with ideas for practical application is usually appreciated by teachers.

8. It is important that consultants give teachers lots of classroom examples of real teachers in real classrooms doing whole language. Sharing stories and anecdotes from experience are very important here. Videos are also wonderful *if* the student populations are similar. (It does no good to show teachers of second language and minority students a video of a whole language classroom with middle class Anglo children.)

9. There needs to be lots of TIME when teachers can interact, plan together, and problem-solve together. Constant talking *at* and not *with* teachers is futile.

10. New teachers who are able to implement whole language successfully may need assistance in learning how not to "put off" their more experienced colleagues.

Linda Henke, Director of Curriculum,
West Des Moines Public Schools
West Des Moines, Iowa

Linda discusses curriculum development in relation to staff development,
then reviews strategies she used in developing a whole language curriculum in
the West Des Moines elementary schools:

In the United States today, one pervasive view of curriculum is that it
originates outside of the classroom. From that perspective, curriculum is
linear and prescriptive; it can be developed in one place by one group of
people and implemented in another place by another group of people.
. . . While it is true that most schools establish curriculum committees
made up of teachers, we have somehow made the giant leap to thinking
that a few teachers developing their own meaning is all that is necessary
. . . ''the other teachers will fall in line.'' Extensive discussion, review of
the research, study of options is done only once by a small group. But
unfortunately, meaning isn't something you can hand out when you
hand out the spiffy new curriculum documents. We all have to make our
own.

Thus, Linda suggests, curriculum development cannot be undertaken prior
to, or separate from, staff development. Instead, the curriculum must evolve
from the growing understanding of the staff. Linda suggests that in the long
run, the most effective way of implementing a whole language philosophy within
a school or school system is to create a whole language ''culture'' that ex-
emplifies the values of the philosophy. So as director of curriculum in the West
Des Moines schools, she became not a dispenser of curriculum guides and
materials, but a nurturer of a culture:

Here are nine strategies that I tried . . . many of them suggested in
other sources . . . that seemed to work with some success:

1. *Support teachers in the acquisiton of knowledge about literacy learning.*
   Build common information in the way of understandings, vocabulary and strategies to be experimented with, modified and
   honed to individual needs. We worked to accomplish this with
   professional libraries both at the building and district level, staff
   development courses with college credit and tailored to the program, monthly grade-level meetings with time to read, write, and
   discuss, and special sessions we called ''highlighters,'' which
   were focused on specific aspects of the program, such as using
   drama in the classroom. We also insured that teachers were given
   time in meetings to write, share their writing with colleagues,
   and talk about books they were reading for personal pleasure.

2. *Give teachers control of their own teaching.* A good curriculum document should encourage experimentation . . . it should be something teachers can grow into and out of. That's what we tried to create. And we used what had formerly been the workbook budget to establish individual budgets for teachers to buy tradebooks, magazines, and other reading materials for their classrooms. In education, money is power. Teachers need access to it in some way if they are to be empowered.

3. *Cultivate networks.* One of my roles became district story-teller, or town crier. I carried my journal everywhere and wrote down what I saw and heard and shared that information with others. "Susan's doing a case study of a writer in her classroom. Why not ask her to discuss it with you at your next building support meeting?" "Sharon's trying an interesting experiment with grouping in her classroom. Why not call her and see how it's working?" One teacher said I was a walking, talking newspaper.

   Two advisory committees were established to help us keep abreast of the program—one focused on individual building needs, the other on concerns and issues brought up at each grade level. These committees became problem-solvers, learning to rely on the expertise that was present in the entire district as we worked to support teachers.

   We also networked with teachers outside the district who were interested in whole language. We held a teacher exchange with a district in Kansas, and a vanload of West Des Moines teachers travelled there for two days of visitation and discussion. And the next month we hosted a return group.

4. *Foster collaboration.* All sessions we planned focused on active participation and discussion. We offered fireside study which allowed ten teachers at a time from around the district to meet to discuss a professional book we had read in common. And we developed "A Guide on the Side," a yearly publication of teachers' writings about literacy and literacy teaching. It included essays, poetry, teacher tips, a whole range of genres. We involved parents in literacy seminars and "write nights," opportunities to explain the program and build connections with the home.

5. *Highlight reflection.* Teaching is such a busy profession that it is easy to fall into the habit of "just doing" without thinking about the doing. Active learners, however, need to reflect, conceptualize, and experiment. In order to learn about teaching, then, we needed to build in time and tools that facilitate the process. The professional journal seemed an ideal place to begin. I encouraged teachers and administrators to find themselves a journal they

could use to organize their thinking about literacy, and to bring the journal to every meeting or staff development session. Keeping notes on scraps of paper and napkins is no way to organize learning. So I role-modeled journalling in meetings, fireside study, classroom visitation, everywhere I could. Frequently we wrote in our journals before we began a meeting, or as we tackled a difficult problem, or before we ended a meeting to help us plan individually.

6. *Create heroes who can emphasize the values inherent in your program.* We encouraged teachers and administrators to become researchers in the classrooms, to write professionally, to present at conferences and serve as resources for other districts. These individuals were recognized at school board meetings and in newsletters sent home to parents.

7. *Bring in shamans to bless your culture.* We learned a great deal from the sessions our district hosted, bringing such well known figures as Ken Goodman and Don Graves to the district. But it was as much the aura they left surrounding the program as what they taught us about literacy that contributed to our work. They had come and they had blessed the program. They had walked through the halls, visited with children and teachers; they had become a part of what we were trying to do.

8. *Create visible symbols of the program's values.* From the moment you step into a school building in West Des Moines, you should know literacy is important. Bulletin boards, book displays, cozy corners in the halls and classrooms, heaps of books and walls covered with children's writing, photographs that show whole language at work . . . the message should be vivid and pervasive: you are entering a community of readers and writers.

9. *Celebrate!* Whole language is hard work. And change is scary. Sometimes in the midst of all of that, it's easy to forget to celebrate each success. Languaging and learning should focus on the joy of being human. A technological view of those processes has stripped away much of that pleasure. Whole language restores it. As a community, we celebrate the accomplishments of every member . . . student, teacher, administrator.

❝As many of us have found, making a commitment to implementing a whole language philosophy means, perhaps first of all, making a commitment to continued professional growth ourselves.**❞**

MAKING A COMMITMENT

As many of us have found, making a commitment to implementing a whole language philosophy means, perhaps first of all, making a commitment to continued professional growth ourselves. This includes, but is not limited to, reading professional literature, and taking risks: that is, experimenting with putting new ideas into practice, and continually evaluating and reconsidering what we are doing and how we're doing it.

Each of us must determine for ourselves what "making a commitment" involves. The following points are simply reminders of what many people have found to be important in trying to implement a whole language philosophy throughout a school or school system:

1. Realize that it will take *time* and energy and resources, both human and monetary.

2. Become a whole language educator, modeling the kinds of change you advocate: for example, become a reader and writer of professional literature; join or start a whole language support group; take risks; empower others; discuss freely the contradictions between your own beliefs and practices and your efforts to narrow the gap between the two.

3. Recognize that whole language teaching cannot merely be mandated, nor can it be brought about merely by adopting policy statements or more holistic kinds of materials, though these can support whole language teaching and the development of a whole language philosophy.

4. Support teachers' professional growth and decision-making, and demonstrate respect for their judgment—in as many ways as possible. This may include developing a whole language "culture" or climate within the school(s).

5. Make provision for the purchase of more holistic educational materials, such as trade books that offer good quality literature and non-fiction, and a variety of materials for writing and publishing in the classroom. Money formerly used for workbooks and basal tests may often be diverted to this purpose.

6. Minimize standardized testing, and downplay the results of standardized tests. Instead, encourage and help teachers develop alternative methods and means of assessment and evaluation, which can form the basis for educational decision-making.

7. Support teachers in taking risks; encourage them to move temporarily into a discomfort zone, but don't expect them to make major changes all at once.

8. Develop with teachers a policy and statement of goals that support and encourage the kind of teaching and learning environment you want to foster. This might include developing your own definition of "time on task" or "effective instruction."

9. Help parents understand what you are doing and why: enlist their support and involvement. The same holds for school board members and others in the community: they too, need to be informed and involved.

10. Above all, perhaps, cultivate respect for one another within and among those in your school community: teachers, students, administrators, parents, school board members, and the public. When we demonstrate respect for the needs and concerns of others, it becomes natural to resolve difficulties through a problem-solving rather than a confrontational approach. This again models the whole language, transactional philosophy of education.

I invite you to join those of us who have already made a commitment to becoming whole language educators and advocates of whole language learning and teaching. For us as well as for our students, whole language is indeed good education.

References

Adams, Marilyn Jager. 1990a. *Beginning to Read: Thinking and Learning about Print.* Cambridge, Mass.: MIT Press.

_____. 1990b. *Beginning to Read: Thinking and Learning about Print: A Summary.* Summarized by Steven A. Stahl, Jean Osborn, and Fran Lehr. Champaign, Ill.: University of Illinois, Center for the Study of Reading.

Allen, JoBeth, and Jana M. Mason, eds. 1989. *Risk Makers, Risk Takers, Risk Breakers: Reducing the Risks for Young Literacy Learners.* Portsmouth, N.H.: Heinemann.

Allington, Richard L. May 1983. The reading instruction provided readers of differing reading abilities. *The Elementary School Journal* 83:548–59.

Altwerger, Bess, Carole Edelsky, and Barbara M. Flores. November 1987. Whole language: What's new? *The Reading Teacher* 41:144–54.

Altwerger, Bess, and V. Resta. 1986. Comparing standardized test scores and miscues. Paper presented at the annual meeting of the International Reading Association, Philadelphia.

Anderson, Richard C., Elfrieda H. Hiebert, Judith A. Scott, and Ian A. G. Wilkinson. 1985. *Becoming a Nation of Readers: The Report of the Commission on Reading.* Champaign, Ill.: Center for the Study of Reading.

Applebee, Arthur N. 1981. *Writing in the Secondary School: English and the Content Areas.* Urbana, Ill.: National Council of Teachers of English.

Applebee, Arthur N., Judith A. Langer, and Ina V. S. Mullis. 1988a. *Learning to Be Literate in America: Reading, Writing, and Reasoning.* The nation's report card. Princeton, N.J.: National Assessment of Educational Progress, Educational Testing Service.

_____. 1988b. *Who Reads Best? Factors Related to Reading Achievement in Grades 3, 7, and 11.* Princeton, N.J.: National Assessment of Educational Progress, Educational Testing Service.

_____. 1989. *Crossroads in American Education.* Princeton, N.J.: National Assessment of Educational Progress, Educational Testing Service.

Applebee, Arthur N., Judith A. Langer, Ina V. S. Mullis, and Lynn B. Jenkins. 1990. *The Writing Report Card, 1984–88.* Princeton, N.J.: Educational Testing Service, National Assessment of Educational Progress.

Atwell, Nancie. 1987. *In the Middle: Writing, Reading, and Learning with Adolescents.* Portsmouth, N.H.: Boynton/Cook.

Avery, Carol S. 1985. Lori "figures it out": A young writer learns to read. In *Breaking Ground: Teachers Relate Reading and Writing in the Elementary School.* Ed. Jane Hansen, Thomas Newkirk, and Donald Graves, pp. 15–28. Portsmouth, N.H.: Heinemann.

Barrett, F. L. 1982. *A Teacher's Guide to Shared Reading.* Richmond Hill, Ontario: Scholastic-TAB.

Barrs, Myra. March 1990. *The Primary Language Record:* Reflection of issues in education. *Language Arts* 67:244–53.

Barrs, Myra, Sue Ellis, Hilary Tester, and Anne Thomas [Centre for Language in Primary Education]. 1989. *The Primary Language Record: A Handbook for Teachers.* Portsmouth, N.H.: Heinemann.

Baskwill, Jane, and Paulette Whitman. 1988. *Evaluation: Whole Language, Whole Child.* Richmond Hill, Ontario: Scholastic-TAB.

Becker, Wesley C., and Russell Gersten. Spring 1982. A follow-up of Follow Through: The later effects of the direct instruction model on children in fifth and sixth grades. *American Educational Research Journal* 19:75–92.

Bennet, Jill, ed. 1987. *Noisy Poems.* Illus. Nick Sharratt. Oxford: Oxford University Press.

Berko, Jean. 1958. The child's learning of English morphology. *Word* 14:150–77.

Bird, Lois Bridges. 1989. *Becoming a Whole Language School: The Fair Oaks Story.* Katonah, N.Y.: Richard C. Owen Publishers.

Bissex, Glenda. 1980. *Gnys at Wrk: A Child Learns to Write and Read.* Cambridge, Mass.: Harvard University Press.

Bloom, Benjamin, George Madaus, and J. Thomas Hastings. 1981. *Evaluation to Improve Learning.* New York: McGraw-Hill.

Bloome, David. 1987. Reading as a social process in a middle school classroom. In *Literacy and Schooling.* Ed. David Bloome, pp. 123–49. Norwood, N.J.: Ablex.

Boder, Elena. 1973. Developmental dyslexia: A diagnostic approach based on three atypical reading-spelling patterns. *Developmental Medicine and Child Neurology* 15:663–87.

Bond, Guy L., and Robert Dykstra. Summer 1967. The Cooperative Research Program in first-grade reading instruction. *Reading Research Quarterly* 2:5–142.

Bookshelf, Stage 1, Teacher's Resource Book. 1986. Jefferson City, Mo.: Scholastic.

Braunger, Jane. May 3, 1989. Personal communication.

Bridge, Connie, Peter Winograd, and Darliene Haley. 1983. Using predictable materials vs. preprimers to teach beginning sight words. *The Reading Teacher* 36:884–91.

Bridge, Connie, and Elfrieda H. Hiebert. November 1985. A comparison of classroom writing practices, teachers' perceptions of their writing instruction, and textbook recommendations on writing practices. *Elementary School Journal* 86:155–72.

Brill, Rhondda. 1985. The remedial reader. In *Teaching Reading: A Language Experience.* Ed. Gordon Winch and Valerie Hoogstad, pp. 142–59. South Melbourne, Australia: Macmillan.

Britton, James. 1970. *Language and Learning.* London: Alen Lane, Penguin Press.

Brophy, Jere E., and Thomas L. Good. 1986. Teacher behavior and student achievement. In *Handbook of Research on Teaching,* 3rd ed. Ed. Merlin C. Wittrock, pp. 328–75. New York: Macmillan.

Brown, Carol S., and Susan L. Lytle. 1988. Merging assessment and instruction: protocols in the classroom. In *Reexamining Reading Diagnosis: New Trends and Procedures.* Ed. Susan M. Glazer, Lyndon W. Searfoss, and Lance M. Gentile, pp. 67–80. Newark, Del.: International Reading Association.

Brummet, Anthony J. January 27, 1989. Policy directions: A response to the Sullivan Royal Commission on Education by the Government of British Columbia. Vancouver, British Columbia.

———. January 27, 1989. Presentation to the British Columbia School Trustees Association. Vancouver, British Columbia.

Buncombe, Fran, and Adrian Peetoom. 1988. *Literature-Based Learning: One School's Journey*. Richmond Hill, Ontario: Scholastic-TAB.

Burke, Carolyn. 1980. The reading interview: 1977. *Reading Comprehension: Resource Guide*. Ed. B. P. Farr and D. J. Strickler. Bloomington: School of Education, Indiana University.

Buscaglia, Leo. 1972. *Love*. New York: Ballantine. [Copyright Charles B. Slack, Inc.]

Bussis, Ann M., and Edward A. Chittenden. March 1987. Research currents: What the reading tests neglect. *Language Arts* 64:302–308.

Butler, Andrea. 1984. *The Story Box in the Classroom*, Stage 1. Melbourne, Australia: Rigby. Also distributed by The Wright Group.

———. n.d. Shared Book Experience. Crystal Lake, Ill.: Rigby. (This is one of a series of booklets accompanying Rigby instructional videos.)

Butler, Kathleen A. November/December 1988. Learning styles. *Learning 88*, pp. 30–34.

Calkins, Lucy McCormick. May 1980. When children want to punctuate: Basic skills belong in context. *Language Arts* 57:567–73. Reprinted in *"Children Want to Write . . ."*: Donald Graves in Australia. Ed. R. D. Walshe, pp. 89–96. Portsmouth, N.H.: Heinemann.

———. 1983. *Lessons from a Child*. Portsmouth, N.H.: Heinemann.

———. 1986. *The Art of Teaching Writing*. Portsmouth, N.H.: Heinemann.

Cambourne, Brian. 1988. *The Whole Story: Natural Learning and the Acquisition of Literacy in the Classroom*. Auckland, New Zealand: Scholastic.

Cameron, Linda. February 10, 1990. Personal communication.

Carbo, Marie. 1981. Case study of Jimmy. Roslyn Heights, N.Y.: Reading Styles Inservice notebook.

———. May 1984. Why most reading tests aren't fair. *Early Years K–8* pp. 73–75.

———. February 1987. Reading style research: "What works" isn't always phonics. *Phi Delta Kappan* 68:431–35.

———. March 1987. Ten myths about teaching reading. *Teaching K-8* 17: 77–80.

———. November 1987. Deprogramming reading failure: Giving unequal learners an equal chance. *Phi Delta Kappan* 69:197–202.

———. October 1988. What reading achievement tests should measure to increase literacy in the U.S. Phi Delta Kappa *Research Bulletin*, No. 7.

———. November 1988. Debunking the great phonics myth. *Phi Delta Kappan* 70:226–40.

Carle, Eric. 1981. *The Very Hungry Caterpillar*. New York: Philomel.

Cazden, Courtney. 1972. *Child Language and Education*. New York: Holt, Rinehart and Winston.

Chall, Jeanne. 1967. *Learning to Read: The Great Debate*. New York: McGraw-Hill.

———. 1983. *Learning to Read: The Great Debate*, updated edition. New York: McGraw-Hill.

————. March 1989. Learning to read: The great debate 20 years later—A response to "Debunking the great phonics myth." *Phi Delta Kappan* 70:521–38.

Chittenden, Edward, and Rosalea Courtney. 1989. Assessment of young children's reading: Documentation as an alternative to testing. In *Emerging Literacy: Young Children Learn to Read and Write*. Ed. Dorothy S. Strickland and Lesley Mandel Morrow, pp. 107–20. Newark, Del.: International Reading Association.

Chomsky, Carol. 1979. Approaching reading through invented spelling. *Theory and Practice of Early Reading*. Ed. Lauren B. Resnick and Phyllis A. Weaver. 2:43–65. Hillsdale, N.J.: Erlbaum.

Clark, Edward T. Spring 1988. The search for a new educational paradigm: The implications of new assumptions about thinking and learning. *Holistic Education* 1:18–30.

Clay, Marie. 1975. *What Did I Write?* Portsmouth, N.H.: Heinemann.

————. 4–5 February 1986. Why reading recovery is the way it is. Paper presented at the Reading Recovery Conference, Ohio Department of Education, Columbus, Ohio. *Proceedings from the First Reading Recovery Conference*, Ohio Department of Education, Columbus, Ohio.

————. 1987. *Writing Begins at Home*. Portsmouth, N.H.: Heinemann.

————. 1988. *The Early Detection of Reading Difficulties*, 4th ed. Portsmouth, N.H.: Heinemann.

Clymer, Theodore L. 1963. The utility of phonic generalizations in the primary grades. *The Reading Teacher* 16:252–58.

Cochrane, Orin, Donna Cochrane, Sharen Scalena, and Ethel Buchanan. 1984. *Reading, Writing and Caring*. Winnipeg: Whole Language Consultants. Distributed by Richard C. Owen Publishers, Katonah, N.Y.

Commission on Reading. 1988a. *Basal Readers and the State of American Reading Instruction: A Call for Action*. Position statement. Urbana, Ill.: National Council of Teachers of English.

————. 1988b. *Report on Basal Readers*. Position statement. Urbana, Ill.: National Council of Teachers of English.

Comprehending Comprehension. 1989. *Home School Helper* 3(2):1–2. Greenville, S.C.: Bob Jones University Press.

Corbett, Marlene. June 1989. *The Testing Dilemma*. SLATE Starter Sheet. Urbana, Ill.: National Council of Teachers of English.

Corder, Reginald. 1971. *An Information Base of Reading: A Critical Review of the Information Base for Current Assumptions Regarding the Status of Instruction and Reading Achievement in the United States*. Berkeley, Calif.: Educational Testing Service, Berkeley Office, U.S. Office of Education Project 0-9031. ERIC ED 054 922.

Council of Chief State School Officers. 1988. *Early Childhood and Family Education: Foundations for Success*. Position statement. Washington, D.C.: Council of Chief State School Officers.

Cowley, Joy. 1988. *Greedy Cat*. Illus. Robyn Belton. Wellington, New Zealand: Department of Education. Distributed by Richard C. Owen Publishers, Katonah, N.Y.

Cramer, Ronald L. 1978. *Writing, Reading, and Language Growth*. Columbus, O.: Charles E. Merrill.

Crowley, Paul. 1989. "They'll grow into 'em": Evaluation, self-evaluation, and self-esteem in special education. In *The Whole Language Evaluation Book*. Ed. Kenneth S. Goodman, Yetta M. Goodman, and Wendy J. Hood, pp. 237–47. Portsmouth, N.H.: Heinemann.

The "Culture Fair" WISC-R I.Q. Test. Spring 1981. *The Testing Digest*, p. 21.

Dalrymple, Karen Sabers. "Well, what about his skills?" Evaluation of whole language in the middle school. In *The Whole Language Evaluation Book*. Ed. Kenneth S. Goodman, Yetta M. Goodman, and Wendy J. Hood, pp. 110–30. Portsmouth, N.H.: Heinemann.

Davidson, Jane L., ed. 1988. *Counterpoint and Beyond: A Response to* Becoming a Nation of Readers. Urbana, Ill.: National Council of Teachers of English.

DeFord, Diane E. September 1981. Literacy: Reading, writing, and other essentials. *Language Arts* 58:652–58.

———. Spring 1985. Validating the construct of theoretical orientation in reading instruction. *Reading Research Quarterly* 20:351–67.

DeFord, Diane E., and Jerome C. Harste. September 1982. Child language research and curriculum. *Language Arts* 59:590–600.

Doake, David B. 1988. *Reading Begins at Birth*. Richmond Hill, Ontario: Scholastic-TAB.

Dobson, Lee. 15 May 1986. Emergent writers in a grade one classroom. Paper presented at the Fourth International Conference on the Teaching of English. Ottawa, Ontario.

———. Fall 1986. Emergent writers in a grade one classroom. *Reading-Canada-Lecture* 4:149–56.

Dunn, Rita, and Kenneth Dunn. 1978. *Teaching Students Through Their Individual Learning Styles: A Practical Approach*. Reston, Va.: Reston Publishing Company.

Durkin, Dolores. April 1987. Testing in the kindergarten. *The Reading Teacher* 40:766–70.

Dykstra, Robert. 1974. Phonics and beginning reading instruction. In *Teaching Reading: A Phonic/Linguistic Approach to Developmental Reading*, by Charles Child Walcutt, Joan Lamport, and Glenn McCracken, pp. 373–97. New York: Macmillan.

"'Early Identification' Efforts Raise Doubts." August 1989. Association for Supervision and Curriculum Development *Update* 31,v:1, 6.

Edelsky, Carole, Kelly Draper, and Karen Smith. Winter 1983. Hookin' 'em in at the start of school in a "whole language" classroom. *Anthropology and Education Quarterly* 14:257–81.

Edelsky, Carole, and Karen Smith. January 1984. "Is that writing—or are those marks just a figment of your curriculum?" *Language Arts* 61:24–32.

Edelsky, Carole, and Susan Harman. October 1988. One more critique of reading tests—with two differences. *English Education* 20:157–71.

Eeds, Maryann, and Deborah Wells. February 1989. Grand conversations: An exploration of meaning construction in literature study groups. *Research in the Teaching of English* 23:4–29.

Elfant, Patricia. In progress. *Cognitive and Metacognitive Strategies of First Graders During a Shared Book Experience*. New York: Unpublished doctoral dissertation, Fordham University.

Elley, Warwick B., and Francis Mangubhai. Fall 1983. The impact of reading on second language learning. *Reading Research Quarterly* 19:53–67.

Emig, Janet. 1983. Non-magical thinking: Presenting writing developmentally in schools. *The Web of Meaning: Essays on Writing, Teaching, Learning, and Thinking*, pp. 133–44. Portsmouth, N.H.: Boynton/Cook. (First published in *Writing: The Nature, Development, and Teaching of Written Communication*, Vol. 2. Ed. Marcia Farr Whiteman. Hillsdale, N.J.: Erlbaum, 1982.)

Engelmann, Siegfried, and Susan Hanner. 1982. *A Direct Instruction Series: Reading Mastery.* Chicago: Science Research Associates.

Enright, D. S., and M. L. McCloskey. 1988. *Integrating English: Developing English Language and Literacy in the Multilingual Classroom.* Reading, Mass.: Addison-Wesley.

Epstein, June, June Factor, Gwendda McKay, and Dorothy Rickards, eds. 1982. *Big Dipper Rides Again.* Victoria, Australia: Oxford University Press Australia.

Factor, June, ed. *Jelly on the Plate.* 1987. Cleveland and Toronto: Modern Curriculum Press.

Farr, Roger. September/October 1987. New trends in reading assessment: Better tests, better uses. *Curriculum Review* 27:21–23.

Farr, Roger, and Robert F. Carey. 1986. *Reading: What Can Be Measured?* 2nd ed. Newark, Del.: International Reading Association.

Ferreiro, Emilia, and Ana Teberosky. 1982. *Literacy Before Schooling.* Tr. Karen Goodman Castro. Portsmouth, N.H.: Heinemann.

Fielding, Linda G., Paul T. Wilson, and Richard C. Anderson. 1986. A new focus on free reading: The role of trade books in reading instruction. In *The Contexts of School-Based Literacy.* Ed. Taffy E. Raphael, pp. 149–60. New York: Random House.

Fitzgerald, Sheila. Spring 1984. Beginning reading and writing through singing: A natural approach. *Highway One* 7, ii:6–12.

Freeman, Yvonne S. Summer 1989. Literature-based or literature: Where do we stand? *Teachers Networking* 9:13–15.

Freppon, Penny. 1988. *An Investigation of Children's Concepts of the Purpose and Nature of Reading in Different Instructional Settings.* Unpublished doctoral dissertation, University of Cincinnati.

Fulwiler, Toby, and Art Young, eds. 1982. *Language Connections: Writing and Reading Across the Curriculum.* Urbana, Ill.: National Council of Teachers of English.

Futrell, Mary Hatwood. March 15, 1989. A most precious resource. *Education Week* 8(25):16.

Galindo, René. 1989. "Así no se pone sí" (That's not how you write "sí"). In *The Whole Language Evaluation Book.* Ed. Kenneth S. Goodman, Yetta M. Goodman, and Wendy J. Hood, pp. 55–67. Portsmouth, N.H.: Heinemann.

Gardner, Howard. 1985. *Frames of Mind: The Theory of Multiple Intelligences.* New York: Basic.

_____. 1987. The Theory of Multiple Intelligences. *Annals of Dyslexia* 37:19–35.

Genishi, Celia, and Anne Dyson. 1984. *Language Assessment in the Early Years.* Norwood, N.J.: Ablex.

Gentile, Lance M., and Merna M. McMillan. 1987. *Stress and Reading Difficulties: Research, Assessment, and Intervention.* Newark, Del.: International Reading Association.

Gentry, Richard R. 1987. *Spel . . . Is a Four-Letter Word.* Richmond Hill, Ontario: Scholastic-TAB. Available in the U.S. from Heinemann, Portsmouth, N.H.

Giacobbe, Mary Ellen. 1984. Helping children become more responsible for their own writing. *LiveWire* 1(i)7–9. National Council of Teachers of English.

Gilles, Carol, Mary Bixby, Paul Crowley, Shirley R. Crenshaw, Margaret Henrichs, Frances E. Reynolds, Donelle Pyle, eds. 1988. *Whole Language Strategies for Secondary Students.* Katonah, N.Y.: Richard C. Owen Publishers.

Glatthorn, Allan A. 1981. *Writing in the Schools: Improvement through Effective Leadership.* Reston, Va.: National Association of Secondary School Principals.

Glazer, Susan Mandel, Lyndon W. Searfoss, and Lance M. Gentile, eds. 1988. *Reexamining Reading Diagnosis: New Trends and Procedures.* Newark, Del.: International Reading Association.

Goelman, Hillel, Antoinette Oberg, and Frank Smith, eds. 1984. *Awakening to Literacy.* Portsmouth, N.H.: Heinemann.

Goetz, Lee. 1966. *A Camel in the Sea.* New York: McGraw-Hill.

Goodman, Kenneth. October 1965. A linguistic study of cues and miscues in reading. *Elementary English* 42:639–43.

————. 1973. *Theoretically Based Studies of Patterns of Miscues in Oral Reading Performance.* Detroit: Wayne State University. Educational Resources Information Center, ED 079 708.

————. April 1986. Basal readers: A call for action. *Language Arts* 63:358–63.

————. 1986. *What's Whole in Whole Language?* Richmond Hill, Ontario: Scholastic-TAB. Available in the U.S. from Heinemann, Portsmouth, N.H.

Goodman, Kenneth S., and Yetta M. Goodman. 1979. Learning to read is natural. *Theory and Practice of Early Reading.* Ed. Lauren B. Resnick and Phyllis A. Weaver, 1:137–54. Hillsdale, N.J.: Erlbaum.

Goodman, Kenneth S., Yetta M. Goodman, and Wendy J. Hood. 1989. *The Whole Language Evaluation Book.* Portsmouth, N.H.: Heinemann.

Goodman, Kenneth S., Patrick Shannon, Yvonne Freeman, and Sharon Murphy. 1988. *Report Card on Basal Readers.* Katonah, N.Y.: Richard C. Owen Publishers.

Goodman, Yetta. June 1978. Kid watching: An alternative to testing. *National Elementary School Principal* 57:41–45.

————. January 1981. Test review: Concepts about print test. *The Reading Teacher* 34:144–49.

————. 1984. The development of initial literacy. In *Awakening to Literacy.* Ed. Hillel Goelman, Antoinette Oberg, and Frank Smith, pp. 102–109. Portsmouth, N.H.: Heinemann.

————. 1989. Evaluation of students: Evaluation of teachers. In *The Whole Language Evaluation Book.* Ed. Kenneth S. Goodman, Yetta M. Goodman, and Wendy J. Hood, pp. 3–14. Portsmouth, N.H.: Heinemann.

Goodman, Yetta, and Bess Altwerger. n.d. Pre-schoolers' book handling knowledge. Unpublished paper, University of Arizona, Tucson. Test of bookhandling knowledge is included in *Bookshelf,* Stage 1 Teacher's Resource Book, from Scholastic.

Goodman, Yetta, and Carolyn L. Burke. 1972. *Reading Miscue Inventory Manual: Procedure for Diagnosis and Evaluation*. New York: Macmillan.

Goodman, Yetta, and Ann Marek. October 1989. *Retrospective Miscue Analysis: Two Papers*. Program in Language and Literacy, Occasional Papers No. 19. Tucson: University of Arizona.

Goodman, Yetta, Dorothy J. Watson, and Carolyn L. Burke. 1987. *Reading Miscue Inventory: Alternative Procedures*. Katonah, N.Y.: Richard C. Owen Publishers.

Goodnow, Jacqueline. 1977. *Children's Drawing*. Cambridge, Mass.: Harvard University Press.

Goswami, Dixie, and Peter R. Stillman, eds. 1987. *Reclaiming the Classroom: Teacher Research as an Agency for Change*. Portsmouth, N.H.: Boynton/ Cook.

Graves, Donald. 1983. *Writing: Teachers and Children at Work*. Portsmouth, N.H.: Heinemann.

Graves, Marilyn. March 6, 1990. Personal communication.

Greene, Graham. 1940. *The Power and the Glory*. New York: Viking Press.

Gregorc, Anthony F. 1986. *An Adult's Guide to Style*. Maynard, Mass.: Gabriel Systems, Inc.

Grundin, Hans U. December 1985. A commission of selective readers: A critique of *Becoming a Nation of Readers*. *The Reading Teacher* 39:262–66.

Gunderson, Lee, and Jon Shapiro. Spring 1987. Some findings on whole language instruction. *Reading-Canada-Lecture* 5(i):22–26.

Hale-Benson, Janice. 1986. *Black Children: Their Roots, Culture, and Learning Styles*. Baltimore: Johns Hopkins.

Hall, MaryAnne. 1986. Teaching and language centered programs. *Roles in Literacy Learning*. Ed. Duane R. Tovey and James E. Kerber, pp. 34–41. Newark, Del.: International Reading Association.

Hall, Nigel. 1987. *The Emergence of Literacy*. Portsmouth, N.H.: Heinemann.

Halliday, M. A. K. 1975. *Learning How to Mean: Explorations in the Development of Language*. London: Edward Arnold.

Haney, Walter, and George Madaus. May 1989. Searching for alternatives to standardized tests: Whys, whats, and whithers. *Phi Delta Kappan* 70:683–87.

Hansen, Jane. 1987. *When Writers Read*. Portsmouth, N.H.: Heinemann.

_____. 1989. Anna evaluates herself. In *Risk Makers, Risk Takers, Risk Breakers*. Ed. JoBeth Allen and Jana M. Mason, pp. 19–29. Portsmouth, N.H.: Heinemann.

_____, Thomas Newkirk, and Donald M. Graves, eds. 1985. *Breaking Ground: Teachers Relate Reading and Writing in the Elementary School*. Portsmouth, N.H.: Heinemann.

Hardt, Ulrich. Fall 1988. One school district's shift to an integrated language arts curriculum. *Oregon English*, pp. 15–20.

Harman, Susan, and Carole Edelsky. April 1989. The risks of whole language literacy: Alienation and connection. *Language Arts* 66:392–406.

Harste, Jerome C. Winter 1978. Understanding the hypothesis, it's the teacher that makes the difference: Part II. *Reading Horizons* 18:89–98.

_____. 1985. Becoming a nation of language learners: Beyond risk. In *Toward Practical Theory: A State of Practice Assessment of Reading Comprehension Instruc-*

tion. Ed. Jerome C. Harste and Diane Stephens, 8:1–122. Indiana University, Language Education Department. ED 264 544.

_____. 1989. *New Policy Guidelines for Reading: Connecting Research and Practice.* Urbana, Ill.: National Council of Teachers of English and ERIC Clearinghouse on Reading and Communication Skills.

_____, Kathy G. Short, and Carolyn Burke. 1988. *Creating Classrooms for Authors: The Reading-Writing Connection.* Portsmouth, N.H.: Heinemann.

Harste, Jerome C., Virginia A. Woodward, and Carolyn L. Burke. February 1984a. Examining our assumptions; A transactional view of literacy and learning. *Research in the Teaching of English* 18:84–108.

_____. 1984b. *Language Stories and Literacy Lessons.* Portsmouth, N.H.: Heinemann.

Hatch, Thomas, and Howard Gardner. November/December 1988. New research on intelligence. *Learning 88* 17:36–39.

Heald-Taylor, Gail. 1989. *The Administrator's Guide to Whole Language.* Katonah, N.Y.: Richard C. Owen Publishers.

Heath, Shirley Bryce. 1983. *Ways with Words: Language, Life, and Work in Communities and Classrooms.* Cambridge: Cambridge University Press.

Heimlich, Joan E., and Susan D. Pittelman. 1986. *Semantic Mapping: Classroom Applications.* Newark, Del.: International Reading Association.

"Helping Underachievers Succeed." August 1989. Association for Supervision and Curriculum Development *Update* 31(v):1–2.

Hill, Mary W. 1989. *Home: Where Reading and Writing Begin.* Portsmouth, N.H.: Heinemann.

Hillerich, Robert L. Summer 1985. Let's pretend. *Michigan Reading Journal* 18:15–18, 20.

Hoffman, Banesh. 1962. *The Tyranny of Testing.* New York: Crowell-Collier.

Holdaway, Don. 1979. *The Foundations of Literacy.* Sydney, Australia: Ashton-Scholastic. Available in the U.S. from Heinemann.

_____. 1984. *Stability and Change in Literacy Learning.* London, Ontario: University of Western Ontario. Available in the U.S. from Heinemann.

_____. 1986. The structure of natural learning as a basis for literacy instruction. In *The Pursuit of Literacy.* Ed. Michael R. Sampson. Dubuque, Iowa: Kendall Hunt Publishing Company.

Hood, Wendy. April 1989. Whole language: A grass roots movement catches on. *Learning 89* 17:60–62.

Hull, Orysia. 1989. Evaluation: The conventions of writing. In *The Whole Language Evaluation Book.* Ed. Kenneth S. Goodman, Yetta M. Goodman, and Wendy J. Hood, pp. 77–83. Portsmouth, N.H.: Heinemann.

International Reading Association and the National Council of Teachers of English. 1989. *Cases in Literacy: An Agenda for Discussion.* Newark. Del.: International Reading Association.

Jachym, Nora K., Richard L. Allington, and Kathleen A. Broikou. October 1989. Estimating the cost of seatwork. *The Reading Teacher* 43:30–33.

Jaggar, Angela, and Trika Smith-Burke, eds. 1985. *Observing the Language Learner.* Newark, Del.: International Reading Association.

Jameson, Fredric. 1986. Metacommentary. In *Contemporary Literary Criticism.* Ed. Robert Con Davis, pp. 112–23. New York and London: Longman.

Jensen, Julie M., ed. 1988. *Stories to Grow On: Demonstrations of Language Learning in K-8 Classrooms*. Portsmouth, N.H.: Heinemann.

Johns, Jerry L., and DiAnn Waksul Ellis. December 1976. Reading: Children tell it like it is. *Reading World* 16:115–28.

Johnson, Dale D., Susan D. Pittelman, and Joan E. Heimlich. April 1986. Semantic mapping. *The Reading Teacher* 39:778–82.

Johnson, D., and D. Roen, eds. 1989. *Richness in Writing: Empowering ESL Students*. New York: Longman.

Johnson, Terry, Robert Anthony, Jim Field, Norma Mickelson, and Alison Preece. 1988. *Evaluation: A Perspective for Change*. Crystal Lake, Ill.: Rigby.

Johnston, Peter. 1983. *Reading Comprehension Assessment: A Cognitive Basis*. Newark, Del.: International Reading Association.

———. April 1987. Teachers as evaluation experts. *The Reading Teacher* 40:744–48.

Joyce, B., and B. Showers. February 1980. Improving inservice training: The messages of research. *Educational Leadership* 37:379–85.

Kamii, Constance, and Marie Randazzo. 1985. Social interaction and invented spelling. *Language Arts* 62:124–33.

King, Dorothy F., and Dorothy J. Watson. 1983. Reading as meaning construction. *Integrating the Language Arts in the Elementary School*. Ed. Beverly A. Busching and Judith I. Schwartz, pp. 70–77. Urbana, Ill.: National Council of Teachers of English.

Klima, E. S., and Ursula Bellugi-Klima. 1966. Syntactic regularities in the speech of children. *Psycholinguistic Papers*. Ed. J. Lyons and R. J. Wales, pp. 183–208. Edinburgh: Edinburgh University Press.

Langer, Judith. Spring 1989. Literate thinking and schooling. *Literacy Research Newsletter* 5:1–2. Excerpts from keynote address given at the 1987 Annual Convention of TESOL, Miami, Florida.

Langer, Judith, and Gordon Pradl. November 1984. Standardized testing: A call for action. *Language Arts* 61:764–67.

Lear, Edward. 1986. *Edward Lear's ABC*. Illus. Carol Pike. Boston: Salem House.

Lee, Dennis. 1983. *Jelly Belly*. Illus. Juan Wijngaard. London: Blackie and Son Ltd., and New York: Peter Bedrick Books.

Lester, Nancy B., and Cynthia S. Onore. 1990. *Learning Change: One School District Meets Language Across the Curriculum*. Portsmouth, N.H.: Boynton/Cook–Heinemann.

Lindfors, Judith W. 1987. *Children's Language and Learning*, 2nd ed. Englewood Cliffs, N.J.: Prentice-Hall.

Lloyd-Jones, Richard, and Andrea A. Lunsford, eds. 1989. *The English Coalition Conference: Democracy through Language*. Urbana, Ill.: National Council of Teachers of English.

Lobel, Arnold. 1963. *Prince Bertram the Bad*. New York: Harper & Row.

Lynch, Priscilla. 1986. *Using Big Books and Predictable Books*. Richmond Hill, Ontario: Scholastic-TAB.

Lynch, Priscilla, and Adrian Peetoom. 1989. *Book Center Program*. New York: Scholastic.

McCarthy, Bernice. 1980. *The 4MAT System: Teaching to Learning Styles with Right/Left Mode Techniques*. Napa, Calif.: Excel.

McKenzie, Moira. 1986. *Journeys into Literacy*. Huddersfield, England: Schofield & Sims Ltd.

McNeill, David. 1966. Developmental psycholinguistics. In *The Genesis of Language: A Psycholinguistic Approach*. Ed. Frank Smith and George A. Miller, pp. 15–84. Cambridge, Mass.: MIT Press.

Madaus, George F. May 1985. Test scores as administrative mechanisms in educational policy. *Phi Delta Kappan* 66:611–17.

Marek, Ann M. 1989. Using evaluation as an instructional strategy for adult readers. In *The Whole Language Evaluation Book*. Ed. Kenneth S. Goodman, Yetta M. Goodman, and Wendy J. Hood, pp. 157–64. Portsmouth, N.H.: Heinemann.

Marshall, Nancy. March 1983. Using story grammar to assess reading comprehension. *The Reading Teacher* 36:616–20.

Mason, Jana, ed. 1989. *Reading and Writing Connections*. Needham Heights, Mass.: Allyn & Bacon.

Medina, Noe, and D. Monty Neill. 1988. *Fallout from the Testing Explosion: How 100 Million Standardized Exams Undermine Equity and Excellence in America's Public Schools*. Cambridge, Mass.: FairTest.

Melser, June, and Joy Cowley. 1980. *In a Dark Dark Wood*. Illus. Christine Ross. Auckland, New Zealand: Shortland. [Included in *The Story Box* program, distributed by The Wright Group]

Menosky, Dorothy M. 1971. A psycholinguistic description of oral reading miscues generated during the reading of varying portions of text by selected readers from grades two, four, six and eight. Doctoral dissertation, Wayne State University.

Michigan State Board of Education. n. d. *Essential Goals and Objectives for Reading Education*. Lansing, Mich.

Moore, David W. November/December 1983. A case for naturalistic assessment of reading comprehension. *Language Arts* 60:957–69.

Morgan, Norah, and Juliana Saxton. 1987. *Teaching Drama*. London: Hutchinson.

Morrow, Lesley Mandel, and Jeffrey K. Smith, eds. 1990. *Assessment for Instruction in Early Literacy*. Englewood Cliffs, N.J.: Prentice Hall.

Mosenthal, Peter B. April 1989. Research views: The whole language approach: Teachers between a rock and a hard place. *The Reading Teacher* 42:628–29.

Mullis, Ina V. S., and Lynn B. Jenkins. 1990. *The Reading Report Card, 1971–88*. Princeton, N.J.: Educational Testing Service, National Assessment of Educational Progress.

National Assessment of Educational Progress. 1985. *The Reading Report Card*. Princeton, N.J.: Educational Testing Service.

National Assessment Governing Board. December 8, 1989. Staff paper on setting goals for national assessment. Washington, D.C.: National Assessment Governing Board.

National Association for the Education of Young Children. 1987. *Developmentally Appropriate Practice in Early Childhood Programs Serving Children from Birth through Age 8*, ed. Sue Bredekamp. As excerpted in *Young Children*, January 1988, pp. 64–84.

National Association of State Boards of Education. 1988. *Right from the Start*. Report of the NASBE Task Force on Early Childhood Education. Alexandria, Va.: National Association of State Boards of Education.

National Council of Teachers of English. January 1989. NCTE to you. *Language Arts* 66:83–90.

———. May 1989. NAEP calls for break with standard curriculum and teaching methods. *Council-Grams* 51:1–2.

Neill, D. Monty, and Noe J. Medina. May 1989. Standardized testing: Harmful to educational health. *Phi Delta Kappan* 70:688–97.

Neisser, Ulric. 1986. New answers to an old question. In *The School Achievement of Minority Children: New Perspectives*. Ed. Ulric Neisser. Hillsdale, N.J.: Erlbaum.

Nelms, Ben F., ed. 1988. *Literature in the Classroom: Readers, Texts, and Contexts*. Urbana, Ill.: National Council of Teachers of English.

Newkirk, Thomas. 1989. *More Than Stories: The Range of Children's Writing*. Portsmouth, N.H.: Heinemann.

Newkirk, Thomas, and Nancie Atwell, eds. 1988. *Understanding Writing: Ways of Observing, Learning, and Teaching*, 2nd ed. Portsmouth, N.H.: Heinemann.

Newman, Judith. 1984. *The Craft of Children's Writing*. Richmond Hill, Ontario: Scholastic-TAB. Available in the U.S. from Heinemann, Portsmouth, N.H.

———. 1985. Insights from recent reading and writing research and their implications for developing whole language curriculum. In *Whole Language: Theory in Use*. Ed. Judith M. Newman, pp. 1–36. Portsmouth, N.H.: Heinemann.

———, ed. 1985. *Whole Language: Theory in Use*. Portsmouth, N.H.: Heinemann.

O'Neill, Cecily, and Alan Lambert. 1982. *Drama Structures*. London: Hutchinson.

Owen, David. 1985. *None of the Above: Behind the Myth of Scholastic Aptitude*. Boston: Houghton Mifflin.

Palincsar, Annemarie Sullivan, and Ann L. Brown. 1989. Instruction for self-regulated reading. In *Toward the Thinking Curriculum: Current Cognitive Research*. Ed. Lauren B. Resnick and Leopold E. Klopfer, pp. 19–39. Alexandria, Va.: Association for Supervision and Curriculum Development.

Pearson, P. David, ed. 1986. Twenty years of research in reading comprehension. In *The Contexts of School-Based Literacy*. Ed. Taffy Raphael, pp. 43–62. New York: Random House.

Peetoom, Adrian. 1986. *Shared Reading: Safe Risks with Big Books*. Richmond Hill, Ontario: Scholastic-TAB.

Peters, Charles W., and Karen K. Wixson. April 1989. Smart new reading tests are coming. *Learning 89* 17:43–44, 53.

Peterson, Mary. Spring 1987. A ghostly evening. *The Michigan Reading Journal* 20:9–23.

Pierce, V. 1984. *Bridging the Gap between Language Research/Theory and Practice: A Case Study*. Unpublished doctoral dissertation, Texas Woman's University, Denton, Texas.

Pinnell, Gay Su. Spring 1985. Helping teachers help children at risk: Insights from the Reading Recovery Program. *Peabody Journal of Education* 62:70–85.

———. 1988. *Success of Children at Risk in a Program That Combines Reading and Writing*. Technical report no. 417. Champaign, Ill.: University of Illinois, Center for the Study of Reading.

———. 1989. Success of at-risk children in a program that combines reading and writing. In *Reading and Writing Connections*. Ed. Jana Mason, pp. 237–60.

Pomerantz, Charlotte. 1984. *Whiff, Sniff, Nibble, and Chew: The Gingerbread Boy Retold*. Illus. Monica Incisa. New York: Greenwillow.

Prelutsky, Jack, ed. 1983. *The Random House Book of Poetry for Children*. Illus. Arnold Lobel. New York: Random House.

Ramist, Leonard, and Solomon Arbeiter. 1984. *Profiles, College-Bound Seniors, 1983*. New York: College Entrance Examination Board.

Reading redefined: A Michigan Reading Association position paper. Winter 1984. *Michigan Reading Journal* 17:4–7.

Reutzel, D. Ray. January 1985. Story maps improve comprehension. *The Reading Teacher* 38:400–404.

Rhodes, Lynn K., and Curt Dudley-Marling. 1988. *Readers and Writers with a Difference: A Holistic Approach to Teaching Learning Disabled and Remedial Students*. Portsmouth, N.H.: Heinemann.

Rhodes, Lynn K., and Nancy L. Shanklin. 1989. A research base for whole language. Denver, Colo.: LINK [LINK, 1430 Larimer Square, Suite 304, Denver, CO 80202; (303) 237-6479]

Ribowsky, Helene. 1985. *The Effects of a Code Emphasis Approach and a Whole Language Approach upon Emergent Literacy of Kindergarten Children*. Alexandria, Va.: Educational Document Reproduction Service, ED 269 720.

Rich, Sharon J. November 1985. Restoring power to teachers: The impact of ''Whole Language.'' *Language Arts* 62:717–24.

Richards, T. S. March 1989. Testmania: The school under siege. *Learning 89* 17:64–66.

Rigg, Pat, and Virginia D. Allen, eds. 1989. *When They Don't All Speak English: Integrating the ESL Student into the Regular Classroom*. Urbana, Ill.: National Council of Teachers of English.

Rigg, Pat, and D. S. Enright. 1986. *Children and ESL: Integrating Perspectives*. Washington, D.C.: Teaching English to Speakers of Other Languages. Distributed by the National Council of Teachers of English.

Roeber, Ed, and Peggy Dutcher. 1989. Michigan's innovative assessment of reading. *Educational Leadership* 46:64–69.

Rosenblatt, Louise. 1938. *Literature as Exploration*. New York: D. Appleton-Century. Reprinted by the National Council of Teachers of English.

_____. 1978. *The Reader, the Text, the Poem: The Transactional Theory of the Literary Work*. Carbondale, Ill.: Southern Illinois University Press.

Rothman, Robert. 11 October 1989. In an effort to boost achievement, Denver abolishes remedial classes. *Education Week* 9(vi):1,27.

Routman, Regie. 1988. *Transitions: From Literature to Literacy*. Portsmouth, N.H.: Heinemann.

Salganki, Laura Hersh. May 1985. Why testing reforms are so popular and how they are changing education. *Phi Delta Kappan* 66:607–10.

Sendak, Maurice. 1963. *Where the Wild Things Are*. New York: Harper & Row.

Seuss, Dr. [Theodore Geissel]. 1960. *Green Eggs and Ham*. New York: Random House.

Shanklin, Nancy. 1982. *Relating Reading and Writing; Developing a Transactional Model of the Writing Process*. Bloomington, Ind.: Monographs in Teaching and Learning, Indiana University School of Education.

———, and Lynn K. Rhodes. March 1989. Transforming literacy instruction. *Educational Leadership* 46:59–63.

Shannon, Patrick. October 1985. Reading instruction and social class. *Language Arts* 62:604–13.

———. 1989. *Broken Promises: Reading Instruction in Twentieth Century America.* Granby, Mass.: Bergin & Garvey Publishers.

Short, Kathy Gnagey, and Kathryn Mitchell-Pierce. 1990. *Talking About Books: Creating Literate Communities.* Portsmouth, N.H.: Heinemann.

Simmons, Jay. March 1990. Portfolios as large-scale assessment. *Language Arts* 67:262–68.

Slaughter, Helen B. October 1988. Indirect and direct teaching in a whole language program. *The Reading Teacher* 42:30–34.

Smith, Frank. 1971, 1978, 1982, 1988. *Understanding Reading.* Hillsdale, N.J.: Erlbaum.

———. 1979, 1985. *Reading without Nonsense.* New York: Teachers College Press.

———. January 1981. Demonstrations, engagement, and sensitivity: A revised approach to language learning. *Language Arts* 58:103–12.

———. September 1981. Demonstrations, engagement, and sensitivity: The choice between people and programs. *Language Arts* 58:634–42.

———. 1983. *Essays into Literacy.* Portsmouth, N.H.: Heinemann.

———. 1988a. *Insult to Intelligence: The Bureaucratic Invasion of Our Classrooms.* Portsmouth, N.H.: Heinemann. Originally published 1986 by Arbor House.

———. 1988b. *Joining the Literacy Club: Further Essays into Education.* Portsmouth, N.H.: Heinemann.

———. January 1989. Overselling literacy. *Phi Delta Kappan* 70:352–59.

Stahl, Steven A., and Patricia D. Miller. Spring 1989. Whole language and language experience approaches for beginning reading: A quantitative research synthesis. *Review of Educational Research* 59:87–116.

Stallings, Jane. 1975. *Implementation and Child Effects of Teaching Practices in Follow Through Classrooms.* Monographs of the Society for Research in Child Development. Chicago: University of Chicago Press.

Stephens, Diane. 1990. *Whole Language: A Research Perspective.* Champaign, Ill.: Richard C. Owen, Publisher, forthcoming.

Stephens, Diane. Forthcoming. *Considering Whole Language: A Review of the Research Literature* (tentative title). Champaign, Ill.: University of Illinois, Center for the Study of Reading.

Sternberg, Robert J. March 1989. The tyranny of testing. *Learning 89* 17:60–63.

Stice, Carole, and Nancy Bertrand. 1989. The texts and textures of literacy learning in whole language versus traditional/skills classrooms. Unpublished manuscript, Tennessee State University, Nashville (Stice) and Middle Tennessee State University (Bertrand).

Stokes, William T. Spring 1989. Naturalistic assessment: A call for action. *The Whole Language Teachers Association Newsletter*, p. 10.

Strickland, Dorothy S., and Lesley Mandel Morrow, eds. 1989. *Emerging Literacy: Young Children Learn to Read and Write.* Newark, Del.: International Reading Association. Distributed also by National Council of Teachers of English.

Suhor, Charles. May 1985. Objective tests and writing samples: How do they affect instruction in composition? *Phi Delta Kappan* 66:635–39.

Sullivan, Barry M. 1988. *A Legacy for Learners*. The report of the Royal Commission on Education. Vancouver, British Columbia: Province of British Columbia.

Sulzby, Elizabeth. Summer 1985. Children's emergent reading of favorite storybooks: A developmental study. *Reading Research Quarterly* 20:458–81.

Taylor, Denny. 1983. *Family Literacy: Young Children Learning to Read and Write*. Portsmouth, N.H.: Heinemann.

_____. November 1989. Toward a unified theory of literacy learning and instructional practices. *Phi Delta Kappan* 71:184–93.

_____. February 1990. Teaching without testing: Assessing the complexity of children's literacy learning. *English Education* 22:4–74.

Taylor, Denny, and Catherine Dorsey-Gaines. 1988. *Growing Up Literate: Learning from Inner-City Families*. Portsmouth, N.H.: Heinemann.

Taylor, Denny, and Dorothy S. Strickland. 1986. *Family Storybook Reading*. Portsmouth, N.H.: Heinemann.

Tchudi, Stephen N. 1986. *Teaching Writing in the Content Areas: College Level*. National Education Association of the United States. Distributed by the National Council of Teachers of English.

_____. 1987. *The Young Learner's Handbook*. New York: Charles Scribner's Sons.

Teale, William H. September 1982. Toward a theory of how children learn to read and write naturally. *Language Arts* 59:550–70.

Teale, William H., Elfrieda H. Hiebert, and Edward A. Chittenden. April 1987. Assessing young children's literacy development. *The Reading Teacher* 40:772–77.

Teale, William H., and Elizabeth Sulzby, eds. 1986. *Emergent Literacy: Writing and Reading*. Norwood, N.J.: Ablex.

Temple, Charles, Ruth Nathan, Nancy Burris, and Frances Temple. 1988. *The Beginnings of Writing*, 2nd ed. Boston: Allyn and Bacon.

Turner, Richard L. December 1989. The ''Great'' debate—Can both Carbo and Chall be right? *Phi Delta Kappan* 71:276–83.

Tyler, Ralph W., and Richard M. Wolf. 1974. *Crucial Issues in Testing*. Berkeley, Calif.: McCutchan.

U.S. Department of Education. 1986. *What Works: Research About Teaching and Learning*. Washington, D.C.: U.S. Department of Education.

_____. June 1988. What we know about phonics. *Research in Brief* series. Office of Educational Research and Improvement, U.S. Department of Education.

Valencia, Sheila, and P. David Pearson. April 1987. Reading assessment: Time for a change. *The Reading Teacher* 40:726–32.

Valencia, Sheila, P. David Pearson, Charles W. Peters, and Karen K. Wixson. April 1989. Theory and practice in statewide reading assessment: Closing the gap. *Educational Leadership* 46:57–63.

Venezky, Richard L., Carl F. Koestle, and Andrew M. Sum. 1987. *The Subtle Danger: Reflections on the Literacy Abilities of America's Young Adults*. Princeton, N.J.: Center for the Assessment of Educational Progress, Educational Testing Service. ED 284 164.

Vygotsky, Lev S. 1978. *Mind in Society: The Development of Higher Psychological Processes*. Ed. Michael Cole, Vera John-Steiner, Sylvia Scribner, and Ellen Souberman. Cambridge, Mass.: Harvard University Press.

_____. 1982. *Thought and Language*. Tr. E. Hanfmann and G. Vakar. Cambridge, Mass.: MIT Press.

Wagner, Betty J. 1976. *Dorothy Heathcote: Drama as a Learning Medium*. Washington, D.C.: National Education Association.

_____. 1983. The expanding circle of informal classroom drama. In Beverley A. Busching and Judith I. Schwartz, eds. *Integrating the Language Arts in the Elementary School*, pp. 155–63. Urbana, Ill.: National Council of Teachers of English.

Watson, Dorothy J., ed. 1987. *Ideas and Insights: Language Arts in the Elementary School*. Urbana, Ill.: National Council of Teachers of English.

_____. 1988. Coming full circle. In *Reading Process and Practice: From Sociopsycholinguistics to Whole Language*, by Constance Weaver, pp. 412–14. Portsmouth, N.H.: Heinemann.

Watson, Dorothy J., Carolyn Burke, and Jerome Harste. 1989. *Whole Language: Inquiring Voices*. Richmond Hill, Ontario: Scholastic.

Watson, Dorothy J., and Paul Crowley. 1988. How can we implement a whole language approach? In *Reading Process and Practice: From Sociopsycholinguistics to Whole Language*, by Constance Weaver, pp. 232–79. Portsmouth, N.H.: Heinemann.

Watson, Dorothy J., and Constance Weaver. May 1988. Basals: Report on the reading commission study. *Teachers Networking* 8(i):10–12.

Weaver, Constance. October 1985. Parallels between new paradigms in science and in reading and literary theories: An essay review. *Research in the Teaching of English* 19:298–316.

_____. 1988. *Reading Process and Practice: From Socio-psycholinguistics to Whole Language*. Portsmouth, N.H.: Heinemann.

_____, versus Patrick Groff. 1989. The basalization of America: A cause for concern. In *Two Responses to the Report Card on Basal Readers*. Bloomington, Ind.: ERIC Clearinghouse on Reading and Communication Skills.

Wells, Gordon. 1986. *The Meaning Makers: Children Learning Language and Using Language to Learn*. Portsmouth, N.H.: Heinemann.

Wiggins, Grant. May 1989. A true test: Toward more authentic and equitable assessment. *Phi Delta Kappan* 70:703–13.

Wilde, Sandra. 1989. Understanding spelling strategies: A kidwatcher's guide to spelling, Part 2. In *The Whole Language Evaluation Book*. Ed. Kenneth S. Goodman, Yetta M. Goodman, and Wendy J. Hood, pp. 227–36. Portsmouth, N.H.: Heinemann.

Wilson, Marilyn. 1985. Testing and literacy: A contradiction in terms? In *Testing in the English Language Arts: Uses and Abuses*. Ed. John Beard and Scott McNabb. Urbana, Ill.: National Council of Teachers of English. Originally published by Michigan Council of Teachers of English.

_____. 1988. How can we teach reading in the content areas? In *Reading Process and Practice: From Socio-psycholinguistics to Whole Language*, by Constance Weaver, pp. 280–320. Portsmouth, N.H.: Heinemann.

Wixson, Karen K., and Charles W. Peters. 1984. Reading redefined: A Michigan Reading Association Position Paper. *Michigan Reading Journal* 17:4–7.

Wixson, Karen K., Charles W. Peters, Elaine M. Weber, and Edward D. Roeber. April 1987. New directions in statewide reading assessment. *The Reading Teacher* 40:749–54.

Woodley, John W., and Carol E. Woodley. 1989. Whole language, Texas style. In *The Whole Language Evaluation Book*. Ed. Kenneth S. Goodman, Yetta M. Goodman, and Wendy J. Hood, pp. 45–54. Portsmouth, N.H.: Heinemann.

Yaden, David B., Jr., and Shane Templeton. 1986. *Metalinguistic Awareness and Beginning Literacy: Conceptualizing What It Means to Read and Write*. Portsmouth, N.H.: Heinemann.

Index

A

Accountability, 182–83, 197–98, 208–
10, 259–61, 277–78
Acquisition of language. *See* language
acquisition/learning
Administrators, 2, 29, 70, 267, 273–76,
279, 284–86
Alternative teaching materials, 264–65
Approximations, successive, 23–24,
81–82, 103–04, 107
Assessment
alternative kinds, 25–26, 28, 211, 260
conferences, conferencing, 160–62,
247–48
dialogue journals and learning logs,
211, 251–52
intertwined with learning and
teaching, 127, 160–62, 176–77,
181, 211–14, 226–28, 237, 241,
243, 253
interviews, 211, 247–49
inventories and questionnaires, 211,
248–50
periodic performance samples, 211
emergent literacy, 218–20, 232–35
reading, 218–20
writing, 232–35
recorded observations, 211, 242–47
self-evaluation, 198, 211, 214–25,
218, 226–27, 232, 252–53
standardized. *See* Standardized tests
student-kept records, 211, 252–53
think-aloud protocols, 211, 242
written conversations, 251–52
"At risk" students, 60, 138, 164
Authentic literacy events (or, authentic
reading and/or writing, authen-

tic texts), 5, 23–24, 30, 39–41,
60–62, 83, 96, 102, 108, 110, 125,
127, 131, 155, 160, 164–67, 179,
201–05

B

Basal reading
position statement(s), 58–59, 69–71
programs, 9–10, 19, 25, 31–32, 36–
37, 56–60, 103–04, 106, 131–32,
140, 195, 246, 265–66
Becoming a Nation of Readers, 36–38,
120–22, 142, 166–67, 175
Behavioral concept of learning, 191,
194; *see also* Transmission
model/philosophy
Bibliographies, starter, 4, 42, 105, 148,
184, 213, 234, 240
Big Books, 134, 149–50, 157, 173, 277–
78, 280
"Blonke" passage, 196

C

Checklists, 243
Code-emphasis approach, 111,
135–36
Comprehension
as constructing meaning, 196, 199–
204, 221–27, 231
described, 169–71
natural development of, 170–72,
176–80
questions, 119, 170, 196, 246
Concepts about print, 91, 121, 135,
138, 150